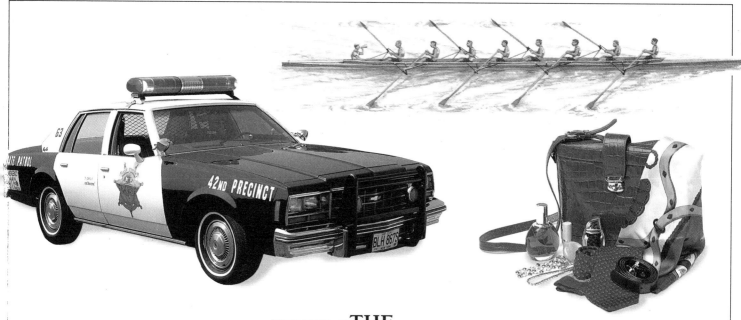

THE
TOP
10
OF EVERYTHING
1998

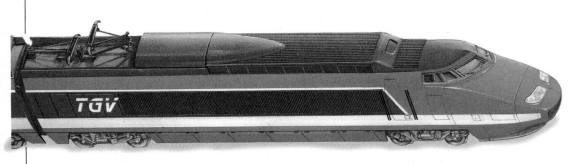

THE
TOP
10
OF EVERYTHING
1998

— RUSSELL ASH —

DK PUBLISHING, INC.

Project Editor Adèle Hayward
US Editors Mary Sutherland, Michael Wise
Project Art Editor Jayne Jones
Editor Julie Oughton
Designer Austin Barlow
Managing Editor Stephanie Jackson
Managing Art Editor Nigel Duffield
Production Controller Alison Jones

Designed and Typeset by Blackjacks Limited
Designer Jonathan Baker
Project Editor Helen Freeman
Senior Editor Jack Buchan
Editor Casey Horton

First American Editon, 1997
2 4 6 8 10 9 7 5 3 1

Published in the United States by
DK Publishing, Inc.
95 Madison Avenue
New York, New York 10016

Visit us on the World Wide Web at http://www.dk.com

Copyright © 1997
Dorling Kindersley Limited, London
Text copyright © 1997 Russell Ash

Library of Congress Cataloging-in-Publication Data
Ash, Russell.
The top ten of everything, 1998 / by Russell Ash.
-- 1st American ed.
p. cm.
Includes index.
ISBN 0-7894-2199-2 -- ISBN 0-7894-2082-1
(pbk. : alk. paper)
1. Curiosities and wonders. 2. World records–Miscellanea.
I. Title.
AG243.A715 1997
031.02--dc21   97-15018
                                                    CIP

Reproduction by HBM Print Ltd, Singapore.
Printed and bound in the United States by
R.R. Donnelley & Sons Company.

CONTENTS

LIFE ON EARTH

THE HUMAN WORLD

SPORTS

THE GOOD & THE BAD

DISASTERS

CULTURE & LEARNING

MUSIC

STAGE, SCREEN & BROADCASTING

INTRODUCTION

This is the 9th annual edition of *The Top 10 of Everything*. If you have never seen one of the previous editions, welcome; if it is already familiar, welcome back. To both groups of readers it is worth mentioning what is new. Every year I try to introduce new categories and lists, and this year I have "starred" some of the lists that have never appeared in a previous edition of *The Top 10 of Everything*. Core lists and old favorites are still included, but this year, as every other year, every list that is featured has been checked and updated, and the book is full of new information. Lists of the best-selling books or the most-watched films of a year, for instance, are replaced in their entirety by those for the latest complete year and are thus completely different. In all other categories, new individual entries have been inserted, or whole lists have been replaced. Even some of the historical lists are revised as new evidence comes to light. In 1997 Hong Kong, a long-standing entry in many Top 10 lists, was handed back to China, and so no longer features as a separate country (although it does, of course, continue to feature in lists that are based on events that occurred when it had the status of a country). Lists on certain subjects alter very dramatically – those of tallest buildings frequently change while I am compiling them, and you will see in the list "10 Longest Passenger Liners" (p. 57) that four of them were launched in 1996 or 1997. During the course of 1998, this list will change yet again as a number of large new vessels are completed.

WHAT'S "TOP"?

Top 10 lists are not "bests" or favorites of mine or anyone else's, but almost invariably measurable rankings. Some are "worsts," as in the case of murder and disaster victims, because these are quantifiable. The lists encompass superlatives in many categories – tallest, longest, fastest, most-produced, richest, most expensive, most common, and so on. Some are "firsts" or "latests": these qualify as a special sort of Top 10 that recognizes, for instance, that the first 10 moonwalkers were leaders in that endeavor. Such lists make up for the fact that most other sources usually give the first entry only, with the result that history's also-rans are in danger of being forgotten. "Latests," as in the case of award winners in certain fields, for example, represent the 10 most recent achievers. Very occasionally an unquantified list of 10 is included if it throws light on a subject that does not readily submit to the Top 10 treatment.

IN THE BEGINNING...

I am often asked how I got the idea for *The Top 10 of Everything*. The vogue for books of lists started in the US with the pioneering *Book of Lists*, which was published in 1977. It was followed by special books of lists on topics from films to food. A few years after this ball started rolling, while on a visit to the US, someone gave me a copy of *The Book of Texas Lists* (which includes such lists as "The 9 worst street names in Dallas," with entries such as Microwave Avenue and Star Trek Lane). Back in England I thought, "If you could do a whole book of lists on Texas, you could certainly do one on London," and so I compiled a book that would have been called *The Book of London Lists* – except that the publishers decided to call it *The Londoner's Almanac*. While I was working on that book, which was published in 1985, it occurred to me that most of these books contained subjective lists that represented someone's opinion or someone's favorites. I asked myself, "What if I included *only* lists that were definitively the biggest, or the fastest, or whatever?" – and the notion of *The Top 10 of Everything* was born. I did not imagine when the first edition was published in 1989 that it would become established as an annual, or that it would receive the interest and attention that it has. I am delighted that it is now published internationally, as a by-product of which I have been interviewed about it on everything from local radio stations to the *Oprah Winfrey Show*.

WHY MAKE LISTS?

Whether we like it or not, we are all bombarded with lists; it's impossible to open a newspaper without seeing lists created by market researchers or pollsters: lists of the safest cars, best-sellers, Oscar winners, annual crime lists, lists of the top schools, and so on, and so on . . . Essentially, lists are a way of simplifying our awareness of everyday activities in a form that we can easily digest and remember. In an age when we are being assailed with information of all kinds (and people are already starting to talk about information overload), lists provide a shorthand way of presenting what might otherwise be an impenetrable mass of data and figures. Lists, especially the sort that you will find in this book, can reflect life – and so, like life itself, they can be serious, bizarre, trivial, important, fascinating, revealing, entertaining, or a combination of all of these attributes. At least, that is my intention.

A VOTE OF THANKS

I would like to thank the many people who have helped with the book since its inception, especially those who have generously contributed information and suggestions. I am always grateful for corrections and owe particular thanks to specialists who have offered constructive advice on lists, or who have even compiled certain lists for me. In contemplating my work on *The Top 10 of Everything*, the analogy of painting the Forth Bridge springs to mind: no sooner have I finished at one end than it's time to start at the beginning again (sometimes, it seems, before the paint is completely dry). If, as a result, I have not found the time to respond to you personally, please take this as a big "thank you."

SUGGESTIONS OR CORRECTIONS

If you have ideas or corrections for future editions, you can contact me on our World Wide Web site at http://www.dk.com (where you will find more Top 10 lists and information about other DK books), e-mail me direct at ash@pavilion.co.uk, or write to me care of the publishers.

PS: Watch for the next edition of *The Top 10 of Everything* – appropriately, it will be the 10th!

TOWN & COUNTRY

T O P   1 0

LEAST POPULATED COUNTRIES IN THE WORLD

	Country	Population
1	Vatican City	738
2	Niue	2,239
3	Tuvalu	9,700
4	Nauru	10,200
5	Wallis and Futuna	13,750
6	Cook Islands	18,300
7	San Marino	24,801
8	Gibraltar	28,800
9	Monaco	29,972
10	Liechtenstein	30,310

These are all independent countries – although some are linked to larger ones. There are numerous dependencies with small populations, among them the Falkland Islands (2,121), and Midway Island (450) and Wake Island (300), both of which are under US military administration. The Pitcairn Islands, which were settled in 1790 by mutineers from the ship *Bounty*, have a population of 54.

T O P   1 0

MOST POPULATED COUNTRIES IN THE WORLD

	Country	Population 1980	1990	1996
1	China	984,736,000	1,133,710,000	1,210,005,000
2	India	692,394,000	855,591,000	952,108,000
3	US	227,726,000	249,913,000	265,563,000
4	Indonesia	154,936,000	187,728,000	206,612,000
5	Brazil	122,830,000	150,062,000	162,661,000
6	Russia	139,045,000	148,081,000	148,078,000
7	Pakistan	85,219,000	113,914,000	129,276,000
8	Japan	116,807,000	123,537,000	125,450,000
9	Bangladesh	88,077,000	110,118,000	123,063,000
10	Nigeria	65,699,000	86,488,000	103,912,000
	World	*4,457,593,000*	*5,281,673,000*	*5,771,939,000*

Source: US Bureau of the Census

The population of China is now more than 4½ times that of the US and represents more than 20 percent of the total population of the world in 1996, proving the commonly stated statistic that "one person in five is Chinese." Although differential rates of population increase result in changes in the order, the members of this Top 10 – which accounts for almost 60 percent of the world's population – remains largely the same from one year to the next and contains every country with a population of more than 100,000,000. The population of the closest runner-up, Mexico, was thought to be 95,772,000 in 1996.

INDIA'S TEEMING MILLIONS
India's high birth rate has resulted in its numbers more than tripling during the 20th century. It is set to exceed one billion by the millennium, closing the gap with China's slower growing population.

T O P 1 0

COUNTRIES WITH THE HIGHEST ESTIMATED POPULATION IN THE YEAR 2000

	Country	Population
1	China	1,253,438,000
2	India	1,012,909,000
3	US	274,943,000
4	Indonesia	219,267,000
5	Brazil	169,545,000
6	Russia	147,938,000
7	Pakistan	141,145,000
8	Bangladesh	132,081,000
9	Japan	126,582,000
10	Nigeria	117,328,000
	World	*6,090,914,000*

According to estimates prepared by the US Bureau of the Census, we will approach the year 2000 with a total world population of over 6 billion. India is scheduled to join China as the second country to achieve a population in excess of one billion, while Mexico is expected to ascend to the 100-million-plus club with a population of 102,912,000. In contrast, the populations of certain countries, such as Russia, are actually set to decline as birth rates fall.

T O P 1 0

COUNTRIES IN WHICH MEN MOST OUTNUMBER WOMEN

	Country	Men per 100 women
1	United Arab Emirates	187
2	Qatar	160
3	Bahrain	138
4	Brunei	133
5	Saudi Arabia	124
6	Vanuatu	114
7	Oman	112
8	Hong Kong	110
9	Libya	109
10	Pakistan	108

T O P 1 0

COUNTRIES IN WHICH WOMEN MOST OUTNUMBER MEN

	Country	Women per 100 men
1=	Cape Verde	114
1=	Latvia	114
1=	Ukraine	114
4	Antigua	113
5	Belarus	112
6=	Lithuania	111
6=	Russia	111
8	Georgia	110
9=	Cambodia	109
9=	Moldova	109

WORLD COUNTRIES

COUNTRIES WITH MOST NEIGHBORS

Country/neighbors	No. of neighbors
1 China	15

Afghanistan, Bhutan, India, Kazakhstan, Kyrgyzstan, Laos, Macao, Mongolia, Myanmar (Burma), Nepal, North Korea, Pakistan, Russia, Tajikistan, Vietnam

2 Russia	14

Azerbaijan, Belarus, China, Estonia, Finland, Georgia, Kazakhstan, Latvia, Lithuania, Mongolia, North Korea, Norway, Poland, Ukraine

3 Brazil	10

Argentina, Bolivia, Colombia, French Guiana, Guyana, Paraguay, Peru, Surinam, Uruguay, Venezuela

4= Germany	9

Austria, Belgium, Czech Republic, Denmark, France, Luxembourg, Netherlands, Poland, Switzerland

4= Sudan	9

Central African Republic, Chad, Egypt, Eritrea, Ethiopia, Kenya, Libya, Uganda, Congo (Zaïre)

4= Congo (Zaïre)	9

Angola, Burundi, Central African Republic, Congo, Rwanda, Sudan, Tanzania, Uganda, Zambia

7= Austria	8

Czech Republic, Germany, Hungary, Italy, Liechtenstein, Slovakia, Slovenia, Switzerland

7= France	8

Andorra, Belgium, Germany, Italy, Luxembourg, Monaco, Spain, Switzerland

7= Saudi Arabia	8

Iraq, Jordan, Kuwait, Oman, People's Democratic Republic of Yemen, Qatar, United Arab Emirates, Yemen Arab Republic

7= Tanzania	8

Burundi, Kenya, Malawi, Mozambique, Rwanda, Uganda, Congo (Zaïre), Zambia

7= Turkey	8

Armenia, Azerbaijan, Bulgaria, Georgia, Greece, Iran, Iraq, Syria

LONGEST BORDERS IN THE WORLD

	Country	km	miles
1	China	22,143	13,759
2	Russia	20,139	12,514
3	Brazil	14,691	9,129
4	India	14,103	8,763
5	US	12,248	7,611
6	Congo (Zaïre)	10,271	6,382
7	Argentina	9,665	6,006
8	Canada	8,893	5,526
9	Mongolia	8,114	5,042
10	Sudan	7,697	4,783

The 7,611 miles/12,248 km of US borders include those shared with Canada (3,987 miles/6,416 km of which comprise the longest continuous border in the world), the 1,539-mile/2,477-km boundary between Canada and Alaska, that with Mexico (2,067 miles/3,326 km), and the border between the US naval base at Guantánamo and Cuba (18 miles/29 km). The total length of the world's land boundaries is estimated to be approximately 274,646 miles/442,000 km.

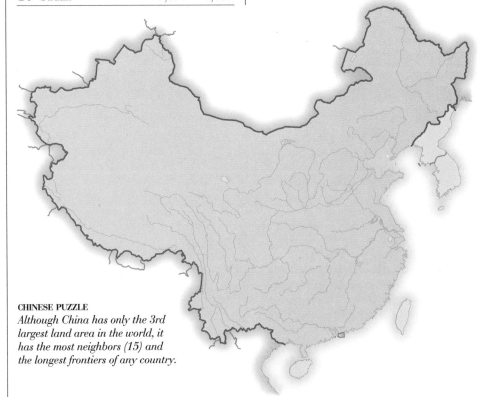

CHINESE PUZZLE
Although China has only the 3rd largest land area in the world, it has the most neighbors (15) and the longest frontiers of any country.

COUNTRIES WITH THE LONGEST COASTLINES

	Country	km	miles		Country	km	miles
1	Canada	243,791	151,485	**6**	Japan	29,751	18,486
2	Indonesia	54,716	33,999	**7**	Australia	25,760	16,007
3	Greenland	44,087	27,394	**8**	Norway	21,925	13,624
4	Russia	37,653	23,396	**9**	US	19,924	12,380
5	Philippines	36,289	22,559	**10**	New Zealand	15,134	9,404

TOP 10

LARGEST LANDLOCKED COUNTRIES IN THE WORLD

	Country	Area sq km	sq miles
1	Kazakhstan	2,717,300	1,049,156
2	Mongolia	1,565,000	604,250
3	Chad	1,284,000	495,755
4	Niger	1,267,080	489,222
5	Mali	1,240,000	478,767
6	Ethiopia	1,128,221	435,609
7	Bolivia	1,098,581	424,165
8	Zambia	752,614	290,586
9	Afghanistan	647,497	250,000
10	Central African Republic	622,984	240,535

TOP 10

LARGEST COUNTRIES IN THE WORLD

	Country	Area sq km	sq miles
1	Russia	17,070,289	6,590,876
2	Canada	9,970,537	3,849,646
3	China	9,596,961	3,705,408
4	US	9,372,614	3,618,787
5	Brazil	8,511,965	3,286,488
6	Australia	7,686,848	2,967,909
7	India	3,287,590	1,269,346
8	Argentina	2,766,889	1,068,302
9	Kazakhstan	2,717,300	1,049,156
10	Sudan	2,505,813	967,500
World total		*136,597,770*	*52,740,700*

The list of the world's largest countries, the Top 10 of which comprise 53.8 percent of the total Earth's land surface, has undergone substantial revision recently: the breakup of the former Soviet Union has effectively introduced two new countries, with Russia taking preeminent position, while Kazakhstan, which enters in 9th position, ousts Algeria (919,595 sq miles/ 2,381,741 sq km) from the list.

TOP 10

LARGEST COUNTRIES IN EUROPE

	Country	Area sq km	sq miles
1	Russia (in Europe)	4,710,227	1,818,629
2	Ukraine	603,700	233,090
3	France	547,026	211,208
4	Spain	504,781	194,897
5	Sweden	449,964	173,732
6	Germany	356,999	137,838
7	Finland	337,007	130,119
8	Norway	324,220	125,182
9	Poland	312,676	120,725
10	Italy	301,226	116,304

MAP OF EUROPE

* Including offshore islands

The United Kingdom falls just outside the Top 10 at 94,247 sq miles/244,101 sq km. Excluding the Isle of Man and Channel Islands, its area comprises England (50,351 sq miles/ 130,410 sq km), Scotland (30,420 sq miles/78,789 sq km), Wales (8,015 sq miles/ 20,758 sq km), and Northern Ireland (5,461 sq miles/14,144 sq km). Geographically, rather than politically, the total area of the British Isles, including the whole island of Ireland (27,136 sq miles/70,283 sq km) is 121,383 sq miles/314,384 sq km.

TOP 10

MOST POPULOUS COUNTRIES NAMED AFTER REAL PEOPLE

	Country	Named after	Population
1	US	Amerigo Vespucci (Italian; 1451–1512)	265,563,000
2	Philippines	Philip II (Spanish; 1527–98)	74,481,000
3	Colombia	Christopher Columbus (Italian; 1451–1506)	36,813,000
4	Saudi Arabia	Abdul Aziz ibn-Saud (Nejd; 1882–1953)	19,409,000
5	Bolivia	Simon Bolivar (Venezuelan; 1783–1830)	7,165,000
6	Marshall Islands	Capt. John Marshall (British; 1748–1818)	53,000
7	Northern Mariana	Maria Theresa (Austrian; 1717–80)	47,000
8	Cook Islands	Capt. James Cook (British; 1728–79)	17,000
9	Wallis and Futuna	Samuel Wallis (British; 1728–95)	14,000
10	Falkland Islands	Lucius Cary, 2nd Viscount Falkland (British; c. 1610–43)	2,000

It is questionable whether China, the world's most populous country, is named after the Emperor Chin. Rhodesia, which was named after the British statesman Cecil Rhodes, was renamed when Zambia was created from Northern Rhodesia in 1964 and Zimbabwe from Southern Rhodesia in 1980. Many countries were named after mythical characters, or were named after saints – often because they were discovered on the saint's day.

WORLD CITIES

12

MOST DENSELY POPULATED CITIES IN THE WORLD

	City/country	Population per sq km	sq mile
1	Hong Kong, China	98,053	253,957
2	Lagos, Nigeria	67,561	174,982
3	Dhaka, Bangladesh	63,900	165,500
4	Jakarta, Indonesia	56,650	146,724
5	Bombay, India	54,997	142,442
6	Ahmadabad, India	50,676	131,250
7	Ho Chi Minh City, Vietnam	50,617	131,097
8	Shenyang, China	44,125	114,282
9	Bangalore, India	43,583	112,880
10	Cairo, Egypt	41,413	107,260

* According to the US Bureau of the Census method of calculating population and population density; includes only cities with populations of over 2,000,000

LARGEST CITIES IN THE WORLD IN THE YEAR 2000

	City/country	Estimated population 2000*
1	Tokyo–Yokohama, Japan	29,971,000
2	Mexico City, Mexico	27,872,000
3	São Paulo, Brazil	25,354,000
4	Seoul, South Korea	21,976,000
5	Bombay, India	15,357,000
6	New York, US	14,648,000
7	Osaka–Kobe–Kyoto, Japan	14,287,000
8	Tehran, Iran	14,251,000
9	Rio de Janeiro, Brazil	14,169,000
10	Calcutta, India	14,088,000

* Based on US Bureau of the Census's unique method of calculating city populations; this gives totals that differ from those calculated by other methods, such as those used by the United Nations

LARGEST NON-CAPITAL CITIES IN THE WORLD*

	City	Country	Population	Capital	Population
1	Shanghai	China	13,400,000	Beijing	10,940,000
2	Bombay	India	12,596,000	New Delhi	284,149
3	Calcutta#	India	11,022,000	New Delhi	284,149
4	São Paulo	Brazil	9,394,000	Brasília	1,864,000
5	Tianjin	China	9,090,000	Beijing	10,940,000
6	Karachi#	Pakistan	8,070,000	Islamabad	320,000
7	New York#	US	7,323,000	Washington, DC	598,000
8	Istanbul#	Turkey	6,293,000	Ankara	2,560,000
9	Rio de Janeiro#	Brazil	5,474,000	Brasília	1,864,000
10	St. Petersburg#	Russia	4,456,000	Moscow	8,967,000

* Based on a comparison of populations within administrative boundaries, hence not comparable with "Top 10 Largest Cities in Europe"
# Former capital city

MOST POPULATED CHINESE CITY
China is the most populous country on the Earth, with Shanghai, its foremost port and industrial center, the world's largest noncapital city, with a total population of 13,400,000.

LARGEST CITIES IN EUROPE

	City/country	Population
1	Moscow*, Russia	10,769,000
2	London*, UK	8,897,000
3	Paris*, France	8,764,000
4	Istanbul#, Turkey	7,624,000
5	Essen, Germany	7,364,000
6	Milan, Italy	4,795,000
7	Madrid*, Spain	4,772,000
8	St. Petersburg, Russia	4,694,000
9	Barcelona, Spain	4,492,000
10	Manchester, UK	3,949,000

* Capital city
# Located in the European part of Turkey

The problem of defining a city's boundaries means that population figures generally relate to "urban agglomerations," which often include suburbs sprawling over very large areas. The US Bureau of the Census's method of identifying city populations produces this list – although one based on cities minus their suburbs would present a very different picture. Using this method with other cities shows that Athens, Rome, and Berlin all have populations in excess of 3,000,000.

NOT BUILT IN A DAY
The building of the Colosseum, Rome, was begun in AD 72. Rome is one of Europe's oldest cities and was the capital of the Roman Empire. It was the first city to attain a population of one million.

THE 10
FIRST CITIES IN THE WORLD WITH POPULATIONS OF MORE THAN ONE MILLION

	City	Country
1	Rome	Italy
2	Angkor	Cambodia
3	Hangchow (Hangzhou)	China
4	London	UK
5	Paris	France
6	Beijing	China
7	Canton (Guangzhou)	China
8	Berlin	Germany
9	New York	US
10	Vienna	Austria

Rome's population was reckoned to have exceeded 1,000,000 some time in the 2nd century BC, and Angkor and Hangchow both reached this figure by about AD 900 and 1200 respectively, but all three subsequently declined. Angkor was completely abandoned in the 15th century.

TOP 10
LARGEST CITIES IN THE US

	City/state	Population
1	New York, New York	7,311,966
2	Los Angeles, California	3,489,779
3	Chicago, Illinois	2,768,483
4	Houston, Texas	1,690,180
5	Philadelphia, Pennsylvania	1,552,572
6	San Diego, California	1,148,851
7	Dallas, Texas	1,022,497
8	Phoenix, Arizona	1,012,230
9	Detroit, Michigan	1,012,110
10	San Antonio, Texas	966,437

TOP 10
OLDEST CITIES IN THE US

	City	Founded
1	St. Augustine, Florida	1565
2	Santa Fe, New Mexico	1609
3	Hampton, Virginia	1610
4	Newport News, Virginia	1621
5=	Albany, New York	1624
5=	New York	1624
7=	Quincy, Massachusetts	1625
8=	Salem, Massachusetts	1626
9=	Jersey City, New Jersey	1629
9=	Lynn, Massachusetts	1629

The oldest permanently inhabited settlements in what is now the United States are the subject of much debate, but the founding years listed are those from which these cities are generally presumed to date. Some sources give Tallahassee, Florida as having been originally settled in 1539, but this date relates only to the winter camp (and the first Christmas Mass celebrated on American soil) of the Spanish explorer Hernando de Soto (c. 1500–42) and his 600 companions, but the city was not founded on this site until 1636.

TOP 10
MOST EXPENSIVE CITIES IN THE WORLD

	City	Country	Index*
1	Tokyo	Japan	176.46
2	Osaka	Japan	164.68
3	Moscow	Russia	142.20
4	Zurich	Switzerland	138.84
5	Geneva	Switzerland	137.15
6	Oslo	Norway	135.33
7	Hong Kong	China	131.44
8	Beijing	China	131.43
9	Libreville	Gabon	131.27
10	Copenhagen	Denmark	130.14

* *Based on New York = 100*

The index on which this ranking is based is derived from research conducted by the Corporate Resources Group. Like the figures published by the United Nations in order to assess allowances for UN officials serving in the various cities, it takes into account the costs of a wide range of consumer goods and services. Runaway inflation and rapid price rises in cities that were once considered economical mean that Moscow and certain African cities now appear in close proximity to others that have traditionally been regarded as expensive.

US STATES

FIRST STATES OF THE US

	State	Entered Union
1	Delaware	December 7, 1787
2	Pennsylvania	December 12, 1787
3	New Jersey	December 18, 1787
4	Georgia	January 2, 1788
5	Connecticut	January 9, 1788
6	Massachusetts	February 6, 1788
7	Maryland	April 28, 1788
8	South Carolina	May 23, 1788
9	New Hampshire	June 21, 1788
10	Virginia	June 25, 1788

The names of two of the first 10 American states commemorate early colonists. Delaware Bay was named after Thomas West, Lord De La Warr, a governor of Virginia. Pennsylvania was called "Pensilvania," or "Penn's woodland," in its original charter, issued in 1681 to the Quaker leader William Penn. Two states were named after places with which their founders had associations: New Jersey was the subject of a deed issued in 1644 by the Duke of York to John Berkeley and Sir George Carteret, who came from Jersey in the Channel Islands, and New Hampshire was called after the English county by settler Captain John Mason. Two names are of Native American origin: Connecticut after the Algonquin Indian name "kuenihtekot," meaning "long river at"; and Massachusetts, which is believed to be native American for "high hill, little plain," the name of a place and of a tribe. The remaining four states' names have royal connections: Virginia after Queen Elizabeth I, the "Virgin Queen," and Georgia, so-called by English soldier and politician James Oglethorpe in honor of King George II, who in 1732 issued a charter allowing him to colonize the area. The colony of Maryland, named after Queen Henrietta Maria, wife of Charles I, was planned by George Calvert, Baron Baltimore, but he died two months before the charter was signed, and it was his son Cecilius who established it. Carolina was originally a French settlement called La Caroline after the French king Charles IX, but the tract of land was issued in 1629 to Sir Robert Heath, who renamed it Carolina after the English king Charles I.

NEWEST STATES OF THE US

	State	Entered Union
1	Hawaii	August 21, 1959
2	Alaska	January 3, 1959
3	Arizona	February 14, 1912
4	New Mexico	January 6, 1912
5	Oklahoma	November 16, 1907
6	Utah	January 4, 1896
7	Wyoming	July 10, 1890
8	Idaho	July 3, 1890
9	Washington	November 11, 1889
10	Montana	November 8, 1889

LARGEST AMERICAN INDIAN TRIBES

	Tribe	Population
1	Cherokee	308,132
2	Navajo	219,198
3	Chippewa	103,826
4	Sioux	103,255
5	Choctaw	82,299
6	Pueblo	52,939
7	Apache	50,051
8	Iroquois	49,038
9	Lumbee	48,444
10	Creek	43,550

The total American Indian population as assessed by the 1990 Census was 1,878,285. Different authorities have estimated that the total North American population at the time of the first European arrivals in 1492 was anything from 1,000,000 to 10,000,000. This declined to a low in 1890 of some 90,000, but has experienced a substantial resurgence in the past century: according to the Census it had risen to 357,000 in 1950, 793,000 in 1970, and 1,479,000 in 1980.

US STATES WITH THE LONGEST SHORELINES

	State	Shoreline km	miles
1	Alaska	54,563	33,904
2	Florida	13,560	8,426
3	Louisiana	12,426	7,721
4	Maine	5,597	3,478
5	California	5,515	3,427
6	North Carolina	5,432	3,375
7	Texas	5,406	3,359
8	Virginia	5,335	3,315
9	Maryland	5,134	3,190
10	Washington	4,870	3,026

New Hampshire's 15-mile/29-km shoreline is the shortest among states that have one – 26 States, plus the District of Columbia, have no shoreline at all.

US STATES WITH THE GREATEST AREA OF TRIBAL LAND

	State	Acres
1	Arizona	20,087,538
2	New Mexico	7,882,619
3	Montana	5,574,835
4	South Dakota	4,520,719
5	Nevada	2,721,000
6	Washington	2,718,516
7	Utah	2,319,286
8	Wyoming	2,059,632
9	Alaska	1,352,205
10	Oklahoma	1,097,004

A total of 34 states contain a total of 56,183,794 acres of tribal land (land owned by tribes and individuals and held in trust by the federal government at the time of the 1990 Census). Some have very small areas (Arkansas has just three acres). The remaining 16 states have no tribal land at all.

TOP 10

US STATES WITH THE GREATEST AREAS OF INLAND WATER

	State	Inland water sq km	sq miles
1	Alaska	222,871	86,051
2	Michigan	103,602	40,001
3	Florida	30,461	11,761
4	Wisconsin	28,982	11,190
5	Louisiana	21,437	8,277
6	California	20,031	7,734
7	Minnesota	18,974	7,326
8	New York	18,780	7,251
9	Texas	17,319	6,687
10	North Carolina	13,217	5,103

TOP 10

LARGEST AMERICAN INDIAN RESERVATIONS

	Reservation/State	Population
1	Navajo, Arizona/ New Mexico/Utah	143,405
2	Pine Ridge, Nevada/ South Dakota	11,182
3	Fort Apache, Arizona	9,825
4	Gila River, Arizona	9,116
5	Papago, Arizona	8,480
6	Rosebud, South Dakota	8,043
7	San Carlos, Arizona	7,110
8	Zuni Pueblo, Arizona/ New Mexico	7,073
9	Hopi, Arizona	7,061
10	Blackfeet, Montana	7,025

TOP 10

LARGEST STATES IN THE US

	State	Area* sq km	sq miles
1	Alaska	1,700,130	656,424
2	Texas	695,673	268,601
3	California	423,999	163,707
4	Montana	380,847	147,046
5	New Mexico	314,937	121,598
6	Arizona	295,274	114,006
7	Nevada	286,367	110,567
8	Colorado	269,618	104,100
9	Oregon	254,819	98,386
10	Wyoming	253,347	97,818

* Total, including water

Alaska, the largest state, has the second smallest population (587,000; Wyoming is the smallest with 453,588). Alaska also has the greatest area of inland water of any state; 222,871 sq miles/86,051 sq km.

TOP 10

SMALLEST STATES IN THE US

	State	Area* sq km	sq miles
1	Rhode Island	4,002	1,545
2	Delaware	6,447	2,489
3	Connecticut	14,358	5,544
4	New Jersey	22,590	8,722
5	New Hampshire	24,219	9,351
6	Vermont	24,903	9,615
7	Massachusetts	27,337	10,555
8	Hawaii	28,313	10,932
9	Maryland	32,135	12,407
10	West Virginia	62,759	24,231

* Total, including water

The District of Columbia has a total area of 176 sq km/68 sq miles.

TOP 10

MOST HIGHLY POPULATED STATES IN THE US

	State	Population 1900	1996
1	California	1,485,053	31,878,234
2	Texas	3,048,710	19,128,261
3	New York	7,268,894	18,184,774
4	Florida	528,542	14,399,985
5	Pennsylvania	6,302,115	12,056,112
6	Illinois	4,821,550	11,846,544
7	Ohio	4,157,545	11,172,782
8	Michigan	2,420,982	9,594,350
9	New Jersey	1,883,669	7,987,933
10	Georgia	2,216,231	7,353,225

The total population of the United States according to the 1900 Census was 76,212,168, compared to the US Bureau of the Census's 1996 estimate of 265,283,783. It has undergone an almost 68-fold expansion in the 206 years since 1790, when it was just 3,929,214. Some states continue to grow faster than others: Florida's population is now 27 times its 1900 figure, and in the 1980s alone increased by 30 percent, while in the same decade that of California grew by more than 20 percent.

TOP 10

STATES WITH THE MOST FOREIGN-BORN RESIDENTS

	State	Residents
1	California	6,458,825
2	New York	2,851,861
3	Florida	1,662,601
4	Texas	1,524,436
5	New Jersey	966,610
6	Illinois	952,272
7	Massachusetts	573,733
8	Pennsylvania	369,316
9	Michigan	355,393
10	Washington	322,144
	Total of all states	*19,767,316*

16

PLACE NAMES

TOP 10

MOST COMMON PLACE NAMES IN THE US

	Name	Occurrences
1	Fairview	287
2	Midway	252
3	Riverside	180
4	Oak Grove	179
5	Five Points	155
6	Oakland	149
7	Greenwood	145
8=	Bethel	141
8=	Franklin	141
10	Pleasant Hill	140

TOP 10

MOST COMMON PLACE NAMES IN THE UK

	Name	Occurrences
1	Newton	150
2	Blackhill/Black Hill	141
3	Mountpleasant/Mount Pleasant	130
4	Castlehill/Castle Hill	127
5	Woodside/Wood Side	116
6	Newtown/New Town	111
7	Greenhill/Green Hill	108
8	Woodend/Wood End	106
9	Burnside	105
10	Beacon Hill	94

TOP 10

LONGEST PLACE NAMES IN THE US*

	Name	Letters
1	El Pueblo de Nuestra Señora la Reina de los Angeles de la Porciuncula, CA (*see* The Top 10 Longest Place Names in the World, No. 5)	57
2	Chargoggagoggmanchauggagogg-chaubunagungamaugg, MA (*see* The Top 10 Longest Place Names in the World, No. 6)	45
3	Villa Real de la Santa Fe de San Francisco de Asis, NM (*see* The Top 10 Longest Place Names in the World, No. 7=)	40
4	Nunathloogagamiutbingoi Dunes, Alaska	28
5	Winchester-on-the-Severn, Maryland	21
6	Scraper-Moechereville, Illinois	20
7	Linstead-on-the-Severn, Maryland	19
8=	Kentwood-in-the-Pines, California	18
8=	Lauderdale-by-the-Sea, Florida	18
8=	Vermilion-on-the-Lake, Ohio	18

TOP 10

COUNTRIES WITH THE LONGEST OFFICIAL NAMES

	Official name*	Common English name	Letters
1	al-Jamāhīrīyah al-ʾArabīya al-Lībīyah ash-Shaʿbīyah al-Ishtirākīyah	Libya	56
2	al-Jumhūrīyah al-Jazāʾirīyah ad-Dīmuqrāṭīyah ash-Shaʾbīyah	Algeria	49
3	United Kingdom of Great Britain and Northern Ireland	United Kingdom	45
4	Sri Lankā Prajathanthrika Samajavadi Janarajaya	Sri Lanka	43
5	Jumhūrīyat al-Qumur al-Ittihādīyah al-Islāmīyah	The Comoros	41
6=	al-Jumhūrīyah al-Islāmīyah al-Mūrītānīyah	Mauritania	36
6=	The Federation of St. Christopher and Nevis	St. Kitts and Nevis	36
8	Jamhuuriyadda Dimuqraadiga Soomaaliya	Somalia	35
9	al-Mamlakah al-Urdunnīyah al-Hāshimīyah	Jordan	34
10	Repoblika Demokratika n'i Madagaskar	Madagascar	32

* *Some official names have been transliterated from languages that do not use the Roman alphabet; their lengths may vary according to the method of transliteration used*

There is clearly no connection between the lengths of names and the longevity of the nation states that bear them. Since this list was first published in 1991, the following three countries have ceased to exist: Socijalisticka Federativna Republika Jugoslavija (Yugoslavia, 45 letters), Soyuz Sovetskikh Sotsialisticheskikh Respublik (USSR, 43), and Ceskoslovenská Socialistická Republika (Czechoslovakia, 36). Uruguay's official name of La República Oriental del Uruguay (29 letters) is sometimes given in full as the 38-letter La República de la Banda Oriental del Uruguay, which would place it in 6th position.

* *Including single-word, hyphenated, and multiple names (not counting hyphens as characters)*

A number of long American place names are of Native American origin, but some are not as long as they once were: in 1916 the US Board on Geographic Names saw fit to reduce the 26-letter New Hampshire stream known as Quohquinapassakessamanagno to "Beaver Creek." There are a number of street names that would qualify for entry, among them a Dr. Martin Luther King Jr. Boulevard in Manhattan, and a Dr. Martin Luther King Jr. Drive in Chicago.

T O P 1 0

MOST COMMON PLACE NAMES OF BIBLICAL ORIGIN IN THE US

	Name/meaning	Occurrences
1	Bethel (house of God)	141
2	Salem (peace)	134
3	Eden (pleasure)	101
4	Shiloh (peace)	98
5	Paradise (pleasure ground)	94
6	Antioch (named for Antiochus, king of Syria)	83
7	Sharon (plain)	72
8	Jordan (descender)	65
9=	Bethany/Bethania (house of affliction)	59
9=	Zion (mount, sunny)	59

An earlier version of this list based on a sampling of more than 60,000 US place names showed Salem to be the most frequent among more than 100 place names of Biblical origin in the US. The name derives from the that of the kingdom ruled over by king Melchizidek (Genesis 14:18), which is often identified with Jerusalem. Salem, Massachusetts, founded in 1628 was the first town in the US to acquire a biblical name. However, this revised version, which takes account of all populated places (cities, towns, and villages) in the US and includes compound names, such as Salemville and Salem Heights, indicates that it falls into second place behind Bethel.

T O P 1 0

LONGEST PLACE NAMES IN THE WORLD*

	Name	Letters
1	Krung thep mahanakhon bovorn ratanakosin mahintharayutthaya mahadilok pop noparatratchathani burirom udomratchanivetma hasathan amornpiman avatarnsa thit sakkathattiyavisnukarmprasit	167

When the poetic name of Bangkok, capital of Thailand, is used, it is usually abbreviated to "Krung Thep" (City of Angels).

2	Taumatawhakatangihangakoauau-otamateaturipukakapikimaunga-horonukupokaiwhenuakitanatahu	85

This is the longer version (the other has a mere 83 letters) of the Maori name of a hill in New Zealand. It translates as "The place where Tamatea, the man with the big knees, who slid, climbed, and swallowed mountains, known as land-eater, played on the flute to his loved one."

3	Gorsafawddacha'idraigodanhed-dogleddollônpenrhynareur-draethceredigion	67

A name contrived by the Fairbourne Steam Railway, Gwynedd, North Wales, UK, for publicity purposes and in order to out do its rival, No. 4. It means "The Mawddach station and its dragon teeth at the Northern Penrhyn Road on the golden beach of Cardigan Bay."

4	Llanfairpwllgwyngyllgogerychwyrn-drobwllllantysiliogogogoch	58

This is the place in Gwynedd, UK, famed especially for the length of its railroad tickets. It means "St. Mary's Church in the hollow of the white hazel near to the rapid whirlpool of Llantysilio of the Red Cave." Its official name comprises only the first 20 letters.

	Name	Letters
5	El Pueblo de Nuestra Señora la Reina de los Angeles de la Porciuncula	57

The site of a Franciscan mission and the full Spanish name of Los Angeles, California, it means "the town of Our Lady the Queen of the Angels of the Little Portion."

6	Chargoggagoggmanchauggagogg-chaubunagungamaugg	45

This is a lake near Webster, Massachusetts. Its Native American name loosely means "You fish on your side, I'll fish on mine, and no one fishes in the middle." An invented extension of its real name (Chagungungamaug Pond, or "boundary fishing place"), this name was devised in the 1920s by Larry Daly, editor of the Webster Times.

7=	Lower North Branch Little Southwest Miramichi	40

Canada's longest place name belongs to a short river in New Brunswick.

7=	Villa Real de la Santa Fe de San Francisco de Asis	40

The full Spanish name of Santa Fe, New Mexico, translates as "Royal city of the holy faith of St. Francis of Assisi."

9	Te Whakatakanga-o-te-ngarehu-o-te-ahi-a-Tamatea	38

The Maori name of Hammer Springs, New Zealand, like the 2nd name in this list, refers to a legend of Tamatea, explaining how the springs were warmed by "the falling of the cinders of the fire of Tamatea."

10	Meallan Liath Coire Mhic Dhubhghaill	32

The longest multiple name in Scotland, this is the name of a place near Aultanrynie, Highland, alternatively spelled Meallan Liath Coire Mhic Dhughaill.

* *Including single-word, hyphenated, and multiple names*

THE LONG SIDE OF THE TRACKS
For the benefit of its many visitors, the original 58-letter version of the name of this Welsh village is spelled phonetically on its station signboard. It is of dubious origin, however, the modern invention of local poet John Evans, and today ranks only as the world's second longest railroad station name, having been overtaken by a similarly contrived Welsh placename.

NATIONAL PARKS

COUNTRIES WITH THE LARGEST PROTECTED AREAS

	Country	Percent of total area	Designated area sq km	sq ml
1	Brazil	16.8	1,430,167	552,191
2	US	10.6	993,547	383,611
3	Greenland	45.2	982,500	379,345
4	Australia	10.9	837,843	323,493
5	Colombia	71.9	818,346	316,158
6	Canada	5.6	554,369	214,092
7	Venezuela	60.7	553,496	213,706
8	Tanzania	38.9	365,115	140,972
9	Indonesia	17.2	330,059	127,437
10	China	3.2	308,970	119,294

The International Union for the Conservation of Nature has defined a National Park as a relatively large area that is not altered by human exploitation and occupation. Many countries have such areas, the Yellowstone National Park in the US being the first, established in 1872. However, since there are also tracts of land that are worthy of protection, but that already have human habitation, the broader definition has evolved of "protected area," which encompasses national parks, nature preserves, natural monuments, and other sites. There are at least 25,000 such designated areas around the world.

THE GRAND CANYON
The Grand Canyon National Park, which comprises 178 miles/286 km of the Colorado River Valley, Arizona, is regarded as one of the great natural wonders of the world and attracts over 4.5 million visitors annually.

MOST VISITED NATIONAL PARKS IN THE US

	Park/location	Visitors (1996)
1	Great Smoky Mountains National Park, North Carolina/Tennessee	9,265,667
2	Grand Canyon National Park, Arizona	4,537,703
3	Yosemite National Park, California	4,046,207
4	Olympic National Park, Washington	3,348,723
5	Yellowstone National Park, Wyoming	3,012,171
6	Rocky Mountain National Park, California	2,923,755
7	Grand Teton National Park, Wyoming	2,733,439
8	Acadia National Park, Maine	2,704,831
9	Zion National Park, Utah	2,498,001
10	Mammoth Cave, Kentucky	1,896,829

FIRST NATIONAL MONUMENTS IN THE US

	National Monument	Established
1	Little Big Horn Battlefield, Montana	Jan 29, 1879
2	Casa Grande Ruins, Arizona	Mar 2, 1889
3	Devils Tower, Wyoming	Sep 24, 1906
4=	El Morro, New Mexico	Dec 8, 1906
4=	Montezuma Castle, Arizona	Dec 8, 1906
6	Gila Cliff Dwellings, New Mexico	Nov 16, 1907
7	Tonto, Arizona	Dec 19, 1907
8	Muir Woods, California	Jan 9, 1908
9	Grand Canyon, Arizona	Jan 11, 1908
10	Pinnacles, California	Jan 16, 1908

There are some 73 National Monuments in the US, covering a total of 3,226 sq miles/ 8,355 sq km/2,064,446 acres. Some sites were identified as of special historical importance earlier than those in this Top 10, but were not officially designated as National Monuments until later dates.

T O P 1 0

LARGEST NATIONAL PARKS IN THE US

	National Park	Established	sq km	Area sq miles	acres
1	Wrangell-St Elias, Alaska	Dec 2, 1980	33,683	13,005	8,323,618
2	Gates of the Arctic, Alaska	Dec 2, 1980	30,448	11,756	7,523,888
3	Denali (formerly Mt. McKinley), Alaska	Feb 26, 1917	19,189	7,409	4,741,910
4	Katmai, Alaska	Dec 2, 1980	14,872	5,742	3,674,794
5	Death Valley, California/Nevada	Oct 31, 1994	13,629	5,262	3,367,628
6	Glacier Bay, Alaska	Dec 2, 1980	13,051	5,039	3,224,794
7	Lake Clark, Alaska	Dec 2, 1980	10,603	4,094	2,619,859
8	Yellowstone, Wyoming/ Montana/Idaho	Mar 1, 1872	8,982	3,468	2,219,791
9	Kobuk Valley, Alaska	Dec 2, 1980	7,086	2,736	1,750,737
10	Everglades, Florida	May 30, 1934	6,102	2,356	1,507,850

Yellowstone National Park was established on March 1, 1872 as the first national park in the world with its role "as a public park or pleasuring ground for the benefit and enjoyment of the people." There are now some 1,200 national parks in more than 100 countries. There are 54 National Parks in the US, with a total area of 83,906 sq miles/217,316 sq km 53,699,743 acres (more than double their area before 1980, when large tracts of Alaska were added). With the addition of various National Monuments, National Historic Parks, National Preserves, and other specially designated areas under the aegis of the National Park Service, the total area is 129,688 sq miles/335,890 sq km (approximately 83 million acres), visited by almost 300,000,000 people a year.

T H E 1 0

FIRST NATIONAL PARKS IN THE US

	National Park	Established
1	Yellowstone, Wyoming/Montana/Idaho	Mar 1, 1872
2	Sequoia, California	Sep 25, 1890
3=	Yosemite, California	Oct 1, 1890
3=	General Grant, California*	Oct 1, 1890
5	Mount Rainier, Washington	Mar 2, 1899
6	Crater Lake, Oregon	May 22, 1902
7	Wind Cave, South Dakota	Jan 9, 1903
8	Mesa Verde, Colorado	Jun 29, 1906
9	Glacier, Montana	May 11, 1910
10	Rocky Mountain, Colorado	Jan 26, 1915

* Name changed to Kings Canyon National Park, March 4, 1940

These are the first 10 National Parks established in the US, even though other National Parks may claim a place in the list because they were founded under different appellations at earlier dates and subsequently redesignated as National Parks.

T H E 1 0

FIRST NATIONAL HISTORIC SITES IN THE US

	National Historic Site	Established*
1	Ford's Theatre, Washington DC	Apr 7, 1866
2	Abraham Lincoln Birthplace, Kentucky	Jul 17, 1916
3	Andrew Johnson, Tennessee	Aug 29, 1935
4	Jefferson National Expansion Memorial, Missouri	Dec 20, 1935
5	Whitman Mission, Washington	Jun 29, 1936
6	Salem Maritime, Massachusetts	Mar 17, 1938
7	Fort Laramie, Wyoming	Jul 16, 1938
8	Hopewell Furnace, Pennsylvania	Aug 3, 1938
9	Vanderbilt Mansion, New York	Dec 18, 1940
10	Fort Raleigh, North Carolina	Apr 5, 1941

* Dates include those for locations originally assigned other designations but later authorized as Historic Sites

Among the most recent of the 74 locations established as Historic Sites were, in 1987, the Plains, Georgia, birthplace and home of President Jimmy Carter, and in 1992 that commemorating the 1954 Brown v Board of Education case, held in Topeka, Kansas, which ruled that racial segregation in public schools was unconstitutional.

TALL BUILDINGS

TALLEST HABITABLE BUILDINGS IN THE WORLD

	Building/location	Stories	Height m	ft
1	Petronas Towers, Kuala Lumpur, Malaysia	96	452	1,482
2	Sears Tower, Chicago, IL _with spires_	110	443 _520_	1,454 _1,707_
3	World Trade Center*, New York, NY	110	417	1,368
4	Jin Mao Building, Shanghai, China _with spire_	93	382 _420_	1,255 _1,378_
5	Empire State Building, New York, NY _with spire_	102	381 _449_	1,250 _1,472_
6	T & C Tower, Kao-hsiung, Taiwan	85	348	1,142
7	Amoco Building, Chicago, IL	80	346	1,136
8	John Hancock Center, Chicago, IL _with spire_	100	344 _450_	1,127 _1,476_
9	Shun Hing Square, Shenzhen, China _with spires_	80	330 _384_	1,082 _1,263_
10	Sky Central Plaza, Guangzhou, China _with spires_	80	323 _391_	1,060 _1,283_

* Twin towers; the second tower, completed in 1973, has the same number of stories but is slightly smaller at 1,362 ft/415 m – although its spire takes it up to 1,710 ft/521 m

Heights are of buildings less their television and radio antennae and uninhabited extensions. The Sears Tower maintains its claim as the tallest building by virtue of having the most floors, the highest occupied floor, and the longest elevator ride.

TALLEST HABITABLE BUILDINGS IN THE SOUTHERN HEMISPHERE

	Building/location	Stories	Height m	ft
1	Rialto Tower, Melbourne, Australia	60	242	794
2	MLC Centre, Sydney, Australia	60	228	748
3	Governor Phillip Tower, Sydney, Australia	54	227	745
4	Central Park Tower, Perth, Australia	52	226	742
5	Bourke Place*, Melbourne, Australia	48	224	735
6=	Carlton Centre, Johannesburg, South Africa	50	220	722
6=	120 Collins Street, Melbourne, Australia	52	220	722
8	Chifley Tower, Sydney, Australia	50	215	705
9	R & I Bank, Perth, Australia	52	214	702
10	Melbourne Central, Melbourne, Australia	55	211	692

* The BHP logo on the top of the building is Australia's highest sign

TALLEST RESIDENTIAL TOWERS IN THE WORLD

	Building/location	Stories	Height m	ft
1	Lake Point Tower, Chicago, IL	70	197	645
2	Central Park Place, New York, NY	56	191	628
3	Olympic Tower, New York, NY	51	189	620
4	Huron Apartments, Chicago, IL	58	183	600
5	May Road Apartments, Hong Kong	58	180	590
6	Marina City Apartments, Chicago, IL	61	179	588
7	30 Broad Street, New York, NY	48	171	562
8	Galleria, New York, NY	57	168	552
9	Ritz Tower, New York, NY	41	165	540
10	Amartapura Condominiums, Tangerang, Indonesia	54	163	535

These towers are all purely residential, rather than office buildings with a proportion given over to residential use. Above its 50 levels of office suites, the 1,127-ft/ 344-m John Hancock Center, Chicago, built in 1968, has 48 levels of apartments (floors 44 through to 92, at 509 ft/155 m to 1,033 ft/315 m above street level), which are thus the tallest apartments in the world. The Metropolitan Tower, New York City, built in 1988, is 716 ft/218 m high with 66 stories, of which the top 48 floors are residential. The 58-story 650-ft/198-m Museum Tower, also in New York, similarly has mixed occupancy, with its top 40 levels residential. The Century Tower, Sydney, Australia, just misses a place in this Top 10.

TALLEST HOTELS IN THE WORLD

	Building/location	Stories	Height m	ft
1	Baiyoke II Tower, Bangkok, Thailand	89	319	1,046
2	Yu Kyong, Pyong Yang, North Korea	105	300	985
3	Raffles Western Hotel, Singapore	73	226	742
4	Westin Peachtree Hotel, Atlanta, GA	71	220	723
5	Westin Hotel, Detroit, MI	71	219	720
6	Shangri-la, Hong Kong	60	215	705
7	Four Seasons Hotel, New York City, NY	52	208	682
8	Trump International Hotel, New York City, NY	45	207	679
9	Trump Tower, New York City, NY	68	202	664
10	Conrad International, Hong Kong	60	200	656

THE TOWERING CENTURY

I ncreasingly tall buildings have been one of the most visible signs of progress during the 20th century. The world's first skyscrapers were built over 100 years ago in Chicago, but the city soon lost its crown to New York. The Empire State Building was to maintain its role as the world's tallest building for more than 40 years, but since the 1980s other US cities, and increasingly those in the Far East, have joined the race. Even the Petronas Tower, Malaysia, the current world record holder, is scheduled to be overtaken by the end of the decade by the Chongqing Tower, China, a 114-story building soaring to 1,500 ft/457 m.

TOP 10

WORLD CITIES WITH MOST SKYSCRAPERS*

	City	Country	Skyscrapers
1	New York City	US	131
2	Chicago	US	47
3	Hong Kong	China	30
4	Houston	US	27
5	Los Angeles	US	21
6	Kuala Lumpur	Malaysia	20
7=	Dallas	US	17
7=	Melbourne	Australia	17
9=	San Francisco	US	15
9=	Shanghai	China	15
9=	Singapore	Singapore	15

* Habitable buildings of over 500 ft/152 m

The word "skyscraper" was first used in the 18th century to mean a high-flying flag on a ship, and later to describe a tall horse or person. It was not used to describe buildings until the 1880s, when the first tall office buildings of 10 stories or more were built in Chicago and New York, with the Eiffel Tower following at the end of the decade. The first modern (i.e. steel-framed) skyscraper was the Woolworth Building, New York, built in 1913.

BANK OF CHINA
Hong Kong's once tallest building prompted a surge of skyscraper construction that has been followed in other Asian cities.

WOOLWORTH BUILDING
Built in 1913, it pioneered New York's passion for skyscrapers.

SEARS TOWER
After 22 years at the top, Chicago's Sears Tower has officially lost its status as "world's tallest."

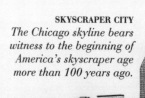

SKYSCRAPER CITY
The Chicago skyline bears witness to the beginning of America's skyscraper age more than 100 years ago.

BRIDGES

LONGEST SUSPENSION BRIDGES IN THE WORLD

	Bridge/location	Year completed	Length of main span m	ft
1	Great Belt, Denmark	1997	1,624	5,328
2	Humber Estuary , UK	1980	1,410	4,626
3	Tsing Ma, Hong Kong, China	1997	1,377	4,518
4	Verrazano Narrows, New York, NY	1964	1,298	4,260
5	Golden Gate, San Francisco, CA	1937	1,280	4,200
6	Höga Kusten, Veda, Sweden	1997	1,210	3,970
7	Mackinac Straits, Michigan	1957	1,158	3,800
8	Minami Bisano-seto, Kojima-Sakaide, Japan	1988	1,100	3,609
9	Fatih Sultan Mehmet (Bosphorus II), Istanbul, Turkey	1988	1,090	3,576
10	Bosphorus I, Istanbul, Turkey	1973	1,074	3,524

If constructed according to plan, the Messina Strait Bridge between Sicily and Calabria, Italy, will have the longest central span at 3,320 m/10,892 ft. However, at 3,910 m/12,828 ft, Japan's Akashi-Kaikyo Bridge, scheduled for completion in 1998, will be the longest overall.

TALLEST BRIDGE TOWERS IN THE WORLD

	Bridge/ location/year completed	Height m	ft
1	East Bridge, Great Belt Fixed Link, Sprogø, Denmark, 1997	254	833
2	Golden Gate, San Francisco, CA, 1937	227	754
3	Ponte de Normandie, Le Havre, France, 1994	214	702
4	Verrazano Narrows, New York City, NY, 1964	210	690
5	Tsing Ma, Hong Kong, China, 1997	206	675
6	Tagus, Lisbon, Portugal, 1965	190	625
7	George Washington, New York City, NY, 1931	183	600
8	Mackinac Straits, Michigan, MI, 1957	168	552
9	Humber Estuary, Hessle-Barton, UK, 1979	162	531
10	Firth of Forth Road, Queensferry, UK, 1964	156	512

HIGHEST-EARNING TOLL BRIDGES AND TUNNELS IN THE US

	Crossing	Annual income ($)
1	Manhattan & Staten Island area crossings, New York	497,546,000
2	Delaware River–Philadelphia, Pennsylvania	106,889,000
3	Chesapeake Bay crossings, Maryland	94,804,000
4	Southern San Francisco Bay Bridges, California	71,396,000
5	Northern San Francisco Bay Bridges, California	54,923,000
6	Delaware Memorial Bridge, Wilmington, Delaware	53,792,000
7	Chesapeake Bay Bridge & Tunnel System, Virginia	33,065,000
8	Delaware River northern crossings, New Jersey	25,981,000
9	Hudson River, New York	20,953,000
10	Greater New Orleans Bridges, Louisiana	19,919,000

LONGEST DRAW BRIDGES IN THE US

	Bridge	Longest span m	ft
1	Fort Madison, Mississippi River, Iowa	166	545
2	George P. Coleman Memorial (US-17), York River, Virginia	152	500
3	S.W. Spokane Street, Seattle, Washington	146	480
4	Duluth, St. Louis Bay, Minnesota	148	486
5	C.M. & N. Railroad, Chicago, Illinois	142	467
6	Route 82, East Haddam, Connecticut	142	465
7	Coos Bay, Oregon	140	458
8	Rigolets Pass, New Orleans, Louisiana	122	400
9	Douglass Memorial, Washington, DC	118	386
10	Lord Delaware, Mattaponi River, Virginia	77	252

LONGEST VERTICAL LIFT BRIDGES IN THE US

	Bridge	Longest span m	ft
1	Arthur Kill, Staten Island, NYC/New Jersey	170	558
2	Pennsylvania Railroad, Kirkwood/Mt Pleasant, DE	167	548
3	Cape Cod Canal, MA,	166	544
4	Delair, Delaware River, NJ	165	542
5	Marine Parkway, Jamaica Bay, NYC	165	540
6	Burlington, Delware River, NJ	163	534
7	Williamette River, Portland, OR	159	521
8	A-S-B Fratt, Kansas City, MO	130	428
9	Harry S. Truman, Kansas City, MO	130	427
10	Roosevelt Island, NYC	126	415

LE PONT DE NORMANDIE
At 2,808 ft/856 m the new bridge crossing the Seine near Le Havre, France, will be the world's longest cable-stayed bridge until the 1999 completion of the 2,920-ft/890-m Tatara

T O P 1 0

LONGEST CANTILEVER BRIDGES IN THE WORLD

	Bridge/location	Year completed	Longest span m	ft
1	Pont de Québec, Canada	1917	549	1,800
2	Firth of Forth, Scotland	1890	521	1,710
3	Minato, Osaka, Japan	1974	510	1,673
4	Commodore John Barry, New Jersey/Pennsylvania	1974	494	1,622
5=	Greater New Orleans 1, Louisiana	1958	480	1,575
5=	Greater New Orleans 2, Louisiana	1988	480	1,575
7	Howrah, Calcutta, India	1943	457	1,500
8	Gramercy, Louisiana	1995	445	1,460
9	Transbay, San Francisco	1936	427	1,400
10	Baton Rouge, Louisiana	1969	376	1,235

T O P 1 0

LONGEST BRIDGES IN THE US

	Bridge	Year completed	Length of main span m	ft
1	Verrazano Narrows, New York	1964	1,298	4,260
2	Golden Gate, San Francisco, California	1937	1,280	4,200
3	Mackinac Straits, Michigan	1957	1,158	3,800
4	George Washington, New York	1931	1,067	3,500
5	Tacoma Narrows II, Washington	1950	853	2,800
6	Transbay, San Francisco, California	1936	704	2,310
7	Bronx-Whitestone, New York	1939	701	2,300
8	Delaware Memorial, Wilmington, Delaware (twin)	1951/68	655	2,150
9	Walt Whitman, Philadelphia, Pennsylvania	1957	610	2,000
10	Ambassador, Detroit, Michigan	1929	564	1,850

All are suspension bridges. The US also has the two longest steel arch bridges in the world, the New River Gorge Bridge, Fayetteville, West Virginia (1977: 1,700 ft/518 m), and the Bayonne in Bayonne, New Jersey (1931: 1,675 ft/511 m) – both of them longer than the next longest in the world, the Sydney Harbour Bridge (1932: 1,670 ft/ 509 m). The Mark Clark Expressway in Charleston, South Carolina (1992: 1,600 ft/488 m) is the world's longest continuous truss bridge.

T O P 1 0

LONGEST CABLE-STAYED BRIDGES IN THE WORLD

	Bridge	Location	Year completed	Length of main span m	ft
1	Pont de Normandie	Le Havre, France	1994	856	2,808
2	Qunghzhou Minjiang	Fozhou, China	1996	605	1,985
3	Yangpu	Shanghai, China	1993	602	1,975
4=	Meiko-Chuo	Nagoya, Japan	1997	590	1,936
4=	Xupu	Shanghai, China	1997	590	1,936
6	Skarnsundet	Trondheim Fjord, Norway	1991	530	1,739
7	Ikuchi	Onomichi-Imabari, Japan	1994	490	1,608
8	Higashi-Kobe	Kobe, Japan	1992	485	1,591
9	Ying Kau	Hong Kong, China	1997	475	1,558
10	Seohae Grand	Asanman, South Korea	1997	470	1,542

TUNNELS

TOP 10

LONGEST UNDERWATER TUNNELS IN THE WORLD

	Tunnel/location	Type	Year completed	Length km	miles
1	Seikan, Japan	Rail	1988	53.90	33.49
2	Channel Tunnel, France/England	Rail	1994	49.94	31.03
3	Dai-Shimizu, Japan	Rail	1982	22.17	13.78
4	Shin-Kanmon, Japan	Rail	1975	18.68	11.61
5	Great Belt Fixed Link (Eastern Tunnel), Denmark	Rail	1997	8.00	4.97
6	Severn, UK	Rail	1886	7.01	4.36
7	Haneda, Japan	Rail	1971	5.98	3.72
8	Kammon, Japan	Rail	1942	3.60	2.24
9	Kammon, Japan	Road	1958	3.46	2.15
10	Mersey, UK	Road	1934	3.43	2.13

The need to connect the Japanese islands of Honshu, Kyushu, and Hokkaido has resulted in a wave of underwater-tunnel building in recent years, with the Seikan the most ambitious project of all. Connecting Honshu and Hokkaido, 14.4 miles/23.3 km of the tunnel are 328 ft/100 m below the sea bed, bored through strata that presented such enormous engineering problems that it took 24 years to complete. The Channel Tunnel's overall length is shorter than the Seikan Tunnel, but the undersea portion, at 23.6 miles/38.0 km, is longer.

TOP 10

LONGEST RAIL TUNNELS IN THE WORLD

	Tunnel/location	Year completed	Length km	miles
1	Seikan, Japan	1988	53.90	33.49
2	Channel Tunnel, France/England	1994	49.94	31.03
3	Moscow Metro (Medvedkovo/Belyaevo section), Russia	1979	30.70	19.07
4	London Underground (East Finchley/Morden, Northern Line), UK	1939	27.84	17.30
5	Dai-Shimizu, Japan	1982	22.17	13.78
6	Simplon II, Italy/Switzerland	1922	19.82	12.31
7	Simplon I, Italy/Switzerland	1906	19.80	12.30
8	Shin-Kanmon, Japan	1975	18.68	11.61
9	Apennine, Italy	1934	18.52	11.50
10	Rokko, Japan	1972	16.25	10.10

TOP 10

LONGEST CANAL TUNNELS IN THE WORLD

	Tunnel	Canal/location	Length km	miles
1	Rôve	Canal de Marseille au Rhône, France	7.12	4.42
2	Bony	Canal de St. Quentin, France	5.67	3.52
3	Standedge	Huddersfield Narrow, UK	5.10	3.17
4	Mauvages	Canal de la Marne et Rhin, France	4.88	3.03
5	Balesmes	Canal Marne à Saône, France	4.82	3.00
6	Ruyaulcourt	Canal du Nord, France	4.35	2.70
7	Strood*	Thames and Medway, UK	3.57	2.22
8	Sapperton	Thames and Severn, UK	3.49	2.17
9	Lappal	Birmingham, UK	3.47	2.16
10	Pouilly-en-Auxois	Canal de Bourgogne, France	3.35	2.08

* *Later converted to a rail tunnel*

After a delay in construction during World War I, the Rôve tunnel on the Canal de Marseilles au Rhône was completed in 1927. Although it has been out of service since June 16, 1963, it remains the longest and the largest canal tunnel in the world, once capable of accommodating ocean-going ships. It is 59 ft/18 m wide and 50.5 ft/15.4 m high, with a bore area of 3,444 sq ft/320 sq m, or about six times the size of a double-track rail tunnel.

TOP 10

LONGEST RAIL TUNNELS IN EUROPE*

	Tunnel/location	Year completed	Length km	miles
1	Channel Tunnel, France/England	1994	49.94	31.03
2	Simplon II, Italy/Switzerland	1922	19.82	12.31
3	Simplon I, Italy/Switzerland	1906	19.80	12.30
4	Apennine, Italy	1934	18.52	11.50
5	Furka Base, Switzerland	1982	15.38	9.55
6	St. Gotthard, Switzerland	1882	15.00	9.32
7	Lötschberg, Switzerland	1913	14.61	9.08
8	Paola, Italy	1988	14.49	9.01
9	Mont-Cenis, France/Italy	1871	13.66	8.49
10	Inn Valley, Austria	1994	12.70	7.89

* *Excluding subways*

T O P 1 0

LONGEST ROAD TUNNELS IN THE WORLD

	Tunnel/location	Year completed	Length km	miles
1	St. Gotthard, Switzerland	1980	16.32	10.14
2	Arlberg, Austria	1978	13.98	8.69
3=	Fréjus, France/Italy	1980	12.90	8.02
3=	Pinglin Highway, Taiwan	*	12.90	8.02
5	Mt. Blanc, France/Italy	1965	11.60	7.21
6	Gudvangen, Norway	1992	11.40	7.08
7	Leirfjord, Norway	*	11.11	6.90
8	Kanetsu, Japan	1991	11.01	6.84
9	Kanetsu, Japan	1985	10.93	6.79
10	Gran Sasso, Italy	1984	10.17	6.32

* *Under construction*

T O P 1 0

LONGEST ROAD AND RAIL TUNNELS IN THE US*

	Tunnel/location	Type	Year completed	Length km	miles
1	Cascade, Washington	Rail	1929	12.54	7.79
2	Flathead, Montana	Rail	1970	12.48	7.78
3	Moffat, Colorado	Rail	1928	10.00	6.21
4	Hoosac, Massachusetts	Rail	1875	7.56	4.70
5	BART Trans-Bay Tubes, San Francisco, California	Rail	1974	5.79	3.50
6	Brooklyn–Battery, New York	Road	1950	2.78	1.73
7	E. Johnson Memorial, Colorado	Road	1979	2.74	1.70
8	Eisenhower Memorial, Colorado#	Road	1973	2.72	1.69
9	Holland Tunnel, New York	Road	1927	2.61	1.62
10	Lincoln Tunnel I, New York	Road	1937	2.51	1.56

* *Excluding subways*
# *The highest-elevation highway tunnel in the world*

At 9.13 miles/14.70 km, Mount McDonald rail tunnel, on the Canadian Pacific line from Calgary, Alberta, to Vancouver, British Columbia, is the longest transport tunnel in North America. In 1979 the US Air Force was reported to have built an experimental 3.73-mile/6.00-km missile transporting tunnel somewhere beneath the Arizona desert. Although longer than any US highway tunnel, its detailed specifications remain a military secret. The New York City West Delaware water tunnel, completed in 1944 and measuring 105.00 miles/168.98 km, is the longest tunnel in the world.

T O P 1 0

LONGEST TUNNELS IN THE UK*

	Tunnel/location	Type	Length km	miles
1	Severn, Avon/Gwent	Rail	7.02	4.36
2	Totley, South Yorkshire	Rail	5.70	3.54
3	Standedge, Manchester/West Yorkshire	Canal	5.10	3.17
4	Standedge, Manchester/West Yorkshire	Rail	4.89	3.04
5	Woodhead New, South Yorkshire	Rail	4.89	3.04
6	Sodbury, Avon	Rail	4.07	2.53
7	Strood, Kent	Rail	3.57	2.22
8	Disley, Cheshire	Rail	3.54	2.20
9	Ffestiniog, Gwynedd	Rail	3.52	2.19
10	Sapperton, Gloucestershire	Canal	3.49	2.17

* *Excluding subways*

THE CHANNEL TUNNEL
First proposed almost 200 years ago, the Channel Tunnel was finally opened in 1994. It is Europe's longest and the world's second longest undersea and rail tunnel.

OTHER STRUCTURES

TOP 10

OLDEST CHURCHES IN THE US

	Church/location	Built
1	Convento de Porta Coeli, San German, Puerto Rico*	1609
2	San Estevan del Rey Mission, Valencia County, New Mexico	1629
3	St. Luke's Church, Isle of Wight County, Virginia	1632
4	First Church of Christ and the Ancient Burying Ground, Hartford County, Connecticut	1640
5	St. Ignatius Catholic Church, St. Mary's County, Maryland	1641
6	Merchant's Hope Church, Prince George County, Virginia	1657
7	Flatlands Dutch Reformed Church, Kings County, New York	1660
8=	0ds House, Essex County, Massachusetts	1661
8=	Church San Blas de Illesces of Coamo, Ponce, Puerto Rico*	1661
8=	St. Mary's Whitechapel, Lancaster County, Virginia	1661

* Not US territory when built, but now a US National Historic Site

TOP 10

OLDEST CATHEDRALS IN THE UK

	Cathedral	Founded
1	Canterbury	1071
2	Lincoln	1073
3	Rochester	1077
4=	Hereford	1079
4=	Winchester	1079
6	York	1080
7	Worcester	1084
8	London (now St. Paul's)	1087
9	Durham	1093
10	Exeter	1114

TOP 10

LARGEST DAMS IN THE WORLD

(Ranked according to the volume of material used in construction)

	Dam	Location	Completed	Volume (m³)
1	Syncrude Tailings	Alberta, Canada	1992	540,000,000
2	Pati	Paraná, Argentina	1990	230,180,000
3	New Cornelia Tailings	Ten Mile Wash, Arizona	1973	209,500,000
4	Tarbela	Indus, Pakistan	1976	105,922,000
5	Fort Peck	Missouri River, Montana	1937	96,050,000
6	Lower Usuma	Usuma, Nigeria	1990	93,000,000
7	Atatürk	Euphrates, Turkey	1990	84,500,000
8	Yacyreta-Apipe	Paraná, Paraguay/Argentina	1991	81,000,000
9	Guri (Raul Leoni)	Caroni, Venezuela	1986	77,971,000
10	Rogun	Vakhsh, Tajikistan	1987	75,500,000

Despite the recent cancellation of several dams on environmental grounds, such as two in the Cantabrian Mountains, Spain, numerous major projects are in development for completion by the end of the century, when this Top 10 will contain some notable new entries. Among several in Argentina is the Chapeton dam under construction on the Paraná, and scheduled for completion this year; it will have a volume of 296,200,000 m³ and will thus become the 2nd largest dam in the world. The Pati, also on the Paraná, will have a volume of 238,180,000 m³, and the Kambaratinsk on the Nayrn, Kyrgyzstan, a volume of 112,000,000 m³. The Cipasang dam under construction on the Cimanuk, Indonesia, will have a volume of 90,000,000 m³.

TOP 10

LARGEST SPORTS STADIUMS IN THE WORLD

	Stadium	Location	Capacity
1	Strahov Stadium	Prague, Czech Republic	240,000
2	Maracaña Municipa Stadium	Rio de Janeiro, Brazil	205,000
3	Rungnado Stadium	Pyongyang, South Korea	150,000
4	Estadio Maghalaes Pinto	Belo Horizonte, Brazil	125,000
5=	Estadio Morumbi	São Paulo, Brazil	120,000
5=	Estadio da Luz	Lisbon, Portugal	120,000
5=	Senayan Main Stadium	Jakarta, Indonesia	120,000
5=	Yuba Bharati Krirangan	nr. Calcutta, India	120,000
9	Estadio Castelão	Fortaleza, Brazil	119,000
10=	Estadio Arrudão	Recife, Brazil	115,000
10=	Estadio Azteca	Mexico City, Mexico	115,000
10=	Nou Camp	Barcelona, Spain	115,000

T O P 1 0

HIGHEST DAMS IN THE WORLD

	Dam	River/location	Completed	Height m	ft
1	Rogun	Vakhsh, Tajikistan	U/C*	335	1,099
2	Nurek	Vakhsh, Tajikistan	1980	300	984
3	Grand Dixence	Dixence, Switzerland	1961	285	935
4	Inguri	Inguri, Georgia	1980	272	892
5=	Chicoasén	Grijalva, Mexico	U/C	261	856
5=	Tehri	Bhagirathi, India	U/C	261	856
7	Kishau	Tons, India	U/C	253	830
8=	Ertan	Yangtse-kiang, China	U/C	245	804
8=	Sayano-Shushensk	Yeniesei, Russia	U/C	245	804
10	Guavio	Guavio, Colombia	U/C	243	797

* Uncompleted at time of publication

T O P 1 0

LARGEST MAN-MADE LAKES IN THE WORLD*

	Dam/lake	Location	Completed	Volume (m³)
1	Owen Falls	Uganda	1954	204,800,000,000
2	Bratsk	Russia	1964	169,900,000,000
3	High Aswan	Egypt	1970	162,000,000,000
4	Kariba	Zimbabwe	1959	160,368,000,000
5	Akosombo	Ghana	1965	147,960,000,000
6	Daniel Johnson	Canada	1968	141,851,000,000
7	Guri (Raul Leoni)	Venezuela	1986	135,000,000,000
8	Krasnoyarsk	Russia	1967	73,300,000,000
9	W.A.C. Bennett	Canada	1967	70,309,000,000
10	Zeya	Russia	1978	68,400,000,000

* Includes only those formed as a result of dam construction

The enlargement of the existing natural lake that resulted from the construction of the Owen Falls created the man-made lake with the greatest surface area: at 26,828 sq miles/69,484 sq km, it is almost as large as the Republic of Ireland.

T O P 1 0

LARGEST BELLS IN THE WESTERN WORLD

	Bell/location	Year cast	Weight (tons)
1	*Tsar Kolokol*, Kremlin, Moscow, Russia	1735	222.56
2	*Voskresenskiy (Resurrection)*, Ivan the Great Bell Tower, Kremlin, Moscow, Russia	1746	72.20
3	*Petersglocke*, Cologne cathedral, Germany	1923	28.00
4	Lisbon cathedral, Portugal	post-1344	26.90
5	St. Stephen's cathedral, Vienna, Austria	1957	23.58
6	Bourdon, Strasbourg cathedral, France	1521	22.05
7	*Savoyarde*, Sacre-Coeur basilica, Paris, France	1891	20.78
8	Bourdon, Riverside Church, New York, NY	1931	20.44
9	Olmütz, Czech Republic	1931	20.05
10	*Campagna gorda*, Toledo cathedral, Spain	1753	19.51

The largest bell in the world is the 20 ft 2 in/6.14 m high, 21 ft 8 in/6.6 m diameter *Tsar Kolokol*, cast in Moscow for the Kremlin. It cracked before it had been installed and has remained there, unrung, ever since. New York's Riverside Church bell (the largest ever cast in England) is the bourdon (that sounding the lowest note) of the 74-bell Laura Spelman Rockefeller Memorial Carillon. This bell is part of one of the world's largest carillons. It is 10 ft 2 in/3.10 m diameter with a total weight of 114.24 tons. Outside the West, large bells exist but were designed to be struck with a beam, not rung with a clapper like Western bells. A 181-ton bell in Osaka, Japan, was destroyed in 1942, but there is a 170-ton bell in the Shi-Tenno-Ji Temple, Kyoto, and an 83-ton bell in Chonan, Japan. The Mingun or Mingoon bell in Mandalay, Myanmar (formerly Burma), cast in 1780, weighs approximately 97 tons, and there is a 60-ton bell in Beijing, China.

T H E 1 0

HIGHEST DAMS IN THE US

	Dam/Location	Height m	ft
1	Oroville, Feather, CA	230	755
2	Hoover, Colorado, AZ/NV	221	725
3	Dworshak, North Fork of Clearwater, ID	219	717
4	Glen Canyon, Colorado, AZ	216	709
5	New Bullard's Bar, North Yuba, CA	194	637
6	New Melones, Stanislaus, CA	191	625
7	Swift, Lewis, WA	186	610
8	Mossyrock, Cowlitz, WA	185	607
9	Shasta, Sacramento, CA	183	602
10	Don Pedro, Tuolumnne, CA	173	568

THE COMMERCIAL WORLD

TOP 10

DUTY-FREE AIRPORTS IN THE WORLD

	Airport	Annual sales ($)
1	London Heathrow Airport	524,100,000
2	Honolulu Airport	419,500,000
3	Hong Kong Airport	400,000,000
4	Singapore Changi Airport	358,800,000
5	Tokyo Narita Airport	340,000,000
6	Amsterdam Schiphol Airport	326,600,000
7	Manila N. Aquino Airport	302,600,000
8	Frankfurt Airport	289,400,000
9	Paris Charles De Gaulle Airport	283,000,000
10	London Gatwick Airport	193,800,000

Although London Heathrow Airport achieved the greatest sales, Honolulu Airport had the highest average sales per passenger ($109.83 compared with $15.79).

TOP 10

DUTY-FREE PRODUCTS

	Product	Annual sales ($)
1	Women's fragrances	2,250,000,000
2	Cigarettes	2,235,000,000
3	Women's cosmetics	1,767,000,000
4	Scotch whisky	1,663,000,000
5	Cognac	1,235,000,000
6	Men's fragrances and toiletries	1,109,000,000
7	Accessories	1,050,000,000
8	Confectionery	1,049,000,000
9	Leather goods (handbags, belts, etc.)	902,000,000
10	Watches	703,000,000

TOP 10

DUTY-FREE COUNTRIES IN THE WORLD

	Country	Annual sales ($)
1	UK	1,827,000,000
2	US	1,447,000,000
3	South Korea	1,052,000,000
4	Germany	1,019,000,000
5	Finland	936,000,000
6	Hong Kong	889,000,000
7	Japan	798,000,000
8	France	718,000,000
9	Denmark	706,000,000
10	Netherlands	668,000,000

In 1995 the UK led the world in duty- and tax-free shopping, accounting for 8.9 percent of total sales. Europe as a whole took 50.4 percent of global sales, Asia and Oceania 30.5 percent, the Americas 18.0 percent, and the whole of Africa just one percent.

TOP 10

EXPORT MARKETS FOR GOODS FROM THE US

	Country	Total value of exports ($)
1	Canada	201,017,080,000
2	Japan	101,661,940,000
3	Mexico	73,141,360,000
4	UK	45,589,320,000
5	South Korea	40,100,400,000
6	Germany	35,382,520,000
7	Taiwan	30,478,200,000
8	Netherlands	26,161,640,000
9	Singapore	24,226,140,000
10	France	22,507,100,000

TOP 10

MOST POPULAR NEW PRODUCTS OF 1996 IN THE US

1	Luvs Stretch Diapers
2	Scott 1000 paper products
3	Pepcid AC antacid
4	Nicorette gum
5	Baked Lays potato chips
6	Pampers Premium diapers
7	Tagament HB/200 antacid
8	Bounty Medleys paper towels
9	DiGiorno self-rising pizza
10	Zantac 75 antacid

Source: Information Resources, Inc.

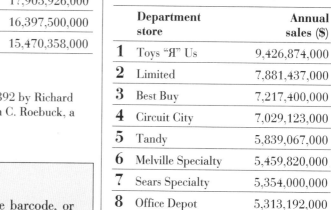

PORT TO PORT
Although service industries have become increasingly significant, the import and export of goods remains the driving force of international trade.

TOP 10

RETAILERS IN THE US

	Retailer	Annual sales ($)		Retailer	Annual sales ($)
1	Wal-Mart Stores	93,627,000,000	6	J.C. Penney Co., Inc.	20,562,000,000
2	KMart Corp.	34,389,000,000	7	American Stores Co.	18,308,894,000
3	Sears Roebuck & Co.	28,020,000,000	8	Price/Costco	17,905,926,000
4	The Kroger Co.	23,937,795,000	9	Safeway Stores	16,397,500,000
5	Dayton Hudson	23,516,000,000	10	Home Depot	15,470,358,000

Source: National Retail Federation

Sears Roebuck, once the No. 1 in this list, was established in Chicago in 1892 by Richard Warren Sears, a former railroad worker turned watch salesman, and Alvah C. Roebuck, a watchmaker, originally exclusively as a mail order company.

THE BIRTH OF THE BARCODE

Now a familiar feature of almost every product we buy, the barcode, or "Universal Product Code," was patented just 25 years ago. Although various similar ideas had been proposed earlier, the design that uses alternating bars was patented on December 11, 1973 by James L. Vanderpool of the Monarch Marking Systems Company of Dayton, Ohio (US Patent No. 3,778,597), establishing the method that is now used internationally. The first barcoded product to pass through a checkpoint was a pack of Wrigley's chewing gum, sold at the Marsh Supermarket, Troy, Ohio, at 8:01am on Wednesday, June 26, 1974.

25 YEARS AGO · YEARS AGO · YEARS AGO ·

TOP 10

SPECIALTY STORES IN THE US (1995)

	Department store	Annual sales ($)
1	Toys "Я" Us	9,426,874,000
2	Limited	7,881,437,000
3	Best Buy	7,217,400,000
4	Circuit City	7,029,123,000
5	Tandy	5,839,067,000
6	Melville Specialty	5,459,820,000
7	Sears Specialty	5,354,000,000
8	Office Depot	5,313,192,000
9	Woolworth Specialty	5,099,000,000
10	TJX	4,447,549,000

Source: National Retail Federation

A toy store heads the list easily, with much of the rest of the Top 10 being equally divided by electronics stores and divisions of major retailers, such as Sears and Woolworths. Others on the list are regional powerhouses, and thus unfamiliar to citizens in other parts of the country.

COMMUNICATION

FIRST PLACES TO ISSUE POSTAGE STAMPS

	Place	Date issued
1	Great Britain	May 1840
2	New York City	Feb 1842
3	Zurich, Switzerland	Mar 1843
4	Brazil	Aug 1843
5	Geneva, Switzerland	Oct 1843
6	Basle, Switzerland	Jul 1845
7	United States	Jul 1847
8	Mauritius	Sep 1847
9	France	Jan 1849
10	Belgium	Jul 1849

The first adhesive postage stamps issued in the US were designed for local delivery and produced by the City Despatch Post, New York City. They were inaugurated on February 15, 1842 and later that year were incorporated into the US Post Office Department. In 1847 the rest of the US followed suit, and the Post Office Department issued its first national stamps.

COUNTRIES SENDING THE MOST LETTERS PER PERSON

	Country	Average*
1	US	670
2=	Liechtenstein	490
2=	Sweden	490
4	Norway	470
5=	Netherlands	420
5=	France	420
7=	Denmark	340
7=	Austria	340
9=	Belgium	330
9=	Luxembourg	330

* *Number of letters mailed per person per annum*

According to the Universal Postal Union's figures the world average for letters mailed per person is 72.

COUNTRIES WITH THE MOST POST OFFICES

	Country	Post offices		Country	Post offices
1	India	153,000	6	Japan	25,000
2	China	64,000	7	UK	20,000
3	US	50,000	8	Germany	19,000
4	Russia	47,000	9	France	17,000
5	Turkey	35,000	10	Ukraine	16,000

COUNTRIES WITH THE MOST TELEPHONES

	Country	Telephones
1	US	155,749,790
2	Japan	60,700,000
3	Germany	40,869,190
4	France	31,600,000
5	UK	28,530,000
6	China	27,230,000
7	Italy	24,542,079
8	Russia	24,097,265
9	South Korea	17,646,614
10	Canada	17,000,000

COUNTRIES WITH THE MOST TELEPHONES PER 100 PEOPLE

	Country	Telephones per 100 people
1	Sweden	68.67
2	Switzerland	61.35
3	Canada	60.74
4	Denmark	60.41
5	US	59.86
6	Luxembourg	57.29
7	Iceland	56.19
8	Norway	55.37
9	Finland	55.36
10	France	54.73

T O P   1 0

COUNTRIES THAT MAKE THE MOST INTERNATIONAL PHONE CALLS

	Country	Calls per person	Total calls per annum
1	US	9.0	2,342,728,000
2	Germany	17.0	1,384,000,000
3	UK	9.1	528,000,000 *
4	Italy	8.7	503,990,000
5	Switzerland	60.0	416,053,000
6	Netherlands	26.5	405,400,000
7	China	0.3	387,350,000
8	Canada	11.9	332,750,000 *
9	Spain	7.5	295,450,000
10	Belgium	29.4	291,037,000

* Estimated

T O P   1 0

COUNTRIES WITH THE MOST CELLULAR PHONE USERS

	Country	Cellular users
1	US	24,134,421
2	Japan	4,331,000
3	UK	3,956,000
4	Germany	2,466,432
5	Australia	2,289,000
6	Italy	2,240,039
7	Canada	1,890,000
8	China	1,566,000
9	Sweden	1,387,000
10	South Korea	960,300

MODERN BUSINESS ON THE LINE
The growth of communications – especially the use of cellular phones – in the 1980s and 1990s has revolutionized global business life.

T O P   1 0

COUNTRIES WITH THE MOST FAX MACHINES

	Country	Fax machines installed
1	US	2,925,000
2	Japan	2,000,000
3	Germany	850,000
4	UK	454,000
5	France	401,000
6	Italy	260,000
7	Canada	199,000
8	China	187,000
9	India	180,000
10	Australia	135,000

Facsimile transmission from one point to another was suggested in the early 19th century and developed in a primitive form soon after the invention of the telephone. As new technology enables transmission from computer to computer, the number of new installations each year, as indicated by this list, will inevitably decline.

T O P   1 0

INTERNET SITES BY TYPE

	Domain name	Type	Number*
1	.com	Commercial	3,965,417
1	.edu	Educational	2,654,129
2	.net	Networks	1,548,575
4	.jp	Japan	734,406
5	.de	Germany	721,847
6	.mil	Military	655,128
7	.ca	Canada	603,325
8	.uk	United Kingdom	591,624
9	.us	United States	587,175
10	.au	Australia	514,760
	Total (including domains not in Top 10)		16,146,360

* As of January, 1997
Source: Network Wizards (http://www.nw.com/)

According to the source used .org is in 12th place with 313,204 sites; .gov is 11th with 387,280.

T O P   1 0

MOST LINKED-TO SITES ON THE WORLD WIDE WEB

	Site	Links
1	Welcome to Netscape	84,052
2	Yahoo	35,818
3	WebCounter Home Page	30,394
4	WebCrawler Searching	25,783
5	The Blue Ribbon Campaign for Online Free Speech	19,667
6	Welcome to Microsoft	17,460
7	Lycos, Inc., Home Page	14,769
8	Infoseek	13,993
9	Discover NCSA: The National Center for Supercomputing Applications	12,478
10	Welcome to Starting Point™	11,195

Source: WebCrawler (http://webcrawler.com/), June 1997

A survey identified those sites on the Internet that were most frequently linked, enabling users to "cruise" to them.

TOYS & GAMES

MOST EXPENSIVE TOYS SOLD AT AUCTION BY CHRISTIE'S EAST, NEW YORK

	Toy/sale	Price ($)*
1	"The Charles," a firehose reel made by American manufacturer George Brown & Co, c. 1875, December 1991	231,000
2	Märklin fire station, December 1991	79,200
3	Horse-drawn, double-decker streetcar, December 1991	71,500
4	Mikado mechanical bank, December 1993	63,000
5	Märklin ferris wheel, June 1994	55,200
6	Girl skipping rope mechanical bank, June 1994	48,300
7	Märklin battleship, June 1994	33,350
8	Märklin battleship, June 1994	32,200
9=	Bing keywind open phaeton tinplate automobile, December 1991	24,200
9=	Märklin fire pumper, December 1991	24,200

Including 10 percent buyer's premium

The firehose reel at No. 1 in this list has the record price paid at auction for any toy other than a doll. Models by the German tinplate maker Märklin, regarded by collectors as the Rolls-Royce of toy manufacturers, similarly feature among the record prices of auction houses in the UK and other countries, where high prices have also been attained.

MOST LANDED-ON SQUARES IN MONOPOLY®*

US game		UK game
Illinois Avenue	1	Trafalgar Square
Go	2	Go
B. & O. Railroad	3	Fenchurch Street Station
Free Parking	4	Free Parking
Tennessee Avenue	5	Marlborough Street
New York Avenue	6	Vine Street
Reading Railroad	7	King's Cross Station
St. James Place	8	Bow Street
Water Works	9	Water Works
Pennsylvania Railroad	10	Marylebone Station

Monopoly® is a registered trade mark of Parker Brothers, a division of Tonka Corporation, US

* Based on a computer analysis of the probability of landing on each square

Monopoly was patented in February 1936. It was devised in Philadelphia during the Great Depression by Charles Darrow, an unemployed heating engineer. Darrow's streets were derived from those of the New Jersey resort, Atlantic City, and with its subtle balance of skill and luck, Monopoly was the first property game that was fun to play. His sales in 1934 rocketed to 20,000, and he entered into a licensing arrangement with Parker Brothers. Darrow rapidly became a millionaire.

TOYS IN THE US IN 1996

1 Barbie*
2 LEGO*
3 Nintendo 64
4 Star Wars*
5 Batman*
6 Hot Wheels*
7 Tickle Me Elmo
8 Sega Saturn
9 Power Rangers*
10 Barney*

* Variety of products within range
Source: Market Focus

MOST EXPENSIVE TEDDY BEARS SOLD AT AUCTION IN THE UK

	Bear/date	Price ($)
1	"Teddy Girl," Steiff bear, December 5, 1994#	170,500
2	"Happy," Steiff Teddy bear, September 19, 1989*	85,250
3	"Eliot," a blue Steiff bear, December 6, 1993#	76,725
4	Black Steiff Teddy bear, May 18, 1990*	37,510
5	"Alfonzo," a red Steiff bear, May 18, 1989#	18,755
6	Rod-jointed Steiff apricot plush Teddy bear, May 9, 1991*	18,244
7	Black Steiff Teddy bear, October 19, 1990+	13,640
8	Apricot-colored Steiff bear, January 31, 1990*	11,935
9=	White plush Steiff Teddy bear January 31, 1990*	9,378
9=	White plush Steiff Teddy bear May 18, 1990*	9,378

* Sold by Sotheby's, London
 # Sold by Christie's, London
+ Sold by Phillip's, London

T O P 1 0

HIGHEST-SCORING WORDS IN SCRABBLE

Word/play	Score
1 Quartzy	(i) 164
	(ii) 162

(i) Play across a triple-word-score (red) square with the Z on a double-letter-score (light blue) square.

(ii) Play across two double-word-score (pink) squares with Q and Y on pink squares.

2= Bezique	(i) 161
4=	(ii) 158

(i) Play across a red square with either the Z or the Q on a light blue square.

(ii) Play across two pink squares with the B and second E on two pink squares.

2= Cazique	(i) 161
4=	(ii) 158

(i) Play across a red square with either the Z or the Q on a light blue square.

(ii) Play across two pink squares with the C and E on two pink squares.

4= Zinkify	158

Play across a red square with the Z on a light blue square.

5= Quetzal	155

Play across a red square with either the Q or the Z on a light blue square.

5= Jazzily	155

Using a blank as one of the Zs, play across a red square with the nonblank Z on a light blue square.

5= Quizzed	155

Using a blank as one of the Zs, play across a red square with the nonblank Z or the Q on a light blue square.

8= Zephyrs	152

Play across a red square with the Z on a light blue square.

8= Zincify	152

Play across a red square with the Z on a light blue square.

8= Zythums	152

Play across a red square with the Z on a light blue square.

These Top 10 words all contain seven letters and therefore earn the premium of 50 for using all the letters in the rack.

T O P 1 0

BESTSELLING CD-ROM TITLES IN THE US, 1996

	Title	Manufacturer
1	*Microsoft Windows95 Upgrade*	Microsoft
2	*Myst*	Broderbund
3	*Warcraft II*	CUC
4	*Duke Nukem 3D*	GT Interactive
5	*Flight Simulator*	Microsoft
6	*Quicken Deluxe*	Intuit
7	*Corel Printhouse*	Corel
8	*Toy Story Animated Storybook*	Disney
9	*Netscape Navigator Personal Edition 3.0*	Netscape
10	*Civilization 2*	MicroProse

Myst drops only one position from its 1994 ranking, outsold during 1995 only by the mega-hyped *Microsoft Windows95*.

FROM PLAYROOM TO SALESROOM
Along with rare toys and teddy bears, fine examples of the doll-maker's craft often attain high prices at auction.

T O P 1 0

MOST EXPENSIVE DOLLS EVER SOLD AT AUCTION IN THE UK

	Doll/sale	Price ($)
1	Kämmer and Reinhardt doll, Sotheby's, London, February 8, 1994	297,800
2	Kämmer and Reinhardt bisque character doll, German, *c.* 1909, Sotheby's, London, October 17, 1996	170,950
3	Kämmer and Reinhardt bisque character doll, German, *c.* 1909, Sotheby's, London, October 17, 1996	144,900
4	Albert Marque bisque character doll, Sotheby's, London, October 17, 1996	112,200
5=	William and Mary wooden doll, English, *c.* 1690, Sotheby's, London, March 24, 1987	105,900
5=	17th-century wooden doll, Christie's, London, May 18, 1989	105,900
7	Albert Marque bisque character doll, Sotheby's, London, October 17, 1996	92,700
8	Mulatto pressed bisque swivel-head Madagascar doll, Sotheby's, London, October 17, 1996	89,000
9	Shellacked pressed bisque swivel-head doll, Sotheby's, London, October 17, 1996	71,900
10	Pressed bisque doll, Sotheby's, London, October 17, 1996	58,000

FUEL & POWER

TOP 10

ENERGY CONSUMERS IN THE WORLD

	Country	Oil	Natural gas	Coal	Nuclear power	Hydro-electric power	Total
						Energy consumption 1995*	
1	US	889.3	616.7	545.0	201.6	28.4	2,281.1
2	China	173.6	17.4	705.8	3.6	17.9	918.3
3	Russia	161.0	350.4	131.6	28.2	16.8	688.1
4	Japan	294.6	60.6	94.7	81.9	8.5	540.3
5	Germany	148.9	73.9	102.0	43.9	2.0	370.6
6	France	98.1	32.6	14.3	107.3	7.2	259.5
7	India	79.9	18.7	141.4	2.2	8.3	250.6
8	Canada	88.2	73.6	27.2	27.6	31.6	248.2
9	UK	90.1	72.5	52.7	25.4	0.6	241.2
10	Italy	104.6	47.4	12.2	–	4.0	168.2
	World	*3,557.0*	*2,076.3*	*2,436.9*	*657.4*	*240.9*	*8,968.4*

* Millions of tons of oil equivalent

TOP 10

NATURAL GAS CONSUMERS IN THE WORLD

	Country	Consumption 1995 billion m³	billion ft³
1	US	621.6	21,952
2	Russia	353.2	12,473
3	Ukraine	76.2	2,691
4	Germany	74.4	2,627
5	Canada	74.2	2,620
6	UK	73.1	2,582
7	Japan	61.2	2,161
8	Italy	47.8	1,688
9	Uzbekistan	42.4	1,497
10	Saudi Arabia	38.6	1,363
	World total	*2,093.0*	*73,914*

TOP 10

HYDROELECTRIC ENERGY CONSUMERS IN THE WORLD

	Country	Consumption 1995 (tons of oil equivalent)
1	Canada	31,600,000
2	US	28,400,000
3	Brazil	24,600,000
4	China	17,900,000
5	Russia	15,200,000
6	Norway	10,500,000
7	Japan	8,500,000
8	India	8,300,000
9	France	7,200,000
10	Sweden	6,400,000
	World total	*240,900,000*

Oil equivalent is the amount of oil that would be required to produce the same amount of energy. 1,000,000 tons of oil is equivalent to approximately 12,000,000,000 kilowatt-hours of electricity.

TOP 10

ELECTRICITY PRODUCERS IN THE WORLD

	Country	Production kW/hr
1	US	3,145,892,000,000
2	Russia	956,587,000,000
3	Japan	906,705,000,000
4	China	839,453,000,000
5	Canada	527,316,000,000
6	Germany	525,721,000,000
7	France	471,448,000,000
8	India	356,519,000,000
9	UK	323,029,000,000
10	Brazil	251,484,000,000

The Top 10 electricity consuming countries are virtually synonymous with these producers, since relatively little electricity is transmitted across national boundaries. Electricity production has burgeoned phenomenally in the postwar era: in 1948 US production was 336,600,000,000 kilowatt-hours, or about one-tenth of its total today, while that of Japan was 33,600,000,000 kilowatt-hours, less than four percent of its present amount.

TOP 10

COUNTRIES WITH THE GREATEST NATURAL GAS RESERVES

	Country	Known reserves (1995) trillion m³	trillion ft³ *
1	Russia	48.1	1,700.0
2	Iran	21.0	741.6
3	Qatar	7.1	250.0
4	United Arab Emirates	5.8	204.6
5	Saudi Arabia	5.3	185.9
6	US	4.6	163.8
7	Venezuela	4.0	139.9
8	Algeria	3.6	128.0
9	Nigeria	3.4	120.0
10	Iraq	3.1	109.7

* One trillion = 1 million million (10^{12})

The world total reserves of natural gas are put at 4,933.6 trillion ft³/139.7 trillion m³ – these Top 10 countries thus hold 76 percent of the world's supplies. At current rates of production, it is reckoned that natural gas supplies will last until 2060.

NORTH SEA OIL AND WATER
*Since 1972 North Sea production platforms
such as this one have extracted the bulk of
the oil produced by Norway and the UK.*

T O P 1 0

OIL PRODUCERS
IN THE WORLD

	Producer	Production 1995 (tons)
1	Saudi Arabia	470,100,000
2	USA	421,600,000
3	Russia	338,200,000
4	Iran	207,200,000
5	Mexico	166,800,000
6	China	164,200,000
7	Venezuela	161,400,000
8	Norway	154,200,000
9	UK	143,600,000
10	United Arab Emirates	124,300,000

Despite its huge output, the US produces
less than half the 889,300,000 tons a year
of oil that it consumes, which is equivalent
to 3 tons per person a year, consumed
directly (through consumption of heating
fuel, motor fuel, etc.) or indirectly (through
consumption of electricity produced by oil-
fired power stations, etc.).

T O P 1 0

COUNTRIES WITH THE LARGEST CRUDE OIL RESERVES

	Country	Reserves (tons)		Country	Reserves (tons)
1	Saudi Arabia	39,400,000,000	6	Venezuela	10,300,000,000
2	Iraq	14,800,000,000	7	Mexico	7,800,000,000
3	Kuwait	14,700,000,000	8	Russia	7,400,000,000
4	United Arab Emirates	14,000,000,000	9	Libya	4,300,000,000
5	Iran	13,200,000,000	10	US	4,100,000,000

Oil accounts for 40 percent of the world energy market. At the end of 1995, the global
known reserves of oil stood at 152,500,000,000 tons, dominated by a Top 10 that controls
129,800,000,000 tons, or 85 percent of the world's oil. At the 1995 rate of production, the
world supply will last for only another 43 years.

T O P 1 0

LARGEST NUCLEAR POWER STATIONS
IN THE WORLD

	Station	Country	Reactors in use	Output (megawatts)
1	Bruce	Canada	1–8	6,910
2	Gravelines	France	1–6	5,706
3	Paluel	France	1–4	5,528
4	Washington	US	1–5	5,326
5	Fukushima Daichi	Japan	1–6	4,696
6	Fukushima Daini	Japan	1–4	4,400
7	Pickering	Canada	1–8	4,328
8	Chinon	France	A3; B1–B4	4,051
9=	Kursk	Russia	1–4	4,000
9=	St. Petersburg	Russia	1–4	4,000

T O P 1 0

COUNTRIES WITH LONGEST
OIL PIPELINES

	Country	Total pipeline length km	miles
1	USA	276,000	171,498
2	Russia	63,000	39,146
3	Mexico	38,350	23,830
4	Canada	23,564	14,642
5	China	10,800	6,711
6	Iran	9,800	6,089
7	Germany	7,590	4,716
8	France	7,546	4,689
9	Argentina	6,990	4,343
10	Algeria	6,910	4,294

DIAMONDS & GOLD

TOP 10

MOST EXPENSIVE COINS EVER SOLD BY SPINK COIN AUCTIONS, LONDON

	Coin/sale	Price ($)
1	George V 1920 Sydney Mint sovereign (March 1, 1992)	156,000
2	Henry III gold penny (June 13, 1985)	97,500
3	Brazilian Coronation peca, 1822 (June 18, 1986)	87,000
4	George III pattern five guineas, 1773 (November 9, 1989)	85,500
5	George III pattern five pounds, 1820 (November 9, 1989)	71,250
6	Charles I triple unite, Oxford Mint, 1643 (May 31, 1989)	66,000
7	Charles II gold pattern crown, 1662 (November 19, 1990)	61,500
8	Edward VIII proof sovereign, 1937 (December 7, 1984)	60,000
9	Henry VIII sovereign (June 2, 1983)	59,000
10	Anne Vigo five guineas, 1703 (November 9, 1989)	58,500

Founded in 1666, the year of the Great Fire of London, Spink & Son Ltd. is the world's oldest-established firm of antique dealers and numismatists. In addition to the coins appearing in the list, on July 3, 1988, in Tokyo, Spink & Son, in association with the Taisei Stamp and Coin Co., achieved the world record price for a British coin when they sold a Victoria proof gothic crown – dating from 1847 and one of only two known – for the equivalent of $189,000.

TOP 10

LARGEST UNCUT DIAMONDS IN THE WORLD

	Diamond	Carats
1	Cullinan	3,106.00

Measuring approximately 4 x 2½ x 2 in/10 x 6.5 x 5 cm, and weighing 1 lb 6 oz/621 gm, the Cullinan was unearthed in 1905. Bought by the Transvaal Government for $750,000, it was presented to King Edward VII. The King decided to have it cut, and the most important of the separate gems are now among the British Crown Jewels.

	Diamond	Carats
2	Braganza	1,680.00

All trace of this enormous stone has been lost.

3	Excelsior	995.20

Cut by the celebrated Amsterdam firm of Asscher in 1903, the Excelsior produced 21 superb stones, which were sold mainly through Tiffany's of New York.

4	Star of Sierra Leone	968.80

Found in Sierra Leone on Valentine's Day, 1972, the uncut diamond weighed 8 oz/225 g and measured 2½ x 1½ in/6.5 x 4 cm.

5	Zale Corporation "Golden Giant"	890.00

Its origin is so shrouded in mystery that it is not even known which country it came from.

	Diamond	Carats
6	Great Mogul	787.50

When found in 1650 in the Gani Mine, India, this diamond was presented to Shah Jehan, the builder of the Taj Mahal. After Nadir Shah conquered Delhi in 1739, it entered the Persian treasury and apparently vanished from history.

7	Woyie River	770.00

Found in 1945 beside the river in Sierra Leone whose name it now bears, it was cut into 30 stones. The largest of these, known as Victory and weighing 31.35 carats, was auctioned at Christie's, New York, in 1984 for $880,000.

8	Presidente Vargas	726.60

Discovered in the Antonio River, Brazil, in 1938, it was named after the then President.

9	Jonker	726.00

In 1934 Jacobus Jonker found this massive diamond after it had been exposed by a heavy storm. Acquired by Harry Winston, it was exhibited in the American Museum of Natural History and attracted enormous crowds.

10	Reitz	650.80

Like the Excelsior, the Reitz was found in the Jagersfontein Mine in South Africa in 1895.

TOP 10

DIAMOND-PRODUCING COUNTRIES

	Country	Production per annum (carats)
1	Australia	41,000,000
2	Congo (Zaïre)	16,500,000
3	Botswana	14,700,000
4	Russia	11,500,000
5	South Africa	9,800,000
6	Brazil	2,000,000
7	Namibia	1,100,000
8=	Angola	1,000,000
8=	China	1,000,000
10	Ghana	700,000
	World total	100,850,000

TOP 10

LARGEST POLISHED GEM DIAMONDS IN THE WORLD

	Diamond/last known whereabouts or owner	Carats
1	"Unnamed Brown" (De Beers)	545.67
2	Great Star of Africa/Cullinan I (British Crown Jewels)	530.20
3	Incomparable/Zale (auctioned in New York, 1988)	407.48
4	Second Star of Africa/Cullinan II (British Crown Jewels)	317.40
5	Centenary (De Beers)	273.85
6	Jubilee (Paul-Louis Weiller)	245.35
7	De Beers (sold in Geneva, 1982)	234.50
8	Red Cross (sold in Geneva, 1973)	205.07
9	Black Star of Africa (unknown)	202.00
10	Anon (unknown)	200.87

South African gold mines have long been the world's No. 1 source, producing almost a quarter of the world's total annual output of almost 2,500 tons.

T O P 1 0

COUNTRIES HOLDING GOLD RESERVES

	Country	Reserves (tons)
1	US	8,974
2	Germany	3,263
3	Switzerland	2,855
4	France	2,806
5	Italy	2,286
6	Netherlands	1,192
7	Japan	831
8	Belgium	666
9	UK	633
10	Austria	628

Gold reserves are the government holdings of gold in each country – and are often far greater than the gold owned by private individuals. In the days of the "Gold Standard," this provided a tangible measure of a country's wealth. Though less significant today, gold reserves remain a component in calculating a country's international reserves, alongside its holdings of foreign exchange and SDRs (Special Drawing Rights).

T O P 1 0

COUNTRIES MAKING GOLD JEWELRY

	Country	Gold used p.a. (tons)
1	Italy	491.6
2	India	441.6
3	China	210.5
4	Saudi Arabia and Yemen	168.8
5	US	163.5
6	Indonesia	146.6
7	Turkey	121.7
8	Taiwan	112.4
9	Hong Kong	90.4
10	Japan	86.0

T O P 1 0

GOLD-MANUFACTURING COUNTRIES

	Country	Gold used in fabrication p.a. (tons)
1	Italy	504.7
2	India	469.7
3	US	275.9
4	China	224.6
5	Japan	206.4
6	Saudi Arabia and Yemen	150.4
7	Indonesia	146.6
8	Turkey	138.4
9	Taiwan	121.3
10	Hong Kong	95.8

Gold fabrication accounted for a world total consumption of 3,590 tons in 1995. This comes from various sources including mined production, scrap, and the release of gold from official stockpiles. In addition to the manufacture of jewelry, 230 tons were used in electronics, 72.4 tons in dentistry, and 120.8 for other industrial and decorative purposes. Issues of official coins also comprise a large sector of the gold market (38 tons in 1995).

T O P 1 0

GOLD-PRODUCING COUNTRIES

	Country	Production 1995 (tons)
1	South Africa	575.8
2	US	363.0
3	Australia	279.4
4	Canada	165.7
5	Russia	156.6
6	China	150.4
7	Indonesia	81.7
8	Brazil	74.3
9	Uzbekistan	70.1
10	Papua New Guinea	60.4

SAVE THE PLANET

THE 10
LARGEST LANDFILL SITES IN THE US

	Site/city	Daily disposal (tons)
1	Fresh Kills, Staten Island, New York	14,000
2	Puente Hills, Whittier, California	13,000
3	G.R.O.W.S., Morrisville, Pennsylvania	10,000
4=	Olinda Alpha Sanitary, Brea, California	6,000
4=	Altamont Sanitary, Livermore, California	6,000
4=	Cincinnati Regional Refuse Facility, Cincinnati, Ohio	6,000
7	Bradley Avenue W. Sanitary, Sun Valley, Idaho	5,600
8	South Side, Indianapolis, Indiana	5,500
9	Apex Regional, Apex, Nevada	5,200
10	Pontiac, Pontiac, Michigan	5,000

Source: Chartwell Information

THE 10
WORST CARBON DIOXIDE EMITTERS IN THE WORLD

	Country	CO_2 emissions per capita per annum (tons)
1	United Arab Emirates	46.61
2	US	21.09
3	Singapore	19.82
4	Kazakhstan	19.26
5	Trinidad and Tobago	17.97
6	Australia	16.80
7	Canada	16.52
8	Russia	15.55
9	Norway	15.46
10	Saudi Arabia	15.27
	World average	*4.52*

CO_2 emissions derive from three principal sources – fossil fuel burning, cement manufacturing, and gas flaring. Since World War II, increasing industrialization in many countries has resulted in huge increases in carbon output, a trend that most countries are now actively attempting to reverse.

SAVE THE CAN
The recycling of aluminum and steel cans has become increasingly common: in the US alone, more than 170 million drink cans and 13 million steel cans are recovered every day.

THE 10
WORST SULFUR DIOXIDE EMITTERS IN THE WORLD

	Country	Annual SO_2 emissions per capita kg	lb	oz
1	Canada	118.7	261	11
2	US	81.2	179	0
3	Germany	70.7	155	14
4	UK	61.8	136	4
5	Spain	56.1	123	11
6	Ireland	52.9	116	10
7	Belgium	41.8	92	2
8	Finland	38.3	84	7
9	Denmark	35.0	77	3
10	Italy	34.4	75	13

Sulfur dioxide, the principal cause of acid rain, is produced by fuel combustion in factories and power stations. Even very small quantities (concentrations as low as 10 to 20 micrograms per cubic meter) can cause severe environmental damage. During the 1980s, even though emissions by all countries declined, some attempts to check pollution in urban areas had an adverse effect on neighboring ecosystems.

TOP 10
MATERIALS IN MUNCIPAL SOLID WASTE IN THE US (1994)

	Material	Amount recovered (tons)	Recovered as % of amount generated	Total generated
1	Paper and paperboard	28,700,000	35.3	81,300,000
2	Other nonferrous metals	1,200,000	0.8	66,100,000
3	Aluminum	3,100,000	1.2	37,600,000
4	Yard trimmings	7,000,000	22.9	30,600,000
5	Plastics	900,000	4.7	19,800,000
6	Wood	1,400,000	9.8	14,600,000
7	Food wastes	500,000	3.4	14,100,000
8	Glass	3,100,000	23.4	13,300,000
9	Ferrous metals	3,700,000	32.3	11,500,000
10	Textiles	800,000	11.7	6,600,000
	Total municipal solid waste (including items not in Top 10)	*49,300,000*	*23.6*	*209,100,000*

TOP 10
STATES WITH THE HIGHEST RECYCLING RATE

	State	Waste recycled (%)
1	New Jersey	56
2	Wisconsin	50
3	Minnesota	41
4	Florida	40
5	Maine	35–40
6=	Ohio	35
6=	Vermont	35
8	Massachusetts	34
9	Virginia	33
10=	New York	32
10=	Oregon	32

Source: National Solid Waste Management Association

Through increasing public awareness and in response to state laws banning various types of packaging or levying additional taxes on the use of certain products, the recycling of solid waste has gathered considerable momentum in the US during the 1990s. All the states in the Top 10 report increased rates – Wisconsin, for example, had a rate of just 24 percent in 1992, and has thus more than doubled its recycling rate (although New Jersey's position at the head of the list may reflect its inclusion of recycled cars, which are omitted from the statistics of most states). Targets of 50 percent or more by the turn of the century or soon afterward have been declared by most states.

THE 10
WORST TRASH PRODUCERS IN THE WORLD

	Country	Domestic waste per capita per annum kg	lb
1	US	730	1,609
2	Australia	690	1,521
3	Canada	660	1,455
4	Finland	620	1,367
5	Iceland	560	1,235
6	Norway	510	1,124
7	The Netherlands	500	1,102
8	Luxembourg	490	1,080
9	France	470	1,036
10	Denmark	460	1,014

TOP 10
US STATES WITH THE HIGHEST BUDGETS FOR RECYCLING*

	State	Budget ($)
1	Wisconsin	45,200,000
2	Florida	25,000,000
3	Minnesota	18–20,000,000
4	Illinois	12,200,000
5	South Carolina	5,500,000
6	Massachusetts	4,800,000
7	Indiana	4,400,000
8	Nebraska	4,000,000
9	Ohio	3,500,000
10=	Hawaii	2,900,000
10=	Oregon	2,900,000

* *1996–7*

THE 10
WORST DEFORESTING COUNTRIES IN THE WORLD

	Country	Average annual forest loss 1981–90 (sq mi)
1	Brazil	14,170
2	Indonesia	4,290
3	Zaïre	2,830
4	Mexico	2,620
5	Bolivia	2,410
6	Venezuela	2,310
7	Thailand	1,990
8	Sudan	1,860
9	Tanzania	1,690
10	Paraguay	1,560

THE BIGGEST DUMP IN THE WORLD

In 1948 the Fresh Kills Landfill site on New York's Staten Island was opened. It has since become the world's largest rubbish dump, covering 2,200 acres to a height of 175 ft/53 m. New York households generate an average of 6.2 lb/2.8 kg of solid waste each per day, 62% of which is landfilled, with the remainder recycled, converted into energy, or incinerated. Every day up to 14,000 tons of this garbage arrives at Fresh Kills. There it is handled by over 500 employees. Environmental concerns have been expressed about the site's future and will continue beyond its closure, which is scheduled for the year 2002.

YEARS AGO • YEARS AGO • YEARS AGO • 50

THE WORLD'S RICHEST

TOP 10

COUNTRIES WITH THE MOST DOLLAR BILLIONAIRES*

	Country	Billionaires
1	US	145
2	Germany	48
3	Japan	34
4=	Hong Kong	12
4=	Thailand	12
6	France	11
7=	Indonesia	10
7=	Mexico	10
9=	Brazil	8
9=	Switzerland	8

* Individuals and families with a net worth of $1,000,000,000 or more
Based on data published in Forbes Magazine

TOP 10

HIGHEST-EARNING ENTERTAINERS IN THE WORLD

	Entertainer	Profession	1995–96 income ($)
1	Oprah Winfrey	TV host/producer	171,000,000
2	Steven Spielberg	Film producer/director	150,000,000
3	The Beatles	Rock group	130,000,000
4	Michael Jackson	Singer	90,000,000
5	The Rolling Stones	Rock group	77,000,000
6	The Eagles	Rock group	75,000,000
7=	David Copperfield	Illusionist	74,000,000
7=	Arnold Schwarzenegger	Actor	74,000,000
9	Jim Carrey	Actor	63,000,000
10=	Michael Crichton	Novelist/screenwriter	59,000,000
10=	Jerry Seinfeld	TV performer	59,000,000

Used by permission of Forbes Magazine

TOP 10

HIGHEST-EARNING SINGERS IN THE WORLD

	Singer(s)	1995–96 income ($)
1	The Beatles	130,000,000
2	Michael Jackson	90,000,000
3	The Rolling Stones	77,000,000
4	The Eagles	75,000,000
5	Garth Brooks	51,000,000
6	R.E.M.	44,000,000
7	Luciano Pavarotti	36,000,000
8	Kiss	35,000,000
9	Mariah Carey	32,000,000
10	Metallica	28,000,000

Used by permission of Forbes Magazine

Even though the Beatles no longer exist as a group, they continue to earn huge revenue from their recordings and videos. The Rolling Stones typify the huge income generated by major rock tours: their *Voodoo Lounge* tour made $300,000,000, while Microsoft paid $4,000,000 to use their song *Start Me Up* to promote Windows95.

TOP 10

HIGHEST-EARNING ACTORS IN THE WORLD

	Actor(s)	1995–96 income ($)
1	Arnold Schwarzenegger	74,000,000
2	Jim Carrey	63,000,000
3	Tom Hanks	50,000,000
4	Tom Cruise	46,000,000
5=	Harrison Ford	44,000,000
5=	Clint Eastwood	44,000,000
5=	Sylvester Stallone	44,000,000
8	Robin Williams	42,000,000
9=	Roseanne	40,000,000
9=	Michael Douglas	40,000,000

Used by permission of Forbes Magazine

Actors with the audience magnetism of Arnold Schwarzenegger, Jim Carrey, and Clint Eastwood today routinely command $20,000,000 or more per movie, while percentage earnings can add further sums: Tom Hanks is thought to have made $35,000,000 from *Apollo 13*, and Tom Cruise could ultimately make over $60,000,000 for his role in *Mission: Impossible*.

TOP 10

HIGHEST-EARNING DECEASED PEOPLE

	Name	Year died
1	Elvis Presley	1977
2	John Lennon	1980
3	James Dean	1955
4	Jimi Hendrix	1970
5	Albert Einstein	1955
6	Marilyn Monroe	1962
7	Jim Morrison	1971
8	Humphrey Bogart	1957
9	Orson Welles	1985
10	Babe Ruth	1948

Under copyright law, the estates of numerous authors, film stars, singers, and songwriters continue to receive posthumous royalty income. Added to this, the commercial exploitation of iconic images in advertisements and other media has become a major business, with Einstein, for example, used to promote everything from whisky to computer software. The estates of innumerable other deceased celebrities accrue substantial income, but the actual amounts are jealously protected by lawyers.

RICHEST PEOPLE IN THE US

In 1996 *Forbes Magazine*, which annually surveys the 400 wealthiest people in the US, ranked 145 American individuals and families as dollar billionaires – that is, with assets in excess of $1,000,000,000, more than double the total for the previous year. The Forbes 400 includes both the inheritors of great family fortunes and self-made individuals. A placing in the list is extremely volatile, however, particularly during recent times, when many who made vast fortunes in a short period lost them with even greater rapidity. At the same time, events such as stock market falls and the decline in property values have led to a fall in the assets of many members of this elite club, while deaths, such as that in 1996 of David Packard, have removed former entrants from the list, which now stands as:

Name	Assets ($)
1 Bill Gates	18,500,000,000

In 1975, at the age of 19, Gates left college (Harvard) to cofound (with Paul G. Allen, who rates 3rd place in this list) the Microsoft Corporation of Seattle, now one of the world's leading computer software companies, and one that has experienced phenomenal growth: a $2,000 investment in 1986 was worth nearly $70,000 in 1993. Gates, a self-described "hard-core technoid," first ascended to number one position in 1992. Formerly a bachelor devoted only to his business and fast cars, on January 1, 1994 he married Microsoft executive Melinda French. The launch of Windows95 the following year further enhanced his fortune, which has since seen him branching into Internet software, cable news, and picture libraries. His book, The Road Ahead, *was a No. 1 best-seller.*

2	Warren Buffett	15,000,000,000

Buffet was born and still lives in Omaha, Nebraska. His professional career started as a pinball service engineer, after which he published a horse race tip sheet. His diverse business interests include the New England textile company Berkshire Hathaway that has in turn acquired major stakes in the Washington Post, Coca-Cola, Gillette, *and other companies. In 1992 Buffett was ranked 4th in the Forbes 400, in 1993 was elevated to first place, but in 1994 dropped back behind Bill Gates.*

3	Paul Allen	7,500,000,000

Cofounder with Bill Gates of Microsoft, Allen has maintained his connections with the computer and multimedia industry. He also pursues such interests as his ownership of the Portland Trail Blazers basketball team, and his passion for musicians such as Jimi Hendrix, one of the subjects of Experience Music Project, a museum founded by Allen.

Name	Assets ($)
4 John Kluge	7,200,000,000

Kluge is founder of the Metromedia Company of Charlottesville, Virginia. The family of German-born Kluge settled in Detroit in 1922, where he worked on the Ford assembly line. He started a radio station and, in 1959, with partners, acquired the Metropolitan Broadcasting Company. This developed into Metromedia, a corporation that owns TV and radio stations and cellular telephone franchises and other varied properties. He also once owned an 80,000-acre estate and castle in Scotland. Kluge, who was placed as America's richest man in 1989, has diversified his interests and is developing Orion Pictures as part of a media group.

5	Larry Ellison	6,000,000,000

California-based Ellison worked with IBM before establishing his own computer software company, Oracle Corporation, which plans to launch interactive television to provide video-on-demand.

6	Phil Knight	5,300,000,000

A former athlete at the University of Oregon, Knight foresaw the burgeoning athletic shoe industry and founded Nike.

7=	Jim Walton	4,800,000,000

Samuel Moore Walton, the founder of Wal-Mart Stores, headed the list of America's richest people for several years. He died in 1992, but the company he founded, today the largest retail chain in the country with 2,200 stores, has annual sales of $95,500,000,000. His widow Helen and four children share the fortune he created.

7=	John Walton	4,800,000,000
9=	Alice Walton	4,700,000,000
9=	Helen Walton	4,700,000,000
9=	S. Robson Walton	4,700,000,000

Five runners-up with assets of more than $4 billion are listed in the *Forbes 400*. They are brothers Donald and Samuel Newhouse ($4,500,000,000 each), sisters Barbara Cox Anthony and Anne Cox Chambers ($4,500,000,000 each), and Ronald Perelman ($4,500,000,000).

GOLDEN GATES OF FORTUNE
Seattle-born Bill Gates's fortune has grown along with the global success of his Microsoft Corporation, making him the world's richest nonroyal with a fortune nudging $19 billion.

YOUNGEST BILLIONAIRES IN THE US

Name/source of wealth/ assets ($)	Age
1 Daniel Morton Ziff (Ziff Brothers Investments), 1,000,000,000	25
2 Robert David Ziff (Ziff Brothers Investments), 1,000,000,000	31
3 Michael Dell (Dell Computer Corp.), 1,100,000,000	32
4 Dirk Edward Ziff (Ziff Brothers Investments), 1,000,000,000	33
5 Theodore W. Waitt (Gateway 2000 Computers), 1,700,000,000	34
6 Abigail Johnson (Fidelity Investments), 2,500,000,000	35
7 Kenneth Tuchman (TeleTech), 1,000,000,000	36
8 Steven Anthony Ballmer (Microsoft Corp.), 3,700,000,000	41
9 Lee Marshall Bass (oil, investments), 2,200,000,000	41
10 Ted Schwartz (APAC Teleservices Inc.), 1,100,000,000	43

THE WEALTH OF NATIONS

THE 10

RICHEST COUNTRIES IN THE WORLD

	Country	GDP per capita ($)
1	Luxembourg	39,833
2	Switzerland	37,179
3	Japan	34,629
4	Bermuda	29,857
5	Denmark	28,104
6	Norway	26,477
7	US	25,860
8	Germany	25,578
9	Austria	24,949
10	Iceland	24,605

GDP (Gross Domestic Product) is the total value of all the goods and services that are produced annually within a country. (Gross National Product, GNP, also includes income from overseas.) Dividing the GDP by the country's population produces the GDP per capita, which is often used as a measure of how "rich" a country is. Some 32 industrialized nations have GDPs in excess of $10,000, while about 15 developing countries, particularly those in Africa, have per capita GDPs of less than $200.

THE 10

COUNTRIES WITH THE HIGHEST PER CAPITA EXPENDITURE

	Country	Expenditure per capita ($)
1	Japan	19,700
2	Switzerland	19,570
3	US	16,500
4	Iceland	15,550
5	Luxembourg	13,880
6	Germany	13,680
7=	France	13,400
7=	Norway	13,400
9	Belgium	13,060
10	Bermuda	12,690

THE 10

POOREST COUNTRIES IN THE WORLD

	Country	GDP per capita ($)
1	Sudan	63
2	Somalia	74
3	Mozambique	80
4	Tanzania	85
5	Afghanistan	111
6	Ethiopia	130
7	Malawi	144
8	Burundi	146
9	Sierra Leone	152
10	Chad	186

THE 10

COUNTRIES WITH THE LOWEST PER CAPITA EXPENDITURE

	Country	Expenditure per capita ($)
1	Somalia	17
2	Tanzania	61
3	Mozambique	87
4	Ethiopia	95
5	Kenya	120
6=	Burundi	130
6=	Malawi	130
8	Nepal	135
9=	Laos	140
9=	Sierra Leone	140

It is difficult for people in Western consumer cultures to comprehend the poverty of the countries appearing in this list, where the total average annual expenditure of an individual would barely cover the cost of a few meals in the West. These poorer economies inevitably rely on a greater degree of self-sufficiency in food production. In such countries, spending on transportation, recreation, and other staple items of the household budgets of developed countries is virtually zero.

THE 10

RICHEST STATES IN THE US

	State	Average income per capita ($)
1	Connecticut	30,303
2	New Jersey	28,858
3	New York	26,782
4	Massachusetts	26,694
5	Maryland	25,927
6	New Hampshire	25,151
7	Nevada	25,013
8	Illinois	24,763
9	Hawaii	24,738
10	Alaska	24,182

The US Bureau of Economic Analysis produces data to show the average income received by each employed resident. In the 20th century, average national incomes in the US have risen steadily from $418 in 1900, to $2,992 in 1950, and $22,788 in 1995.

THE 10

POOREST STATES IN THE US

	State	Average income per capita ($)
1	Mississippi	16,531
2	Arkansas	17,429
3	West Virginia	17,915
4	New Mexico	18,055
5	Oklahoma	18,152
6	Utah	18,223
7	Montana	18,482
8	Kentucky	18,612
9	North Dakota	18,663
10	Alabama	18,781

Historically, the southern states of the US have tended to be the poorest, with the average annual income in Mississippi barely half that of the annual income in the prosperous District of Columbia. The national average income ($22,788 in 1995) was exceeded in just 21 of the 50 states.

T O P 1 0

COINS AND BILLS IN CIRCULATION IN THE US*

	Unit	Value in circulation ($)
1	$100 bill	252,311,216,200
2	$20 bill	82,060,900,480
3	$50 bill	47,052,728,150
4	$10 bill	13,512,717,430
5	$1 bill	8,219,481,212
6	$5 bill	7,322,233,410
7	Dime	2,821,930,000
8	Quarter	1,831,908,000
9	Nickel	1,647,068,000
10	$2 bill	1,075,448,118

* As of January 1, 1997

As well as the denominations in this Top 10, there are 289,502 $500 bills (value $144,751,000), 168,006 $1,000 bills ($168,006,000), 354 $5,000 bills ($1,770,000), and 345 $10,000 bills ($3,450,000), along with 13,123,260,000 pennies ($13,123,260,000) in circulation. In 1996, 19,473,352,000 coins were minted at the US Mint production facilities.

THE 10 COUNTRIES MOST IN DEBT

	Country	Debt ($)
1	Brazil	151,104,000,000
2	Mexico	128,302,000,000
3	China	100,535,000,000
4	India	98,990,000,000
5	Indonesia	96,500,000,000
6	Russia	94,232,000,000
7	Argentina	77,387,000,000
8	Turkey	66,332,000,000
9	Thailand	60,990,000,000
10	South Korea	54,542,000,000

The World Bank's annual *World Debt Tables* estimated the total indebtedness (including "official" debt which is guaranteed by governments, and "private" debt which is not) of developing countries in 1995 at $2,067,722,000,000, equivalent to $362 for every person in the world. A country's debt is usually considered in relation to its Gross National Product (GNP), and hence its ability to repay it: China's total debt, for example, is less than one-fifth of its GNP.

TOP 10 US COMPANIES MAKING THE GREATEST PROFIT PER SECOND

	Company	Profit per second ($)
1	General Motors	218
2	General Electric	208
3	Exxon Corporation	205
4	Philip Morris	172
5	IBM	132
6	Ford Motor Co.	131
7	Intel	113
8	Citicorp	109
9	Merck	105
10	E. I. Du Pont de Nemours	104

TOP 10 COUNTRIES IN WHICH IT IS EASIEST TO BE A MILLIONAIRE

	Country/ currency unit	Value of 1,000,000 units $
1	Ukraine, Karbovanets	5.52
2	Turkey, Lira	11.44
3	Zaïre, Zaïre	19.90
4	Angola, Kwanza	31.25
5	Guinea-Bissau, Peso	55.07
6	Belarus, Rouble	57.82
7	Mozambique, Metical	89.16
8	Vietnam, Dông	90.14
9	Russia, Rouble	185.10
10	Afghanistan, Afghani	209.11

Runaway inflation in many countries has reduced the value of their currencies to such an extent that they make them virtually worthless. Thus with an exchange rate running at an average of 428,287.55 Ukrainian Karbovanets to the dollar, total assets of just $5.52 will qualify a person as a millionaire in the Ukraine.

TOP 10 COUNTRIES WITH MOST CURRENCY IN CIRCULATION 100 YEARS AGO

	Country	Currency in circulation 100 years ago ($)			
		gold	silver	paper	total
1	France	863,300,000	727,500,000	557,750,000	2,148,550,000
2	US	683,850,000	421,950,000	1,008,800,000	2,114,600,000
3	Germany	591,700,000	218,250,000	344,350,000	1,154,300,000
4	India	48,500,000	824,500,000	58,200,000	931,200,000
5	Russia	189,150,000	67,900,000	596,550,000	853,600,000
6	UK	494,700,000	106,700,000	189,150,000	790,550,000
7	China	–	727,500,000	–	727,500,000
8	Austria	38,800,000	92,150,000	368,600,000	499,550,000
9	Italy	106,700,000	53,350,000	276,450,000	436,500,000
10	Spain	92,150,000	116,400,000	145,500,000	354,050,000

It is interesting to consider that there are now individuals in these countries who, on paper at least, own more than the entire country's money supply in the late 1890s. Today there is in excess of $1,000,000,000,000 in circulation in the US.

CANDY IS DANDY

CANDY-CONSUMING COUNTRIES IN THE WORLD

	Country	Consumption per capita (per annum lb) chocolate	other sweets	total
1	Denmark	15	22	37
2	Ireland	18	13	31
3=	UK	18	11	29
3=	Switzerland	22	7	29
5=	Germany	15	13	28
6=	Austria	18	7	25
7=	Belgium/Luxembourg	13	11	24
7=	Netherlands	11	13	24
7=	Australia	11	13	24
10	US	11	11	22

ICE CREAM-CONSUMING COUNTRIES IN THE WORLD

	Country	Production per capita quarts	pints
1	US	28.09	46.78
2	Finland	22.90	38.13
3	Denmark	20.87	34.76
4	Australia	19.60	32.64
5	Canada	17.55	29.22
6	Sweden	17.32	28.84
7	Norway	16.87	28.10
8	Belgium/Luxembourg	15.11	25.16
9	UK	13.19	21.96
10	New Zealand	13.13	21.87

Source : International Dairy Foods Association

Global statistics for ice cream consumption are hard to come by, but this list presents recent and reliable International Ice Cream Association estimates for per capita production of ice cream and related products (frozen yogurt, sherbert, water ices, etc.) – and since only small amounts of such products are exported, consumption figures can be presumed to be similar.

ICE CREAM BRANDS IN THE US

	Brand	Sales ($)*
1	Private labels	773,100,000
2	Good Humor-Breyer's	375,600,000
3	Breyer's Grand	371,200,000
4	Blue Bell Creameries	174,300,000
5	Häagen-Dazs	138,500,000
6	Ben & Jerry's	113,300,000
7	Turkey Hill Dairy	63,000,000
8	Conagra	55,900,000
9	Marigold Foods	45,200,000
10	Friendly	44,900,000

* Year to September 8, 1996
Source: International Dairy Foods Association

The memorably titled Häagen-Dazs ice cream was the brainchild of Reuben Mattus, who in 1961 created a range of high quality ice creams, choosing a meaningless but Danish-sounding name to emphasize the rich, creamy nature of his product.

BEN & JERRY'S ICE CREAM/FROZEN YOGURT FLAVORS

1	Chocolate Chip Cookie Dough
2	Cherry Garcia
3	Cherry Garcia Low Fat Frozen Yogurt
4	Phish Food
5	Chocolate Fudge Brownie
6	New York Super Fudge Chunk
7	Chunky Monkey
8	Vanilla Caramel Fudge
9	Peanut Butter Cup
10	Chocolate Fudge Brownie Frozen Yogurt

The late Grateful Dead founder Jerry Garcia is probably the only rock musician to have two best-selling ice cream or frozen yogurt flavors named in his honor.

THE HOLE STORY

Life Savers were first made in the early years of this century by Clarence A. Crane of Cleveland, Ohio, who named them after their resemblance to a life ring and registered the trademark. He sold his business in 1913 for $2,900 to Edward John Noble. After changing the packaging and by ingenious marketing, Noble relaunched the product to become the world's best-selling candy. Polo Mints, "the mint with the hole," were launched in the UK in 1948, and are today Britain's best-selling mint. They are the British version of Life Savers, using a similar slogan, and became familiar in the UK when GIs were seen consuming them during World War II.

50 YEARS AGO • YEARS AGO • YEARS AGO • YEARS AGO •

TOP 10

COCOA-CONSUMING COUNTRIES IN THE WORLD

	Country	Total cocoa consumption (tons)
1	US	599,767
2	Germany	269,735
3	UK	202,825
4	France	172,512
5	Russian Federation	158,622
6	Japan	124,230
7	Brazil	111,003
8	Italy	94,137
9	Belgium/Luxembourg	68,453
10	Spain	66,359

Cocoa is the principal ingredient of chocolate, and its consumption is therefore closely linked to the production of chocolate in each consuming country. Like coffee, the consumption of chocolate tends to occur mainly in the Western world and in relatively affluent countries. Since some of these Top 10 consuming nations also have large populations, the list for cocoa consumption per capita is somewhat different in composition, being dominated by those countries with a long-established tradition of manufacturing chocolate products:

	Country	Consumption per capita	
		lb	oz
1	Belgium/ Luxembourg	13	0
2	Iceland	9	13
3	Switzerland	7	11
4	UK	6	15
5	Denmark	6	14
6	Austria	6	12
7	Germany	6	10
8	Norway	6	2
9	Malta	6	0
10	France	5	15

TOP 10

CANDY BRANDS IN THE US

	Brand	Market share percent
1	Reese's Peanut Butter Cup	5.0
2	Snickers Original	4.8
3	M&M's Plain	3.5
4	M&M's Peanut	3.2
5	Hershey's Kit Kat	2.4
6=	Hershey Kisses Milk	2.3
6=	Nestlé Butterfinger	2.3
8	Hershey's Milk Chocolate and Nougats Regular	2.1
9	Life Savers Original "Five Flavor"	2.0
10	Milky Way Original	2.0

TOP 10

GUM BRANDS IN THE US

	Brand	Sales ($)*
1	Wrigley's Doublemint	62,600,000
2	Winter Fresh	53,400,000
3	Freedent	50,800,000
4	Wrigley's Big Red	44,000,000
5	Wrigley's Spearmint	39,100,000
6	Wrigley's Juicy Fruit	37,500,000
7	Bubblicious	29,000,000
8	Bubble Yum	25,400,000
9	Dentyne Cinn A Burst	23,100,000
10	Dentyne	18,200,000

* *Through grocery stores only – total sales of some brands through drug stores, mass merchandisers, and other outlets including vending machines, gas stations, etc., may more than double these figures*

Source: Information Resources, Inc.

TOP 10

HONEY-PRODUCING STATES AND PROVINCES IN NORTH AMERICA

	State/Province	Honey production (lbs p.a.)		State/Province	Honey production (lbs p.a.)
1	California	45,000,000	6	Idaho	9,443,000
2	South Dakota	24,010,000	7	Texas	8,610,000
3	Florida	22,600,000	8	Montana	8,526,000
4	North Dakota	19,800,000	9	Wisconsin	8,200,000
5	Minnesota	14,400,000	10	Michigan	6,930,000

FOOD FOR THOUGHT

T O P   1 0

CALORIE-CONSUMING COUNTRIES IN THE WORLD

	Country	Average daily consumption per capita
1	Ireland	3,847
2	Greece	3,815
3	Cyprus	3,779
4	US	3,732
5	Spain	3,708
6	Belgium/Luxembourg	3,681
7	New Zealand	3,669
8	Denmark	3,664
9	Portugal	3,634
10	France	3,633
	UK	*3,317*
	World average	*2,718*

The calorie requirement of the average man is 2,700 and of the average woman, 2,500. Inactive people need fewer calories, while those engaged in heavy labor might need to increase, perhaps even to double, these figures. Calories that are not consumed as energy are stored as fat – which is why calorie-counting is one of the key aspects of most diets.

T O P   1 0

SUGAR-CONSUMING COUNTRIES IN THE WORLD

	Country	Consumption per capita per annum kg		lb	oz
1	Swaziland	203.5		448	10
2	Singapore	82.5		181	14
3	Fiji	78.8		173	12
4	Malta	62.9		138	11
5	Belize	61.6		135	13
6	Israel	59.9		132	1
7	Tobago	59.7		131	10
8	Iceland	59.5		131	3
9	Denmark	57.2		126	2
10	Costa Rica	56.4		124	5

THE SWEET TASTE OF SUCCESS
The name of its first product, the Milky Way bar, and successors such as Galaxy, reflect the name of the Mars company's founder.

T H E   1 0

FIRST MARS PRODUCTS

	Product	Introduced
1=	Milky Way bar	1923
1=	Snickers bar (nonchocolate)	1923
3	Snickers bar (chocolate)	1930
4	3 Musketeers bar	1932
5	Maltesers	1937
6	Kitekat (cat food; now Whiskas)	1939
7	Mars almond bar	1940
8	M&M's plain chocolate candies	1941
9	Uncle Ben's Converted brand rice	1942
10=	M&M's peanut chocolate candies	1954
10=	Pal (dog food)	1954

American candy manufacturer Franklin C. Mars established his first business in Tacoma, Washington, in 1911 and formed the Mar-O-Bar company in Minneapolis (later moving it to Chicago) in 1922 with the first of its internationally known products, the Milky Way bar. The founder's son Forrest E. Mars set up in the UK in 1932, merging the firm with its American counterpart in 1964.

T O P   1 0

HOTTEST CHILIES

	Typical example	Scoville Units
1	Datil, Habanero, Scotch Bonnet	100,000–350,000
2	Chiltepin, Santaka, Thai	50,000–100,000
3	Aji, Cayenne, Piquin, Tabasco	30,000–50,000
4	Arbol	15,000–30,000
5	Serrano, Yellow Wax	5,000–15,000
6	Chipolte, Jalapeno, Mirasol	2,500–5,000
7	Cascabel, Sandia, Rocotillo	1,500–2,500
8	Ancho, Espanola, Pasilla, Poblano	1,000–1,500
9	Anaheim, New Mexico	500–1,000
10	Cherry, Peperoncini	100–500

Hot peppers contain substances called capsaicinoids, which determine how "hot" they are. In 1912 pharmacist Wilbur Scoville pioneered a test, based on which chilies are ranked by Scoville Units according to which one part of capsaicin, the principal capsaicinoid, per million equals 15,000 Scoville Units.

T H E   1 0

FIRST HEINZ PRODUCTS

	Product	Introduced
1	Horseradish	1869
2=	Sour gherkins	1870
2=	Sour mixed pickles	1870
2=	Chow chow pickle	1870
2=	Sour onions	1870
2=	Prepared mustard	1870
2=	Sauerkraut in crocks	1870
8=	Heinz & Noble catsup	1873
8=	Vinegar	1873
10=	Green pepper sauce	1879
10=	Red pepper sauce	1879
10=	Worcestershire sauce	1879

THE 10

LARGEST CHEESES EVER MADE

1 57,508 lb/26,085 kg

Making gigantic cheeses is not a modern eccentricity: in his Natural History, *the Roman historian Pliny the Elder (AD 23–79) describes a 1,000-lb/454-kg cheese that was made in the Tuscan town of Luni. The current world record holder is this monster Cheddar made in 1995 in Quebec, Canada, by Loblaws Supermarkets and Agropur Dairies.*

2 40,060 lb/18,171 kg

This former world record holder was manufactured on March 13–14, 1988 by Simon's Specialty Cheese of Little Chute, Wisconsin. It was then taken on tour in a refrigerated "cheesemobile."

3 34,591 lb/15,690 kg

Made on January 20–22, 1964 for the World's Fair, New York, by the Wisconsin Cheese Foundation, it was 14½ ft/4.35 m long, 6½ ft/1.95 m wide, and 6 ft/1.8 m high. It toured and was displayed until 1968, when it was cut up to be sold.

4 13,440 lb/6,096 kg

Using the milk from 6,000 cows, production started on July 12, 1937. The cheese was exhibited at the New York State Fair.

5 11,815 lb/5,359 kg

This Cheddar was made in January 1957 in Flint, Michigan, from the milk pooled by a group of 367 farmers from their 6,600 cows.

6 8,000 lb/3,629 kg

This large Canadian Cheddar was made especially for the 1883 Toronto Fair.

7 1,474 lb/669 kg

A cheese 13 ft/3.90 m in circumference was made by James Elgar of Peterborough, UK, in 1849.

8 1,400 lb/653 kg

This Cheddar was given to President Jackson. After maturing for two years in the White House, it was given to the people of Washington, DC, on George Washington's birthday.

9= 1,200 lb/544 kg

A huge Cheshire presented to President Thomas Jefferson by a preacher, John Leland, in 1801, it was appropriately made by the town of Cheshire, Massachusetts.

9= 1,200 lb/544 kg

Made on March 3, 1989 in the village of West Pennard, Somerset, UK, by John Green, to recreate the 19th-century "Great Pennard Cheese," which was a 1,100-lb/499-kg, 9-ft/2.7-m circumference Cheddar named after the Somerset village in which it was made. It was presented to Queen Victoria as a wedding gift in 1840 and exhibited at the Egyptian Hall in Piccadilly, London. Its modern counterpart was shown at the May 1989 Festival of British Food and Farming. It took 1,200 gallons/5,455 liters of milk and measured 3 ft/75 cm in diameter and 9 ft/2.7 m in circumference.

TOP 10

PASTA PRODUCTS

	Pasta	Percentage market share
1	Spaghetti	26.0
2	Twists	18.0
3	Assorted shapes	13.5
4	Lasagne	9.2
5	Shells	9.0
6	Tagliatelle	8.0
7	Noodles	7.1
8	Macaroni	6.3
9	Tortellini	2.5
10	Cannelloni	0.4

THE 10

FIRST 10 COCA-COLA PRODUCTS

	Product	Introduced
1	Coca-Cola	1886
2	Fanta	1960
3	Sprite	1961
4	TAB	1963
5	Fresca	1966
6	Mr. PiBB	1972
7	Hi-C Soft Drinks	1977
8	Mello Yello	1979
9	Ramblin' Root Beer	1979
10	Diet Coke	1982

TOP 10

CONSUMERS OF KELLOGG'S CORN FLAKES*

1	Ireland		**6**	Norway
2	UK		**7**	Canada
3	Australia		**8**	US
4	Denmark		**9**	Mexico
5	Sweden		**10**	Venezuela

* Based on per capita consumption

In 1894 Dr. John Harvey and Will Keith Kellogg were running their Sanatorium. Attempting to devise healthy foods for their patients, they experimented with corn dough that they boiled and passed through rollers. By accident, they discovered that if the dough was left overnight it came out as flakes, and that when these were baked they turned into a tasty cereal.

TOP 10

COUNTRIES WITH THE MOST McDONALDS RESTAURANTS

	Country	Restaurants (1996)
1	US	12,094
2	Japan	2,004
3	Canada	992
4	Germany	743
5	UK	650
6	Australia	608
7	France	541
8	Brazil	337
9	Taiwan	163
10	Netherlands	151

ALCOHOLIC BEVERAGES

T O P 1 0

WINE PRODUCERS IN THE US

	Vintner	Storage capacity (gallons)
1	E. & J. Gallo Winery	330,000,000
2	Canandaigua Wine Co.	261,300,000
3	Grand Metropolitan, plc	110,000,000
4	The Wine Group	81,000,000
5	Vie-Del Company	59,200,000
6	JFJ Bronco	52,350,000
7	Golden State Vintners & Golden State Vintners, Napa	51,900,000
8	Delicato Vineyards	40,000,000
9	F. Korbel & Bros/ Heck Cellars	33,000,000
10	Robert Mondavi Winery	20,000,000

Source: Wines & Vines

Grand Metropolitan, a UK-owned company, is the only non-American winery in this Top 10.

FROM RUSSIA WITH LOVE

The first occasion on which the name of Smirnoff vodka appeared in print in English was on April 26, 1948, when the Official Gazette of the US Patent Office referred to the trademark. The Smirnovs were a family of Moscow distillers who established their company in the early 19th century. They were purveyors of vodka until the Russian Revolution of 1917, when Vladimir Smirnov was imprisoned and condemned to death. He escaped and fled to France, changing the spelling of his name to "Smirnoff." The family's vodka formula was later taken to the US by a friend, Rudolph Kunnett, and acquired by Heublein.

50 YEARS AGO

T O P 1 0

HARD LIQUOR-DRINKING COUNTRIES IN THE WORLD

	Country	Annual consumption per capita (pure alcohol) quarts
1	Russia	4.86
2	Romania	4.18
3=	China	4.02
3=	Poland	4.02
5	Cyprus	3.80

	Country	Annual consumption per capita (pure alcohol) quarts
6	Slovakia	2.96
7	Hungary	2.93
8	Bulgaria	2.91
9	Greece	2.85
10	France	2.66

T O P 1 0

WINE-DRINKING COUNTRIES IN THE WORLD

	Country	Annual consumption per capita 75 cl quarts	bottles
1	France	67.1	84.7
2	Italy	63.8	80.5
3	Portugal	61.7	78.9
4	Luxembourg	61.5	77.6
5	Argentina	46.3	58.4
6	Switzerland	46.1	58.1
7	Spain	38.4	48.4
8	Hungary	36.7	46.3
9	Greece	36.5	46.0
10	Austria	33.8	42.7
	US	*7.2*	*9.1*

T O P 1 0

BEER-DRINKING COUNTRIES IN THE WORLD

	Country	Annual consumption per capita quarts
1	Czech Republic	169.1
2	Ireland	149.3
3	Germany	145.5
4	Denmark	126.9
5	Austria	122.2
6	Belgium	109.9
7	UK	103.5
8	Hungary	103.2
9	Luxembourg	105.0
10	New Zealand	104.4
	US	*90.7*

T O P 1 0

LARGEST BREWERIES IN THE WORLD

	Brewery	Location	Annual sales quarts
1	Anheuser-Busch, Inc.	US	11,012,000,000
2	Heineken NV	Netherlands	5,653,000,000
3	Miller Brewing Co.	US	5,380,000,000
4	Kirin Brewery Co. Ltd.	Japan	3,424,000,000
5	Foster's Brewing Group	Australia	3,223,000,000
6	Companhia Cervejaria Brahma	Brazil	2,673,000,000
7	Groupe BSN	France	2,642,000,000
8	Coors Brewing Co.	US	2,533,000,000
9	South Africa Breweries Ltd.	South Africa	2,399,000,000
10	Companhia Antartica Paulista	Brazil	2,113,000,000

T O P 1 0

MOST EXPENSIVE BOTTLES OF WINE EVER SOLD AT AUCTION

	Wine/sale	Price ($)
1	Château Lafite 1787, Christie's, London, December 5, 1985	140,700
2	Château d'Yquem 1784, Christie's, London, December 4, 1986	56,608
3	Château Mouton Rothschild 1945 (jeroboam – equivalent to 4 bottles), Christie's, Geneva, May 14, 1995 (S.Fr 68,200)	56,229
4	Château Lafite Rothschild 1832 (double magnum), International Wine Auctions, London, April 9, 1988	40,320
5	Château Pétrus 1945 (jeroboam), Sotheby's, New York, September 16, 1995	37,375
6	Château Mouton Rothschild 1986 (Nebuchadnezzar – equivalent to 20 bottles), Sotheby's, New York, April 22, 1995	36,800
7	Château Lafite 1806, Sotheby's, Geneva, November 13, 1988 (S.Fr 57,200)	36,456
8=	Château Mouton Rothschild 1985 (Nebuchadnezzar), Sotheby's, Los Angeles, October 12, 1996	33,350
8=	Château Mouton Rothschild 1989 (Nebuchadnezzar), Sotheby's, Los Angeles, October 12, 1996	33,350
10	Cheval-blanc 1947 (Imperial – equivalent to eight bottles), Christie's, London, December 1, 1994	33,248

After surviving for over 200 years, the first entry in this list, and another bottle that had been sold in 1987 for $29,500 – both of which were initialed by America's third President Thomas Jefferson – suffered disastrous fates in New York. The first was exhibited in a cabinet where the heat from the display light dried out the cork, allowing the contents to evaporate. The other, a bottle of Château Margaux 1784, had been bought by Jefferson when he was ambassador to France and had his initials scratched into the glass. This association had increased its post-auction price tag to $500,000, and an offer approaching $300,000 had been refused. On April 25, 1989 it was displayed at a tasting in the Four Seasons restaurant, New York, when it was inadvertently smashed by a waiter's tray. A small quantity of the wine was salvaged, but, as the wine merchant who drank it reported, "It tasted like it still had wine taste, but not very good." Fortunately, it was insured.

T O P 1 0

BREWERIES IN THE US

	Brewery	Total sales 1995 (barrels)*
1	Anheuser-Busch	87,400,000
2	Miller Brewing Company	42,700,000
3	Coors	20,100,000
4	Stroh	11,000,000
5	G. Heileman	7,600,000
6	S&P Industries	7,500,000
7	Heineken USA	2,800,000
8	Molson	2,200,000
9	Genesee	1,900,000
10	Labatts	800,000

*   Wholesale sales; a barrel contains 31.5 gallons

Anheuser-Busch total annual sales accounts for 2,753,100,000 gallons – equivalent to more than 10 gallons for every inhabitant of the US.

SOFT DRINKS

T O P 1 0

SOFT-DRINK CONSUMERS IN THE WORLD

	Country	Annual consumption per capita liters	quarts
1	Switzerland	105.0	110.0
2	Barbados	81.4	86.0
3	Bahamas	75.0	79.3
4	US	74.7	78.9
5	Australia	73.9	78.1
6	Germany	72.0	76.1
7	Canada	69.3	73.2
8=	Belgium	65.0	68.7
8=	Japan	65.0	68.7
10	Singapore	61.4	69.9

As one might expect, affluent Western countries feature prominently in this list. Despite the spread of the so-called "Coca-Cola culture," former Eastern Bloc and developing countries rank very low – some African nations recording consumption of less than one quart/.95 liter per annum.

T O P 1 0

SOFT DRINKS IN THE US

	Brand	1994 sales (gallons)*
1	Coca-Cola Classic	2,621,000,000
2	Pepsi	2,066,000,000
3	Diet Coke	1,268,000,000
4	Dr. Pepper	768,000,000
5	Diet Pepsi	760,000,000
6	Mountain Dew	683,000,000
7	Sprite	581,000,000
8	7-Up	381,000,000
9	Caffeine Free Diet Coke	265,000,000
10	Caffeine Free Diet Pepsi	153,000,000

* Wholesale sales

Source: Beverage Marketing Corporation

A total of 13,275,000,000 gallons of soft drinks was sold in the US in 1994. Such is the international nature of the soft drink market that a comparative British list would show Coca-Cola, Pepsi, and 7-Up in identical positions. Alongside them in a UK list, however, would be long-established domestic brands that include Lucozade and Schweppes products.

T O P 1 0

CONSUMERS OF COCA-COLA

	Country	Servings consumed per person (1995)
1	US	343
2	Mexico	322
3	Germany	201
4=	Argentina	179
4=	Spain	179
6	South Africa	147
7	Japan	136
8	Brazil	122
9	UK	114
10	Philippines	105

The first Coca-Cola was served in Jacob's Pharmacy in Atlanta, Georgia, on May 8, 1886. The first advertisement appeared in the *Atlanta Journal*, describing Coca-Cola as "Delicious! Refreshing! Exhilarating! Invigorating!" The new drink proved an immediate success – especially after a local prohibition act of July 1886 banned alcohol. "Coke" was first served in bottles in 1894.

T O P 1 0

CONSUMERS OF PERRIER WATER IN THE WORLD

	Country
1	France
2	US
3	Belgium
4	Canada
5	UK
6	Greece
7	Germany
8	Hong Kong
9	Switzerland
10	Japan

In 1903, St. John Harmsworth, a wealthy Englishman on a tour of France, visited Vergèze, a spa town near Nîmes. Its spring, Les Bouillens (which was believed to have been discovered by the Carthaginian soldier Hannibal *c.* 218 BC), was notable for the occurrence of carbon dioxide, which is released from the surrounding rock, permeating through the water and making it naturally sparkling. Harmsworth recognized the potential for selling the spa water and proceeded to buy the spring. He named it after Dr. Louis Perrier, a local doctor, and bottling it in green bottles said to have been modeled on the Indian clubs with which he exercised. The company was sold back to the French in 1948, and in 1992 the firm was bought by the Swiss company Nestlé. Perrier water has maintained a reputation as a popular drink in sophisticated circles. Perrier is now drunk in 145 countries around the world, and its name has become synonymous with mineral water.

T O P 1 0

MILK-DRINKING COUNTRIES IN THE WORLD

	Country*	Annual consumption per capita liters	quarts
1	Iceland	174.2	184.1
2	Finland	165.1	174.5
3	Norway	142.9	151.0
4	Sweden	122.5	129.4
5	Spain	111.6	117.9
6	UK	111.5	117.8
7	Denmark	111.3	117.6
8	Switzerland	98.3	103.9
9	New Zealand	97.9	103.4
10	Australia	95.6	101.0
	US	89.9	95.0

* Those reporting to the International Dairy Federation only

COFFEE-DRINKING COUNTRIES IN THE WORLD

	Country	Annual consumption per capita			
		kg	lb	oz	cups*
1	Norway	9.04	19	15	1,356
2	Denmark	8.70	19	3	1,305
3	Finland	8.62	19	0	1,293
4	Austria	8.47	18	11	1,271
5	Belgium/Luxembourg#	8.34	18	6	1,251
6	Sweden	8.17	18	0	1,226
7	Switzerland	7.97	17	9	1,196
8	Germany	7.38	16	4	1,107
9	Netherlands	6.67	14	11	1,001
10	France	5.48	12	1	822
	US	4.02	8	13	603

* Based on 150 cups per kg/2 lb 3 oz
# Combined for statistical purposes

AN AWFUL LOT OF COFFEE
Within the Top 10 alone, national tastes create a pattern of coffee consumption that varies from averages of almost four cups a day down to just two.

CADBURY SCHWEPPES' WORLD BRANDS

1 Dr. Pepper*

2 7-Up*

3 Schweppes Mixers

4 Canada Dry Ginger Ale

5 Crush Orange

6 A&W* (US – root beer and cream soda)

7 Sunkist*

8 Penafiel (Mexico – mineral waters)

9 Squirt (US – fruit sodas)

10 Cottee's (Australia)

* *Internationally available*

German-born Jean Jacob Schweppe (1740–1821) moved to Geneva where he worked as a jeweler. An amateur scientist, he became interested in the manufacture of artificial mineral waters. He moved to London in 1792 and began producing his own brand of soda water, forming Schweppe & Co. By the 1870s the company was also making ginger ale and "Indian Tonic Water" by adding quinine to sweetened soda water (after the style of the British in India who drank it as an antidote to malaria, thus beginning the fashion for gin and tonic). Schweppes established its first overseas factory in Brooklyn, New York, in 1885. It consolidated its position in the United States in the 1950s by means of an advertising campaign that featured the distinctive and imposing figure of Commander Edward Whitehead, a real Schweppes employee.

TEA-DRINKING COUNTRIES IN THE WORLD

	Country	Annual consumption per capita			
		kg	lb	oz	cups*
1	Irish Republic	3.16	7	0	1,390
2	UK	2.53	5	9	1,113
3	Kuwait	2.52	5	9	1,109
4	Turkey	2.02	4	7	889
5	Qatar	1.76	3	14	774
6	Bahrain	1.67	3	11	735
7	Syria	1.55	3	8	682
8	Hong Kong	1.48	3	4	651
9	Iran	1.32	2	15	581
10	Sri Lanka	1.29	2	13	568
	US	0.34	0	12	150

* Based on 440 cups per kg/2 lb 3 oz

Despite the UK's traditional passion for tea, during recent years its consumption has consistently lagged behind that of Ireland. In the same period, Qatar's tea consumption has dropped from its former world record of 8 lb 12 oz/3.97 kg (1,747 cups) per head.

COFFEE BRANDS IN THE US*

	Brand	Sales ($)
1	Folgers	504,200,000
2	Maxwell House	394,900,000
3	Private label	135,800,000
4	Maxwell House Master Blend	89,500,000
5	Hills Bros	80,700,000
6	Chock Full o' Nuts	57,500,000
7	Maxwell House Lite	50,300,000
8	Yuban	45,700,000
9	Folgers Coffee Singles	46,600,000
10	MJB	38,000,000

* *Plain ground*

Source: Information Research Inc.

Total sales of plain ground coffee for 1996 were $1,800,000,000, down 14.9% from 1995.

TRANSPORTATION & TOURISM

THE 10

FIRST MANNED BALLOON FLIGHTS

Date of flight

1 November 21, 1783

François Laurent, Marquis d'Arlandes, and Jean-François Pilâtre de Rozier took off in a hot-air balloon designed by the Montgolfiers.

2 December 1, 1783

The first-ever flight in a hydrogen balloon.

3 January 19, 1784

This flight included the first aerial stowaway.

4 February 25, 1784

The first-ever flight outside France.

5 March 2, 1784

Flown by Jean-Pierre François Blanchard.

6 April 14, 1784

The first ascent in the British Isles.

7 April 25, 1784

Guyton de Morveau, a French chemist, and L'Abbé Bertrand flew at Dijon.

8 May 8, 1784

Bremond and Maret flew at Marseilles.

9 May 12, 1784

Brun and Comte Xavier de Maistre – both just 20 years old – ascended at Chambéry.

10 May 15, 1784

This balloon crash-landed near Strasbourg.

THE 10

FIRST PEOPLE TO FLY IN HEAVIER-THAN-AIR AIRCRAFT

Pilot/nationality

1 Orville Wright (1871–1948), US

On December 17, 1903 at Kitty Hawk, North Carolina, Wright made the first-ever manned flight in his Wright Flyer I. It lasted 12 seconds and covered a distance of 120 ft/37 m.

2 Wilbur Wright (1867–1912), US

On the same day, Orville's brother made his first flight in the Wright Flyer I (59 seconds).

3 Alberto Santos-Dumont (1873–1932), Brazil

At Bagatelle, Bois de Boulogne, Paris, Santos-Dumont made a 193-ft/60-m hop on October 23, 1906 in his clumsy No. 14-bis.

4 Charles Voisin (1882–1912), France

Voisin made a short, six-second hop of 197 ft/ 60 m at Bagatelle on March 30, 1907. The aircraft was built by him and his brother.

Pilot/nationality

5 Henri Farman (1874–1958), UK (later a French citizen)

Farman first flew on October 7, 1907 and by October 26 had achieved 2,530 ft/771 M.

6 Léon Delagrange (1873–1910), France

On November 5, 1907 at Issy-les-Moulineaux, Delagrange flew his Voisin-Delagrange I for 40 seconds at 1,640 ft/500 m.

7 Robert Esnault-Pelterie (1881–1957), France

On November 16, 1907 at Buc, he first flew his REP 1 for 55 sec at 1,969 ft/600 m.

8 Charles W. Furnas (1880–1941), US

On May 14, 1908 at Kitty Hawk, Wilbur Wright took Furnas, his mechanic, up in the Wright Flyer III for 29 sec at 1,968 ft/600 m.

9 Louis Blériot (1872–1936), France

After some earlier short hops, on June 29, 1908 at Issy, Blériot flew his Blériot VIII. On July 25, 1909 he became the first to fly across the English Channel.

10 Glenn Hammond Curtiss (1878–1930), US

On July 4, 1908 at Hammondsport, New York, Curtiss flew an AEA June Bug for 1 min 42.5 sec at 5,090 ft/1,551 m, the first "official" flight in the US that was watched by a crowd.

FLIGHT TO FAME
Wilbur Wright flies the Wright Brothers' 1901 glider: their experiments led the way to the first powered aircraft.

T H E 1 0

FIRST TRANSATLANTIC FLIGHTS

Date*/crossing/aircraft

1 May 16–27, 1919,
Trepassy Harbor,
Newfoundland to Lisbon, Portugal,
US Navy/Curtiss flying boat NC-4

2 June 14–15, 1919,
St. John's, Newfoundland
to Galway, Ireland,
Twin Rolls-Royce-engined
converted Vickers Vimy bomber

3 July 2–6, 1919,
East Fortune, Scotland to
Roosevelt Field, New York,
British R-34 airship

4 March 30–June 5, 1922,
Lisbon, Portugal to Recife, Brazil,
Fairey IIID seaplane *Santa Cruz*

5 August 2–31, 1924,
Orkneys, Scotland to
Labrador, Canada,
Two Douglas seaplanes, *Chicago*
and *New Orleans*

6 October 12–15, 1924
Friedrichshafen, Germany to
Lakehurst, New Jersey,
Los Angeles, a renamed, German-built
ZR 3 airship

7 January 22–February 10, 1926,
Huelva, Spain to Recife, Brazil,
Plus Ultra, a Dornier Wal
twin-engined flying boat

8 February 8–24, 1927,
Cagliari, Sardinia to Recife, Brazil,
Santa Maria, a Savoia-Marchetti
S.55 flying boat

9 March 16–17, 1927,
Lisbon, Portugal to Natal, Brazil,
Dornier Wal flying boat

10 April 28–May 14, 1927,
Genoa, Italy to Natal, Brazil,
Savoia-Marchetti flying boat

* *All dates refer to the actual Atlantic legs of*
the journeys; some started earlier and ended
beyond their first transatlantic landfalls

FIRST FIGHTER
The German Messerschmitt 262
first flew in 1942 and became the
first jet fighter in military use.

T H E 1 0

FIRST ROCKET AND JET AIRCRAFT

	Aircraft	Country	First flight
1	Heinkel He 176*	Germany	June 20, 1939
2	Heinkel He 178	Germany	August 27, 1939
3	DFS 194*	Germany	#August 1940
4	Caproni-Campini N-1#	Italy	August 28, 1940
5	Heinkel He 280V-1	Germany	April 2, 1941
6	Gloster E.28/39	UK	May 15, 1941
7	Messerschmitt Me 163 Komet*	Germany	August 13, 1941
8	Messerschmitt Me 262V-3	Germany	July 18, 1942
9	Bell XP-59A Airacomet	US	October 1, 1942
10	Gloster Meteor F Mk 1	UK	March 5, 1943

* *Rocket-powered*
# *Precise date unknown*

Prototypes of the rocket-powered Heinkel 176 and the turbojet Heinkel 178 first flew prior to the outbreak of World War II. The first operational jets were developed in the early years of the war, with the Messerschmitt Me 262 the first jet fighter in service. The German Arado Ar 234V-1Blitz ("Lightning"), which first flew on June 15, 1943, was the world's first jet bomber.

DEATH OF A PIONEER

Orville Wright died on January 30, 1948 at the age of 76. With his elder brother Wilbur, who had died in 1912, Orville had achieved fame when, on December 17, 1903 at Kitty Hawk, North Carolina, he become the first person in the world to fly a powered aircraft. The Wright Brothers went on to achieve total mastery of the air: no one else succeeded in getting airborne until 1906, by which time the Wrights were already regularly flying long distances under full control. The Smithsonian Institution in Washington, DC, long refused to accept the Wrights claims as the first to fly, and as a result their first aircraft, *Flyer I*, was "exiled" and exhibited in the Science Museum, London, but was finally returned to the US in the year of Orville's death.

YEARS AGO • 50 • YEARS AGO

AIR TRAVEL

TOP 10

BUSIEST AIRPORTS IN THE US

	Airport/location	Total enplaned passengers (1995)
1	Chicago O'Hare International, Illinois	31,433,002
2	Atlanta (Hartsfield), Georgia	28,090,978
3	Dallas/Fort Worth International, Texas	26,962,940
4	Los Angeles International, California	26,133,795
5	San Francisco International, California	17,187,766
6	Miami International, Florida	16,065,673
7	Denver (Stapleton), Colorado	14,858,763
8	John F. Kennedy International, New York	14,601,827
9	Detroit Metropolitan, Michigan	14,082,598
10	Phoenix Sky Harbor International, Arizona	13,738,433

Source: Federal Aviation Administration

THE WORLD'S LARGEST AIRPORT OPENS

In 1948, the year that aviation pioneer Orville Wright died, the airline industry that he and his brother Wilbur had made possible took an important step forward with the opening on July 31 of Idlewild Airport, New York. Developed on a site reclaimed from the marshland of Jamaica Bay, the international airport, then the largest in the world, derived its name from a golf course that had been swallowed up by its construction. In the same year, the Atlantic was crossed by jets for the first time, heralding the era the modern airliner. On Christmas Eve 1963, Idlewild was renamed John F. Kennedy International Airport to honor the assassinated US president.

TOP 10

INTERNATIONAL FLIGHT ROUTES WITH MOST AIR TRAFFIC

	City A	City B	Passengers per route A to B	Passengers per route B to A	Total passengers
1	Hong Kong	Taipei	2,055,000	2,045,000	4,100,000
2	London	Paris	1,711,000	1,842,000	3,553,000
3	London	New York	1,322,000	1,311,000	2,633,000
4	Dublin	London	1,268,000	1,269,000	2,537,000
5	Kuala Lumpur	Singapore	1,196,000	1,119,000	2,315,000
6	Honolulu	Tokyo	1,157,000	1,137,000	2,294,000
7	Amsterdam	London	1,107,000	1,101,000	2,208,000
8	Seoul	Tokyo	1,089,000	1,081,000	2,170,000
9	Bangkok	Hong Kong	993,000	910,000	1,903,000
10	Hong Kong	Tokyo	940,000	937,000	1,877,000

TOP 10

BUSIEST AIRPORTS IN THE WORLD

	Airport	Location	Passengers per annum
1	Chicago O'Hare	Chicago, IL	66,468,000
2	Hartsfield Atlanta Int.	Atlanta, GA	53,630,000
3	DFW Int.	Dallas/Fort Worth, TX	52,601,000
4	London Heathrow	London, UK	51,368,000
5	LA Int.	Los Angeles, CA	51,050,000
6	Frankfurt	Frankfurt, Germany	34,376,000
7	San Francisco Int.	San Francisco, CA	33,965,000
8	Miami Int.	Miami, FL	30,203,000
9	J.F. Kennedy Int.	New York, NY	28,807,000
10	Charles De Gaulle	Paris, France	28,363,000

TOP 10

BUSIEST AIRPORTS IN EUROPE

	Airport	Location	Passengers per annum
1	London Heathrow	London, UK	51,368,000
2	Frankfurt	Frankfurt, Germany	34,376,000
3	Charles de Gaulle	Paris, France	28,363,000
4	Orly	Paris, France	26,497,000
5	Schiphol	Amsterdam, Netherlands	23,069,000
6	London Gatwick	London, UK	21,045,000
7	Fiumicino	Rome, Italy	19,911,000
8	Madrid	Madrid, Spain	18,223,000
9	Palma	Mallorca, Spain	14,051,000
10	Zurich	Zurich, Switzerland	14,044,000

GIANTS OF THE SKIES
The increasing carrying capacity and distances flown by airliners such as Boeing 747 jumbo jets have resulted in a huge growth in international air traffic.

TOP 10
AIRLINE-USING COUNTRIES IN THE WORLD

	Country	Passenger km p.a.*	Passenger miles p.a.*
1	US	853,389,000,000	530,271,000,000
2	UK	152,453,000,000	94,730,000,000
3	Japan	129,981,000,000	80,766,000,000
4	Australia	67,145,000,000	41,722,000,000
5	France	66,932,000,000	41,590,000,000
6	China	64,204,000,000	39,895,000,000
7	Germany	62,158,000,000	38,623,000,000
8	Russia	61,035,000,000	37,925,000,000
9	Canada	49,288,000,000	30,626,000,000
10	Netherlands	48,474,000,000	30,120,000,000

* *Total distance traveled by scheduled aircraft of national airlines multiplied by number of passengers carried*

TOP 10
BUSIEST INTERNATIONAL AIRPORTS IN THE WORLD

	Airport	Location	International passengers per annum
1	London Heathrow	London, UK	44,262,000
2	Frankfurt	Frankfurt, Germany	27,546,000
3	Charles de Gaulle	Paris, France	25,690,000
4	Hong Kong International	Hong Kong	25,248,000
5	Schiphol	Amsterdam, Netherlands	22,943,000
6	New Tokyo International (Narita)	Tokyo, Japan	20,681,000
7	Singapore International	Singapore	20,203,000
8	London Gatwick	Gatwick, UK	19,417,000
9	J.F. Kennedy International	New York	15,898,000
10	Bangkok	Bangkok, Thailand	13,747,000

Other than New York's JFK, only five airports in the United States handle more than 5,000,000 international passengers a year, namely Miami (13,071,000), Los Angeles (12,679,000), Chicago O'Hare (6,174,000), Honolulu (5,504,000), and San Francisco (5,238,000).

COCKPIT OF A BOEING 727-200

WATERWAYS

TOP 10

SHIPPING COUNTRIES IN THE WORLD

	Country	Ships*
1	Panama	3,488
2	Russia	1,579
3	Liberia	1,534
4	Cyprus	1,436
5	China	1,387
6	Greece	981
7	Malta	925
8	Bahamas	910
9	Japan	812
10	Norway	678
	US	543
	World total, including those not in this Top 10	25,092

* *The list includes only ships of more than 1,000 GRT – Gross Registered Tonnage*

The Top 10 countries in this list account for 55 percent of the world's merchant ships of more than 1,000 gross tons.

TOP 10

BUSIEST PORTS IN THE WORLD

	Port	Location	Goods handled p.a. (tons)
1	Rotterdam	Netherlands	385,800,000
2	Singapore	Singapore	319,700,000
3	South Louisiana	Louisiana	204,482,591
4	Chiba	Japan	191,500,000
5	Kobe	Japan	188,500,000
6	Hong Kong	Hong Kong	162,300,000
7	Houston	Texas	156,500,000
8	Shanghai	China	153,900,000
9	Nagoya	Japan	151,300,000
10	Yokohama	Japan	141,400,000

This Top 10 accounts for all but one of the world's ports handling more than 120,000,000 tons of goods a year: Kawasaki, Japan (115,900,000 tons per annum), which, along with Chiba, serves the urban area of Tokyo.

THE IMPORTANCE OF THE ORIENTAL PORT
With the rise of the economies of the Far East, ports such as Singapore have steadily eclipsed many of those in Europe and the US, and now account for half the world's Top 10 busiest ports.

TOP 10

LARGEST OIL TANKERS IN THE WORLD

	Tanker	Year built	Country of origin	Deadweight tonnage*
1	*Jahre Viking*	1979	Japan	564,650
2	*Kapetan Giannis*	1977	Japan	516,895
3	*Kapetan Michalis*	1977	Japan	516,423
4	*Nissei Maru*	1975	Japan	484,276
5	*Stena King*	1978	Taiwan	457,927
6	*Stena Queen*	1977	Taiwan	457,841
7	*Kapetan Panagiotis*	1977	Japan	457,062
8	*Kapetan Giorgis*	1976	Japan	456,368
9	*Sea Empress*	1976	Japan	423,677
10	*Mira Star*	1975	Japan	423,642

* *The total weight of the vessel, including its cargo, crew, passengers, and supplies*

The 1,504 ft/485.45 m long *Jahre Viking* (formerly called *Happy Giant* and *Seawise Giant*) is the longest vessel ever built – it is as long as more than 20 tennis courts end-to-end and is 226 ft/68.8 m wide. It was extensively damaged during the Iran–Iraq War but was salvaged, refitted, and relaunched in 1991. Economic demands and technological improvements have enabled the size of oil tankers to increase progressively in the second half of the 20th century. The largest tanker afloat in the 1950s was the 104,521-ton Japanese-built Universe Apollo, launched in 1958. The dangerous operation of entering the relatively shallow water of ports to load and unload was overcome by advances in deep-water facilities, as a result of which the size of tankers grew to such an extent that the largest of vessel of the 1960s was the Universe Iran, of 326,933 tons. A deadweight tonnage of 400,000 tons was first exceeded in 1972 with the launch of the Globtik Tokyo (483,662 tons), heralding the age of the "supertanker" with oil tankers of 500,000 tons or more.

TOP 10

LONGEST SHIP CANALS IN THE WORLD

	Canal/country/opened	Length km	ml
1	St. Lawrence Seaway, Canada/US, 1959	304	189
2	Main-Danube, Germany, 1992	171	106
3	Suez, Egypt, 1869	162	101
4=	Albert, Belgium, 1939	129	80
4=	Moscow-Volga, Russia, 1937	129	80
6	Kiel, Germany, 1895	99	62
7	Trollhätte, Sweden, 1916	87	54
8	Alphonse XIII, Spain, 1926	85	53
9	Panama, Panama, 1914	82	51
10	Houston, TX, 1914	81	50

The longest ship canal in the world is the St. Lawrence Seaway (Canada/US). It opened in 1959 and is 189 miles/304 km in length. The Main-Danube Canal, Germany, completed in 1992, is the second longest at 106 miles/171 km. The Suez Canal, Egypt, opened in 1869, measures 101 miles/162 km – almost double the length of the Panama Canal (1914; 51 miles/82 km).

DID YOU KNOW

"THE BIGGEST SHIP IN THE WORLD"

The 692-ft/211-m steamship *Great Eastern*, designed by Isambard Kingdom Brunel, was five times bigger than any vessel ever built, a record held for nearly 50 years. Built in Millwall, London, and almost as long as the Thames was wide, it was decided to launch it sideways. Thousands turned out for the event, but the ship would not budge. She was finally launched in 1858 and in 1866 laid the first commercially successful transatlantic telegraph cable. However, the ship was dogged by misfortune, and 30 years after her launch the *Great Eastern* was broken up for scrap.

TOP 10

PORTS IN THE US (1995)

	Port/state	Goods handled p.a. (tons)
1	South Lousiana, Louisiana	204,482,591
2	Houston, Texas	135,231,322
3	New York, New York/New Jersey	119,341,574
4	Baton Rouge, Louisiana	83,612,788
5	Valdez, Alaska	80,955,084
6	New Orleans, Louisiana	76,984,036
7	Plaquemine, Louisiana	72,897,301
8	Corpus Christi, Texas	70,456,033
9	Long Beach, California	53,227,940
10	Tampa, Florida	51,911,335

Source: Waterborne Commerce of the US, Department of the Army Corps of Engineers, Water Resources Support Center

TOP 10

COUNTRIES WITH THE LONGEST INLAND WATERWAY NETWORKS*

	Country	km	miles
1	China	138,600	86,122
2	Russia	101,000	62,758
3	Brazil	50,000	31,069
4	US#	41,009	25,482
5	Indonesia	21,579	13,409
6	Vietnam	17,702	11,000
7	India	16,180	10,054
8	Zaïre	15,000	9,321
9	France	14,932	9,278
10	Colombia	14,300	8,886

* *Canals and navigable rivers*
\# *Excluding Great Lakes*

TOP 10

LONGEST PASSENGER LINERS IN THE WORLD

	Ship/year built/country of origin	Length m	ft	in
1	*Norway* (former *France*), 1961, France	315.53	1,035	2
2	*United States*, 1952, USA	301.76	990	0
3	*Queen Elizabeth 2*, 1969, UK	293.53	963	0
4=	*Grandeur of the Seas*, 1996, Finland	279.10	915	8
4=	*Enchantment of the Seas*, 1997, Finland	279.10	915	8
6	*Rhapsody of the Seas*, 1997, France	279.00	915	4
7	*Carnival Destiny*, 1996, Italy	272.35	893	6
8	*Sovereign of the Seas*, 1987, France	268.33	880	4
9=	*Monarch of the Seas*, 1991, France	268.32	880	4
9=	*Majesty of the Seas*, 1992, France	268.32	880	4

Source: Lloyds Register

THE MAJESTIC OCEAN LINER *QE2*
The QE2 was built as a replacement for the liner Queen Elizabeth. *It offers luxury accommodations for up to 1,700 passengers and made its maiden voyage in 1969.*

ON THE ROAD

TOP 10

FASTEST PRODUCTION CARS IN THE WORLD

	Model	Maximum speed km/h	mph
1	Lamborghini Diablo	325	202
2	Ferrari Testarossa	290	180
3=	Ferrari 348ts	277	172
3=	Ferrari 348tb	277	172
5	Porsche 928 GT	274	170
6	Porsche 911 Turbo	270	168
7	Porsche 928S Series 4	266	165
8	Porsche 911 Carrera 2	259	161
9=	Lotus Esprit Turbo SE	257	160
9=	TVR 450SEAC	257	160

TOP 10

MAKES OF CAR IMPORTED TO THE US

	Manufacturer	Total sales (1995)
1	Toyota	295,336
2	Honda	229,443
3	Nissan	220,374
4	Mazda	117,859
5	Hyundai	107,371
6	Volvo	88,505
7	BMW	87,115
8	Mercedes-Benz	76,752
9	Mitsubishi	74,194
10	Ford	59,191

TOP 10

MODELS OF CAR IN THE US

	Make/model	Total sales (1995)		Make/model	Total sales (1995)
1	Ford Taurus	366,266	6	Pontiac Grand Am	234,226
2	Honda Accord	293,898	7	Honda Civic	217,146
3	GM Saturn	285,674	8	Chevrolet Lumina	214,595
4	Ford Escort	285,570	9	Chevrolet Cavalier	212,767
5	Toyota Camry	248,188	10	Toyota Corolla	184,002

WHEELS OF FORTUNE

Although the manufacture of automobiles was in its infancy in 1898 it was a milestone year for a number of innovations: the pneumatic tire valve with a replaceable core was invented by George H.F. Schrader of New York, and in the same year the Goodyear Tire & Rubber Company was started in Akron, Ohio by brothers Frank and Charles Seiberling. They chose to name it after Charles Goodyear (1800-60), the American inventor of the process for vulcanizing rubber, which made tire manufacture technically and commercially possible. Today Goodyear is the leading tire manufacturer in the US, making almost one in three of all tires.

100 YEARS AGO

TOP 10

CAR MANUFACTURERS IN NORTH AMERICA*

	Company	Production (1995)
1	Ford	1,602,959
2	Chevrolet	1,138,032
3	Honda	659,128
4	Pontiac	623,604
5	Toyota	607,049
6	Buick	495,240
7	Lincoln-Mercury	484,267
8	Dodge	414,687
9	Oldsmobile	391,216
10	Nissan	333,234

* *US/Canada*

Based on group total sales, General Motors is the largest manufacturer by a considerable margin, with US and Canada production of 3,137,723.

TOP 10

CAR COLORS IN THE US

	Color	% (1995)
1	White	18.9
2	Dark green	17.3
3	Medium red	11.2
4	Light brown	9.7
5	Black	5.9
6	Silver	5.4
7	Teal/Aqua	4.6
8=	Medium blue	4.4
8=	Bright red	4.4
10	Light blue	4.3

TOP 10

CAR IMPORTS BY COUNTRY OF ORIGIN

	Country	Imports (1995)
1	Canada	1,678,276
2	Japan	1,387,193
3	Mexico	463,305
4	South Korea	216,618
5	Germany	206,892
6	Sweden	82,634
7	UK	42,176
8	Belgium	20,907
9	Taiwan	3,674
10	Italy	973

ROAD TO RUIN

The first passenger cars took to the road little over 100 years ago. There are now thought to be some 500 million cars and 150 million commercial vehicles in the world. As well as the many benefits brought by the inexorable advance of motoring, road safety and the problems of pollution, road building, and the consumption of raw materials are engaging manufacturers as they seek improved safety, fuel economy, environmental friendliness, and the potential to recycle every component as increasing numbers of vehicles reach the end of their useful lives.

"TIN LIZZIE"
At one time, more than half the cars in the world were Model T Fords.

PRODUCTION LINE
The growth of mass production enabled the growth of the car culture that has dominated the 20th century.

TOP 10
BEST-SELLING CARS OF ALL TIME

	Model	Year first produced	Estimated no. made
1	Volkswagen Beetle	1937*	21,220,000
2	Toyota Corolla	1963	20,000,000
3	Ford Model T	1908	15,536,075
4	Volkswagen Golf/Rabbit	1974	14,800,000
5	Lada Riva	1970	13,500,000
6	Ford Escort/Orion	1967	12,000,000
7	Nissan Sunny/Pulsar	1966	10,200,000
8	Mazda 323	1977	9,500,000
9	Renault 4	1961	8,100,000
10	Honda Civic	1972	8,000,000

* Still produced in Mexico and Brazil

Estimates of manufacturers' output of their best-selling models vary from the vague to the unusually precise 26,536,075 of the Model T Ford, with 15,007,033 produced in the US.

BEETLEMANIA
Designed by Ferdinand Porsche in 1937, production of the first Beetles began in 1945. Within 10 years, more than one million had been sold.

FOR ESCORT
First produced in 1967, the Ford Escort and Orion were among the most popular cars of the postwar period.

GOLF COURSE
Volkswagen's successor to the Beetle, the Golf is the best-selling European car.

ON THE RIGHT TRACK

T O P 1 0

BUSIEST RAIL NETWORKS
IN THE WORLD

Country	Passenger/ km (million) per annum	miles (million) per annum
1 Japan	396,332	246,269
2 China	354,700	219,965
3 India	319,400	198,500
4 Russia	191,900	119,200
5 Ukraine	75,900	47,200
6 France	58,380	36,276
6 Germany	58,003	36,041
6 Egypt	47,992	29,821
6 Italy	47,100	29,270
6 South Korea	30,216	18,775

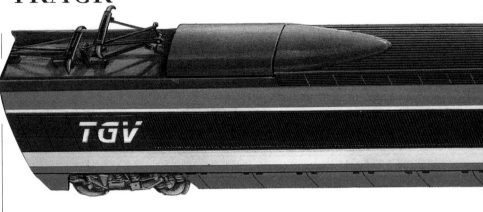

T O P 1 0

LONGEST UNDERGROUND RAIL NETWORKS IN THE WORLD

Location	Opened	Stations	Total track length km	miles
1 London, UK	1863	270	401	251
2 New York, NY	1904	469	398	249
3 Paris, France*	1900	432	323	202
4 Tokyo, Japan#	1927	250	289	181
5 Moscow, Russia	1935	150	244	153
6 Mexico City, Mexico	1969	154	178	112
7 Chicago, IL	1943	145	173	108
8 Copenhagen, Denmark+	1934	79	170	106
9 Berlin, Germany	1902	135	167	104
10 Seoul, South Korea	1974	130	165	103

* Metro + RER
\# Through-running extensions raise total to 391 miles/683 km, with 502 stations
+ Only partly undergound

GOING UNDERGROUND
London's Metropolitan Railway, the world's first underground service, opened on January 10, 1863. The wide gauge track (7-ft/ 2.134-m) seen here at Bellmouth, Praed Street, was used in its early years.

T O P 1 0

OLDEST UNDERGROUND RAIL NETWORKS IN THE WORLD

Location	Opened
1 London, UK	1863
2 Budapest, Hungary	1896
3 Glasgow, UK	1896
4 Boston, MA	1897
5 Paris, France	1900
6 Wuppertal, Germany	1901
7 Berlin, Germany	1902
8 New York, NY	1904
9 Philadelphia, PA	1907
10 Hamburg, Germany	1912

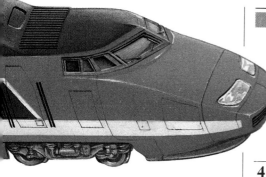

TRAIN À GRANDE VITESSE
The French TGV (Train à Grande Vitesse, or high-speed train) began service between Paris and Lyons in 1981. Its world record scheduled speed is set to be exceeded by even faster "bullet trains" now entering service in Japan.

T O P 1 0

COUNTRIES WITH THE FASTEST RAIL JOURNEYS*

	Country/journey/train	Distance km	miles	Speed km/h	mph
1	France, Paris–Lille (TGV 587)	204.2	126.9	250.0	155.3
2	Japan, Hiroshima–Kokuru (31 *Nozomi*)	192.0	119.3	230.4	143.2
3	Spain, Madrid–Ciudad Real (AVE 9744)	170.7	106.1	217.9	135.4
4	Germany, Fulda–Kassel (ICE *Frankfurter Römer*)	90.0	55.9	200.0	124.3
5	UK, Stevenage–Doncaster (InterCity 225)	206.6	128.4	177.1	110.0
6	Sweden, Hallsberg–Skövde (X2000 429)	113.8	70.7	175.1	108.8
7	Italy, Rome–Florence (*Cristoforo Colombo*)	261.9	162.7	162.0	100.7
8	US, Baltimore–Wilmington (*Metroliner*)	110.1	68.4	153.6	95.4
9	Canada, Toronto–Dorval (*Metropolis*)	519.5	322.8	144.3	89.7
10	Russia, St. Petersburg–Moscow (ER 200)	649.9	403.8	130.4	81.0

* *Fastest journey for each country; all those in this Top 10 have other similarly or equally fast services*

The fastest international journeys are those on the Eurostar London–Paris route, via Eurotunnel (307.9 miles at 106.6 mph) and the TGVs between Paris and Brussels (206.4 miles at 92.5 mph). During 1997–98, two revolutionary high-speed trains, the E2 and E3, are scheduled to enter service in Japan, raising the speed to about 171 mph/275 km/h.

T O P 1 0

SURVIVING STEAM LOCOMOTIVES IN THE US

	Class	No. surviving
1	2-8-0	206
2	0-4-0	202
3	0-6-0	143
4	2-8-2	131
5	4-6-0	108
6	2-6-0	83
7	2-6-2	78
8	4-6-2	76
9	Shay	74
10	4-4-0	58

The number of surviving steam locomotives bears a close relation to the numbers of each class built – in the case of the 2-8-0s, some 21,000. Of these survivors, only a relatively small number is operational – again led by the 2-8-0s with 35 functioning examples, down to just 12 in the case of the 4-4-0s. There are instances of classes built in the thousands, such as the 2,200 2-10-2s, where fewer than 10 have survived and none are operational. The Shay was a geared, rather than wheeled, locomotive, introduced in 1880 and designed for steep gradients.

T O P 1 0

BUSIEST AMTRAK RAIL STATIONS IN THE US

	Station	Boardings (1996)
1	New York-Penn	5,483,923
2	Washington-Union	3,021,281
3	Philadelphia-30th St.	2,928,502
4	Chicago-Union	1,961,211
5	Los Angeles-Union	1,008,361
6	Baltimore-Penn	834,149
7	Boston-South	786,337
8	San Diego	655,420
9	Emeryville	566,991
10	Sacramento	548,056

T O P 1 0

LONGEST RAIL NETWORKS IN THE WORLD

	Location	Total rail length km	miles
1	US	240,000	149,129
2	Russia	154,000	95,691
3	Canada	70,176	43,605
4	India	62,462	38,812
5	China	58,399	36,287
6	Germany	43,966	27,319
7	Australia	38,563	23,962
8	Argentina	37,910	23,556
9	France	33,891	21,059
10	Brazil	27,418	17,037

Although remaining at the head of this list, US rail mileage has declined considerably since its 1916 peak of 254,000 miles/408,773 km, as the majority of people now travel by road. The total of all world networks is today reckoned to be some 746,476 miles/1,201,337 km.

TOURISM

TOP 10
AMUSEMENT AND THEME PARKS IN THE WORLD

	Park/location	Estimated visitors (1996)
1	Tokyo Disneyland, Tokyo, Japan	16,980,000
2	Disneyland, Anaheim, California	15,000,000
3	Magic Kingdom at Walt Disney World, Lake Buena Vista, Florida	13,803,000
4	Disneyland Paris, Marne-la-Vallée, France	11,700,000
5	EPCOT at Walt Disney World, Lake Buena Vista, Florida	11,235,000
6	Disney-MGM Studios Theme Park at Walt Disney World, Lake Buena Vista, Florida	9,975,000
7	Universal Studios Florida, Orlando, Florida	8,400,000
8	Everland, Kyonggi-Do, South Korea	8,000,000
9	Blackpool Pleasure Beach, Blackpool, UK	7,500,000
10	Yokohama Hakkeijima Sea Paradise, Japan	6,926,000

Source: Amusement Business

ITALIAN ATTRACTION
Famous historic buildings such as the Leaning Tower of Pisa contribute to Italy's appeal, making it one of the world's most popular tourist destinations.

TOP 10
AMUSEMENT AND THEME PARKS IN EUROPE

	Park/location	Estimated visitors (1996)
1	Disneyland Paris, Marne-la-Vallée, France	11,700,000
2	Blackpool Pleasure Beach, Blackpool, UK	7,500,000
3	Tivoli Gardens, Copenhagen, Denmark	3,100,000
4	De Efteling, Kaatsheuvel, Netherlands	3,000,000
5=	Alton Towers, Staffordshire, UK	2,700,000
5=	Port Aventura, Salou, Spain	2,700,000
7	Europa Park, Rust, Germany	2,500,000
8=	Gardaland, Casteinuovo Del Garda, Italy	2,400,000
8=	Liseberg, Gothenburg, Sweden	2,400,000
10	Bakken, Klampenborg, Denmark	2,100,000

Source: Amusement Business

Despite appearing at the top of this list, Disneyland Paris continues to lose money at an alarming rate (in the six months to March 1997 its loss increased from F.Fr169,000,000/$33,400,000 to F.Fr210,000,000/ $41,500,000). Meanwhile, competition is mounting both from existing theme parks, among which those in the UK are especially well represented, and from newly-opened complexes, such as Spain's Port Aventura and Warner Brothers' Movie World in Bottrop-Krichhellen, Germany, which opened in 1996.

TOP 10
COUNTRIES EARNING MOST FROM TOURISM

	Country	Total ($) receipts (1996)
1	US	64,400,000,000
2	Spain	28,400,000,000
3	France	28,200,000,000
4	Italy	27,300,000,000
5	UK	20,400,000,000
6	Austria	15,100,000,000
7	Germany	13,200,000,000
8	Hong Kong	11,200,000,000
9	China	10,500,000,000
10	Singapore	9,900,000,000

TOP 10
COUNTRIES OF ORIGIN OF TOURISTS TO THE US

	Country	Visitors per annum
1	Japan	3,506,000
2	UK	2,461,000
3	Germany	1,450,000
4	Mexico	1,324,000
5	France	686,000
6	Brazil	507,000
7	Italy	457,000
8	Korea	361,000
9=	China	353,000
9=	Venezuela	353,000

The enumeration methods of the US Immigration and Naturalization Service differ from those of the World Tourism Organization, presenting the contradictory conclusion that, in the latest year for which figures are available, the US received either 17,155,000 or 44,791,000 tourists.

TOP 10

TOURIST SPENDING COUNTRIES IN THE WORLD

	Tourist country of origin	World total %	Total expenditure ($) (1996)
1	Germany	14.2	50,675,000,000
2	US	12.9	45,855,000,000
3	Japan	10.3	36,792,000,000
4	UK	6.9	24,737,000,000
5	France	4.6	16,328,000,000
6	Italy	3.5	12,419,000,000
7	Austria	3.3	11,687,000,000
8	Russia	3.3	11,599,000,000
9	Netherlands	3.2	11,445,000,000
10	Canada	2.9	10,220,000,000

Source: World Tourism Organization

TOP 10

TOURIST COUNTRIES IN THE WORLD

	Country	World total %	Total visitors (1996)
1	France	10.3	61,500,000
2	US	7.5	44,791,000
3	Spain	6.9	41,295,000
4	Italy	5.5	32,853,000
5	UK	4.4	26,025,000
6	China	3.8	22,765,000
7	Mexico	3.7	21,732,000
8	Hungary	3.5	20,670,000
9	Poland	3.3	19,420,000
10	Canada	2.9	17,345,000

Source: World Tourism Organization

TOP 10

MOST COMMON TYPES OF LOST PROPERTY ON NEW YORK TRANSIT AUTHORITY

1	Backpacks
2	Radios/Walkmans
3	Eyeglasses
4	Wallets and purses
5	Cameras
6	Keys
7	Cellular phones
8	Watches
9	Inline skates
10	Jewelry

Although the New York Transit Authority does not keep itemized records in the same detail as London Transport (which encompasses London's buses and

"Tube" trains), a comparison of the ranking of the two lists reveals both interesting similarities (keys feature at No. 6 in both lists) and differences. In the case of the London list there is a clear decline in total articles handed in from year to year. Books have figured in the No. 1 position for several years, but changes in fashion have meant that hats, once one of the commonest lost items, no longer even warrant a separate category, while often expensive electronic calculators, laptop computers, and cellular phones are now lost in increasing numbers in both London and New York. Auctions of NYTA's unclaimed property have included such bizarre items as five wheelchairs, while false teeth and artificial limbs feature among the stranger items that have been lost in recent years in both cities. London's weird list includes a skeleton, a box of glass eyes, breast implants, an outboard motor, a complete double bed, a theatrical coffin, 280 pounds of currants and raisins, a stuffed gorilla, and an urn containing human ashes (the latter was never claimed, and the ashes were ceremoniously scattered in a flowerbed in a nearby park).

TOP 10

US TRANSIT AUTHORITIES

	Authority	Annual revenue ($)*
1	New York-MTA-New York City Transit Authority	3,360,166,205
2	New Jersey Transit Corporation	927,990,319
3	Chicago-RTA-Chicago Transit Authority	765,157,156
4	Boston-Massachusetts Bay Transit Authority	742,149,248
5	Los Angeles County Metropolitan Transit Authority	717,418,906
6	Washington Metropolitan Area Transit Authority	677,321,233
7	New York-MTA-Long Island Rail Road Company	662,423,543
8	Philadelphia-South East Pennsylvania Transportation Authority	659,252,795
9	New York-MTA-Metro North Commuter Railroad	489,192,947
10	Chicago-RTA-North Eastern Illinois Regional Commuter Rail Road Corporation	309,699,671

* Passenger Fares, Local and State Funds, Federal Assistance, and other funds

THE UNIVERSE & THE EARTH

TOP 10

BRIGHTEST STARS

	Star	Constellation	Distance*	Apparent magnitude
1	Sun	Solar System	92,952,666 mi	–26.8
2	Sirius	Canis Major	8.64	–1.46
3	Canopus	Carina	1,200	–0.73
4	Alpha Centauri	Centaurus	4.35	–0.27
5	Arcturus	Boötes	34	–0.04
6	Vega	Lyra	26	+0.03
7	Capella	Auriga	45	+0.08
8	Rigel	Orion	900	+0.12
9	Procyon	Canis Minor	11.4	+0.38
10	Achernar	Eridanus	85	+0.46

* From the Earth in light years, unless otherwise stated

Based on apparent visual magnitude as viewed from the Earth – the lower the number, the brighter the star – Sirius, which has a diameter of 900,988 miles/1,450,000 km, is actually over 24 times brighter than the Sun, but its distance from the Earth relegates it into 2nd place. If the Sun is excluded, the 10th brightest star is Beta Centauri in the constellation of Centaurus. At its brightest, the star Betelgeuse is brighter than some of these, but as it is variable its average brightness disqualifies it from this Top 10. The jury is out on a star known as VI Cygni No. 12 in the constellation of Cygnus; it was discovered in 1992 and is arguably the brightest star in the galaxy. However, this still awaits verification.

TOP 10

GALAXIES NEAREST THE EARTH

	Galaxy	Distance (light years)
1	Large Cloud of Magellan	169,000
2	Small Cloud of Magellan	190,000
3	Ursa Minor dwarf	250,000
4	Draco dwarf	260,000
5	Sculptor dwarf	280,000
6	Fornax dwarf	420,000
7=	Leo I dwarf	750,000
7=	Leo II dwarf	750,000
9	Barnard's Galaxy	1,700,000
10	Andromeda Spiral	2,200,000

These, and a number of other galaxies, are members of the so-called "Local Group." With such vast distances as these, "local" is clearly a relative term.

MOST FREQUENTLY SEEN COMETS

	Comet	Orbit period (years)
1	Encke	3.302
2	Grigg–Skjellerup	4.908
3	Honda–Mrkós–Pajdusáková	5.210
4	Tempel 2	5.259
5	Neujmin 2	5.437
6	Brorsen	5.463
7	Tuttle–Giacobini–Kresák	5.489
8	Tempel–L. Swift	5.681
9	Tempel 1	5.982
10	Pons–Winnecke	6.125

The comets in this Top 10, and several others, return with regularity, while others have such long periods of absence that they may not be seen again for many thousands – or even millions – of years. The most frequent visitor is Encke's Comet, which was named after the German astronomer Johann Franz Encke (1791–1865), who in 1818 calculated the period of its elliptical orbit. It had first been observed shortly before his birth, but without its orbit being calculated, and has been seen on almost all its subsequent returns. Encke's Comet is becoming extremely faint, and after its most recent return in 1994 it may very well be considered "lost."

MOST COMMON ELEMENTS IN THE UNIVERSE

	Element	Parts per 1,000,000
1	Hydrogen	739,000
2	Helium	240,000
3	Oxygen	10,700
4	Carbon	4,600
5	Neon	1,340
6	Iron	1,090
7	Nitrogen	970
8	Silicon	650
9	Magnesium	580
10	Sulfur	440

STARS NEAREST TO THE EARTH
(Excluding the Sun)

	Star	Light years*	Distance from the Earth km	miles
1	Proxima Centauri	4.22	39,923,310,000,000	24,792,500,000,000
2	Alpha Centauri	4.35	41,153,175,000,000	25,556,250,000,000
3	Barnard's Star	5.98	56,573,790,000,000	35,132,500,000,000
4	Wolf 359	7.75	73,318,875,000,000	45,531,250,000,000
5	Lalande 21185	8.22	77,765,310,000,000	48,292,500,000,000
6	Luyten 726-8	8.43	79,752,015,000,000	49,526,250,000,000
7	Sirius	8.64	81,833,325,000,000	50,818,750,000,000
8	Ross 154	9.45	89,401,725,000,000	55,518,750,000,000
9	Ross 248	10.40	98,389,200,000,000	61,100,000,000,000
10	Epsilon Eridani	10.80	102,173,400,000,000	63,450,000,000,000

* One light year = 5,878,812,000 miles
9,460,528,404,000 km

A spaceship traveling at a speed of 25,000 mph/40,237 km/h – which is faster than any speed yet achieved in space by a manufactured object – would take more than 113,200 years to reach Earth's closest star, Proxima Centauri.

THE MILKY WAY
Often referred to as just "the Galaxy," the Milky Way is a giant spiral made up of several billion stars, including our sun. Its true nature has been discovered by astronomers only in the 20th century.

NEW ELEMENTS DISCOVERED

The British chemist Sir William Ramsay (1852–1916) knew that when nitrogen was extracted from air, it appeared to be heavier than nitrogen prepared chemically. From this he concluded that there must be other gases present. He duly confirmed the presence of argon and helium, and in 1898, working with Morris W. Travers, discovered three more previously unknown gases, krypton, xenon, and neon. In 1904 Ramsay was awarded the Nobel Prize for Chemistry for his discoveries. As well as other uses for these gases, the wavelength of krypton is now used as the basis for the international standard measurement of a meter.

100 YEARS AGO

THE SOLAR SYSTEM

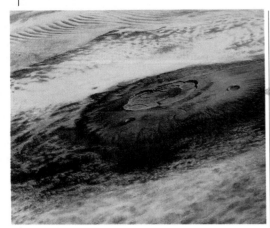

LIFE ON MARS?
Recent studies of a Martian meteorite have once again raised the idea that life may once have existed on the seventh largest planet.

TOP 10
LARGEST BODIES IN THE SOLAR SYSTEM

	Body	Maximum diameter km	miles
1	The Sun	1,392,140	865,036
2	Jupiter	142,984	88,846
3	Saturn	120,536	74,898
4	Uranus	51,118	31,763
5	Neptune	49,532	30,778
6	The Earth	12,756	7,926
7	Venus	12,103	7,520
8	Mars	6,794	4,222
9	Ganymede	5,269	3,274
10	Titan	5,150	3,200

Most of the planets are visible with the naked eye. The exceptions are Uranus, discovered on March 13, 1781 by the British astronomer Sir William Herschel; Neptune, found by the German astronomer Johann Galle on September 23, 1846; and, outside this Top 10, Pluto, located using photographic techniques by American astronomer Clyde Tombaugh. Its discovery was announced on March 13, 1930; its diameter is uncertain but is thought to be approximately 1,430 miles/2,302 km. Mercury, also outside this Top 10, has a diameter of 3,032 miles/4,880 km. Ganymede is the largest of Jupiter's satellites, and Titan the largest of Saturn's.

TOP 10
BODIES IN THE SOLAR SYSTEM WITH THE GREATEST ESCAPE VELOCITY*

	Body	Escape velocity (ft/s)
1	The Sun	2,025,848
2	Jupiter	197,565
3	Saturn	105,836
4	Neptune	78,409
5	Uranus	73,816
6	Earth	36,679
7	Venus	33,988
8	Mars	16,502
9	Mercury	13,943
10	Pluto	3,871

*	Excluding satellites

TOP 10
BODIES IN THE SOLAR SYSTEM WITH THE GREATEST SURFACE GRAVITY*

	Body	Surface gravity	Weight#
1	The Sun	27.90	3,998.10
2	Jupiter	2.64	378.32
3	Neptune	1.20	171.96
4	Uranus	1.17	167.66
5	Saturn	1.16	166.23
6	Earth	1.00	143.00
7	Venus	0.90	129.00
8=	Mars	0.38	54.45
8=	Mercury	0.38	54.45
10	Pluto	0.06	8.60

*	Excluding satellites
#	Of a 143 lb adult on the body's surface

TOP 10
MOST COMMON SOURCES OF ASTEROID NAMES

	Sources	Asteroids			Sources	Asteroids
1	Astronomers	1,172		6	Historical persons	360
2	Places	833		7	Writers	275
3	Scientists other than astronomers	551		8	Composers and musicians	130
4	Mythological characters	439		9	Literary characters	112
5	Astronomers' family members and friends	406		10	Organizations	93

SATURN'S NINTH MOON IS DISCOVERED

The first of Saturn's moons, Titan, was discovered in 1655, followed by seven more between 1671 and 1848, but in 1898 the American astronomer William Pickering (1858–1938) found the most remarkable of them, Phoebe, Saturn's outermost moon, which lies some 8,048,000 miles/12,952,000 km distant from Saturn, taking 550 days to complete one orbit. Phoebe is 137 miles/220 km in diameter, but orbits in a direction opposite from all the other satellites, suggesting that it may in fact be an asteroid captured by Saturn's gravitational pull. Since Pickering's discovery, more moons have been observed, bringing Saturn's total to 18 satellites.

YEARS AGO 100 YEARS AGO

T O P   1 0

LARGEST PLANETARY MOONS IN THE SOLAR SYSTEM

	Moon	Planet	Diameter km	miles
1	Ganymede	Jupiter	5,269	3,274

Discovered by Galileo in 1609–10 and believed to be the largest moon in the Solar System, Ganymede – one of Jupiter's 16 satellites – is thought to have a surface of ice about 60 miles/97 km thick.

2	Titan	Saturn	5,150	3,200

Titan, the largest of Saturn's 18 confirmed moons, is actually larger than Mercury and Pluto. It was discovered by the Dutch astronomer Christian Huygens in 1655.

3	Callisto	Jupiter	4,820	2,995

Possessing a composition similar to Ganymedes, Callisto is heavily pitted with craters, perhaps more than any other body in the Solar System.

4	Io	Jupiter	3,632	2,257

Most of what we know about Io was reported by the 1979 Voyager probe, which revealed a crust of solid sulfur, with massive eruptions hurling sulfurous material into space.

5	The Moon	Earth	3,475	2,159

Our own satellite is a quarter of the size of the Earth, the 5th largest in the Solar System, and the only moon explored by humans.

6	Europa	Jupiter	3,126	1,942

Although Europa's ice-covered surface is apparently smooth and crater-free, it is covered with mysterious black lines, some of them 40 miles/64 km wide, resembling canals.

7	Triton	Neptune	2,750	1,708

This moon was discovered on October 10, 1846, by amateur astronomer William Lassell. Triton is the only known satellite in the Solar System that revolves around its planet in the direction opposite to the planet's rotation.

8	Titania	Uranus	1,580	982

The largest of Uranus's 15 moons, Titania was discovered by William Herschel in 1787 and has a snowball-like surface of ice.

9	Rhea	Saturn	1,530	951

Saturn's second largest moon was discovered by 17th-century Italian-born French astronomer Giovanni Cassini.

10	Oberon	Uranus	1,516	942

Oberon, also discovered by Herschel, was given the name of the fairy-king husband of Queen Titania, both characters in Shakespeare's A Midsummer Night's Dream.

T O P   1 0

LARGEST PLANETARY MOONS IN THE SOLAR SYSTEM DISCOVERED IN THE 20TH CENTURY

	Moon	Planet	Year discovered	Discoverer	Diameter km	mi
1	Charon	Pluto	1978	James Christy	1,240	771
2	Miranda	Uranus	1948	Gerard Kuiper	472	293
3	Proteus	Neptune	1989	*Voyager 2*	403	250
4	Nereid	Neptune	1949	Gerard Kuiper	340	211
5	Larissa	Neptune	1989	*Voyager 2*	192	119
6	Janus	Saturn	1966	Audouin Dollfus	190	118
7	Himalia	Jupiter	1904	Charles Perrine	184	114
8	Puck	Uranus	1985	*Voyager 2*	170	106
9	Galatea	Neptune	1989	*Voyager 2*	158	98
10	Despina	Neptune	1989	*Voyager 2*	148	92

T O P   1 0

COLDEST BODIES IN THE SOLAR SYSTEM*

	Body	Lowest temperature (°F)
1	Pluto	–382
2	Uranus	–369
3	Neptune	–364
4	Mercury	–328
5	Saturn	–256
6	Jupiter	–229
7	Mars	–220
8	Earth	–128
9	Venus	+867
10	The Sun	+9,932

* Excluding satellites and asteroids

Absolute zero, which has almost been attained on the Earth under laboratory conditions, is –459.67°F, only 100.67°F below the surface temperature of Triton, a moon of Neptune. At the other extreme, it has been calculated theoretically that the core of Jupiter attains 54,000°F, while the core of the Sun reaches 27,720,032°F.

T O P   1 0

LARGEST ASTEROIDS IN THE SOLAR SYSTEM

	Asteroid	Year discovered	Diameter km	miles
1	Ceres	1801	936	582
2	Pallas	1802	607	377
3	Vesta	1807	519	322
4	Hygeia	1849	450	279
5	Euphrosyne	1854	370	229
6	Interamnia	1910	349	217
7	Davida	1903	322	200
8	Cybele	1861	308	192
9	Europa	1858	288	179
10	Patienta	1899	275	171

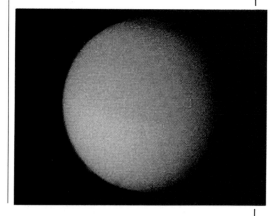

GIANT MOON
Titan, the first of Saturn's satellites to be discovered, is bigger than the planet Mercury.

SPACE FIRSTS

FIRST PEOPLE IN ORBIT

Name	Orbits	Duration hr:min	Spacecraft/ country	Date
1 Yuri Alekseyivich Gagarin	1	1:48	*Vostok I* (USSR)	Apr 12, 1961
2 Gherman Stepanovich Titov	17	25:18	*Vostok II* (USSR)	Aug 6–7, 1961
3 John Herschel Glenn	3	4:56	*Friendship 7* (US)	Feb 20, 1962
4 Malcolm Scott Carpenter	3	4:56	*Aurora 7* (US)	May 24, 1962
5 Andrian Grigoryevich Nikolayev	64	94:22	*Vostok III* (USSR)	Aug 11–15, 1962
6 Pavel Romanovich Popovich	48	70:57	*Vostok IV* (USSR)	Aug 12–15, 1962
7 Walter Marty Schirra	6	9:13	*Sigma 7* (US)	Oct 3, 1962
8 Leroy Gordon Cooper	22	34:19	*Faith 7* (US)	May 15–16, 1963
9 Valeri Fyodorovich Bykovsky	81	119:60	*Vostok V* (USSR)	Jun 14–19, 1963
10 Valentina Vladimirovna Tereshkova	48	70:50	*Vostok VI* (USSR)	Jun 16–19, 1963

No. 2 was the youngest-ever astronaut, aged 25 years 329 days, and No. 10 was the first woman in space. Among early pioneering flights, neither Alan Shepard (May 5, 1961: *Freedom 7*) nor Gus Grissom (July 21, 1961: *Liberty Bell 7*) actually orbited, achieving altitudes of only 115 miles/185 km and 118 miles/190 km respectively.

FIRST MOONWALKERS

Name/ spacecraft	Mission dates
1 Neil A. Armstrong (*Apollo 11*)	Jul 16–24, 1969
2 Edwin E. ("Buzz") Aldrin (*Apollo 11*)	Jul 16–24, 1969
3 Charles Conrad, Jr. (*Apollo 12*)	Nov 14–24, 1969
4 Alan L. Bean (*Apollo 12*)	Nov 14–24, 1969
5 Alan B. Shepard (*Apollo 14*)	Jan 31–Feb 9, 1971
6 Edgar D. Mitchell (*Apollo 14*)	Jan 31–Feb 9, 1971
7 David R. Scott (*Apollo 15*)	Jul 26–Aug 7, 1971
8 James B. Irwin (*Apollo 15*)	Jul 26–Aug 7, 1971
9 John W. Young (*Apollo 16*)	Apr 16–27, 1972
10 Charles M. Duke (*Apollo 16*)	Apr 16–27, 1972

SHANNON W. LUCID
The US's 6th woman in space, and the most experienced, Lucid holds the record for time in space by an American woman. In 1996 she traveled 75.2 million miles/121 million km in 188 days in orbit, during which she transferred to the Russian Mir space station.

FIRST WOMEN IN SPACE

	Name/country/mission	Date
1	Valentina Vladimirovna Tereshkova, USSR, *Vostok VI*	Jun 16–19, 1963

Tereshkova (b. Mar 6, 1937) was the first and, at 26, the youngest woman in space.

2	Svetlana Savitskaya, USSR, *Soyuz T7*	Aug 19, 1982

On July 25, 1984 Savitskaya (b. Aug 4, 1948) also walked in space (from Soyuz T12*).*

3	Sally K. Ride, US, *STS-7*	Jun 18–24, 1983

Ride (b. May 26, 1951) was the first American woman and, at age 32, the youngest.

4	Judith A. Resnik, US, *STS-41-D*	Aug 30–Sep 5, 1984

Resnik (b. Apr 5, 1949) was later killed in the STS-51-L Shuttle *disaster.*

5	Kathryn D. Sullivan, US, *STS-41-G*	Oct 5–13, 1984

Sullivan (b. Oct 3, 1951) was the first American woman to walk in space.

6	Anna L. Fisher, US, *STS-51-A*	Nov 8–16, 1984

Fisher (b. Aug 24, 1949) was the first American mother in space.

7	Margaret Rhea Seddon, US, *STS-51-D*	Apr 12–19, 1985

Seddon (b. Nov 8, 1947) flew again in STS-40 (Jun 5–14, 1991) and STS-58 (Oct 18–Nov 1, 1993).

8	Shannon W. Lucid, US, *STS-51-G*	Jun 17–24, 1985

Lucid (b. Jan 14, 1943) also flew in STS-34 (Oct 18–23, 1989), STS-43 (Aug 2–11, 1991), STS-58 (Oct 18–Nov 1, 1993). From STS-76 she transferred to the Russian Mir space station, then returned to Earth with STS-79 (Mar 22–Sep 26, 1996).

9	Bonnie J. Dunbar, US, *STS-61-A*	Oct 30–Nov 6, 1985

Dunbar (b. Mar 3, 1949) also flew in STS-32 (Jan 9–20, 1990), STS-50 (Jun 25–Jul 9, 1992), and STS-71 (Jun 27–Jul 7, 1995).

10	Mary L. Cleave, US, *STS-61-B*	Nov 26–Dec 3, 1985

Cleave (b. Feb 5, 1947) also flew in STS-30 (May 4–8, 1989).

THE 10

FIRST ARTIFICIAL SATELLITES

	Satellite	Country	Launch date
1	*Sputnik 1*	USSR	Oct 4, 1957
2	*Sputnik 2*	USSR	Nov 3, 1957
3	*Explorer 1*	US	Feb 1, 1958
4	*Vanguard 1*	US	Mar 17, 1958
5	*Explorer 3*	US	Mar 26, 1958
6	*Sputnik 3*	USSR	May 15, 1958
7	*Explorer 4*	US	Jul 26, 1958
8	*SCORE*	US	Dec 18, 1958
9	*Vanguard 2*	US	Feb 17, 1959
10	*Discoverer 1*	US	Feb 28, 1959

Artificial satellites for use as radio relay stations were first proposed by the British science fiction writer Arthur C. Clarke in the October 1945 issue of *Wireless World*.

THE 10

FIRST BODIES TO HAVE BEEN VISITED BY SPACECRAFT

	Body	Spacecraft/country	Year
1	Moon	*Pioneer 4* (US)	1959
2	Venus	*Mariner 2* (US)	1962
3	Mars	*Mariner 4* (US)	1965
4	Sun	*Pioneer 7* (US)	1966
5	Jupiter	*Pioneer 10* (US)	1973
6	Mercury	*Mariner 10* (US)	1974
7	Saturn	*Pioneer 11* (US)	1979
8	Comet Giacobini-Zinner	*International Sun-Earth Explorer 3* (International Cometary Explorer US)	1985
9	Uranus	*Voyager 2* (US)	1986
10	Halley's Comet	*Giotto* (Europe)	1986

MARINER 9
More than six months after launch, Mariner 9 became the first probe to orbit another planet, sending back new data about Mars.

THE 10

FIRST COUNTRIES TO HAVE ASTRONAUTS OR COSMONAUTS IN ORBIT

	Country	Name	Date*
1	USSR	Yuri Alekseyiviech Gagarin	Apr 12, 1961
2	US	John Herschell Glenn	Feb 20, 1962
3	Czechoslovakia	Vladimir Remek	Mar 2, 1978
4	Poland	Miroslaw Hermaszewski	Jun 27, 1978
5	East Germany	Sigmund Jahn	Aug 26, 1978
6	Bulgaria	Georgi I. Ivanov	Apr 10, 1979
7	Hungary	Bertalan Farkas	May 26, 1980
8	Vietnam	Pham Tuan	Jul 23, 1980
9	Cuba	Arnaldo T. Mendez	Sep 18, 1980
10	Mongolia	Jugderdemidiyn Gurragcha	Mar 22, 1981

* Of first space entry of a national of that country

Since the Soviet Union and the United States began and have dominated the exploration of space, all missions by non-Soviet and non-US citizens have been as guests of one of these countries. Especially since the era of the space shuttle and *Mir* space station, the list of nations with spaceflight experience has lengthened considerably and now includes Afghanistan, Austria, Belgium, Canada, France, Germany, India, Italy, Japan, Mexico, Netherlands, Romania, Saudi Arabia, Switzerland, Syria, and the UK.

THE 10

FIRST PLANETARY PROBES

	Probe/country	Planet	Arrival*
1	*Venera 4* (USSR)	Venus	Oct 18, 1967
2	*Venera 5* (USSR)	Venus	May 16, 1969
3	*Venera 6* (USSR)	Venus	May 17, 1969
4	*Venera 7* (USSR)	Venus	Dec 15, 1970
5	*Mariner 9* (US)	Mars	Nov 13, 1971
6	*Mars 2* (USSR)	Mars	Nov 27, 1971
7	*Mars 3* (USSR)	Mars	Dec 2, 1971
8	*Venera 8* (USSR)	Venus	Jul 22, 1972
9	*Venera 9* (USSR)	Venus	Oct 22, 1975
10	*Venera 10* (USSR)	Venus	Oct 25, 1975

* Successfully entered orbit or landed

This list excludes "fly-bys" – those probes that passed by but did not land on the surface of another planet. The US's *Pioneer 10*, for example, which was launched on March 2, 1972, flew past Jupiter on December 4, 1973 but did not land. *Venera 4* was the first unmanned probe to land on a planet, and *Venera 9* the first to transmit pictures from a planet's surface. *Mariner 9* was the first probe to orbit another planet; earlier and later Mariners were not designed to land. These probes either are now in orbit around the Sun or have traveled beyond the Solar System.

ASTRONAUTS & COSMONAUTS

TOP 10

MOST EXPERIENCED NON-US AND NON-RUSSIAN ASTRONAUTS AND COSMONAUTS

	Name/country	No. of missions	Duration of missions			
			day	hr	min	sec
1	Thomas Reiter, Germany	1	179	02	41	37
2	Talgat A. Musabeyev, Kazakhstan	1	125	22	53	36
3	Ulf D. Merbold, Germany	3	49	21	38	04
4	Claude Nicollier, Switzerland	3	34	12	53	58
5	Jean-Loup Chrétien, France	2	32	15	59	00
6	Jean-Pierre Haignere, France	1	20	16	09	02
7	Marc J. Garneau, Canada	2	18	06	04	05
8=	Jean-Jacques Favier, France	1	16	21	47	47
8=	Robert B. Thirsk, Canada	1	16	21	47	47
10	Claudie André-Deshays, France	1	15	18	23	37

TOP 10

COUNTRIES WITH MOST SPACEFLIGHT EXPERIENCE*

	Country	Astronauts	Duration of missions			
			day	hr	min	sec
1	USSR/Russia*	83	12,112	20	27	05
2	US	221	5,133	14	29	01
3	Germany	8	278	18	56	53
4	Kazakhstan	2	133	21	06	06
5	France	7	117	19	27	55
6	Canada	5	61	06	33	35
7	Japan	4	39	12	18	06
8	Italy	3	39	10	35	47
9	Switzerland	1	34	12	53	58
10	Bulgaria	2	11	19	11	06

* *Russia became a separate independent state on December 25, 1991*

TOP 10

MOST EXPERIENCED US ASTRONAUTS*

	Name#	Duration of missions			
		day	hr	min	sec
1	Shannon W. Lucid	223	02	52	26
2	Norman E. Thagard	140	13	26	59
3	John E. Blaha	139	12	24	44
4=	Gerald P. Carr	84	01	16	00
4=	Edward G. Gibson	84	01	16	00
4=	William R. Pogue	84	01	16	00
7	Owen K. Garriott	69	18	56	23
8	Alan L. Bean	69	15	45	25
9	Jack R. Lousma	67	11	13	46
10	F. Story Musgrave	53	09	58	27

* *To January 1, 1997*

UNTETHERED SPACE WALK
On an eight-day US space mission in 1984, astronauts made their first untethered space walks, using their hands as instruments in guiding a nitrogen-propelled maneuvering unit.

TOP 10

YOUNGEST US ASTRONAUTS

	Astronaut	First flight	Age*
1	Janice E. Voss	Jun 21, 1993	27
2	Kenneth D. Bowersox	Jun 25, 1984	28
3	Sally K. Ride	Jun 18, 1983	32
4	Tamara E. Jernigan	Jun 5, 1991	32
5	Eugene A. Cernan	Jun 3, 1966	32
6	Koichi Wakata	Jan 11, 1996	32
7	Steven A. Hawley	Aug 30, 1984	32
8	Mary E. Weber	Jul 13, 1995	32
9	Kathryn D. Sullivan	Oct 5, 1984	33
10	Ronald E. McNair#	Feb 3, 1984	33

* *Those of apparently identical age have been ranked according to their precise age in days at the time of their first flight*
\# *Killed in Challenger disaster, January 1986*

TOP 10

OLDEST US ASTRONAUTS

	Astronaut	Last flight	Age*
1	F. Story Musgrave	Dec 7, 1996	61
2	Vance D. Brand	Dec 11, 1990	59
3	Karl G. Henize	Aug 6, 1985	58
4	William E. Thornton	May 6, 1985	56
5	Don L. Lind	May 6, 1985	54
6	Henry W. Hartsfield	Nov 6, 1988	54
7	John E. Blaha	Dec 7, 1996	54
8	William G. Gregory	Mar 18, 1995	54
9	Robert A. Parker	Dec 11, 1990	53
10	Shannon W. Lucid	Mar 31, 1996	53

* *Those of apparently identical age have been ranked according to their precise age in days at the time of their last flight*

SPACE SALVAGE OPERATION
Discovery *Space Shuttle 51-A astronaut Dale A. Gardner uses his MMU (Manned Maneuvering Unit) to recover the malfunctioning Weststar VI communications satellite.*

TOP 10

MOST EXPERIENCED SPACEWOMEN*

	Name#	No. of missions	Duration of missions days	hr	min	sec
1	Shannon W. Lucid	5	223	02	52	26
2	Yelena V. Kondakova	1	169	05	21	35
3	Tamara E. Jernigan	4	53	06	12	39
4	Bonnie J. Dunbar	4	41	12	37	50
5	Kathryn C. Thornton	4	40	15	15	18
6	Susan J. Helms	3	33	29	16	31
7	Marsha S. Ivins	3	32	19	32	22
8	Margaret Rhea Seddon	3	30	02	22	15
9	Ellen S. Baker	3	28	14	31	42
10	Linda M. Godwin	3	26	10	38	07

* *To January 1, 1997*
\# *All US except 2 (Russian)*

Already a veteran of four missions, Shannon Lucid became America's most experienced astronaut and the world's most experienced female astronaut in 1996. She took off in US Space Shuttle *STS-76 Atlantis* on March 22 and transferred to the Russian *Mir* Space Station, returning on board *STS-79 Atlantis* on September 26 after traveling 75,200,000 miles/121,000,000 km.

TOP 10

LONGEST SPACE SHUTTLE FLIGHTS*

	Flight	Dates	Duration of flights hr	min	sec
1	*STS-80 Columbia*	Nov 19–Dec 7, 1996	423	53	18
2	*STS-78 Columbia*	Jun 20–Jul 7, 1996	405	48	30
3	*STS-67 Endeavor*	Mar 2–18, 1995	399	9	46
3	*STS-73 Columbia*	Oct 20–Nov 5, 1995	381	53	16
5	*STS-75 Columbia*	Feb 22–Mar 9, 1996	377	41	25
6	*STS-65 Columbia*	Jul 8–23, 1994	353	55	00
7	*STS-58 Columbia*	Oct 18–Nov 1, 1993	336	12	32
8	*STS-62 Columbia*	Mar 9–18, 1994	335	16	41
9	*STS-50 Columbia*	Jun 25–Jul 9, 1992	331	30	04
10	*STS-59 Endeavor*	Apr 9–20, 1994	269	49	30

* *To January 1, 1997*

The acronym STS (Space Transportation System) has been used throughout the Shuttle programme. The first nine flights were simply numbered *STS-1* (April 12–14, 1981) to *STS-9.* Thereafter a more complex system was employed, until the digital system was reinstated after the ill-fated *Challenger* launch.

THE FACE OF THE EARTH

TOP 10

MOST COMMON ELEMENTS IN THE EARTH'S CRUST

	Element	Percentage*
1	Oxygen	45.6
2	Silicon	27.3
3	Aluminum	8.4
4	Iron	6.2
5	Calcium	4.7
6	Magnesium	2.8
7	Sodium	2.3
8	Potassium	1.8
9	Hydrogen	1.5
10	Titanium	0.6

* *Totals more than 100 percent due to rounding*

This is based on the average percentages of the elements in igneous rock. At an atomic level, out of every million atoms, some 205,000 are silicon, 62,600 are aluminum, and 29,000 are hydrogen. However, in the Universe as a whole, hydrogen is by far the most common element, comprising some 927,000 out of every million atoms, followed by helium at 72,000 per million.

TOP 10

LIGHTEST ELEMENTS*

	Element	Year discovered	Density#
1	Lithium	1817	0.533
2	Potassium	1807	0.859
3	Sodium	1807	0.969
4	Calcium	1808	1.526
5	Rubidium	1861	1.534
6	Magnesium	1808	1.737
7	Phosphorus	1669	1.825
8	Beryllium	1798	1.846
9	Cesium	1860	1.896
10	Sulfur	Prehistoric	2.070

* *Solids only*
\# *Grams per cubic centimeter at 20°C*

TOP 10

ELEMENTS WITH THE HIGHEST MELTING POINTS

	Element	Melting point (°F)
1	Carbon	6,606
2	Tungsten	6,170
3	Rhenium	5,756
4	Osmium	5,513
5	Tantalum	5,424
6	Molybdenum	4,742
7	Niobium	4,474
8	Iridium	4,370
9	Ruthenium	4,190
10	Hafnium	4,040

Other elements that melt when heated to high temperatures include chromium (3,373°F), iron (2,795°F), and gold (1,947°F). For comparison, the surface of the Sun attains a temperature of 9,626°F.

TOP 10

HEAVIEST ELEMENTS

	Element	Year discovered	Density*
1	Osmium	1804	22.59
2	Iridium	1804	22.56
3	Platinum	1748	21.45
4	Rhenium	1925	21.01
5	Neptunium	1940	20.47
6	Plutonium	1940	20.26
7	Gold	Prehistoric	19.29
8	Tungsten	1783	19.26
9	Uranium	1789	19.05
10	Tantalium	1802	16.67

* *Grams per cubic centimeter at 20°C*

The two heaviest elements, the metals osmium and iridium, were discovered at the same time by the British chemist Smithson Tennant (1761–1815), who was also the first to prove that diamonds are made of carbon. A cubic foot (0.028317 m^3) of osmium weighs 1,410 lb/640 kg – equivalent to 10 people each weighing 141 lbs/64 kg.

TOP 10

ELEMENTS WITH THE LOWEST MELTING POINTS*

	Element	Melting point (°F)
1	Mercury	-38.0
2	Francium	80.6#
3	Cesium	83.1
4	Gallium	85.6
5	Rubidium	102.0
6	Phosphorus	111.4
7	Potassium	145.9
8	Sodium	208.0
9	Sulfur	235.0
10	Iodine	236.3

* *Solids only*
\# *Approximate*

Among other familiar elements that melt at relatively low temperatures are tin (449.6°F) and lead (621.5°F).

TOP 10

LARGEST METEORITES EVER FOUND

	Location	Estimated weight (tons)
1	Hoba West, Grootfontein, Namibia	60.0
2	*Ahnighito ("the Tent")*, Cape York, West Greenland	34.0
3	Bacuberito, Mexico	29.8
4	Mbosi, Tanganyika	28.7
5	Agpalik, Cape York, West Greenland	22.2
6	Armanti, Western Mongolia	22.1
7=	Willamette, Oregon	15.3
7=	Chupaderos, Mexico	15.3
9	Campo del Cielo, Argentina	14.3
10	Mundrabila, Western Australia	13.2

Meteorites have been known since early times: fragments of meteorite have been found mounted in a necklace in an Egyptian pyramid and in ancient Native American burial sites.

DEAD LOW
DEAD LOW
The shore of the Dead Sea is the lowest point on the world's surface. It takes its name from the scarcity of plants and animals that results from its high salt content.

T O P 1 0

DEEPEST DEPRESSIONS IN THE WORLD

	Depression/location	Maximum depth below sea level	
		m	ft
1	Dead Sea, Israel/Jordan	400	1,312
2	Turfan Depression, China	154	505
3	Qattâra Depression, Egypt	133	436
4	Poluostrov Mangyshlak, Kazakhstan	132	433
5	Danakil Depression, Ethiopia	117	383
6	Death Valley, US	86	282
7	Salton Sink, US	72	235
8	Zapadny Chink Ustyurta, Kazakhstan	70	230
9	Prikaspiyskaya Nizmennost', Kazakhstan/Russia	67	220
10	Ozera Sarykamysh, Turkmenistan/Uzbekistan	45	148

The shore of the Dead Sea, Israel/Jordan is the lowest exposed ground below sea level. However, its bed, at 2,388 ft/728 m below sea level, is only half as deep as that of Lake Baikal, Russia, which is 4,872 ft/ 1,485 m below sea level.

T O P 1 0

LARGEST DESERTS IN THE WORLD

	Desert	Location	Approx. area	
			sq km	sq miles
1	Sahara	North Africa	9,000,000	3,500,000
2	Australian	Australia	3,800,000	1,470,000
3	Arabian	Southwest Asia	1,300,000	502,000
4	Gobi	Central Asia	1,036,000	400,000
5	Kalahari	Southern Africa	520,000	201,000
6	Turkestan	Central Asia	450,000	174,000
7	Takla Makan	China	327,000	125,000
8=	Namib	Southwest Africa	310,000	120,000
8=	Sonoran	US/Mexico	310,000	120,000
10=	Somali	Somalia	260,000	100,000
10=	Thar	India/Pakistan	260,000	100,000

THE NORTON COUNTY METEORITE

On February 18, 1948, people in New Mexico, Oklahoma, and Kansas reported seeing the spectacle of a fireball followed by a trail of smoke. It came to earth in Norton County, Kansas, and on investigation was discovered to be a meteorite weighing 2,360 lb/1,070 kg. Almost white, it is one of the largest stone meteorites ever discovered. Meteorites are composed principally of either iron or stone. More stone than iron meteorites fall to earth, but they usually break up on impact, and consequently all the largest known meteorites are iron. The Norton County Meteorite is now the prize exhibit in the Meteorite Museum of the University of New Mexico in Albuquerque.

YEARS AGO · YEARS AGO · YEARS AGO · YEARS AGO ·
50

This Top 10 presents the approximate areas and ranking of the world's great deserts. These are often broken down into smaller desert regions – the Australian Desert into the Gibson, Simpson, and Great Sandy Desert, for example. Of the total land surface of the Earth, as much as one-quarter may be considered "desert," or land where more water is lost through evaporation than is acquired through precipitation. However, deserts may range from the extremely arid and barren sandy desert, through arid, to semiarid. Nearly every desert exhibits features that encompass all of these degrees of aridity without a precise line of demarcation between them.

RIVERS & WATERFALLS

GREATEST* RIVERS IN THE WORLD

	River/outflow/sea	Average flow (m³/sec)
1	Amazon, Brazil/South Atlantic	175,000
2	Congo, Angola–Congo (Zaïre)/ South Atlantic	39,000
3	Negro, Brazil/South Atlantic	35,000
4	Yangtze–Kiang, China/Yellow Sea	32,190
5	Orinoco, Venezuela/South Atlantic	25,200
6	Plata–Paraná–Grande, Uruguay/South Atlantic	22,900
7	Madeira–Mamoré–Grande, Brazil/South Atlantic	21,800
8	Yenisey–Angara–Selenga, Russia/Kara Sea	18,000
9	Brahmaputra, Bangladesh/Bay of Bengal	16,290
10	Lena–Kirenga, Russia/Arctic Ocean	16,100

Based on rate of discharge at mouth

LONGEST RIVERS IN NORTH AMERICA

	River/location	Length km	miles
1	Mackenzie–Peace, Canada	4,241	2,635
2	Mississippi, US	3,779	2,348
3	Missouri, US	3,726	2,315
4	Yukon, Canada/US	3,185	1,979
5	St. Lawrence, Canada	3,130	1,945
6	Rio Grande, US	2,832	1,760
7	Nelson, Canada	2,575	1,600
8	Arkansas, US	2,348	1,459
9	Colorado, US	2,334	1,450
10	Atchafalaya-Red	2,305	1,432

THE WORLD'S LONGEST RIVER?

The Nile's source was discovered in 1858 when British explorer John Hanning Speke reached lake Victoria Nyanza. The river is today generally accepted to be the world's longest, with an overall length of 4,145 miles/ 6,670 km. It was not until almost 100 years later, in 1953, that the source of the Amazon was identified as a stream called Huarco flowing from the Misuie glacier in the Peruvian Andes. It joins the Amazon's main tributary at Ucayali, Peru, giving a total length of 4,007 miles/6,448 km. However, by following the Amazon from its source and up the Rio Pará it is possible to sail for some 4,195 miles/6,750 km, a greater distance than the length of the Nile, but since this route is not considered geologically part of the Amazon basin, the Nile maintains its preeminence.

LONGEST RIVERS IN SOUTH AMERICA

	River/location	Length km	miles
1	Amazon, Peru/Brazil	6,448	4,007
2	Plata–Paraná, Brazil/ Paraguay/Argentina/ Uruguay	4,000	2,485
3	Madeira–Mamoré– Grande, Bolivia/Brazil	3,380	2,100
4	Purus, Peru/Brazil	3,207	1,993
5	São Francisco, Brazil	3,198	1,987
6	Orinoco, Colombia/Venezuela	2,736	1,700
7	Tocantins, Brazil	2,699	1,677
8	Paraguay, Paraguay/ Brazil/Argentina/Bolivia	2,549	1,584
9	Japurá–Caquetá, Colombia/Brazil	2,414	1,500
10	Negro, Colombia/ Venezuela/Brazil	2,253	1,400

LONGEST RIVERS IN THE WORLD

	River/location	Length km	miles
1	Nile, Tanzania/Uganda/ Sudan/Egypt	6,670	4,145
2	Amazon, Peru/Brazil	6,448	4,007
3	Yangtze–Kiang, China	6,300	3,915
4	Mississippi–Missouri– Red, US	5,971	3,710
5	Yenisey–Angara–Selenga, Mongolia/Russia	5,540	3,442
6	Huang Ho (Yellow River), China	5,464	3,395
7	Ob–Irtysh, Mongolia/ Kazakhstan/Russia	5,410	3,362
8	Congo, Angola/Congo (Zaïre)	4,700	2,920
9	Lena–Kirenga, Russia	4,400	2,734
10	Mekong, Tibet/China/ Myanmar (Burma)/Laos/Thailand Cambodia/Vietnam	4,350	2,703

LONGEST RIVERS IN ASIA

	River/location	Length km	miles
1	Yangtze–Kiang, China	6,300	3,915
2	Yenisey–Angara–Selenga, Mongolia/Russia	5,540	3,442
3	Huang Ho, China	5,464	3,395
4	Ob–Irtysh, Mongolia/ Kazakhstan/Russia	5,410	3,362
5	Lena–Kirengal, Russia	4,400	2,734
6	Mekong, Tibet/China/ Myanmar/Laos/Thailand Cambodia/Vietnam	4,350	2,703
7	Amur–Argun, China/Russia	4,345	2,700
8	Syr Darya–Naryn, Kyrgyzstan/Tajikistan/ Uzbekistan/Kazakhstan	3,019	1,876
9	Nizhnyaya Tunguska, Russia	2,989	1,857
10	Indus, Pakistan	2,880	1,790

THE RIVER RHINE AT ST. GOAR
The Rhine, the longest river in Western Europe, is easily navigable. As a consequence it is the busiest waterway on the continent.

T O P 1 0

RIVERS PRODUCING THE MOST SEDIMENT

	River	Sediment discharged (tons per annum)
1	Yellow	2,090,000,000
2	Ganges	1,600,000,000
3	Brahmaputra	800,000,000
4	Yangtze	551,000,000
5	Indus	480,000,000
6	Amazon	397,000,000
7	Mississippi–Missouri	342,000,000
8	Irrawaddy	331,000,000
9	Mekong	187,000,000
10	Colorado	150,000,000

T O P 1 0

GREATEST* WATERFALLS IN THE WORLD

	Waterfall/country	Average flow (m³/sec)
1	Boyoma (Stanley), Congo (Zaïre)	17,000
2	Khône, Laos	11,610
3	Niagara, Canada/US	5,830
4	Grande, Uruguay	4,500
5	Paulo Afonso, Brazil	2,890
6	Urubupungá, Brazil	2,750
7	Iguaçu, Argentina/Brazil	1,700
8	Maribondo, Brazil	1,500
9	Churchill (Grand), Canada	1,390
10	Kabalega (Murchison), Uganda	1,200

* Based on volume of water

With an average flow rate of 13,000 m³/sec, and a peak of 50,000 m³/sec, the Guaíra, or Salto das Sete Quedas formerly occupied second place in this list, but following the completion of the Itaipú dam in 1982, it was submerged.

T O P 1 0

LONGEST RIVERS IN EUROPE

	River	Location	Length km	miles
1	Danube	Germany/Austria/Slovakia/ Hungary/Serbia/Romania/Bulgaria	2,842	1,766
2	Rhine	Switzerland/Germany/Holland	1,368	850
3	Elbe	Czech Republic/Germany	1,167	725
4	Loire	France	1,014	630
5	Tagus	Portugal	1,009	627
6	Meuse	France/Belgium/Holland	950	590
7	Ebro	Spain	933	580
8	Rhône	Switzerland/France	813	505
9	Guadiana	Spain/Portugal	805	500
10	Seine	France	776	482

T O P 1 0

HIGHEST WATERFALLS IN THE WORLD

	Waterfall	River	Location	Total drop m	ft
1	Angel	Carrao	Venezuela	979	3,212 *
2	Tugela	Tugela	South Africa	948	3,110
3	Utigård	Jostedal Glacier	Nesdale, Norway	800	2,625
4	Mongefossen	Monge	Mongebekk, Norway	774	2,540
5	Yosemite	Yosemite Creek	California	739	2,425
6	Østre Mardøla Foss	Mardals	Eikisdal, Norway	657	2,154
7	Tyssestrengane	Tysso	Hardanger, Norway	646	2,120
8	Cuquenán	Arabopo	Venezuela	610	2,000
9	Sutherland	Arthur	South Island, New Zealand	580	1,904
10	Kjellfossen	Naero	Gudvangen, Norway	561	1,841

* Longest single drop 2,648 ft/807 m

OCEANS, SEAS & LAKES

TOP 10

LARGEST OCEANS AND SEAS IN THE WORLD

	Ocean/sea	Approx. area	
		sq km	sq miles
1	Pacific Ocean	165,241,000	63,800,000
2	Atlantic Ocean	82,439,000	31,830,000
3	Indian Ocean	73,452,000	28,360,000
4	Arctic Ocean	13,986,000	5,400,000
5	Arabian Sea	3,864,000	1,492,000
6	South China Sea	3,447,000	1,331,000
7	Caribbean Sea	2,753,000	1,063,000
8	Mediterranean Sea	2,505,000	967,000
9	Bering Sea	2,269,000	876,000
10	Bay of Bengal	2,173,000	839,000

Geographers hold differing opinions as to whether certain bodies of water are regarded as seas in their own right or as parts of larger oceans – the Coral, Weddell, and Tasman Seas would be eligible for this list, but most authorities consider them part of the Pacific Ocean.

THE GREAT LAKES OF NORTH AMERICA
The vast expanse of the Great Lakes is particularly impressive when viewed from space. Lakes Superior and Huron are partly within Canada, making Lake Michigan the largest lake wholly situated within the US.

TOP 10

DEEPEST OCEANS AND SEAS IN THE WORLD

	Ocean/sea	Greatest depth		Average depth	
		m	ft	m	ft
1	Pacific Ocean	10,924	35,837	4,028	13,215
2	Indian Ocean	7,455	24,460	3,963	13,002
3	Atlantic Ocean	9,219	30,246	3,926	12,880
4	Caribbean Sea	6,946	22,788	2,647	8,685
5	South China Sea	5,016	16,456	1,652	5,419
6	Bering Sea	4,773	15,659	1,547	5,075
7	Gulf of Mexico	3,787	12,425	1,486	4,874
8	Mediterranean Sea	4,632	15,197	1,429	4,688
9	Sea of Japan	3,742	12,276	1,350	4,429
10	Arctic Ocean	5,625	18,456	1,205	3,953

The deepest point in the deepest ocean is the Marianas Trench in the Pacific at a depth of 35,837 ft/10,924 m, according to a recent hydrographic survey, although a slightly lesser depth of 35,814 ft/ 10,916 m was recorded on January 23, 1960 by Jacques Piccard and Donald Walsh in their 58-ft/17.7-m long bathyscaphe *Trieste 2* during the deepest-ever ocean descent. Whichever measurement is correct, it is still close to 6.8 miles/11 km down, or almost 29 times the height of the Empire State Building.

T O P 1 0

MOST COMMON ELEMENTS IN SEAWATER

	Element	Tons per mi³
1	Water*	4,553,000,000
2	Chlorine	90,000,000
3	Sodium	50,000,000
4	Magnesium	6,430,000
5	Sulfur	4,227,000
6	Calcium	1,930,000
7	Potassium	1,792,000
8	Bromine	308,000
9	Carbon	133,248
10	Strontium	38,000

* Composed of hydrogen and oxygen

A typical cubic mile of seawater is a treasury of often valuable elements, but sodium and chlorine (combined as sodium chloride, or common salt) are the only two that are extracted in substantial quantities. The cost of extracting such elements as gold (approximately 37 pounds of which are found in the average mi³ of seawater) would be prohibitively expensive.

T O P 1 0

LARGEST FRESHWATER LAKES IN THE US*

	Lake/state	Approx. area sq km	sq miles
1	Michigan, Illinois/Indiana/Michigan/Wisconsin	57,700	22,278
2	Iliamna, Alaska	2,590	1,000
3	Okeechobee, Florida	1,813	700
4	Becharof, Alaska	1,186	458
5	Red, Minnesota	1,168	451
6	Teshepuk, Alaska	816	315
7	Naknek, Alaska	627	242
8	Winnebago, Wisconsin	557	215
9	Mille Lacs, Minnesota	536	207
10	Flathead, Montana	510	197

* Excluding those partly in Canada

T O P 1 0

LARGEST LAKES IN THE WORLD

	Lake	Location	Approx. area sq km	sq miles
1	Caspian Sea	Azerbaijan/Iran/Kazakhstan/Russia/Turkmenistan	378,400	146,101
2	Superior	Canada/US	82,100	31,699
3	Victoria	Kenya/Tanzania/Uganda	62,940	24,301
4	Huron	Canada/US	59,580	23,004
5	Michigan	US	57,700	22,278
6	Aral Sea	Kazakhstan/Uzbekistan	40,000	15,444
7	Tanganyika	Burundi/Tanzania/Congo (Zaïre)/Zambia	31,987	12,350
8	Baikal	Russia	31,494	12,160
9	Great Bear	Canada	31,153	12,028
10	Great Slave	Canada	28,570	11,031

T O P 1 0

COUNTRIES WITH THE GREATEST AREA OF INLAND WATER

	Country	Percentage of total area	Water area sq km	sq miles
1	Canada	7.60	755,170	291,573
2	India	9.56	314,400	121,391
3	China	2.82	270,550	104,460
4	US	2.20	206,010	79,541
5	Ethiopia	9.89	120,900	46,680
6	Colombia	8.80	100,210	38,691
7	Indonesia	4.88	93,000	35,908
8	Russia	0.47	79,400	30,657
9	Australia	0.90	68,920	26,610
10	Tanzania	6.25	59,050	22,799

Large areas of some countries are occupied by major rivers and lakes. Lake Victoria, for example, raises the water area of Uganda to 15.39 percent of its total. In Europe, three Scandinavian countries have considerable areas of water: Sweden has 15,072 sq miles/39,036 sq km (8.68 percent), Finland has 12,185 sq miles/31,560 sq km (9.36 percent), and Norway has 6,317 sq miles/16,360 sq km (5.05 percent).

DID YOU KNOW

TALLER THAN EVEREST?

Mountains are conventionally measured from sea level. Thus Everest, at 29,022 ft/8,846 m above sea level is the world's tallest mountain. However, the bases of some mountains lie far beneath the sea. The Hawaiian volcano Mauna Kea is 13,796 ft/4,206 m tall but has even greater height below sea level, some 19,683 ft/6,000 m, bringing its total height to 33,481 ft/10,206 m, or 4,461 ft/1,360 m taller than Everest. Its neighbor, Mauna Loa, at 13,681 ft/4,171 m tall with a further 18,043 ft/5,500 m below sea level, is also taller than Everest and is thought to be the world's most voluminous mountain at 10,076 mi³/42,000 km³. The tallest mountain wholly beneath the sea is in the Pacific Ocean's Tonga Trench, rising to 28,510 ft/8,690 m.

ON TOP OF THE WORLD

T O P 1 0

HIGHEST MOUNTAINS IN THE WORLD

(Height of principal peak; lower peaks of the same mountain are excluded)

	Mountain	Location	m	ft
1	Everest	Nepal/Tibet	8,846	29,022
2	K2	Kashmir/China	8,611	28,250
3	Kangchenjunga	Nepal/Sikkim	8,598	28,208
4	Lhotse	Nepal/Tibet	8,501	27,890
5	Makalu I	Nepal/Tibet	8,470	27,790
6	Dhaulagiri I	Nepal	8,172	26,810
7	Manaslu I	Nepal	8,156	26,760
8	Cho Oyu	Nepal	8,153	26,750
9	Nanga Parbat	Kashmir	8,126	26,660
10	Annapurna I	Nepal	8,078	26,504

Dhaulagiri was believed to be the world's tallest mountain until Kangchenjunga was surveyed and declared to be even higher. However, when the results of the so-called Great Trigonometrical Survey of India were studied, it became apparent that Everest (then called "Peak XV") was the tallest, its height being computed as 29,002 ft/8,840 m. Errors in measurement were corrected in 1955, giving the height as 29,029 ft/8,848 m. On April 20, 1993, using the latest measuring techniques, this was again revised to the current "official" figure. The mountain's name was suggested in 1865 as a tribute to Sir George Everest, the Surveyor General of India who had led the Great Trigonometrical Survey.

T O P 1 0

HIGHEST MOUNTAINS IN NORTH AMERICA

	Mountain/location	m	ft
1	McKinley (Denali), US	6,194	20,320
2	Logan, Canada	6,050	19,850
3	Citlaltépetl (Orizaba), Mexico	5,700	18,700
4	St. Elias, US/Canada	5,489	18,008
5	Popocatépetl, Mexico	5,452	17,887
6	Foraker, US	5,304	17,400
7	Ixtaccihuatl, Mexico	5,286	17,343
8	Lucania, Canada	5,226	17,147
9	King, Canada	5,173	16,971
10	Steele, Canada	5,073	16,644

T O P 1 0

HIGHEST ACTIVE VOLCANOES IN THE WORLD

	Volcano	Location	Latest activity	m	ft
1	Guallatiri	Chile	1987	6,060	19,882
2	Lááscar	Chile	1991	5,990	19,652
3	Cotopaxi	Ecuador	1975	5,897	19,347
4	Tupungatito	Chile	1986	5,640	18,504
5	Popocatépetl	Mexico	1995	5,452	17,887
6	Ruiz	Colombia	1992	5,400	17,716
7	Sangay	Ecuador	1988	5,230	17,159
8	Guagua Pichincha	Ecuador	1988	4,784	15,696
9	Purace	Colombia	1977	4,755	15,601
10	Kliuchevskoi	Russia	1995	4,750	15,584

This list includes all volcanoes that have been active at some time during the 20th century. Although it does not qualify for the list above, the highest currently active volcano in Europe is Mt. Etna in Italy (10,855 ft/3,311 m), which was responsible for numerous deaths in earlier times. Although still active, Etna's last major eruption took place on March 11, 1669, killing at least 20,000.

T O P 1 0

HIGHEST DORMANT VOLCANOES IN THE WORLD

	Volcano	Location	Latest activity	m	ft
1	Llullaillaco	Chile	1877	6,723	22,057
2	El Misti	Peru	c. 1870	5,822	19,101
3	Orizaba	Mexico	1687	5,610	18,405
4	Rainier	US	c. 1894	4,392	14,410
5	Shasta	US	1786	4,317	14,162
6	Fuji	Japan	1708	3,776	12,388
7	Tolbachik	Russia	1876	3,682	12,080
8	Turrialba	Costa Rica	1866	3,246	10,650
9	Baitoushan	China/Korea	1702	2,774	9,003
10	Bandai	Japan	1888	1,819	5,968

This list comprises the world's tallest volcanoes that are known to have been active at some time before the 20th century, but which now appear to be dormant – although some, including Mt. Rainier, Mt. Shasta, and Mt. Fuji still emit steam. Mt. Rainier and Mt. Fuji are both classic examples of "composite cones" or "strato-volcanoes" – those that have been built up during sequential eruptions over many thousands of years.

TOP 10
HIGHEST MOUNTAINS IN SOUTH AMERICA

	Mountain/location	m	ft
1	Cerro Aconcagua, Argentina	6,960	22,834
2	Ojos del Salado, Argentina/Chile	6,885	22,588
3	Bonete, Argentina	6,873	22,550
4	Pissis, Argentina/Chile	6,780	22,244
5	Huascarán, Peru	6,768	22,205
6	Llullaillaco, Argentina/Chile	6,723	22,057
7	Libertador, Argentina	6,721	22,050
8	Mercadario, Argentina/Chile	6,670	21,884
9	Yerupajá, Peru	6,634	21,765
10	Tres Cruces, Argentina/Chile	6,620	21,720

TOP 10
HIGHEST MOUNTAINS* IN EUROPE

	Mountain/country	m	ft
1	Mont Blanc, France/Italy	4,807	15,771
2	Monte Rosa, Italy/Switzerland	4,634	15,203
3	Dom, Switzerland	4,545	14,911
4	Liskamm, Italy/Switzerland	4,527	14,853
5	Weisshorn, Switzerland	4,505	14,780
6	Täschorn, Switzerland	4,491	14,734
7	Matterhorn, Italy/Switzerland	4,477	14,688
8	La Dent Blanche, Switzerland	4,357	14,293
9	Nadelhorn, Switzerland	4,327	14,196
10	Le Grand Combin Switzerland	4,314	14,153

* Height of principal peak; lower peaks of the same mountain are excluded

DID YOU KNOW
HIGH FLIERS

On April 3, 1933, 20 years before any climbers had reached the top of Mount Everest, British pilots Lord Clydesdale, in a Westland P.V3, and Flt. Lt. David McIntyre, in a Westland Wallace biplane, succeeded in flying over it. Using oxygen and wearing electrically-heated flying suits, they battled against high winds, almost crashed, and suffered from failed oxygen equipment, but both achieved their objective and landed safely.

TOP 10
COUNTRIES WITH THE HIGHEST ELEVATIONS IN THE WORLD*

	Country/mountain	m	ft
1	Nepal#, Everest	8,846	29,022
2	Pakistan, K2	8,611	28,250
3	India, Kangchenjunga	8,598	28,208
4	Bhutan, Khula Kangri	7,554	24,784
5	Tajikistan, Mt. Garmo (formerly Kommunizma)	7,495	24,590
6	Afghanistan, Noshaq	7,499	24,581
7	Kyrgyzstan, Pik Pobedy	7,439	24,406
8	Kazakhstan, Khan Tengri	6,995	22,949
9	Argentina, Cerro Aconcagua	6,960	22,834
10	Chile, Ojos del Salado	6,885	22,588

* Based on the tallest peak in each country
# Everest straddles Nepal and Tibet, which – now known as Xizang – is a province of China

While an elevation of more than 1,000 ft/ 305 m is commonly regarded as a mountain, there is no international agreement. Using this criterion, almost every country in the world can claim to have at least one mountain.

TOP 10
STATES WITH THE HIGHEST ELEVATIONS IN THE US

	State/peak	m	ft
1	Alaska, Mount McKinley (Denali)	6,194	20,320
2	California, Mount Whitney	4,418	14,494
3	Colorado, Mount Elbert	4,399	14,433
4	Washington, Mount Rainier	4,392	14,410
5	Wyoming, Gannett Peak	4,207	13,804
6	Hawaii, Mauna Kea	4,205	13,796
7	Utah, Kings Peak	4,123	13,528
8	New Mexico, Wheeler Peak	4,011	13,161
9	Nevada, Boundary Peak	4,005	13,140
10	Montana, Granite Peak	3,901	12,799

TOP 10
COUNTRIES WITH THE LOWEST ELEVATIONS IN THE WORLD

	Country	m	ft
1	Maldives, Unnamed	3	10
2=	Marshall Islands, Unnamed	6	20
2=	Tuvalu, Unnamed	6	20
4	Gambia, Unnamed	43	141
5	Bahamas, Mount Alvernia	63	206
6	Nauru, Unnamed	68	225
7	Qatar, Dukhan Heights	73	240
8	Kiribati, Banaba	81	270
9	Bahrain, Jabal al-Dukhan	134	440
10	Denmark, Yding Skovhøj	173	568

These 10 countries are definitely off the agenda if you are planning a climbing holiday, none of them possessing a single elevation taller than a medium-sized skyscraper.

WORLD WEATHER

THE 10
LAYERS OF CLOUDS

	Cloud layer	Altitude of layer m	ft
1	Stratus	below 450	below 1,456
2=	Cumulus	450–2,000	1,476–6,562
2=	Stratocumulus	450–2,000	1,476–6,562
2=	Cumulonimbus	450–2,000	1,476–6,562
5	Nimbostratus	900–3,000	2,953–9,843
6=	Altostratus	2,000–7,000	6,562–22,966
6=	Altocumulus	2,000–7,000	6,562–22,966
8=	Cirrus	5,000–13,500	16,404–44,291
8=	Cirrostratus	5,000–13,500	16,404–44,291
8=	Cirrocumulus	5,000–13,500	16,404–44,291

TOP 10
WETTEST INHABITED PLACES IN THE WORLD

	Location	Average annual rainfall mm	in
1	Buenaventura, Colombia	6,743	265.47
2	Monrovia, Liberia	5,131	202.01
3	Pago Pago, American Samoa	4,990	196.46
4	Moulmein, Myanmar, Burma	4,852	191.02
5	Lae, Papua New Guinea	4,645	182.87
6	Baguio, Luzon Island, Philippines	4,573	180.04
7	Sylhet, Bangladesh	4,457	175.47
8	Conakry, Guinea	4,341	170.91
9=	Bogor, Java, Indonesia	4,225	166.34
9=	Padang, Sumatra, Indonesia	4,225	166.34

WET, WET, WET
All 10 of the world's wettest places receive more than 12 feet/4 meters of rain each year, with the rainiest of all experiencing over 22 feet /6.7 meters.

TOP 10
HOTTEST CITIES IN THE WORLD*

	City	Highest recorded temperature °F	°C
1	Arouane, Mali	130	54.4
2=	Abadan, Iran	127	52.8
2=	Cloncurry, Australia	127	52.8
2=	Wadi Halfa, Sudan	127	52.8
5=	Aswan, Egypt	124	51.1
5=	Fort Flatters, Algeria	124	51.1
5=	Mosul, Iraq	124	51.1
8=	Cufra, Libya	122	50.0
8=	Gabes, Tunisia	122	50.0
8=	Multan, Pakistan	122	50.0

* Hottest city in each country only

Phoenix, Arizona (118°F/47.8°C) and Seville, Spain (117°F/47.2°C) are the hottest cities in the US and Europe.

TOP 10
HOTTEST INHABITED PLACES IN THE WORLD

	Location	Average temperature °F	°C
1	Djibouti, Djibouti	86.0	30.0
2=	Timbuktu, Mali	84.7	29.3
2=	Tirunelveli, India	84.7	29.3
2=	Tuticorin, India	84.7	29.3
5=	Nellore, India	84.6	29.2
5=	Santa Marta, Colombia	84.6	29.2
7=	Aden, South Yemen	84.0	28.9

	Location	Average temperature °F	°C
7=	Madurai, India	84.0	28.9
7=	Niamey, Niger	84.0	28.9
10=	Hudaydah, North Yemen	83.8	28.8
10=	Ouagadougou, Burkina Faso	83.8	28.8
10=	Thanjāvūr, India	83.8	28.8

TOP 10

HIGHEST TEMPERATURES RECORDED IN THE US

	Weather station/state	Date	°F	°C
1	Greenland Ranch, California	July 10, 1913	134	56.7
2	Lake Havasu City, Arizona	June 29, 1994	128	53.3
3	Laughlin, Nevada	June 29, 1994	125	51.7
4	Waste Isolation Pilot Plant, New Mexico	June 27, 1994	122	50.0
5=	Alton, Kansas	July 24, 1936	121	49.5
5=	Steele, North Dakota	July 6, 1936	121	49.5
7=	Ozark, Arkansas	August 10, 1936	120	48.9
7=	Tipton, Oklahoma	June 27, 1994	120	48.9
7=	Gannvalley, South Dakota	July 5, 1936	120	48.9
7=	Seymour, Texas	August 12, 1936	120	48.9

TOP 10

LOWEST TEMPERATURES RECORDED IN THE US

	Weather station/state	Date	°F	°C
1	Prospect Creek, Alaska	January 23, 1971	−80	−62.2
2	Rogers Pass, Montana	January 20, 1954	−70	−56.7
3	Peter's Sink, Utah	February 1, 1985	−69	−56.1
4	Riverside R.S, Wyoming	February 9, 1933	−66	−54.4
5	Maybell, Colorado	February 1, 1985	−61	−51.7
6=	Island Park Dam, Idaho	January 18, 1943	−60	−51.1
6=	Parshall, North Dakota	February 15, 1936	−60	−51.1
8	Pokegama Dam, Minnesota	February 16, 1903	−59	−50.6
9	McIntosh, South Dakota	February 17, 1936	−58	−50.0
10=	Seneca, Oregon	February 10, 1933	−54	−47.8
10=	Danbury, Wisconsin	January 24, 1922	−54	−47.8

TOP 10

DRIEST INHABITED PLACES IN THE WORLD

	Location	Average annual rainfall mm	in
1	Aswan, Egypt	0.5	0.02
2	Luxor, Egypt	0.7	0.03
3	Arica, Chile	1.1	0.04
4	Ica, Peru	2.3	0.09
5	Antofagasta, Chile	4.9	0.19
6	Minya el Qamn, Egypt	5.1	0.20
7	Asyût, Egypt	5.2	0.20
8	Callao, Peru	12.0	0.47
9	Trujillo, Peru	14.0	0.54
10	Fayyum, Egypt	19.0	0.75

TOP 10

COLDEST INHABITED PLACES IN THE WORLD

	Location	Average temperature °F	°C
1	Norlísk, Russia	12.4	−10.9
2	Yakutsk, Russia	13.8	−10.1
3	Yellowknife, Canada	22.3	−5.4
4	Ulaanbator, Mongolia	23.9	−4.5
5	Fairbanks, Alaska,	25.9	−3.4
6	Surgut, Russia	26.4	−3.1
7	Chita, Russia	27.1	−2.7
8	Nizhnevartosvsk, Russia	27.3	−2.6
9	Hailar, Mongolia	27.7	−2.4
10	Bratsk, Russia	28.0	−2.2

TOP 10

SNOWIEST CITIES IN THE US

	City	Average annual snowfall in	mm
1	Blue Canyon, CA	240.8	6,116
2	Marquette, MI	129.2	3,282
3	Sault Ste. Marie, MI	116.1	2,949
4	Syracuse, NY	114.0	2,896
5	Caribou, ME	110.0	2,794
6	Mount Shasta, CA	104.9	2,664
7	Lander, WY	102.2	2,596
8	Flagstaff, AZ	100.8	2,560
9	Sexton Summit, OR	97.8	2,484
10	Muskegon, MI	97.1	2,466

TOP 10

HOTTEST CITIES IN THE US

	City	Average temperature °F	°C		City	Average temperature °F	°C
1	Key West, Florida	77.8	25.4	6	Brownsville, Texas	73.8	23.1
2	Miami, Florida	75.9	24.2	7=	Tampa, Florida	72.4	22.2
3	West Palm Beach, Florida	74.7	23.7	7=	Vero Beach, Florida	72.4	22.4
4	Fort Myers, Florida	74.4	23.5	9	Corpus Christi, Texas	71.6	22.3
5	Yuma, Arizona	74.2	23.3	10	Daytona Beach, Florida	70.4	21.3

LIFE ON EARTH

TOP 10

LARGEST DINOSAURS EVER DISCOVERED

1 *Seismosaurus*
Length: 98–119 ft/ 30–36 m
Estimated weight: 50–80 tons

A skeleton of this colossal plant-eater was excavated in 1985 near Albuquerque, New Mexico, by US paleontologist David Gillette, and given a name that means "earth-shaking lizard." It is being studied by the New Mexico Museum of Natural History, which may confirm its position as the largest dinosaur, with some claiming a length of up to 170 ft/52 m.

2 *Supersaurus*
Length: 80–100 ft/24–30 m
Estimated weight: 50 tons

The remains of Supersaurus *were found in Colorado, in 1972. Some scientists have suggested a length of up to 138 ft/42 m.*

3 *Antarctosaurus*
Length: 60–98 ft/18–30 m
Estimated weight: 40–50 tons

Named Antarctosaurus *("southern lizard") by German paleontologist Friedrich von Huene in 1929, this creature's thigh bone alone measures 7 ft 6 in/ 2.3 m.*

4 *Barosaurus*
Length: 75–90 ft/23–27.5 m
Height and Weight uncertain

Barosaurus (meaning "heavy lizard," so named by US paleontologist Othniel C. Marsh in 1890) has been found in both North America and Africa, thus proving the existence of a land link between these continents in Jurassic times (205–140 million years ago).

5 *Mamenchisaurus*
Length: 89 ft/27 m
Weight uncertain

An almost complete skeleton discovered in 1972 showed it had the longest neck of any known animal, comprising more than half its total body length. It was named by Chinese paleontologist Yang Zhong-Jian (known in paleontological circles as "C.C. Young") after the place in China where it was found.

6 *Diplodocus*
Length: 75–89 ft/23–27 m
Estimated weight: 12 tons

Diplodocus *was probably one of the most stupid dinosaurs, having the smallest brain in relation to its body size.*

7 *Ultrasauros*
Length: Over 82 ft/25 m
Estimated weight: 50 tons

Ultrasauros *was discovered by James A. Jensen in Colorado in 1979 but has not yet been fully studied. It was originally called "Ultrasaurus" ("ultra lizard"), which, it turned out, was a name also given to another, smaller dinosaur. To avoid confusion, its spelling was altered.*

8 *Brachiosaurus*
Length: 82 ft/25 m
Estimated weight: 50 tons

Some paleontologists have put the weight of Brachiosaurus *as high as 190 tons, but this seems improbable.*

9 *Pelorosaurus*
Length: 80 ft/24 m
Height and Weight uncertain

The first fragments of Pelorosaurus *("monstrous lizard") were found in Sussex and named by British doctor and geologist Gideon Algernon Mantell as early as 1850.*

10 *Apatosaurus*
Length: 66–70 ft/20–21 m
Estimated weight: 20–30 tons

Apatosaurus *(its name means "deceptive lizard") is better known by its former name of* Brontosaurus *("thunder reptile"). The bones of the first one ever found, in Colorado in 1879, caused great confusion for many years because its discoverer attached a head from a different species to the rest of the skeleton.*

DIPLODOCUS

FIRST DINOSAURS TO BE NAMED

Name/meaning/named by	Year
1 *Megalosaurus*, Great lizard, William Buckland	1824
2 *Iguanodon*, Iguana tooth, Gideon Mantell	1825
3 *Hylaeosaurus*, Woodland lizard, Gideon Mantell	1832
4 *Macrodontophion*, Large tooth snake, A. Zborzewski	1834
5= *Thecodontosaurus*, Socket-toothed lizard, Samuel Stutchbury and H. Riley	1836
5= *Palaeosaurus*, Ancient lizard, Samuel Stutchbury and H. Riley	1836
7 *Plateosaurus*, Flat lizard, Hermann von Meyer	1837
8= *Cladeiodon*, Branch tooth, Richard Owen	1841
8= *Cetiosaurus*, Whale lizard, Richard Owen	1841
10 *Pelorosaurus*, Monstrous lizard, Gideon Mantell	1850

The first 10 dinosaurs were all identified and named within a quarter of a century – although subsequent research has since cast doubt on the authenticity of certain specimens. The name *Megalosaurus*, the first to be given to a dinosaur, was proposed by William Buckland (1784–1856), an English geologist who was also Dean of Westminster and a noted eccentric. Acknowledging that the name had been suggested to him by another clergyman-geologist, the Rev. William Daniel Conybeare, Buckland first used it in an article, "Notice on the *Megalosaurus* or Great Fossil Lizard of Stonesfield," which was published in 1824. The *Iguanodon*, the second dinosaur to be named, was identified by Gideon Algernon Mantell (1790–1852). Mantell found the first *Iguanodon* teeth in 1822 in a pile of stones being used for road repairs in the Tilgate Forest area of Sussex. After detailed study, he concluded that they resembled an enormous version of the teeth of the Central American iguana lizard, and hence suggested the name *Iguanodon*.

AS DEAD AS A DODO
The dodo, a flightless member of the dove family, was discovered in 1598, and specimens were taken to Europe where its ungainly appearance was greeted with astonishment. Within 100 years, entirely as a result of human activity in hunting them down, the dodo had disappeared, its name becoming a synonym for "extinct."

FINAL DATES THAT 10 ANIMALS WERE LAST SEEN ALIVE

Animal	Last seen alive
1 Aurochs	1627

This giant wild ox, once described by Julius Caesar, was last recorded in central Europe after the advance of agriculture forced it to retreat from its former territory, which once stretched to the west as far as Britain. It was extensively hunted, and the last few specimens died on the Jaktorow Forest in Poland.

2 Aepyornis	1649

Also known as the "Elephant bird," the 10 ft/3 m wingless bird was a native of Madagascar.

3 Dodo	1681

Discovered by European travelers in 1507, specimens of this curious bird were extensively collected – its lack of flight and tameness making it extremely vulnerable to being caught. Its name comes from the Portuguese word duodo, meaning "stupid." The last dodo seen alive was on the island of Mauritius in 1681, where it was observed by English naturalist Benjamin Harry.

4 Steller's sea cow	1768

This large marine mammal, named after its 1741 discoverer, German naturalist Georg Wilhelm Steller, and one of the creatures that gave rise to the legend of the mermaid, was rapidly hunted to extinction. The spectacled cormorant, which Steller also found, became extinct at about the same time.

5 Great auk	1844

The last pair in the world of Pinguinus impennis, a flightless North Atlantic seabird, was killed on June 4, 1844 on Eldey island on behalf of an Icelandic collector called Carl Siemsen. A stuffed example, collected in 1821 by Count F.C. Raben, was sold at Sotheby's, London, in 1971 to the Natural History Museum of Iceland. Another example was sold by the University of Durham on September 21, 1977 for $6,600. There are possibly as many as 80 specimens in natural history collections around the world.

6 Tarpan	1851

This European wild horse was last seen in the Ukraine. Przewalski's horse, another wild horse thought to be extinct, has been rediscovered in Mongolia. New, captive-bred stock has been reintroduced into its former range around the fringes of the Gobi Desert.

7 Quagga	1883

This zebralike creature, found in South Africa and first recorded in 1685, was hunted by European settlers for food and leather to such an extent that by 1870 the last specimen in the wild had been killed. Examples sent to European collectors and zoos survived but failed to reproduce in captivity and steadily died out. The last example, a female in Amsterdam Zoo, died on August 12, 1883.

8 Pilori muskrat	1902

The species became extinct following the May 8, 1902 eruption of Mont Pelée, Martinique, which destroyed its habitat.

9 Passenger pigeon	1914

The passenger pigeon's last moment can be stated precisely. At 1:00pm on September 1, 1914 at Cincinnati Zoo, a 29-year-old bird named Martha expired. There had once been vast flocks of passenger pigeons, with estimated totals running to a staggering five to nine billion in the 19th century. However, as they were remorselessly killed for food and to protect farm crops in the US, and since the bird laid just one egg each season, its decline was almost inevitable. By March 24, 1900 (when the last passenger pigeon in the wild was shot), it was virtually extinct, with only a few specimens, such as Martha, in zoos.

10 Heath hen	1932

The grouselike prairie chicken known as the heath hen (Tympanuchus cupido cupido) was extensively hunted in the New England states until only a few specimens survived, all on the island of Martha's Vineyard, Massachusetts. Despite conservation measures to protect them, many birds were killed in a forest fire in 1916, and a virus decimated the survivors, the last of them dying on March 11, 1932.

ENDANGERED ANIMALS

THE 10

MOST ENDANGERED MAMMALS IN THE WORLD

Mammal	Estimated no.
1= Tasmanian wolf	?
1= Halcon fruit bat	?
1= Ghana fat mouse	?
4 Javan rhinoceros	50
5 Iriomote cat	60
6 Black lion tamarin	130
7 Pygmy hog	150
8 Kouprey	100–200
9 Tamarau	200
10 Indus dolphin	400

THE 10

MOST ENDANGERED BIRDS IN THE US

1	Golden-cheeked Warbler
2	Kirtland's Warbler
3	Bachman's Warbler
4	Black-capped Vireo
5	Cerulean Warbler
6	Colima Warbler
7	Golden-winged Warbler
8	Black Swift
9	Baird's Sparrow
10	Cassin's Sparrow

Source: US Fish and Wildlife Service

TOP 10

RAREST MARINE MAMMALS

Mammal	Estimated no.
1 Caribbean monk seal	200
2 Mediterranean monk seal	400
3 Juan Fernandez fur seal	750
4 West Indian manatee	1,000
5 Guadeloupe fur seal	1,600
6 New Zealand fur seal	2,000
7= Hooker's sea lion	4,000
7= Right whale	4,000
9 Fraser's dolphin	7,800
10 Amazon manatee	8,000

The hunting of seals for their fur and of whales for oil and other products has resulted in a sharp decline in their populations. Populations of some species of seal formerly numbering millions have shrunk to a few thousand, and it has been estimated that the world population of humpback whales has dwindled from 100,000 to 10,000.

PYGMY HOG
It is hoped that the smallest known pig, the pygmy hog, a rare inhabitant of the Himalayan foothills, will be rescued through the creation of a forest preserve in India.

THE 10

COUNTRIES FORMERLY IMPORTING MOST RAW IVORY

Country	Weight per annum lb	kg
1 Hong Kong	395,967	179,608
2 Japan	222,634	100,985
3 China	111,078	50,384
4 Belgium	85,385	38,730
5 Singapore	39,070	17,722
6 US	10,589	4,803
7 France	9,890	4,486
8 UK	9,308	4,222
9 India	8,552	3,879
10 Taiwan	6,515	2,955

Most elephant ivory comes from Africa and goes to the Far East as raw material for a carving industry that then re-exports its products worldwide. Western countries such as Belgium have acted as conduits for this trade, as have several African countries, including Burundi and Djibouti, which have virtually no wild elephants of their own.

THE 10

COUNTRIES FORMERLY EXPORTING MOST IVORY

Country	Weight per annum lb	kg
1 Hong Kong	299,692	135,938
2 Singapore	100,586	221,754
3 Japan	33,139	73,059
4 Belgium	24,034	52,986
5 Somalia	22,638	49,908
6 Tanzania	22,581	49,783
7 Congo (Zaire)	18,806	41,460
8 Gabon	13,542	29,855
9 Zaïre	11,009	24,271
10 Djibouti	10,901	24,033

SAVING NATURE

The US Endangered Species Act is regarded as one of the most important pieces of legislation ever enacted to protect animals and plants. The Act made it an offense to destroy species or their habitats, or to engage in such activities as importing or trading in certain animals, birds' eggs, and rare plants, and established recovery plans for many species. Endangered species that are at risk of extinction and threatened species (at risk of becoming endangered) are included. Animals on the list encompass large, popular creatures, such as bears and deer, and rare but less familiar birds, reptiles, fish, and insects: on January 31, 1997, the total stood at 444 animals and 623 plants.

25 YEARS AGO

ELEPHANTS UNDER THREAT

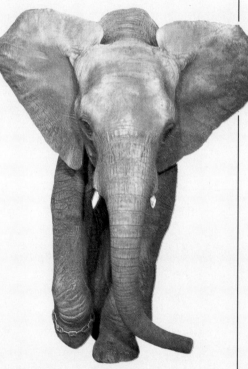

The elephant has been associated with humans for thousands of years and has been used for hunting, in warfare, for transportation, and in the logging industry. There were once millions of African elephants, and as recently as the beginning of this century there were at least 100,000 Asian elephants. Destruction of natural habitats, extensive poaching for ivory and hide and, in Asia, for use in traditional medicine, has reduced the populations of both African and Asian elephants. In 1996 their total populations were estimated to be 286,234 and between 37,860 and 48,740 respectively. Extensive programs have been established to rescue them from their threatened status.

TUSK TRADE
Despite an international ban since 1991, the illegal poaching and smuggling of ivory continues to endanger the elephant populations of certain countries.

BABY ELEPHANT
Protected in game preserves, elephants now have the opportunity to breed without threat.

TOP 10

COUNTRIES WITH THE MOST ELEPHANTS

	Country	Elephants
1	Tanzania	73,459*
2	Zaïre	65,974#
3	Botswana	62,998*
4	Gabon	61,794+
5	Zimbabwe	56,297*
6	Congo	32,563#
7	India	20,000★
8	Zambia	19,701*
9	Kenya	13,834*
10	South Africa	9,990*

* Definite
\# Probable
\+ Possible
★ Minimum

BIG GAME
Once numbered in the millions, hunting has decimated the huge herds of elephants that once roamed Africa and Asia.

LAND ANIMALS

SLOTHFUL SLOTH
One of nature's most somnolent creatures, even the name of the sloth has become a synonym for extreme laziness – exceeded only by the almost inert koala.

T O P 1 0
DEADLIEST SNAKES IN THE WORLD

	Snake	Native region
1	Saw-scales or carpet viper	Africa and Asia

This snake is considered the most dangerous for various reasons: it is relatively common, prone to biting, and injects a large amount of highly toxic venom. It probably kills as many as 8,000 people a year in Asia alone.

	Snake	Native region
2=	Taipan	Australia and New Guinea

Taipans have very long fangs and are able to deliver a large quantity of venom. Mortality is practically 100 percent unless antivenin is administered immediately.

	Snake	Native region
2=	Black mamba	Southern and Central Africa

Death is nearly 100 percent without antivenin.

	Snake	Native region
4	Tiger snake	Australia

Mortality is very high without antivenin.

	Snake	Native region
5	Common krait	South Asia

Even with antivenin mortality is up to 50 percent.

	Snake	Native region
6	Death adder	Australia

Without antivenin mortality is over 50 percent, but prompt treatment saves most victims.

	Snake	Native region
7	Yellow or Cape cobra	Southern Africa

This is the most dangerous type of cobra in the world, with a high mortality rate.

	Snake	Native region
8	King cobra	India and Southeast Asia

At up to 19 ft/5.8 m long, the king cobra is the largest poisonous snake in the world. It also injects the most venom into its victims.

	Snake	Native region
9=	Bushmaster	Central and South America
9=	Green mamba	Africa

Most people fear snakes, but only a few dozen of the 3,500-odd snake species that exist cause serious harm. Measuring the strength of the venom of snakes is technically possible, but this factor does not indicate how dangerous they may be. This Top 10 takes account of the degree of threat posed by those snakes that have a record of causing fatalities.

T O P 1 0
LAZIEST ANIMALS IN THE WORLD

	Animal	Average hours of sleep		Animal	Average hours of sleep
1	Koala	22	**6=**	Hamster	14
2	Sloth	20	**6=**	Squirrel	14
3=	Armadillo	19	**8=**	House cat	13
3=	Opossum	19	**8=**	Pig	13
5	Lemur	16	**10**	Spiny anteater	12

This list excludes periods of hibernation, which can last up to several months among creatures such as the ground squirrel. At the other end of the scale comes the frantic shrew, which has to hunt and eat constantly, or else perish: it literally has no time for sleep. The incredible swift contrives to sleep on the wing, "turning off" alternate halves of its brain for shifts of two hours or more. Flight control is entrusted to whichever hemisphere of the brain is on duty at the time.

T O P 1 0
LONGEST SNAKES IN THE WORLD

	Snake	Maximum length m	ft
1	Reticulated (Royal) python	10.7	35
2	Anaconda	8.5	28
3	Indian python	7.6	25
4	Diamond python	6.4	21
5	King cobra	5.8	19
6	Boa constrictor	4.9	16
7	Bushmaster	3.7	12
8	Giant brown snake	3.4	11
9	Diamondback rattlesnake	2.7	9
10	Indigo or gopher snake	2.4	8

Although the South American anaconda is sometimes claimed to be the longest snake, this has not been authenticated, and therefore the python remains at No. 1.

T O P 1 0
LONGEST LAND ANIMALS IN THE WORLD

	Animal	Maximum length m	ft
1	Reticulated (Royal) python	10.7	35
2	Tapeworm	10.0	33
3	African elephant	7.3	24
4	Crocodile	5.9	19
5	Giraffe	5.8	19
6	White rhinoceros	4.2	14
7	Hippopotamus	4.0	13
8	American bison	3.9	13
9	Arabian camel (dromedary)	3.5	12
10	Siberian tiger	3.3	11

T O P 1 0

HEAVIEST WILD TERRESTRIAL MAMMALS IN THE WORLD*

	Mammal	Length m	ft	Weight kg	lb
1	African elephant	7.3	24	7,000	14,432
2	White rhinoceros	4.2	14	3,600	7,937
3	Hippopotamus	4.0	13	2,500	5,512
4	Giraffe	5.8	19	1,600	2,527
5	American bison	3.9	13	1,000	2,205
6	Arabian camel (dromedary)	3.5	12	690	1,521
7	Polar bear	3.0	10	600	1,323
8	Moose	3.0	10	550	1,213
9	Siberian tiger	3.3	11	300	661
10	Gorilla	2.0	7	220	485

* *Excluding domesticated cattle and horses*

T O P 1 0

MOST COMMON MAMMALS IN THE UK

	Mammal	Estimated number
1	Common rat	76,790,000
2	House mouse	75,192,000
3	Field vole	75,000,000
4	Common shrew	41,700,000
5	Wood mouse	38,000,000
6	Rabbit	37,500,000
7	Mole	31,000,000
8	Bank vole	23,000,000
9	Pygmy shrew	8,600,000
10	Grey squirrel	2,520,000

T O P 1 0

MOST PROLIFIC WILD MAMMALS IN THE WORLD

	Animal	Average litter
1	Malagasy tenrec	25
2	Virginian opossum	22
3	Golden hamster	11
4	Ermine	10
5	Prairie vole	9
6	Coypu	8.5
7=	European hedgehog	7
7=	African hunting dog	7
9=	Meadow vole	6.5
9=	Wild boar	6.5

T O P 1 0

FASTEST MAMMALS IN THE WORLD

	Mammal	Maximum recorded speed km/h	mph
1	Cheetah	105	65
2	Pronghorn antelope	89	55
3=	Mongolian gazelle	80	50
3=	Springbok	80	50
5=	Grant's gazelle	76	47

	Mammal	Maximum recorded speed km/h	mph
5=	Thomson's gazelle	76	47
7	Brown hare	72	45
8	Horse	69	43
9=	Greyhound	68	42
9=	Red deer	68	42

T O P 1 0

MOST INTELLIGENT MAMMALS

1	Human
2	Chimpanzee
3	Gorilla
4	Orangutan
5	Baboon
6	Gibbon
7	Monkey
8	Smaller toothed whale
9	Dolphin
10	Elephant

This list is based on research conducted by Edward O. Wilson, Professor of Zoology at Harvard University, who defined intelligence as speed and extent of learning performance over a wide range of tasks, also taking account of the ratio of an animal's brain size to its body bulk. It may come as a surprise that the dog does not make it into this Top 10; a recent study of 133 dog breeds by the US psychologist Stanley Coren showed that there is a wide range of intelligence within the species.

DID YOU KNOW

WORLD CHAMPION SPRINTER

Although animals such as pronghorn antelopes can sustain high speeds for longer periods of time, the cheetah is the fastest animal over short distances. It can accelerate to 60 mph/96 km/h in three seconds from a standing start. Tests conducted in 1937 at Harringay Stadium, a greyhound racing track in London, and additional tests carried out in the US in 1960 were inconclusive since cheetahs in captivity are reluctant to run. However, analysis of films of cheetahs in the wild indicate that they can easily cover 23ft/7m with a single stride of 0.28 seconds duration – equivalent to 56 mph/90 km/h – and exceed that in short bursts of speed.

MARINE ANIMALS

T O P   1 0

HEAVIEST MARINE MAMMALS

	Mammal	Length m	ft	in	Weight (tons)
1	Blue whale	33.5	110	0	143.3
2	Fin whale	25.0	82	0	49.6
3	Right whale	17.5	57	5	44.1
4	Sperm whale	18.0	59	0	39.7
5	Gray whale	14.0	46	0	36.0
6	Humpback whale	15.0	49	2	29.2
7	Baird's whale	5.5	18	0	12.1
8	Southern elephant seal	6.5	21	4	4.0
9	Northern elephant seal	5.8	19	0	3.7
10	Pilot whale	6.4	21	0	3.2

Probably the largest animal that ever lived, the blue whale dwarfs even the other whales listed here, all but one of which far outweigh the biggest land animal, the elephant.

T O P   1 0

FISHING COUNTRIES

	Country	Annual catch (tons)
1	China	19,365,304
2	Peru	9,315,192
3	Japan	8,959,720
4	Chile	6,655,739
5	US	6,547,001
6	Russia	4,906,801
7	India	4,665,048
8	Indonesia	4,009,878
9	Thailand	3,690,703
10	South Korea	2,920,019

T O P   1 0

LARGEST TURTLES AND TORTOISES

	Turtle/tortoise	Maximum weight kg	lb
1	Pacific leatherback turtle	865	1,908
2	Atlantic leatherback turtle	454	1,000
3=	Green sea turtle	408	900
3=	Aldabra giant tortoise	408	900
5	Loggerhead turtle	386	850
6	Galapagos giant or elephant tortoise	385	849
7	Alligator snapping turtle	183	403
8	Black sea turtle	126	278
9	Flatback turtle	84	185
10	Hawksbill turtle	68	150

Both the size and the longevity of turtles and tortoises remain hotly debated by zoologists. Although the weights on which this Top 10 are ranked are from corroborated sources, there are many claims of even larger specimens among the 265 living species of *Chelonia* (turtles and tortoises). The largest are marine turtles, while the Aldabra giant tortoises are the largest of the land-dwellers – and probably the longest-lived land creatures of all, at more than 150 years. The alligator snapping turtle is the largest freshwater species. However, all living examples would be dwarfed in size by prehistoric monster turtles such as *Stupendemys geographicus*, that measured up to 10 ft/3 m in length and weighed over 4,497 lb/2,040 kg.

T O P   1 0

FASTEST FISH IN THE WORLD

	Fish	Maximum recorded speed km/h	mph
1	Sailfish	110	68
2	Marlin	80	50
3	Bluefin tuna	74	46
4	Yellowfin tuna	70	44
5	Blue shark	69	43
6	Wahoo	66	41
7=	Bonefish	64	40
7=	Swordfish	64	40
9	Tarpon	56	35
10	Tiger shark	53	33

Flying fish have a top speed in the water of only 23 mph/37 km/h, but airborne they can reach 35 mph/56 km/h. Many sharks qualify for this list; only two are listed here to prevent the list becoming overly shark-infested. But just in case you thought it was safe to go back in the water, the great white shark (of *Jaws* fame) can manage speeds of 30 mph/48 km/h with ease. For any smaller fish (up to the size of a pike or salmon) a handy formula for estimating an individual's top speed is just over 10 times its own length in centimeters per second: thus a trout 5½ in/15 cm long swims at 58 in/160 cm per second, or 3.6 mph/5.8 km/h.

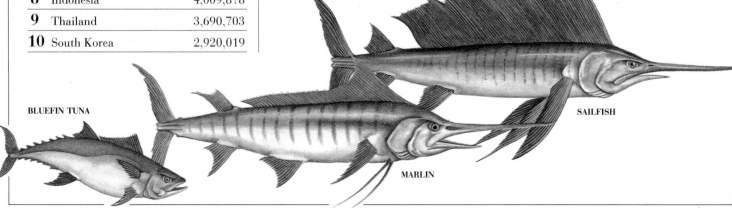

BLUEFIN TUNA

SAILFISH

MARLIN

T O P 1 0

LARGEST SPECIES OF SALTWATER FISH CAUGHT IN THE WORLD

	Species	Angler/location/date	kg	Weight g	lb	oz
1	Great white shark	Alfred Dean, Ceduna, South Australia, 1959	1,208	39	2,664	0
2	Tiger shark	Walter Maxwell, Cherry Grove, California, 1964	807	41	1,780	0
3	Greenland shark	Terje Nordtvedt, Trondheimsfjord, Norway, 1987	775	0	1,708	9
4	Black marlin	A. C. Glassell, Jr., Cabo Blanco, Peru, 1953	707	62	1,560	0
5	Bluefin tuna	Ken Fraser, Aulds Cove, Nova Scotia, 1979	678	59	1,496	0
6	Pacific blue marlin	Jay W. de Beaubien, Kaaiwi Point, Kona, Hawaii, 1982	624	15	1,376	0
7	Atlantic blue marlin	Larry Martin, St. Thomas, Virgin Islands, 1977	581	52	1,282	0
8	Swordfish	L. Marron, Iquique, Chile, 1953	536	16	1,182	0
9	Mako shark	Patrick Guillanton, Black River, Mauritius, 1988	505	76	1,115	0
10	Hammerhead shark	Allen Ogle, Sarasota, Florida, 1982	449	52	991	0

IN THE CAN
Sardines, along with other species of herring and pilchard, are components of a world fishing industry that in the 1990s first topped 100 million tons a year.

T O P 1 0

SPECIES OF FISH MOST CAUGHT WORLDWIDE

	Species	Tons caught per annum
1	Anchoveta	13,113,986
2	Alaska pollock	4,738,416
3	Chilean jack mackerel	4,689,926
4	Silver carp	2,572,430
5	Atlantic herring	2,079,075
6	Grass carp	2,007,977
7	South American pilchard	1,976,913
8	Common carp	1,793,679
9	Chubb mackerel	1,661,731
10	Skipjack tuna	1,612,281

The Food and Agriculture Organization of the United Nations estimates the volume of the world's fishing catch, which totals almost 122,000,000 tons a year, of which about 83,000,000 tons is figured to be destined for human consumption – equivalent to approximately 29 lbs/13 kg a year for every inhabitant. The foremost species, anchoveta, are small anchovies used principally as bait to catch tuna. In recent years, the amount of carp has increased markedly. Among broader groupings, some 3,300,000 tons of shrimp and a similar tonnage of squid, cuttlefish, and octopus, are caught annually.

T O P 1 0

LARGEST SPECIES OF FRESHWATER FISH CAUGHT IN THE WORLD

	Species	Angler/location/date	kg	Weight g	lb	oz
1	White sturgeon	Joey Pallotta III, Benicia, California, 1983	212	28	468	0
2	Alligator gar	Bill Valverde, Rio Grande, Texas, 1951	126	55	279	0
3	Nile perch	Kurt M. Fenster, Tende Bay, Entebbe, Uganda, 1989	68	98	152	1
4	Chinook salmon	Les Anderson, Kenai River, Arkansas, 1985	44	11	97	4
5=	Blue catfish	Edward B. Elliott, Missouri River, South Dakota, 1959	44	00	97	0
5=	Tigerfish	Raymond Houtmans, Congo River, Kinshasa, Zaïre, 1988	44	00	97	0
7	Lake sturgeon	James M. DeOtis, Kettle River, Montana, 1986	41	84	92	4
8	Flathead catfish	Mike Rogers, Lake Lewisville, Texas, 1982	41	39	91	4
9	Atlantic salmon	Henrik Henrikson, Tana River, Norway, 1928	35	89	79	2
10	Carp	Leo van der Gugten, Lac de St-Cassien, France, 1987	34	33	75	11

FLYING ANIMALS

T O P 1 0
SMALLEST BATS IN THE WORLD

Bat/habitat	Weight gm	oz	Length cm	in
1 Kitti's hognosed bat (*Craseonycteris thonglongyai*), Thailand	2.0	0.07	2.9	1.1
2 Proboscis bat (*Rhynchonycteris naso*), Central and South America	2.5	0.09	3.8	1.5
3= Banana bat (*Pipistrellus nanus*), Africa	3.0	0.11	3.8	1.5
3= Smoky bat (*Furiptera horrens*), Central and South America	3.0	0.11	3.8	1.5
5= Little yellow bat (*Rhogeessa mira*), Central America	3.5	0.12	4.0	1.57
5= Lesser bamboo bat (*Tylonycteris pachypus*), Southeast Asia	3.5	0.12	4.0	1.57
7 Disk-winged bat (*Thyroptera tricolor*), Central and South America	4.0	0.14	3.6	1.42
8 Lesser horseshoe bat (*Rhynolophus hipposideros*), Europe and Western Asia	5.0	0.18	3.7	1.46
9 California myotis (*Myotis californienses*), North America	5.0	0.18	4.3	1.69
10 Northern blossom bat (*Macroglossus minimus*), Southeast Asia to Australia	15.0	0.53	6.4	2.52

T O P 1 0
LARGEST FLIGHTED BIRDS

Bird	Weight kg	lb	oz
1 Great bustard	20.9	46	1
2 Trumpeter swan	16.8	37	1
3 Mute swan	16.3	35	15
4= Albatross	15.8	34	13
4= Whooper swan	15.8	34	13
6 Manchurian crane	14.9	32	14
7 Kori bustard	13.6	30	0
8 Gray pelican	13.0	28	11
9 Black vulture	12.5	27	8
10 Griffon vulture	12.0	26	7

T O P 1 0
LARGEST BIRDS OF PREY*

Bird	Length cm	in
1 California condor	124	49
2= Steller's sea eagle	114	45
2= Lammergeier	114	45
4 Bald eagle	109	43
5= Andean condor	107	42
5= European black vulture	107	42
5= Ruppell's griffon	107	42
8 Griffon vulture	104	41
9 Wedge-tailed eagle	102	40
10 Lappet-faced vulture	100	39

* Diurnal only – hence excluding owls

The entrants in this Top 10 all measure more than 39 in (1 m) from beak to tail, but birds of prey generally have smaller body weights than those appearing in the list of 10 largest flighted birds. All of these raptors, or aerial hunters, have remarkable eyesight and can spot their victims from great distances. However, even if they kill animals heavier than themselves, they are generally unable to take wing with them: stories of eagles carrying off lambs and small children are usually fictitious.

GROUNDED
Some of the largest living birds – as well as some that are now extinct – are incapable of flight and have become adapted to life on the ground.

OSTRICH
108 in (274.3 cm)

CASSOWARY
60 in (152.4 cm)

EMPEROR PENGUIN
45 in (114 cm)

T O P 1 0
LARGEST FLIGHTLESS BIRDS

Bird	Weight kg	lb	oz	Height cm	in
1 Ostrich	156.5	345	0	274.3	108
2 Emu	40.0	88	3	152.4	60
3 Cassowary	33.5	73	14	152.4	60
4 Rhea	25.0	55	2	137.1	54
5 Emperor penguin	29.4	64	13	114.0	45
6 Flightless cormorant	4.5	9	15	95.0	37⅓
7 Flightless steamer	5.5	12	2	84.0	33
8 Kakapo	2.5	5	8	66.0	26
9 Kagu	5.0	11	0	59.9	23⅗
10 Kiwi	3.5	7	12	55.9	22

TOP 10
LARGEST BIRDS IN THE UK

Bird	Beak to tail length cm	in
1= Mute swan	145–160	57–63
1= Whooper swan	145–160	57–63
3 Bewick's swan	116–128	46–50
4 Canada goose	up to 110	up to 43
5 Gray heron	90–100	35–39
6 Cormorant	84–98	33–39
7 Gannet	86–96	34–38
8 Golden eagle	76–91	30–36
9 White-tailed sea eagle	69–91	27–36
10 Capercaillie (male)	82–90	32–35

TOP 10
BIRDS WITH THE LARGEST WINGSPANS

Bird	Maximum wingspan m	ft
1 Marabou stork	4.0	13
2 Albatross	3.7	12
3 Trumpeter swan	3.4	11
4= Mute swan	3.1	10
4= Whooper swan	3.1	10
4= Gray pelican	3.1	10
4= Californian condor	3.1	10
4= Black vulture	3.1	10
9= Great bustard	2.7	9
9= Kori bustard	2.7	9

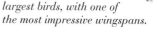

WINGED WONDER
The albatross is among the world's largest birds, with one of the most impressive wingspans.

TOP 10
MOST COMMON BREEDING BIRDS IN THE US

1 Red-winged blackbird
2 House sparrow
3 Mourning dove
4 European starling
5 American robin
6 Horned lark
7 Common grackle
8 American crow
9 Western meadowlark
10 Brown-headed cowbird

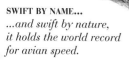

SWIFT BY NAME...
...and swift by nature, it holds the world record for avian speed.

TOP 10
FASTEST BIRDS IN THE WORLD

Bird	Maximum recorded speed km/h	mph
1 Spine-tailed swift	171	106
2 Frigate bird	153	95
3 Spur-winged goose	142	88
4 Red-breasted merganser	129	80
5 White-rumped swift	124	77
6 Canvasback duck	116	72
7 Eider duck	113	70
8 Teal	109	68
9= Mallard	105	65
9= Pintail	105	65

Until pilots cracked 190 mph/306 km/h in 1919, birds were the fastest creatures on the Earth: diving peregrine falcons clock up speeds approaching 185 mph/ 298km/h. However, most comparisons of the air speed of birds rule out diving or wind-assisted flight: most small birds on migration can manage a ground speed of 60 mph/97 km/h to 70 mph/113 km/h. This list therefore picks out star performers among the medium- to large-sized birds that do not need help from wind or gravity to hit their top speed.

TOP 10
LONGEST AERIAL MIGRATIONS

Bird	Maximum migration km	miles
1 Arctic tern	20,117	12,500
2 Parasitic jaeger	16,093	10,000
3= Baird's sandpiper	15,450	9,600
3= Pectoral sandpiper	15,450	9,600
5= Gray-headed albatross	14,967	9,300
5= Hudsonian godwit	14,967	9,300
5= Lesser yellowlegs	14,967	9,300
5= Light-mantled sooty albatross	14,967	9,300
5= Northern giant petrel	14,967	9,300
5= Pomarine jaeger	14,967	9,300
5= Red phalarope	14,967	9,300
5= Royal albatross	14,967	9,300
5= Ruddy turnstone	14,967	9,300
5= Southern polar skua	14,967	9,300
5= Surfbird	14,967	9,300
5= Wandering tattler	14,967	9,300
5= Whimbrel	14,967	9,300
5= White-rumped sandpiper	14,967	9,300

LIVESTOCK

T O P 1 0

TYPES OF LIVESTOCK IN THE WORLD

	Livestock	World total
1	Chickens	12,664,000,000
2	Cattle	1,306,476,000
3	Sheep	1,067,566,000
4	Pigs	900,480,000
5	Ducks	715,000,000
6	Goats	639,400,000
7	Turkeys	230,000,000
8	Buffaloes	151,514,000
9	Horses	60,894,000
10	Donkeys	43,762,000

The 17,779,092,000 animals accounted for by this Top 10 outnumber the world's human population by three to one. The world's chicken population is more than double the human population, while the world's cattle population outnumbers the population of China.

COUNTING SHEEP
Ranking third in the global livestock inventory, sheep are widely distributed and actually outnumber the human population in certain countries.

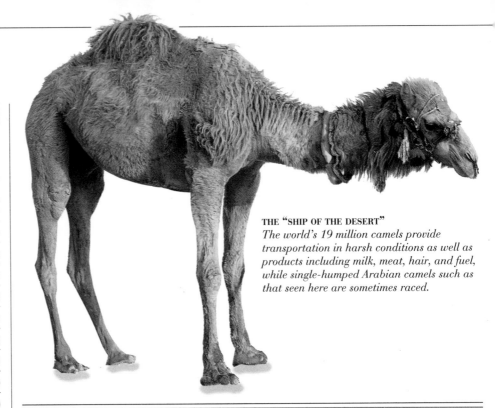

THE "SHIP OF THE DESERT"
The world's 19 million camels provide transportation in harsh conditions as well as products including milk, meat, hair, and fuel, while single-humped Arabian camels such as that seen here are sometimes raced.

T O P 1 0

COUNTRIES WITH MOST CAMELS

	Country	Camels		Country	Camels
1	Somalia	6,200,000	6	Ethiopia	1,000,000
2	Sudan	2,903,000	7	Kenya	810,000
3	India	1,520,000	8	Chad	600,000
4	Pakistan	1,119,000	9	Saudi Arabia	418,000
5	Mauritania	1,087,000	10	Mongolia	390,000
				World total	*19,241,000*

T O P 1 0

COUNTRIES WHERE SHEEP MOST OUTNUMBER PEOPLE

	Country	Sheep	Human population	Sheep per person
1	Falkland Islands	717,000	2,121	338.05
2	New Zealand	47,144,000	3,494,300	13.49
3	Uruguay	22,685,000	3,116,800	7.28
4	Australia	120,651,000	18,114,000	6.66
5	Mongolia	13,719,000	2,363,000	5.81
6	Mauritania	5,288,000	2,217,000	2.39
7	Kazakhstan	33,524,000	16,963,600	1.98
8	Iceland	470,000	266,786	1.76
9	Namibia	2,620,000	1,500,000	1.75
10	Somalia	13,500,000	9,077,000	1.49

The estimated total world sheep population is 1,067,566,000 – a global average of one sheep for every 5.62 people (or 0.2 sheep per person) – but as this Top 10 shows, there are a number of countries where the tables are turned and sheep considerably outnumber humans.

T O P 1 0

WOOL-PRODUCING COUNTRIES

	Country	Annual production (tons)
1	Australia	772,000
2	New Zealand	309,000
3	China	267,000
4	Russia	103,720
5	Argentina	101,400
6	Kazakhstan	99,210
7	Uruguay	94,075
8	South Africa	73,538
9	UK	67,350
10	Pakistan	58,642
	World total	*2,855,238*

T O P 1 0

COUNTRIES WITH MOST TURKEYS

	Country	Turkeys
1	US	88,000,000
2	France	36,000,000
3	Italy	22,000,000
4	UK	10,000,000
5=	Brazil	6,000,000
5=	Canada	6,000,000
5=	Mexico	6,000,000
8=	Portugal	5,000,000
8=	Germany	5,000,000
10=	Argentina	4,000,000
10=	Israel	4,000,000
10=	Madagascar	4,000,000
	World total	*230,000,000*

T O P 1 0

COUNTRIES WITH MOST PIGS

	Country	Pigs
1	China	424,680,000
2	US	59,992,000
3	Brazil	35,350,000
4	Germany	24,698,000
5	Russia	22,631,000
6	Poland	20,418,000
7	Spain	18,332,000
8	Mexico	18,000,000
9	Vietnam	16,500,000
10	France	14,593,000
	World total	*900,480,000*

The distribution of the world's pig population is determined by cultural, religious, and dietary factors – few pigs are found in African and Islamic countries, for example – with the result that there is a disproportionate concentration of pigs in countries that do not have such prohibitions – 73 percent of the world total is found in these Top 10 countries. Denmark, with 11,190,000 pigs and a human population of 5,215,718, is the country in which the pig population most outnumbers the human population (there are others with marginally more pigs than people, such as Tuvalu, with 13,000 pigs and 12,000 humans). The UK has 7,879,000 pigs, or one pig for every eight people.

BRINGING HOME THE BACON
The omnivorous pig has long been domesticated and figures prominently in the mythology and literature of many nations – as well as in their diets.

T O P 1 0

EGG-PRODUCING COUNTRIES

	Country	Annual hen egg production (eggs)
1	China	205,659,107,000
2	US	73,305,401,000
3	Japan	42,848,286,000
4	Russia	31,148,754,000
5	India	25,665,640,000
6	Brazil	23,332,400,000
7	Mexico	20,133,861,000
8	France	17,099,316,000
9	Spain	11,566,204,000
10	Italy	10,516,246,000

World annual total hen egg production is estimated to be 49,785,672 tons, or 692,240,842,592 individual eggs – enough for everyone on the planet to eat an egg every three days.

T O P 1 0

BEEF-PRODUCING COUNTRIES

	Country	Annual production (tons)
1	US	12,734,000
2	Brazil	5,093,000
3	China	3,829,000
4	Russia	3,085,000
5	Argentina	2,718,000
6	France	2,093,000
7	Australia	1,987,000
8	Germany	1,551,000
9	Mexico	1,465,000
10	India	1,424,000
	World total	*58,661,000*

China's beef production has increased almost 15-fold since the period 1979–81, during which it was estimated to be 252,000 tons per annum. The UK's recent concerns with BSE, or "mad cow disease," have resulted in a decline in beef production that has evicted it from its place in this Top 10.

CATS, DOGS & OTHER PETS

TOP 10

TYPES OF PET IN THE US

	Pet	Estimated number
1	Cats	66,150,000
2	Dogs	58,200,000
3	Parakeets	14,190,000
4	Small animal pets*	12,740,000
5	Freshwater fish	10,800,000#
6	Reptiles	7,540,000
7	Finches	7,350,000
8	Cockatiels	6,320,000
9	Canaries	2,580,000
10	Parrots	1,550,000

* Includes rabbits, ferrets, hamsters,
  guinea pigs, and gerbils
\# Number of households owning, rather than
  individual specimens

Source: Pet Industry Joint
Advisory Council

TOP 10

PEDIGREE CAT BREEDS IN THE US

	Breed	No. registered*
1	Persian	42,578
2	Maine Coon	4,747
3	Siamese	2,865
4	Abyssinian	2,383
5	Exotic	1,981
6	Oriental	1,371
7	Scottish Fold	1,264
8	American Shorthair	1,032
9	Birman	933
10	Ocicat	868

Of the 36 different breeds of cats listed with the Cat Fancier's Association, these were the Top 10 registered in 1996 out of a total of 68,948. The biggest increase in popularity since the 1980s has been for the Exotic, the rank of which has leapt from 14th in 1982. The Maine Coon has also consolidated its popularity. Many legends attach to this breed: for example, that it is so-called because it resulted from crossbreeding a cat and a raccoon; and that it descends from the Angora cats that were owned by Marie Antoinette and escaped to Maine during the French Revolution.

* To year ending December 31, 1996

TOP 10

DOG BREEDS IN THE US

	Breed	No. registered by American Kennel Club, Inc. 1996		Breed	No. registered by American Kennel Club, Inc. 1996
1	Labrador Retriever	149,505	6	Poodle	56,803
2	Rottweiler	89,867	7	Dachshund	48,426
3	German Shepherd	79,076	8	Cocker Spaniel	45,305
4	Golden Retriever	68,993	9	Yorkshire Terrier	40,216
5	Beagle	56,946	10	Pomeranian	39,712

Source: The American Kennel Club

TOP 10

STICK INSECTS' NAMES

1	Sticky	6	Stick
2	Fred	7	Sam
3	Twiggy	8	Billy
4	Tom	9	Freddie
5	George	10	Charlie

TOP 10

BRANDS OF CANNED DOG FOOD IN THE US

	Brand	Sales in 1995 ($)
1	Kal Kan Pedigree	216,100,000
2	Alpo	96,300,000
3	Mighty Dog	84,200,000
4	Friskies Gourmet	72,100,000
5	Alpo Prime Cuts	68,000,000
6	Gravy Train	67,000,000
7	Pedigree Choice Cuts	65,000,000
8	Skippy, Premium	63,000,000
9	Cycle	59,000,000
10	Pedigree Select Dinners	42,000,000

Source: Petfood Industry Magazine/Pet Industry Joint Advisory Council

TOP 10

BRANDS OF CANNED CAT FOOD IN THE US

	Brand	Sales ($)
1	Friskies Buffet	295,300,000
2	9-Lives	266,000,000
3	Fancy Feast	177,300,000
4	Whiskas	106,500,000
5	Alpo Canned Cat Food	88,600,000
6	Purina Premium	50,500,000
7	Sheba	38,800,000
8	Amore	32,000,000
9	Kozy Kitten	12,000,000
10	Figaro	8,000,000

Source: Petfood Industry Magazine/Pet Industry Joint Advisory Council

TOP 10

BRANDS OF DRY DOG FOOD IN THE US

	Brand	Sales in 1995 ($)
1	Dog Chow	290,100,000
2	Puppy Chow	155,000,000
3	Meal Time	101,200,000
4	Come 'N Get It	81,000,000
5	ONE	70,500,000
6	Gravy Train	67,000,000
7	Kibbles & Chunks	64,500,000
8	Field Trial	63,000,000
9	Dry Cycle	60,000,000
10	Fit & Trim	56,200,000

Source: Petfood Industry Magazine/Pet Industry Joint Advisory Council

TOP 10

CATS' NAMES IN THE US

1	Kitty		7	Missy
2	Smokey		8	Shadow
3	Tigger		9	Samantha
4	Tiger		10=	Baby
5	Max		10=	Callie
6	Patches		10=	Midnight

TOP 10

GOLDFISH NAMES

1	Jaws		6	George
2	Goldie		7	Flipper
3	Fred		8	Ben
4	Tom		9	Jerry
5	Bubbles		10	Sam

TOP 10

BRANDS OF DRY CAT FOOD IN THE US

	Brand	Sales ($)
1	Cat Chow	146,500,000
2	Friskies	126,400,000
3	Meow Mix	100,300,000
4	9-Lives	67,000,000
5	Chef's Blend	51,500,000
6	Alley Cat	43,200,000
7	Deli-Cat	38,100,000
8	Kitten Chow	33,100,000
9	Kozy Kitten	28,000,000
10	Crave Whiskas	27,800,000

Source: Petfood Industry Magazine/Pet Industry Joint Advisory Council

TOP 10

BUDGERIGARS' NAMES

1	Joey		8	Magic
2	Billy		9	George
3	Bluey		10	Tweety
4	Bobby			
5	Snowy			
6	Peter			
7	Charlie			

PLANT LIFE

T O P 1 0

COUNTRIES WITH THE LARGEST AREAS OF FOREST

	Country	Forest area acres
1	Russia	1,892,607,000
2	Canada	1,220,699,000
3	Brazil	1,205,872,000
4	US	731,406,000
5	Zaïre	429,468,000
6	Australia	358,302,000
7	China	322,462,000
8	Indonesia	276,199,000
9	Peru	209,545,000
10	India	169,267,000
	World total	*10,225,227,000*

Despite the felling of trees for commercial use and to clear land for other human settlement and agriculture, particularly in the world's rainforests, the planet's total area of forests and woodlands has barely fluctuated in the past quarter-century. In 1972, the forested proportion stood at just over 32 percent of the world's total land area, and today it is only fractionally under 32 percent.

T O P 1 0

LARGEST NATIONAL FORESTS IN THE US

	Forest/location	Acres
1	Tongass National Forest, Sitka, Alaska	16,719,874
2	Chugach National Forest, Anchorage, Alaska	5,404,414
3	Toiyabe National Forest, Sparks, Nevada	3,212,229
4	Tonto National Forest, Phoenix, Arizona	2,874,593
5	Boise National Forest, Boise, Idaho	2,647,740
6	Humboldt National Forest, Elko, Nevada	2,478,102
7	Challis National Forest, Challis, Idaho	2,464,524
8	Shoshone National Forest, Cody, Wyoming	2,436,834
9	Flathead National Forest, Kalispell, Montana	2,354,511
10	Payette National Forest, McCall, Idaho	2,323,232

This list's No. 1 is actually larger than all 10 of the smallest states combined and the District of Columbia. Even the much smaller No. 2 is larger than Massachusetts.

THE MIGHTY REDWOOD
Originally there were 40 species of redwood (Sequoia), but now there are only three – two in the US and one in China.

T O P 1 0

TALLEST TREES IN THE US

(*The tallest known example of each of the 10 tallest species*)

	Tree	Location	m	ft
1	Coast Douglas fir	Coos County, Oregon	100.3	329
2	Coast redwood	Humboldt Redwoods State Park, California	95.4	313
3	General Sherman giant sequoia	Sequoia National Park, California	83.8	275
4	Noble fir	Mount St. Helens National Monument, Washington	82.9	272
5	Grand fir	Olympic National Park, Washington	76.5	251
6	Western hemlock	Olympic National Park, Washington	73.5	241
7	Sugar pine	Dorrington, California	70.7	232
8	Ponderosa pine	Plumas National Forest, California	68.0	223
9	Port-Orford cedar	Siskiyou National Forest, Oregon	66.8	219
10	Pacific silver fir	Forks, Washington	66.1	217

A coast redwood known as the Dyerville Giant (from Dyerville, California), which stood 362 ft/110.3 m high, fell in a storm on March 27, 1991, and a slightly taller (363-ft/110.6-m) coast redwood, which formerly topped this list, fell during 1992. The General Sherman giant sequoia is thought to be the planet's most colossal living thing, weighing some 1,400 tons, which is equivalent to the weight of nine blue whales or 360 elephants.

OLDEST BOTANIC GARDENS IN NORTH AMERICA

	Garden	Founded
1	Pierce's Park,* Kennett Square, Pennsylvania	1800
2	United States Botanic Garden, Washington, DC	1820
3	Painter's Arboretum,# Media, Pennsylvania	1830
4	Missouri Botanical Garden, St. Louis, Missouri	1859
5	Arnold Arboretum, Jamaica Plain, Massachusetts	1872
6	Beal-Garfield Botanic Garden, East Lansing, Michigan	1873
7	Dominion Arboretum & Botanic Garden, Ottawa, Ontario, Canada	1886
8	University of California – Berkeley Botanic Garden, Berkeley, California	1890
9	New York Botanical Garden, Bronx, New York	1891
10	Botanic Garden of Smith College, Northampton, Massachusetts	1893

* *Now Longwood Gardens*
\# *Now Tyler Arboretum*

MOST FORESTED COUNTRIES IN THE WORLD
(By percent of forest cover)

	Country	Forest cover		Country	Forest cover
1	Surinam	92	6	Gabon	74
2	Papua New Guinea	91	7	Finland	69
3	Solomon Islands	85	8=	Bhutan	66
4	French Guiana	81	8=	Japan	66
5	Guyana	77	10	North Korea	65

RAIN FOREST IN SOUTH AMERICA

BIGGEST TREES IN THE US*

	Tree	Location	Points		Tree	Location	Points
1	General Sherman giant sequoia	Sequoia National Park, California	1,300	6	White oak	Wye Mills State Park, Maryland	479
2	Coast redwood	Prairie Creek, California	1,183	7	American elm	Louisville, Kansas	419
3	Coast Douglas fir	Coos County, Oregon	782	8	Loblolly pine	Warren, Arizona	357
4	Sugar pine	Dorrington, California	681	9	Sugar maple	Kingston, New Hampshire	345
5	Black willow	Grand Traverse County, Michigan	499	10	Pinyon pine	Cuba, New Mexico	295

* *By species (i.e. the biggest known example of each of the 10 big species)*
Source: National Register of Big Trees, American Forestry Association

The American Forestry Association operates a National Register of Big Trees, which is constantly updated as new "champion trees" are nominated. Their method of measurement, or points, which gives this Top 10 by species, is based not solely on height but also takes account of the thickness of the trunk and spread of the upper branches and leaves, or crown. The formula adds the circumference in inches of the tree at 4.5 feet above the ground to the total height of the tree in feet and to one-quarter of the average crown spread in feet. The General Sherman giant sequoia is 998 inches in circumference, 275 feet tall and with an average crown spread of 107 feet, hence 998 + 275 + 27 = 1,300 points.

FOOD FROM THE LAND

T O P 1 0

WORLD VEGETABLE RECORDS*

(As held by Bernard Lavery)

	Vegetable/ record year	Weight kg	lb	oz
1	Pumpkin (1989 – held for 3 days)	322.06	710	0
2	Cabbage (1989)	56.24	124	0
3	Summer squash (1990)	49.04	108	2
4	Zucchini (1990)	29.25	64	8
5	Kohlrabi (1990)	28.18	62	2
6	Celery (1990)	20.89	46	1
7	Radish (1990)	12.73	28	1
8	Cucumber (1991)	9.10	20	1
9	Brussels sprout (1992)	8.25	18	3
10	Carrot (1996)	5.20	11	7½

* *Current world record unless otherwise stated*

Bernard Lavery, who lives in Llanharry, Mid Glamorgan, UK, holds 19 world and 10 British records for his giant vegetables. Through books and a telephone helpline, he offers practical advice to enable others to achieve similar results.

T O P 1 0

BANANA-PRODUCING COUNTRIES IN THE WORLD

	Country	Annual production (tons)
1	India	10,472,000
2	Brazil	6,260,000
3	Ecuador	6,066,000
4	China	3,647,000
5	Philippines	3,527,000
6	Colombia	2,755,000
7	Indonesia	2,535,000
8	Mexico	2,360,000
9	Costa Rica	2,200,000
10	Thailand	1,873,000
	World total	*60,044,000*

T O P 1 0

VEGETABLE CROPS IN THE WORLD

	Crop	Annual production (tons)
1	Sugarcane	1,265,561,000
2	Rice	606,539,000
3	Wheat	596,537,000
4	Corn	567,197,000
5	Potatoes	309,424,000
6	Sugar beet	293,166,000
7	Cassava	180,549,000
8	Barley	153,364,000
9	Soybeans	138,826,000
10	Sweet potatoes	134,532,000

T O P 1 0

FRUIT CROPS IN THE WORLD

	Crop	Annual production (tons)
1	Oranges	63,715,000
2	Bananas	60,044,000
3	Grapes	59,731,000
4	Apples	54,769,000
5	Coconuts	49,683,000
6	Plantains	33,280,000
7	Mangoes	20,982,000
8	Melons	15,454,000
9	Tangerines, clementines, satsumas	14,930,000
10	Pears	12,784,000

T O P 1 0

COCONUT-PRODUCING COUNTRIES IN THE WORLD

	Country	Annual production (tons)		Country	Annual production (tons)
1	Indonesia	15,288,000	**6**	Mexico	1,323,000
2	Philippines	11,354,000	**7**	Malaysia	1,149,000
3	India	8,819,000	**8**	Vietnam	1,102,000
4	Sri Lanka	2,201,000	**9**	Brazil	1,047,000
5	Thailand	1,614,000	**10**	Papua New Guinea	771,000

TOP 10

RICE-PRODUCING COUNTRIES IN THE WORLD

	Country	Annual production (tons)
1	China	206,362,000
2	India	134,904,000
3	Indonesia	54,966,000
4	Bangladesh	27,184,000
5	Vietnam	26,458,000
6	Thailand	23,293,000
7	Myanmar	22.168,000
8	Japan	13,917,000
9	Brazil	12,386,000
10	Philippines	12,128,000
	World total	*606,539,000*

World production of rice has risen dramatically during this century. It remains the staple diet for a huge proportion of the global population, especially in Asian countries. Relatively small quantities are grown elsewhere: the US's output is 8,696,000 tons, and the total for the whole of Europe is just 2,331,000 tons, with Italy the leading producer at 1,415,000 tons.

TOP 10

COFFEE-PRODUCING COUNTRIES IN THE WORLD

	Country	Annual production (tons)
1	Brazil	1,025,000
2	Colombia	892,000
3	Mexico	449,000
4	Indonesia	381,000
5	Ethiopia	251,000
6	Uganda	242,000
7	Guatemala	231,000
8	Ecuador	217,000
9	Côte d'Ivoire	213,000
10	Vietnam	203,000
	World total	*6,176,000*

In recent years there has been a decline in coffee production from the former world peak of over 6,600,000 tons. While this list continues to prove the saying, "There's an awful lot of coffee in Brazil," Kenya, perhaps surprisingly, does not appear, since its annual total of 103,000 tons ranks the country in only 17th place.

TOP 10

TEA-PRODUCING COUNTRIES IN THE WORLD

	Country	Annual production (tons)
1	India	788,000
2	China	675,000
3	Kenya	270,000
4	Sri Lanka	266,000
5	Indonesia	154,000
6	Turkey	148,000
7	Japan	105,000
8	Georgia	81,000
9	Iran	61,000
10	Bangladesh	56,000
	World total	*2,895,000*

FLOWER POWER
Sunflowers come from North and Central America, but the plant has been successfully introduced into many other parts of the world. The oil derived from its seeds is used in cooking and for manufacturing food products such as margarine, while the residue is made into animal feed.

TOP 10

SUNFLOWER SEED-PRODUCING COUNTRIES IN THE WORLD

	Country	Annual production (tons)
1	Argentina	6,084,000
2	Russia	4,629,000
3	Ukraine	2,954,000
4	France	2,196,000
5	US	2,002,000
6	India	1,620,000
7	China	1,398,000
8	Romania	1,028,000
9	Turkey	992,000
10	Hungary	856,000
	World total	*28,867,000*

THE HUMAN WORLD

T O P 1 0

MOST COMMON PHOBIAS

	Object of phobia	Medical term
1	Spiders	Arachnephobia or arachnophobia
2	People and social situations	Anthropophobia or sociophobia
3	Flying	Aerophobia or aviatophobia
4	Open spaces	Agoraphobia, cenophobia, or kenophobia
5	Confined spaces	Claustrophobia, cleisiophobia, cleithrophobia, or clithrophobia
6	Vomiting	Emetophobia or emitophobia
7	Heights	Acrophobia, altophobia, hypsophobia, or hypsiphobia
8	Cancer	Carcinomaphobia, carcinophobia, carcinomatophobia, cancerphobia, or cancerophobia
9	Thunderstorms	Brontophobia or keraunophobia; related phobias are those associated with lightning (astraphobia), cyclones (anemophobia), and hurricanes and tornadoes (lilapsophobia)
10	Death	Necrophobia or thanatophobia

A phobia is a morbid fear that is out of all proportion to the object of the fear. Many people would admit to being uncomfortable about these principal phobias, as well as others such as snakes (ophiophobia), injections (trypanophobia), or ghosts (phasmophobia), but most do not become obsessive about them or allow such fears to rule their lives. True phobias often arise from some incident in childhood when a person has been afraid of some object and has developed an irrational fear that has persisted into adulthood.

T O P 1 0

MOST COMMON ALLERGENS

(Substances that cause allergies)

Food allergen		Environmental allergen
Nuts	1	House dust mite (*Dermatophagoides pteronyssinus*)
Shellfish/seafood	2	Grass pollens
Milk	3	Tree pollens
Wheat	4	Cats
Eggs	5	Dogs
Fresh fruit (apples, oranges, strawberries, etc.)	6	Horses
Fresh vegetables (potatoes, cucumbers, etc.)	7	Molds (*Aspergillus fumigatus, Alternaria, Cladosporium*, etc.)
Cheese	8	Birch pollen
Yeast	9	Weed pollen
Soy protein	10	Wasp/bee venom

An allergy has been defined as "an unpleasant reaction to foreign matter, specific to that substance, which is altered from the normal response and peculiar to the individual concerned." Allergens, the substances that cause allergies, are usually foods but may also be environmental agents such as pollen, which causes hay fever. Reactions can cause symptoms ranging from severe mental or physical disability to minor irritations such as a mild headache. "Elimination dieting" to pinpoint and avoid food allergens, and identifying and avoiding environmental allergens, can often result in the effective treatment of many allergies.

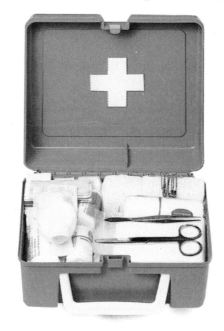

TOP 10
CAUSES OF STRESS-RELATED ILLNESSES

	Event	Value
1	Death of spouse	100
2	Divorce	73
3	Marital separation	65
4=	Detention in prison or other institution	63
4=	Death of close family member	63
6	Major personal injury or illness	53
7	Marriage	50
8	Losing one's job	47
9=	Marital reconciliation	45
9=	Retirement	45

Psychiatrists Dr. Thomas Holmes and Dr. Richard Rahe joined forces and devised what they called the "Social Readjustment Rating Scale" to place a value on the likelihood of illness occurring as a result of stress caused by various "life events." The cumulative effect of several incidents increases the risk factor – if an individual's points total over 300 in a given year, he is thought to have a 79 percent chance of major illness.

TOP 10
DRUGS MOST PRESCRIBED IN THE US

	Drug	Prescriptions per annum
1	Amoxicillin	34,952,000
2	Acetaminophen	27,877,000
3	Albuterol	14,660,000
4	Aspirin	13,786,000
5	Ibuprofen	13,260,000
6	Hydrochlorothiazide	12,676,000
7	Multivitamins	11,823,000
8	Furosemide	11,766,000
9	Erythromycin	11,387,000
10	Guaifenesin	11,275,000

Source: National Center for Health Statistics

TOP 10
COSTS OF GETTING SICK

	Condition	Cost ($ billion)
1	Cardiovascular	80
2	Injuries	69
3=	Cancer	49
3=	Kidney and diabetes	49
5	Pregnancy and birth	40
6	Respiratory	38
7	Digestive	36
8	Musculoskeletal	28
9	Circulatory	20
10	Mental Health	19

Source: National Center for Health Statistics

TOP 10
REASONS FOR VISITS TO DOCTORS IN THE US

	Principal reason	Visits per annum
1	General medical examination	39,789,000
2	Progress visit, or unspecified	29,109,000
3	Cough	23,936,000
4	Routine prenatal examination	22,136,000
5	Postoperative visit	19,136,000
6	Throat symptoms	16,446,000
7	Well-baby examination	13,204,000
8	Depression	13,180,000
9	Earache/ear infection	12,204,000
10	Stomach pain/cramps/ spasms	11,632,000

Source: National Center for Health Statistics

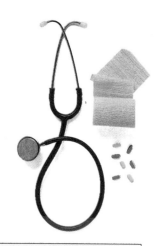

PAINKILLER PATENTED

Although it was discovered in 1853, acetyl salicylic acid was disregarded for 40 years until Felix Hoffman, a chemist working for the German company Bayer, rediscovered it and used it to treat his father's arthritis. Bayer patented the process for producing it commercially in 1898, and it was first sold the following year. It was given the name "aspirin" ("a" for acetyl, "spir" from the Latin name of the flower meadowsweet, while "in" was a popular ending for the names of drugs). After its defeat in World War I, Germany's patents lapsed and other companies began making aspirin, which became the world's best-selling over-the-counter drug.

YEARS AGO · YEARS AGO · YEARS AGO · YEARS AGO
100

MATTERS OF LIFE & DEATH

COUNTRIES WITH THE HIGHEST MALE LIFE EXPECTANCY

	Country	Life expectancy at birth (years)
1	San Marino	77.2
2	Iceland	76.8
3	Japan	76.1
4	Andorra	76.0
5	Hong Kong	75.4
6	Israel	75.1
7	Canada	74.9
8	Sweden	74.8
9=	Martinique	74.7
9=	Switzerland	74.7
	US	72.0

The relatively high, and generally increasing, life expectancy for males in these Top 10 countries contrasts sharply with that in many developing countries, particularly most African countries, where it rarely exceeds 45 years. Sierra Leone is at the bottom of the league with an average life expectancy of 37.5 years.

COUNTRIES WITH THE HIGHEST FEMALE LIFE EXPECTANCY

	Country	Life expectancy at birth (years)
1	San Marino	85.3
2	Japan	82.2
3	Andorra	82.0
4	Switzerland	81.4
5	France	81.1
6=	Canada	81.0
6=	Hong Kong	81.0
6=	Martinique	81.0
9	Australia	80.8
10	Iceland	80.7
	US	78.9

Female life expectancy in all the Top 10 countries – as well as an additional seven – now exceeds 80 years. The comparative figure for such developing countries as Sierra Leone where it is 40.6 years for women, makes for less encouraging reading. The world over, women generally live longer than men – in certain countries, such as Iraq, by as much as 11 years.

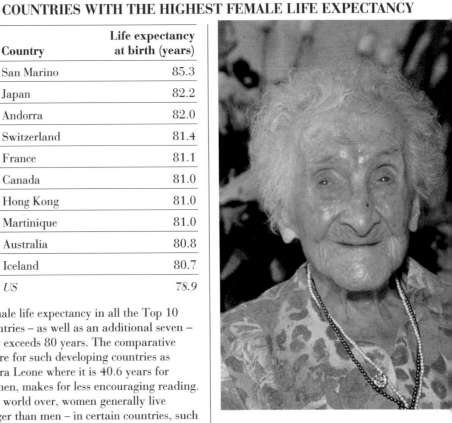

BORN IN 1875
At her 122nd birthday on February 21, 1997, Jeanne Louise Calment of Arles, France, became the world's oldest living person.

COUNTRIES WITH THE MOST DEATHS FROM HEART DISEASE

	Country	Death rate per 100,000
1	Czech Republic	314.4
2	Scotland	258.3
3	New Zealand	248.6
4	Finland	243.2
5	Hungary	240.0
6	Bulgaria	230.1
7	Denmark	211.1
8	England & Wales	210.0
9	Sweden	209.3
10	Australia	200.5
	US	188.1

COUNTRIES WITH THE LOWEST INFANT MORTALITY

	Country	Death rate per 1,000 live births
1	Iceland	3.2
2	Sweden	3.4
3	Singapore	4.3
4	Finland	4.4
5=	Japan	4.5
5=	Norway	4.5
7=	Hong Kong	4.8
7=	Taiwan	4.8
9	Liechtenstein	5.3
10	Denmark	5.6
	US	8.5

COUNTRIES WITH THE HIGHEST INFANT MORTALITY

	Country	Death rate per 1,000 live births
1	Sierra Leone	166.0
2	Afghanistan	161.0
3	Western Sahara	149.0
4	Mozambique	148.0
5	Guinea	147.0
6	Malawi	144.0
7	Guinea-Bissau	140.0
8	Central African Republic	137.2
9	Gambia	132.0
10	Liberia	126.0

THE 10

MOST COMMON CAUSES OF DEATH IN THE US

	Cause	Deaths
1	Diseases of the heart	938,750
2	Cancer	536,330
3	Cerebrovascular diseases	156,500
4	Chronic obstructive pulmonary diseases and allied conditions	102,940
5	Accidents and adverse effects	89,960
6	Pneumonia and influenza	79,630
7	Diabetes	58,450
8	Human Immunodeficiency Virus infection	42,690
9	Suicide	30,350
10	Chronic liver disease and cirrhosis	25,650

Source: National Center for Health Statistics.

Figures are for 1995, based on a total number of 2,312,203 deaths estimated in the US for that year. "Accidents and adverse effects" includes 41,786 deaths resulting from motor vehicle accidents. The category "Homicide and legal intervention" (which includes murders, executions, and deaths resulting from actions by members of the police force), formerly at No. 10, fell to 11th place with 22,230 deaths.

THE 10

MOST COMMON CAUSES OF DEATH IN THE WORLD

	Cause	Deaths
1	Infectious and parasitic diseases*	10,726,000
2	Diseases of the circulatory system	9,676,000
3	Unknown causes	8,124,000
4	Malignant neoplasms (cancers)	6,013,000
5	Acute lower respiratory infections#	4,110,000
6	External causes (injuries, etc)	3,996,000
7	Perinatal and neonatal causes	3,180,000
8	Diarrhea and dysentery	3,010,000
9	Chronic lower respiratory diseases	2,888,000
10	Tuberculosis	2,709,0004

* Other than those listed
 # Among children under 5

Collectively, according to the World Health Organization's figures, infectious and parasitic diseases (which include diseases listed in the Top 10 as well as such killers as malaria – approximately 2,000,000 deaths a year, and measles – 1,160,000) are the principal causes of deaths worldwide, an overall total of 16,445,000.

TOP 10

COUNTRIES WITH THE MOST CREMATIONS

	Country	% of deaths	Cremations (1995)
1	Japan	98.55	963,540
2	US	21.15	488,224
3	UK	70.60	445,574
4	Germany	35.80	316,524
5	Czech Republic	72.50	85,494
6	Canada*	36.11	72,600
7	The Netherlands	48.21	65,637
8	Australia	52.00	65,438
9	France	11.76	62,212
10	Sweden	64.74	60,824

* 1994

No information is available for China, which is believed to have 1,288 crematoria, and where cremation is common.

THE 10

SHORTEST-LIVED PROFESSIONS

	Profession	SMR*
1	Deckhands, engine-room hands, bargemen, boatmen	304
2	Hairdressers and barbers	263
3	General laborers	243
4	Foremen on ships, barges, and other vessels	236
5	Fishermen	234
6	Steel erectors, scaffolders, etc.	180
7	Foremen in product inspection and packaging	160
8	Chemical and petroleum processing-plant operators	154
9	Travel stewards and attendants, hospital and hotel porters	150
10	Foremen on production lines	149

* Standard Mortality Ratio; figures for men in the UK only

HEALTH FOR ALL

The World Health Organization came into being on April 7, 1948. An arm of the United Nations, the WHO now has 189 member states. Its primary objective is "the attainment by all peoples of the highest possible level of health," and for the past 20 years has been operating a program with the ambitious aim of "Health for All by the Year 2000." This it proposes to achieve through education and activities in such areas as the combating of high levels of infant mortality, smoking, and the international spread of infectious diseases by means of measures such as the provision of safe drinking water and immunization in developing countries. The WHO spearheaded the campaign that successfully eradicated smallpox and has adopted a similar program to eliminate polio by the end of the century.

YEARS AGO • YEARS AGO • YEARS AGO • YEARS AGO •
50

FOR BETTER OR FOR WORSE

TOP 10

PROFESSIONS OF COMPUTER-DATING MEMBERS

MEN

	Profession	Percent of those registered
1	Engineers	6.1
2	Company directors	5.0
3	Computer programmers	4.7
4	Architects/designers	4.6
5	Accountants	4.4
6	Teachers	4.2
7	Doctors	4.0
8	Managers	3.7
9	Civil servants	2.5
10	Farmers	1.4

WOMEN

	Profession	Percent of those registered
1	Teachers	7.8
2	Lawyers	5.1
3	Nurses	4.9
4	Accountants	4.5
5	Civil servants	3.9
6	Secretaries	3.8
7	Women at home	3.5
8	Doctors	3.1
9	Social workers	2.8
10	Students	1.3

TOP 10

US STATES WITH THE MOST MARRIAGES

	State	Marriages (1995)
1	California	203,897
2	Texas	185,642
3	New York	151,477
4	Florida	142,937
5	Nevada	123,184
6	Illinois	91,579
7	Ohio	88,864
8	Pennsylvania	76,679
9	Tennessee	73,052
10	Michigan	71,222

TOP 10

COUNTRIES WITH THE HIGHEST MARRIAGE RATE

	Country	Marriages per 1,000 p.a.*
1	Cuba	17.7
2	Bermuda	15.1
3	Philippines	14.0
4	Liechtenstein	13.1
5	Benin	12.8
6	Seychelles	12.7
7	Puerto Rico	12.6
8	Maldives	11.7
9=	Bangladesh	10.7
9=	Turkmenistan	10.7
	US	8.9

* *During latest period for which figures available*

The apparent world record marriage rate of 31.2 per 1,000 often reported for the US territory of the Northern Mariana Islands – which has a total population of under 44,000 – and that of 18.0 for the US Virgin Islands are statistical "blips" and have not been included.

TOP 10

MONTHS FOR MARRIAGES IN THE US

	Month	Marriages
1	June	263,000
2	August	254,000
3	May	238,000
4=	July	224,000
4=	October	224,000
6	September	219,000
7	November	174,000
8	December	169,000
9	April	165,000
10	March	148,000

Source: National Center for Health Statistics

Figures are estimates for 1995 from a US total of some 2,336,000 weddings, a one percent decline compared with the previous year (in 1995 the US marriage rate of 8.9 per 1,000 of the population hit its lowest level since 1963). February was at No. 11 with 146,000, and January the least popular with only 111,000.

THE 10

FIRST WEDDING ANNIVERSARY GIFTS

1	Cotton
2	Paper
3	Leather
4	Fruit and flowers
5	Wood
6	Sugar (or iron)
7	Wool (or copper)
8	Bronze (or electrical appliances)
9	Pottery (or willow)
10	Tin (or aluminum)

TOP 10

SINGLES REQUESTED AT WEDDINGS

	Title/artist	Year
1	*Endless Love*, Diana Ross and Lionel Richie	1981
2	*Your Song*, Elton John	1971
3	*Everything I Do (I Do It for You)*, Bryan Adams	1991
4	*The Best*, Tina Turner	1989
5	*Crazy for You*, Madonna	1985
6	*(Where Do I Begin) Love Story*, Andy Williams	1971
7	*I Will Always Love You*, Whitney Houston	1992
8	*Love Me Tender*, Elvis Presley	1956
9	*I Just Can't Stop Loving You*, Michael Jackson	1987
10	*Unchained Melody*, Righteous Brothers	1965

TOP 10

OVERSEAS HONEYMOON DESTINATIONS FOR US COUPLES

	Destination	Percent
1	Mexico	10.7
2	Jamaica	9.6
3	Virgin Islands	7.0
4	The Bahamas	6.3
5	Europe	4.1
6	St. Lucia	3.9
7	Puerto Rico	3.6
8	Aruba	3.1
9	St. Maarten	3.0
10=	Barbados	2.5
10=	Canada	2.5
10=	Cayman Islands	2.5

Source: Modern Bride

TOP 10

HONEYMOON DESTINATIONS IN THE US FOR US COUPLES

	State	Percent
1	Florida	17.0
2	Hawaii	13.9
3	California	7.2
4	Pennsylvania	3.6
5	Nevada	3.2
6=	Colorado	1.8
6=	Georgia	1.8
8	North Carolina	1.3
9=	New York	1.2
9=	Virginia	1.2

Source: Modern Bride

THE 10

COUNTRIES WITH THE HIGHEST DIVORCE RATE

	Country	Divorces per 1,000 p.a.
1	Latvia	5.6
2	Russia	4.5
3	Belarus	4.3
4=	Cuba	4.2
4=	Ukraine	4.2
6	US	4.1
7	Puerto Rico	4.0
8	Estonia	3.8
9	Lithuania	3.7
10	Moldova	3.3

THE 10

US STATES WITH THE MOST DIVORCES

	State*	Divorces (1995)
1	Texas	98,373
2	Florida	79,528
3	New York	55,999
4	Ohio	48,682
5	Michigan	39,910
6	Pennsylvania	39,439
7	Illinois	38,784
8	Georgia	37,209
9	North Carolina	36,978
10	Tennessee	33,081

* *Figures not available for California, Indiana, and Louisiana*

Source: National Center for Health Statistics

THE 10

COUNTRIES WITH THE LOWEST DIVORCE RATES

	Country	Divorce rate per 1,000 p.a.
1	Mozambique	0.01
2=	Western Samoa	0.2
2=	Sri Lanka	0.2
2=	North Korea	0.2
2=	Guatemala	0.2
2=	Antigua and Barbuda	0.2
7=	St. Lucia	0.3
7=	Pakistan	0.3
7=	Macedonia	0.3
7=	Bosnia and Herzegovina	0.3

WHAT'S IN A NAME?

TOP 10

GIRLS' AND BOYS' NAMES IN THE US

Girls		Boys
Brittany	1	Michael
Ashley	2	Christopher
Jessica	3	Matthew
Amanda	4	Joshua
Sarah	5	Andrew
Megan	6	James
Caitlin	7	John
Samantha	8	Nicholas
Stephanie	9	Justin
Katherine	10	David

American name fashions are highly volatile and vary considerably according to a child's ethnic background and the influences of popular culture. Jennifer, for example, once rose to the No. 2 position because the heroine of the book and 1970 film *Love Story* had this name, and Tiffany entered this Top 10 in 1980 in the wake of the TV series *Charlie's Angels* and its character Tiffany Welles. This pattern has been mirrored in the 1990s with Brittany, a name that does not even make an appearance among the Top 100 British girls' names. In contrast, three of the Top 10 US boys' names (Matthew, Joshua, and James) also appear in the British Top 10.

TOP 10

GIRLS' AND BOYS' NAMES IN THE US 100 YEARS AGO

Girls		Boys
Mary	1	John
Ruth	2	William
Helen	3	Charles
Margaret	4	Robert
Elizabeth	5	Joseph
Dorothy	6	James
Catherine	7	George
Mildred	8	Samuel
Frances	9	Thomas
Alice/Marion	10	Arthur

TOP 10

GIRLS' AND BOYS' NAMES 50 YEARS AGO IN THE US

Girls		Boys
Mary	1	Robert
Patricia	2	James
Barbara	3	John
Judith	4	William
Carol/Carole	5	Richard
Sharon	6	Thomas
Nancy	7	David
Joan	8	Ronald
Sandra	9	Donald
Margaret	10	Michael

TOP 10

MOST COMMON LAST NAMES OF GERMAN ORIGIN IN THE US*

1	Myers	6	Schwarz
2	Schmidt	7	Schneider
3	Hoffman (n)	8	Zimmerman
4	Wagner#	9	Keller
5	Meyer	10	Klein

* Excluding those that have been anglicized, such as Schmidt/Smith

 # Sometimes of English origin

TOP 10

MOST COMMON LAST NAMES OF LATINO ORIGIN IN THE US

1	Rodriguez	6	Martinez
2	Gonzalez	7	Hernandez
3	Garcia	8	Perez
4	Lopez	9	Sanchez
5	Rivera	10	Torres

TOP 10

GIRLS' AND BOYS' NAMES 50 YEARS AGO IN THE UK

Girls		Boys
Margaret	1	John
Patricia	2	David
Christine	3	Michael
Mary	4	Peter
Jean	5	Robert
Ann	6	Anthony
Susan	7	Brian
Janet	8	Alan
Maureen	9	William
Barbara	10	James

TOP 10

MOST COMMON LAST NAMES OF SCANDINAVIAN ORIGIN IN THE US*

1	Anderson	6	Hansen
2	Peterson	7	Carlson
3	Neilsen	8	Larson
4	Christianson	9	Erikson
5	Olson	10	Swanson

* Includes variant spellings, such as Andersen, Andersson, etc

TOP 10

MOST COMMON LAST NAMES OF IRISH ORIGIN IN THE US

1	Murphy	6	Kelley*
2	Kelly*	7	Burke
3	Sullivan	8	Riley
4	Kennedy#	9	O'Brien
5	Bryant	10	McCoy

* Sometimes of Scottish or English origin

 # Sometimes of Scottish origin

TOP 10

MOST COMMON LAST NAMES IN THE US

	Surname	Number
1	Smith	2,382,509
2	Johnson	1,807,263
3	Williams/Williamson	1,568,939
4	Brown	1,362,910
5	Jones	1,331,205
6	Miller	1,131,205
7	Davis	1,047,848
8	Martin/Martinez/ Martinson	1,046,297
9	Anderson/Andersen	825,648
10	Wilson	787,825

Over 20 years ago the United States Social Security Administration published its survey of the most common surnames. It was based on the number of people for whom it had more than 10,000 files, which covered a total of 3,169 names. The SSA has not repeated the exercise, but it is probable that the ranking order has remained very similar.

TOP 10

MOST COMMON LAST NAMES DERIVED FROM OCCUPATIONS IN THE US

1	Smith
2	Miller
3	Taylor
4	Clark (cleric)
5	Walker (cloth worker)
6	Wright (workman)
7	Baker
8	Carter (driver or maker of carts)
9	Stewart (steward)
10	Turner (woodworker)

It is reckoned that about one in six US surnames recalls the occupation of the holder's ancestors. Several US Presidents have borne such surnames, including Zachary Taylor and Jimmy Carter, both of which feature in this Top 10.

TOP 10

MOST COMMON NAMES OF MOVIE CHARACTERS

1	Jack		6	George
2	John		7	Michael
3	Frank		8	Tom
4	Harry		9	Mary
5	David		10	Paul

Based on Simon Rose's One FM Essential Film Guide *(1993) survey of feature films released in the period* 1983–93.

TOP 10

MOST COMMON LAST NAMES IN THE MANHATTAN TELEPHONE DIRECTORY

1	Smith/Smyth/Smythe
2	Lee/Lea/Leigh/Ley/Li
3	Brown/Browne
4	Cohen/Coan/Coen/Cohn/Cone/Kohn
5	Johnson/Johnston/Johnsen
6	Rodriguez
7	Miller
8	Williams
9	Jones
10	Davis/Davies

TOP 10

MOST COMMON PATRONYMS IN THE US

1	Johnson ("son of John")
2	Williams/Williamson ("son of William")
3	Jones ("son of John")
4	Davis ("son of Davie/David")
5	Martin/Martinez/Martinson ("son of Martin")
6	Anderson/Andersen ("son of Andrew")
7	Wilson ("son of Will")
8	Harris/Harrison ("son of Harry")
9	Thomas
10	Thomson/Thompson ("son of Thomas")

TOP 10

MOST COMMON DESCRIPTIVE LAST NAMES IN THE US

1	Brown (brown-haired)
2	White (light-skinned, or white-haired)
3	Young (youthful, or a younger brother)
4	Gray (gray-haired)
5	Long (tall)
6	Russell (red-haired)
7	Black/Blake (black-haired, or dark-skinned)
8	Little (small)
9	Reid (red-haired)
10	Curtis (courteous, or well-educated)

As many as one in ten of all US surnames may be derived from a physical description that was once applied to an ancestor. The list is headed by the Browns, whose role as laborers and pioneers was recognized by the 19th-century British author Thomas Hughes in his novel *Tom Brown's Schooldays* (1857), writing: "For centuries, in their quiet, dogged, homespun way, they have been subduing the earth in most English counties, and leaving their mark in American forests and Australian uplands."

TOP 10

TERMS OF ENDEARMENT USED IN THE US*

1	Honey
2	Baby
3	Sweetheart
4	Dear
5	Lover
6	Darling
7	Sugar
8=	Angel
8=	Pumpkin
10=	Beautiful
10=	Precious

* *Based on survey of romance conducted by a US champagne company*

ORGANIZATIONS & CHARITIES

ROBERT BADEN-POWELL
After serving in the army in India and Africa, Robert Baden-Powell, known as "BP," founded the worldwide scouting movement.

TOP 10

MEMBERSHIP ORGANIZATIONS IN THE US

	Organization	Approximate membership
1	American Automobile Association	35,291,651
2	American Association of Retired Persons	32,000,000
3	YMCA of America	14,447,270
4	National Congress of Parents and Teachers	6,500,000
5	National Right to Life Committee	6,000,000
6	National Committee to Preserve Social Security and Medicare	5,500,000
7	Evangelical Lutheran Church in America	5,200,000
8	National Council of Senior Citizens	5,000,000
9	American Farm Bureau Federation	4,700,000
10	Boy Scouts of America	4,602,844

TOP 10

COUNTRIES WITH THE HIGHEST BOY SCOUT MEMBERSHIP

	Country	Membership*
1	Indonesia	10,059,131
2	US	4,602,844
3	Philippines	2,685,767
4	India	1,657,780
5	Thailand	1,000,348
6	UK	637,905
7	Bangladesh	602,492
8	Pakistan	420,775
9	Republic of Korea	273,046
10	Canada	270,402

* As of December 1, 1996

Following an experimental camp held in 1907 on Brownsea Island, Dorset, England, Sir Robert Baden-Powell (1857–1941) launched the scouting movement. There are believed to be just 13 countries in the world where scouting either does not exist or is forbidden for political reasons; of the later, China is among the largest.

TOP 10

COUNTRIES OWING MOST TO THE UN

	Country	Owed ($)
1	US	1,615,976,258
2	Russian Federation	278,169,189
3	Ukraine	247,216,193
4	Japan	152,608,079
5	Germany	66,773,309
6	Brazil	33,996,512
7	UK	31,745,354
8	France	30,308,319
9	Italy	22,417,874
10	Spain	9,945,703

As of March 31, 1997, a total of $2,861,404,043 was owed to the UN by its members, including money outstanding to its regular budget, peace-keeping operations, and international tribunals.

TOP 10

COUNTRIES WITH THE HIGHEST GIRL GUIDE AND GIRL SCOUT MEMBERSHIP

	Country	Membership
1	US	3,390,130
2	Philippines	1,250,928
3	India	758,575
4	UK	707,651
5	Canada	273,681
6	South Korea	184,993
7	Pakistan	101,634
8	Indonesia	98,636
9	Malaysia	92,539
10	Japan	88,331

TOP 10

STATES WITH THE MOST GIRL SCOUTS

	State	Girl Scouts
1	California	222,184
2	New York	180,015
3	Texas	158,405
4	Illinois	154,499
5	Pennsylvania	152,004
6	Ohio	141,638
7	Michigan	116,021
8	New Jersey	97,664
9	Florida	94,281
10	Missouri	94,140

The Girl Guides of the United States of America was founded by Juliet Gordon Low in Savannah, Georgia, on March 12, 1912, taking the British Girl Guides, founded in 1910, as its model. It changed its name to Girl Scouts in 1913. Total membership declined in the mid-1980s, but has steadily increased again in recent years to levels approaching those of the early 1970s. Approximately one girl in nine between the ages of five and 17, one girl in four age six to eight and one girl in seven age nine to 11 belongs to the Girl Scouts.

TOP 10

US FOUNDATIONS

	Foundation	Annual donations ($)
1	The Ford Foundation	288,660,188
2	W.K. Kellogg Foundation	222,691,781
3	The Pew Charitable Trusts	193,081,614
4	Soros Humanitarian Foundation	168,359,909
5	John D. & Catherine T. MacArthur Foundation	123,953,670
6	The Annenberg Foundation	112,996,033
7	Lilly Endowment Inc.	111,652,675
8	The Andrew W. Mellon Foundation	110,606,687
9	The New York Community Trust	107,795,883
10	The Rockefeller Foundation	102,008,668

TOP 10

CORPORATE FOUNDATIONS IN THE US

	Foundation	Annual donations ($)
1	AT&T Foundation	34,597,537
2	US WEST Foundation	26,546,048
3	General Motors Foundation	22,655,604
4	Ford Motors Company Fund	22,267,753
5	Coca-Cola Foundation	21,327,452
6	Procter & Gamble Fund	21,131,938
7	GTE Foundation	20,669,814
8	Amoco Foundation	19,838,667
9	Exxon Education Foundation	19,427,367
10	SBC Foundation	19,191,453

TOP 10

CHARITIES IN THE US

	Charity	Total revenue 1995 ($)	Donations ($)
1	YMCA of the US	2,060,000,000	249,400,000
2	Catholic Charities US	1,942,000,000	334,100,000
3	American Red Cross	1,724,000,000	465,600,000
4	Salvation Army	1,421,000,000	741,700,000
5	Shriners Childrens' Hospital	1,254,000,000	198,300,000
6	Goodwill Industries International	1,037,000,000	113,400,000
7	YWCA of the US	570,000,000	145,900,000
8	United Cerebral Palsy Associations	543,000,000	57,900,000
9	Boy Scouts of America	515,000,000	225,000,000
10	Girl Scouts of America	513,000,000	89,100,000

TOP 10

COMMUNITY FOUNDATIONS IN THE US

	Foundation	Annual donations ($)
1	New York Community Trust	50,965,342
2	Cleveland Foundation	30,723,125
3	San Francisco Foundation	28,762,376
4	Marin Community Foundation	28,241,000
5	Chicago Community Trust	26,957,224
6	Communities Foundation of Texas	25,166,739
7	Columbus Foundation and Affiliated Organizations	24,010,918
8	California Community Foundation	16,213,754
9	Greater Kansas City Community Foundation & Affiliated Trust	15,752,474
10	Boston Foundation	14,493,655

TOP 10

ENVIRONMENTAL ORGANIZATIONS IN THE US

	Organization	Membership		Organization	Membership
1	National Wildlife Federation	5,600,000	6	The Wilderness Society	330,000
2	Greenpeace	1,400,000	7=	Environmental Defense Fund	125,000
3	Sierra Club	553,246	7=	Natural Resources Defense Council	125,000
4	National Audubon Society	516,220	9	National Parks and Conservation Association	100,000
5	Ducks Unlimited	500,000	10	Defenders of Wildlife	80,000

Panda device © 1986 WWF – World Wide Fund for Nature (formerly World Wildlife Fund).

ROYAL HIGHNESSES & PRESIDENTS

TOP 10

LONGEST-REIGNING MONARCHS IN THE WORLD

	Monarch	Country	Reign	Age at accession	Years reigned
1	Louis XIV	France	1643–1715	5	72
2	John II	Liechtenstein	1858–1929	18	71
3	Franz-Josef	Austria-Hungary	1848–1916	18	67
4	Victoria	UK	1837–1901	18	63
5	Hirohito	Japan	1926–89	25	62
6	George III	UK	1760–1820	22	59
7	Louis XV	France	1715–74	5	59
8	Pedro II	Brazil	1831–89	6	58
9	Wilhelmina	Netherlands	1890–1948	10	58
10	Henry III	England	1216–72	9	56

Extravagant claims have been made for long-reigning monarchs in the ancient world. One example is the alleged 94-year reign of Phiops II, a 6th Dynasty Egyptian pharaoh. Since his dates cannot be verified, he has not been included in this Top 10.

TOP 10

MEMBERS OF THE ROYAL FAMILY IN LINE TO THE BRITISH THRONE

	Title	Date of Birth
1	The Prince of Wales	November 14, 1948
2	Prince William of Wales	June 21, 1982
3	Prince Henry of Wales	September 15, 1984
4	The Duke of York	February 19, 1960
5	Princess Beatrice of York	August 8, 1988
6	Princess Eugenie of York	March 23, 1990
7	Prince Edward	March 10, 1964
8	The Princess Royal	August 15, 1950
9	Master Peter Mark Andrew Phillips	November 15, 1977
10	Miss Zara Anne Elizabeth Phillips	May 15, 1981

The birth in 1988 of Princess Beatrice altered the order of succession, ousting Viscount Linley from the No. 10 position, while the birth in 1990 of her sister, Princess Eugenie, evicted HRH Princess Margaret, Countess of Snowdon, from the Top 10.

TOP 10

CURRENT MONARCHIES* WITH MOST RULERS

	Monarchy	Line commenced	No. rulers#
1	Japan	40 BC	125
2	England	802	64
3	Sweden	980	59
4	Denmark	940	55
5	Norway	858	42
6	Monaco	1458	20
7	Spain	1516	18
8=	Netherlands	1572	14
8=	Liechtenstein	1699	14
10	Thailand	1782	9

* *Including principalities*
\# *Monarchs deposed and later restored counted once only*

Among the dwindling ranks of monarchies, these are the longest-established, at least according to the number of successive incumbents. There are many other countries that had innumerable monarchs but that no longer have hereditary rulers, among them China, France, and Russia.

TOP 10

BUSIEST MEMBERS OF THE BRITISH ROYAL FAMILY

	Member	Events attended
1	Princess Royal	514
2	The Queen	509
3	Prince of Wales	417
4	Duke of Edinburgh	364
5	Duke of Kent	206
6	Duke of Gloucester	151
7	Duchess of Gloucester	128
8	Princess Alexandra	119
9	Prince Edward	115
10	Princess Margaret	114

In 1996 the members of the Royal Family appearing in this list attended a total of 2,637 events in the UK, while three other members (the Duke of York, the Duchess of Kent, and the Queen Mother) attended 199 events between them. In addition, those in this Top 10 carried out a total of 813 engagements while abroad on official tours, the Duke of Edinburgh carrying out the greatest number, 255.

TOP 10

HIGHEST-PAID MEMBERS OF THE BRITISH ROYAL FAMILY

	Member	Annual payment (£)
1	The Queen	7,900,000
2	The Queen Mother	643,000
3	The Duke of Edinburgh	359,000
4	The Duke of York	249,000
5	The Duke of Kent	236,000
6	The Princess Royal	228,000
7	Princess Alexandra	225,000
8	Princess Margaret	219,000
9	The Duke of Gloucester	175,500
10	Prince Edward	96,000

The Civil List is not technically the Royal Family's "pay," but the allowance made by the Government for their staff and the costs incurred in the course of performing their public duties. The amount of the Civil List was fixed for 10 years from January 1, 1991 and provides a total annual allocation of £10,417,000. Of that sum, £1,515,000 is refunded to the Treasury. Prince Charles receives his income largely from the Duchy of Cornwall, not the Civil List.

THE 10
FIRST PRESIDENTS OF THE US

	President/dates	Period of office
1	George Washington (1732–99)	1789–97
2	John Adams (1735–1826)	1797–1801
3	Thomas Jefferson (1743–1826)	1801–09
4	James Madison (1751–1836)	1809–17
5	James Monroe (1758–1831)	1817–25
6	John Quincy Adams (1767–1848)	1825–29
7	Andrew Jackson (1767–1845)	1829–37
8	Martin Van Buren (1782–1862)	1837–41
9	William H. Harrison (1773–1841)	1841
10	John Tyler (1790–1862)	1841–45

TOP 10
LONGEST-SERVING US PRESIDENTS

	President	Period in office years	days
1	Franklin D. Roosevelt	12	39
2=	Grover Cleveland	8*	
2=	Dwight D. Eisenhower	8*	
2=	Ulysses S. Grant	8*	
2=	Andrew Jackson	8*	
2=	Thomas Jefferson	8*	
2=	James Madison	8*	
2=	James Monroe	8*	
2=	Ronald Reagan	8*	
2=	Woodrow Wilson	8*	

* Two four-year terms – now the maximum any US president may be elected to office

PRESIDENT OF THE US, BILL CLINTON
As well as featuring in the list of tallest US presidents, Bill Clinton would appear in a list of the youngest and in a list of the most popular US presidents.

THE 10
LATEST US PRESIDENTS AND VICE PRESIDENTS TO DIE IN OFFICE

	Name/date of death	Office		Name/date of death	Office
1	John F. Kennedy* November 22, 1963	P	6	Garret A. Hobart November 21, 1899	VP
2	Franklin D. Roosevelt April 12, 1945	P	7	Thomas A. Hendricks November 25, 1885	VP
3	Warren G. Harding August 2, 1923	P	8	James A. Garfield* September 19, 1881	P
4	James S. Sherman October 30, 1912	VP	9	Henry Wilson, November 10, 1875	VP
5	William McKinley* September 14, 1901	P	10	Abraham Lincoln* April 15, 1865	P

* Assassinated

TOP 10
TALLEST US PRESIDENTS

	President	Height m	ft in
1	Abraham Lincoln	1.93	6 4
2	Lyndon B. Johnson	1.91	6 3
3=	Bill Clinton	1.89	6 2½
3=	Thomas Jefferson	1.89	6 2½
5=	Chester A. Arthur	1.88	6 2
5=	George Bush	1.88	6 2
5=	Franklin D. Roosevelt	1.88	6 2
5=	George Washington	1.88	6 2
9=	Andrew Jackson	1.85	6 1
9=	Ronald Reagan	1.85	6 1

TOP 10
US PRESIDENTS WITH THE MOST ELECTORAL VOTES

	President	Year	Votes
1	Ronald Reagan	1984	525
2	Franklin D. Roosevelt	1936	523
3	Richard Nixon	1972	520
4	Ronald Reagan	1980	489
5	Lyndon B. Johnson	1964	486
6	Franklin D. Roosevelt	1932	472
7	Dwight D. Eisenhower	1956	457
8	Franklin D. Roosevelt	1940	449
9	Herbert Hoover	1928	444
10	Dwight D. Eisenhower	1952	422

HUMAN ACHIEVEMENTS

THE 10

FIRST EXPLORERS TO LAND IN THE AMERICAS

	Explorer	Nationality	Discovery/ exploration	Year
1	Christopher Columbus	Italian	West Indies	1492
2	John Cabot	Italian/ English	Nova Scotia/ Newfoundland	1497
3	Alonso de Hojeda	Spanish	Brazil	1499
4	Vicente Yañez Pinzón	Spanish	Amazon	1500
5	Pedro Alvarez Cabral	Portuguese	Brazil	1500
6	Gaspar Corte Real	Portuguese	Labrador	1500
7	Rodrigo de Bastidas	Spanish	Central America	1501
8	Vasco Nuñez de Balboa	Spanish	Panama	1513
9	Juan Ponce de León	Spanish	Florida	1513
10	Juan Díaz de Solís	Spanish	Río de la Plata	1515

THE 10

FIRST PEOPLE TO GO OVER NIAGARA FALLS

	Name	Method	Date
1	Annie Edison Taylor	Barrel	Oct 24, 1901
2	Bobby Leach	Steel barrel	Jul 25, 1911
3	Jean Lussier	Rubber ball fitted with oxygen cylinders	Jul 4, 1928
4	William Fitzgerald (aka Nathan Boya)	Rubber ball	Jul 15, 1961
5	Karel Soucek	Barrel	Jul 3, 1984
6	Steven Trotter	Barrel	Aug 18, 1985
7	Dave Mundy	Barrel	Oct 5, 1985
8=	Peter deBernardi	Metal container	Sep 28, 1989
8=	Jeffrey Petkovich	Metal container	Sep 28, 1989
10	Dave Mundy	Diving bell	Sep 26, 1993

Source: Niagara Falls Museum

THE 10

LAST *TIME* MAGAZINE "MEN OF THE YEAR"

	Recipient	Year
1	Dr. David Ho (1952–), AIDS researcher	1996
2	Newt Gingrich (1943–), US politician	1995
3	Pope John Paul II (1920–)	1994
4	Yasser Arafat (1929–), F.W. de Klerk (1936–), Nelson Mandela (1918–), Yitzhak Rabin (1922–95), "Peacemakers"	1993
5	Bill Clinton (1946–), US President	1992
6	George Bush (1924–), US President	1991
7	Ted Turner (1938–), US businessman	1990
8	Mikhail Gorbachev (1931–), Soviet leader	1989
9	"Endangered Earth"	1988
10	Mikhail Gorbachev, Soviet leader	1987

THE 10

FIRST PEOPLE TO REACH THE NORTH POLE

Name/nationality	Date	Name/nationality	Date
1= Robert Edwin Peary (US)	Apr 6, 1909	**7=** Pavel Afanaseyevich Geordiyenko (USSR)	Apr 23, 1948
1= Matthew Alexander Henson (US)	Apr 6, 1909	**7=** Mikhail Yemel'yenovich Ostrekin (USSR)	Apr 23, 1948
1= Ooqueah (Eskimo)	Apr 6, 1909	**7=** Pavel Kononovich Sen'ko (USSR)	Apr 23, 1948
1= Ootah (Eskimo)	Apr 6, 1909	**7=** Mikhail Mikhaylovich Somov (USSR)	Apr 23, 1948
1= Egingwah (Eskimo)	Apr 6, 1909		
1= Seegloo (Eskimo)	Apr 6, 1909		

There remains some doubt as to the validity of Peary's team's claim. The first undisputed "conquest," that of the 1948 Soviet team, was achieved by landing in an aircraft.

THE FIRST SOLO CIRCUMNAVIGATION OF THE EARTH

Although there have now been several hundred solo voyages round the world, the first ever was completed on July 3, 1898 when 54-year-old Captain Joshua Slocum arrived in Fairhaven, Massachusetts, after a voyage of more than three years. The Canadian-born professional sailor had set off from Boston on April 24, 1895 in *Spray*, an 36-ft-9 in/11.2-mm replica of an old oyster boat he had built himself at a cost of $553.32. Slocum was hailed as a hero, and wrote a book about his exploit. At the end of 1909, he embarked on another solo journey in *Spray*, this time to the Orinoco, but was never seen again.

100 YEARS AGO

CONQUEST OF EVEREST

As early as the mid-nineteenth century it was realized that Mount Everest was the world's highest peak, but it was 100 years before it was successfully climbed. No attempts were made until the 1920s, and in 1922 the second expedition reached a height of 27,297 ft/8,320 m. Although a member of the third expedition attained 28,150 ft/ 8,580 m, two members of the party vanished. The first successful ascent, that of Hillary and Tenzing, culminated on May 29, 1953. The first woman to climb Everest was Junko Tabei of Japan on May 16, 1975, and on August 20, 1980 Italian climber Reinhold Messner became the first to climb solo, and without oxygen.

THE 10
FIRST MOUNTAINEERS TO CLIMB EVEREST

	Mountaineer	Nationality	Date
1	Edmund Hillary	New Zealander	May 29, 1953
2	Tenzing Norgay	Nepalese	May 29, 1953
3	Jürg Marmet	Swiss	May 23, 1956
4	Ernst Schmied	Swiss	May 23, 1956
5	Hans-Rudolf von Gunten	Swiss	May 24, 1956
6	Adolf Reist	Swiss	May 24, 1956
7	Wang Fu-chou	Chinese	May 25, 1960
8	Chu Ying-hua	Chinese	May 25, 1960
9	Konbu	Tibetan	May 25, 1960
10=	Nawang Gombu	Indian	May 1, 1963
10=	James Whittaker	US	May 1, 1963

Nawang Gombu and James Whittaker are 10th equal because, neither wishing to deny the other the privilege of being first, they ascended the last feet to the top side by side.

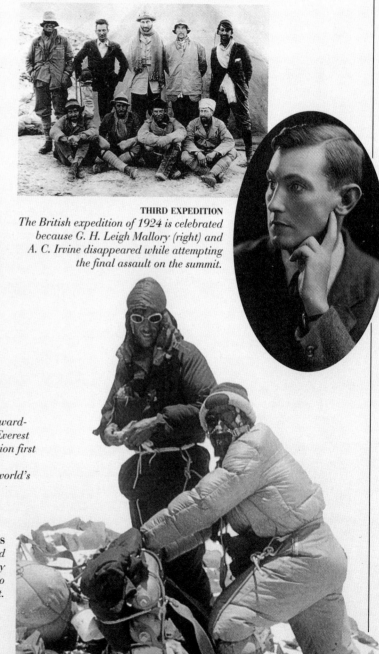

THIRD EXPEDITION
The British expedition of 1924 is celebrated because G. H. Leigh Mallory (right) and A. C. Irvine disappeared while attempting the final assault on the summit.

FIRST EXPEDITION
Led by Lt. Col. C.K. Howard-Bury, the 1921 British Everest Reconnaissance Expedition first assessed the scale of the challenge posed by the world's tallest mountain.

PEAK OF SUCCESS
Edmund Hillary and Sherpa Tenzing Norgay became the first to conquer Everest.

NOBEL PRIZE WINNERS

T O P 1 0
NOBEL PRIZE-WINNING COUNTRIES

	Country	Phy	Che	Ph/Med	Lit	Pce	Eco	Total
1	US	63	41	74	10	17	25	230
2	UK	21	23	24	8	11	7	94
3	Germany	19	27	15	6	4	1	72
4	France	11	7	7	12	9	1	47
5	Sweden	4	4	7	7	5	2	29
6	Switzerland	2	5	6	2	3	–	18
7	Former USSR	7	1	2	3	2	1	16
8	Stateless institutions	–	–	–	–	15	–	15
9=	Italy	3	1	3	5	1	–	13
9=	Netherlands	6	3	2	–	1	1	13

Phy – Physics; Che – Chemistry; Ph/Med – Physiology or Medicine; Lit – Literature; Pce – Peace; Eco – Economic Sciences. Germany includes the united country before 1948, West Germany to 1990, and the united country since 1990.

DID YOU KNOW

THE ULTIMATE PRIZE

Having made a fortune through his invention of dynamite, and many other patents, the Swedish scientist Alfred Nobel (1833–96) left his wealth to a fund to sponsor the prizes that bear his name. Winners in the six categories each receive a sum of money: in 1901 this amounted to 150,800 Swedish krona, but today it is worth 7,400,000 krona, or approximately $1,119,000. Winners also receive a 2.6-in/66-mm diameter 18-carat gold medal weighing about 6.2 oz/ 175 gm, which is engraved with the laureate's name. All the medals feature a portrait of Alfred Nobel, but their design and inscriptions vary according to the prize: that of the Physics, Chemistry, Physiology or Medicine, and Literature Prizes has a quotation in Latin from Virgil's *Aeneid*, "Inventions enhance life, which is beautified through art," while the Peace medal states "For the peace and brotherhood of men." The Economics Sciences Prize is inscribed "The Bank of Sweden, in Memory of Alfred Nobel, 1968" – the year that the prize was established.

T H E 1 0
LATEST WINNERS OF THE NOBEL PRIZE FOR LITERATURE

	Winner/country/dates	Prize year
1	Wislawa Szymborska (Poland, 1923–)	1996
2	Seamus Heaney (Ireland, 1939–)	1995
3	Kenzaburo Oe (Japan, 1935–)	1994
4	Toni Morrison (US, 1931–)	1993
5	Derek Walcott (Saint Lucia, 1930–)	1992
6	Nadine Gordimer (South Africa, 1923–)	1991
7	Octavio Paz (Mexico, 1914–)	1990
8	Camilo José Cela (Spain, 1916–)	1989
9	Naguib Mahfouz (Egypt, 1911–)	1988
10	Joseph Brodsky (Russia/US, 1940–96)	1987

T H E 1 0
LATEST WINNERS OF THE NOBEL PRIZE FOR ECONOMIC SCIENCES

	Winner/country/dates	Prize year
1=	James A. Mirrlees (UK, 1936–)	
1=	Professor William Vickrey (Canada, 1914–96)	1996

The analysis of informational asymmetries.

3	Robert E. Lucas (US, 1937–)	1995

The hypothesis of rational expectations as an aid to macroeconomic analysis and economic policy.

4=	John C. Harsanyi (Hungary/US, 1920–)	
4=	Reinhard Selten (Germany, 1930–)	
4=	John F. Nash (US, 1928–)	1994

The analysis of equilibria in the theory of noncooperative games.

7=	Robert W. Fogel (US, 1926–)	
7=	Douglass C. North (US, 1920–)	1993

The application of economic theory and quantitative methods to explain economic and institutional change.

9	Gary S. Becker (US, 1930–)	1992

Extending microeconomic analysis to a wide range of human behaviors and interactions.

10	Ronald H. Coase (UK/US, 1910–)	1991

The discovery and clarification of the significance of transaction costs and property rights for the traditional structure and functioning of the economy.

The Nobel Prize for Economic Science is a recent addition to the Nobel Prizes, first awarded in 1969. It is presented annually by the Royal Swedish Academy of Sciences and consists of a gold medal, a diploma, and a sum of money. The Nobel laureate for Economic Sciences, along with that of the other prizes, is announced annually in October, and the presentation is made to the winner on December 10, which is the anniversary of Alfred Nobel's death.

T H E 1 0

LATEST WINNERS OF THE NOBEL PEACE PRIZE

Winner/country/dates	Prize year	Winner/country/dates	Prize year
1= Carlos Filipe Ximenes Belo (East Timor, 1948–)	1996	**4=** Itzhak Rabin (Israel, 1922–1995)	1994
1= José Ramos-Horta (East Timor, 1949–)	1996	**7=** Nelson Rolihlahla Mandela (South Africa, 1918–)	1993
3 Joseph Rotblat (UK, 1908–)	1995	**7=** Frederik Willem de Klerk (South Africa, 1936–)	1993
4= Yasir Arafat (Palestine, 1929–)	1994	**9** Rigoberta Menchú (Guatemala, 1959–)	1992
4= Shimon Peres (Israel, 1923–)	1994	**10** Aung San Suu Kyi (Myanmar, 1945–)	1991

T H E 1 0

LATEST WINNERS OF THE NOBEL PRIZE FOR CHEMISTRY

Winner/country/dates	Prize year
1= Sir Harold W. Kroto (UK, 1939–)	
1= Richard E. Smalley (US, 1943–)	1996

The discovery of new forms of carbon known as fullerenes.

3= Paul Crutzen (Netherlands, 1933–)	
3= Mario Molina (Mexico, 1943–)	
3= Frank Sherwood Rowland (US, 1927–)	1995

Work in atmospheric chemistry concerning the formation and decomposition of ozone.

6 George A. Olah (Hungary/US, 1927–)	1994

The preparation of positively charged hydrocarbons, or "carbocations."

7= Michael Smith (UK/Canada, 1932–)	1993

The development of site-specific mutagenesis.

7= Kary Banks Mullis (US, 1944–)	1993

The invention of the polymerase chain reaction.

9 Rudolph A. Marcus (US, 1923–)	1992

Theories of electron transfer.

10 Richard Robert Ernst (Switzerland, 1933–)	1991

The development of high-resolution nuclear magnetic resonance (NMR) spectroscopy.

T H E 1 0

LATEST WINNERS OF THE NOBEL PRIZE FOR PHYSIOLOGY OR MEDICINE

Winner/country/dates	Prize year
1= Peter C. Doherty (Australia, 1940–)	
1= Rolf M. Zinkernagel (Switzerland, 1944–)	1996

The discovery of how the immune system recognizes virus-infected cells.

3= Christiane Nüsslein-Volhard (Germany, 1942–)	
3= Eric F. Wieschaus (US, 1947–)	
3= Edward B. Lewis (US, 1918–)	1995

Discoveries about the involvement of genes in the spatial organization of organisms.

6= Alfred G. Gilman (US, 1941–)	
6= Martin Rodbell (US, 1925–)	1994

Discovery of G-proteins and their role in signal transduction within cells.

8= Richard J. Roberts (US, 1943–)	
8= Phillip A. Sharp (US, 1944–)	1993

The discovery of mosaic genes.

10= Edmond H. Fischer (US, 1920–)	
10= Edwin G. Krebs (US, 1918–)	1992

The discovery of mechanisms for the regulation of proteins in the human body.

T H E 1 0

LATEST WINNERS OF THE NOBEL PRIZE FOR PHYSICS

Winner/country/dates	Prize year
1= David M. Lee (US, 1931–)	
1= Douglas D. Osheroff (US, 1945–)	
1= Robert C. Richardson (US, 1937–)	1996

The discovery of superfluidity of helium-3.

4= Martin L. Perl (US, 1927–)	1995

The discovery of the tau lepton.

4= Frederick Reines (US, 1918–)	1995

The detection of the neutrino.

6= Bertram Neville Brockhouse (Canada, 1918–)	
6= Clifford G. Shull (US, 1915–)	1994

Studies of neutron beams.

8= Russell A. Hulse (US, 1950–)	
8= Joseph H. Taylor, Jr. (US, 1941–)	1993

The discovery of a new type of pulsar.

10 Georges Charpak (France, 1924–)	1992

The invention of detectors for the detection of interactions of elementary particles.

SPORTS

TOP 10

HIGHEST-EARNING GOLFERS ON THE PGA TOUR

	Player	Winnings ($)
1	Tom Lehman	1,780,159
2	Phil Mickelson	1,697,799
3	Mark Brooks	1,429,396
4	Steve Stricker	1,383,739
5	Mark O'Meara	1,255,749

	Player	Winnings ($)
6	Fred Couples	1,248,694
7	Davis Love III	1,211,139
8	Brad Faxon	1,055,050
9	Scott Hoch	1,039,564
10	David Duval	977,079

Source: ESPNET Sports Zone

TOP 10

PLAYERS TO WIN THE MOST MAJORS IN A CAREER

	Player	Country	British Open	US Open	Masters	PGA	Total
1	Jack Nicklaus	US	3	4	6	5	18
2	Walter Hagen	US	4	2	0	5	11
3=	Ben Hogan	US	1	4	2	2	9
3=	Gary Player	South Africa	3	1	3	2	9
5	Tom Watson	US	5	1	2	0	8
6=	Harry Vardon	UK	6	1	0	0	7
6=	Gene Sarazen	US	1	2	1	3	7
6=	Bobby Jones	US	3	4	0	0	7
6=	Sam Snead	US	1	0	3	3	7
6=	Arnold Palmer	US	2	1	4	0	7

TOP 10

BIGGEST WINNING MARGINS IN THE US MASTERS

	Player*	Year	Winning margin
1	Tiger Woods	1997	12
2	Jack Nicklaus	1965	9
3	Raymond Floyd	1976	8
4	Cary Middlecoff	1955	7
5	Arnold Palmer	1964	6
6=	Claude Harmon	1948	5
6=	Ben Hogan	1953	5
6=	Nick Faldo (UK)	1996	5
9=	Jimmy Demaret	1940	4
9=	Sam Snead	1952	4
9=	Severiano Ballesteros (Spain)	1980	4
9=	Severiano Ballesteros (Spain)	1983	4
9=	Bernhard Langer (Germany)	1993	4

* All golfers from the United States unless otherwise stated

WINNERS OF WOMEN'S MAJORS

	Player	Titles
1	Patty Berg	16
2=	Mickey Wright	13
2=	Louise Suggs	13
4	Babe Didrikson Zaharias	12
5	Betsy Rawls	8
6	JoAnne Gunderson Carner	7
7=	Kathy Whitworth	6
7=	Pat Bradley	6
7=	Julie Simpson Inkster	6
7=	Glenna Collett Vare	6

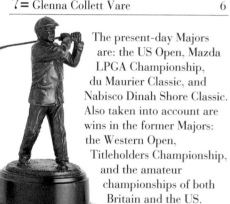

The present-day Majors are: the US Open, Mazda LPGA Championship, du Maurier Classic, and Nabisco Dinah Shore Classic. Also taken into account are wins in the former Majors: the Western Open, Titleholders Championship, and the amateur championships of both Britain and the US.

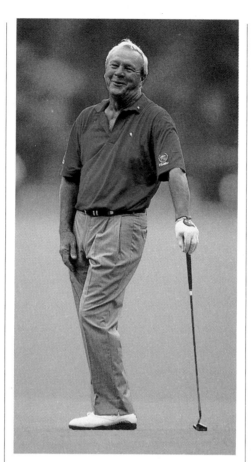

HAPPY GOLFER
Arnold Palmer has remained the world's highest-earning golfer for many years, his income in 1996 being over $15 million.

LOWEST WINNING SCORES IN THE US MASTERS

	Player*	Year	Score
1	Tiger Woods	1997	270
2=	Jack Nicklaus	1965	271
2=	Raymond Floyd	1976	271
4=	Ben Hogan	1953	274
5=	Ben Crenshaw	1995	274
6=	Severiano Ballesteros (Spain)	1980	275
6=	Fred Couples	1992	275
8=	Arnold Palmer	1964	276
8=	Jack Nicklaus	1975	276
7=	Tom Watson	1977	276
8=	Nick Faldo (UK)	1996	276

* All US players unless otherwise stated

The US Masters is the only Major played on the same course each year, at Augusta, Georgia. The course was built on the site of an old nursery, and the abundance of flowers and shrubs is a reminder of its former days, with each of the holes named after the plants growing adjacent to it.

LOWEST WINNING SCORES IN THE US OPEN

	Player	Country	Year	Venue	Score
1=	Jack Nicklaus	US	1980	Baltusrol	272
1=	Lee Janzen	US	1993	Baltusrol	272
3	David Graham	Australia	1981	Merion	273
4=	Jack Nicklaus	US	1967	Baltusrol	275
4=	Lee Trevino	US	1968	Oak Hill	275
6=	Ben Hogan	US	1948	Riviera	276
6=	Fuzzy Zoeller	US	1984	Winged Foot	276
8=	Jerry Pate	US	1976	Atlanta	277
8=	Scott Simpson	US	1987	Olympic Club	277
10=	Ken Venturi	US	1964	Congressional	278
10=	Billy Casper	US	1966	Olympic Club	278
10=	Hubert Green	US	1977	Southern Hills	278
10=	Curtis Strange	US	1988	Brookline	278
10=	Curtis Strange	US	1989	Oak Hill	278
10=	Steve Jones	US	1996	Oakland Hills	278

PLAYERS WITH MOST WINS ON THE US TOUR IN A CAREER

	Player*				Player*	
1	Sam Snead	81		6	Billy Casper	51
2	Jack Nicklaus	71		7=	Walter Hagen	40
3	Ben Hogan	63		7=	Cary Midlecoff	40
4	Arnold Palmer	60		9	Gene Sarazen	38
5	Byron Nelson	52		10	Lloyd Mangrum	36

* All US

For many years Sam Snead's wins were believed to total 84, but the PGA Tour amended this figure in 1990 after discrepancies had been found in their previous lists. They deducted 11 wins from his total but added eight others, which should have been included, for a revised total of 81. The highest-placed current member of the regular Tour is Tom Watson, in joint 11th place with 32 wins. The highest-placed overseas player is Gary Player (South Africa), with 22 wins. Sam Snead, despite being the most successful golfer on the US Tour, never won the US Open.

WORLD TENNIS

WINNERS OF MEN'S GRAND SLAM SINGLES TITLES

	Player/country	A	F	W	US	Total
1	Roy Emerson (Australia)	6	2	2	2	12
2=	Björn Borg (Sweden)	0	6	5	0	11
2=	Rod Laver (Australia)	3	2	4	2	11
4=	Jimmy Connors (US)	1	0	2	5	8
4=	Ivan Lendl (Czechoslovakia)	2	3	0	3	8
4=	Fred Perry (UK)	1	1	3	3	8
4=	Ken Rosewall (Australia)	4	2	0	2	8
4=	Pete Sampras (US)	2	0	3	3	8
8=	René Lacoste (France)	0	3	2	2	7
8=	William Larned (US)	0	0	0	7	7
8=	John McEnroe (US)	0	0	3	4	7
8=	John Newcombe (Australia)	2	0	3	2	7
8=	William Renshaw (UK)	0	0	7	0	7
8=	Richard Sears (US)	0	0	0	7	7
8=	Mats Wilander (Sweden)	3	3	0	1	7

A = *Australian Open;* F = *French Open;* W = *Wimbledon;* US = *US Open*

WINNERS OF WOMEN'S GRAND SLAM SINGLES TITLES

	Player/country	A	F	W	US	Total
1	Margaret Court (Australia)	11	5	3	5	24
2	Steffi Graf (Germany)	4	5	7	7	21
3	Helen Wills-Moody (US)	0	4	8	7	19
4=	Chris Evert-Lloyd (US)	2	7	3	6	18
4=	Martina Navratilova (Czechoslovakia/US)	3	2	9	4	18
6	Billie Jean King (US)	1	1	6	4	12
7=	Maureen Connolly (US)	1	2	3	3	9
7=	Monica Seles (Yugoslavia/US)	4	3	0	2	9
9=	Suzanne Lenglen (France)	0	2	6	0	8
9=	Molla Mallory (US)	0	0	0	8	8

A = *Australian Open;* F = *French Open;* W = *Wimbledon;*
US = *US Open*

MALE PLAYERS IN THE WORLD*

	Player	Country
1	Pete Sampras	US
2	Thomas Muster	Austria
3	Michael Chang	US
4	Yevgeny Kafelnikov	Russia
5	Goran Ivanisevic	Croatia
6	Richard Krajicek	Netherlands
7	Thomas Enqvist	Sweden
8	Carlos Moya	Spain
9	Marcelo Rios	Chile
10	Wayne Ferreira	South Africa

* *ATP rankings as of March 17, 1997*

WIMBLEDON RECORD-HOLDER
Martina Navratilova's nine singles wins from 1978 to 1990 make her Wimbledon's unrivaled singles champion.

FEMALE PLAYERS IN THE WORLD*

	Player	Country
1	Steffi Graf	Germany
2	Martina Hingis	Switzerland
3	Arantxa Sanchez Vicario	Spain
4	Jana Novotna	Czech Republic
5	Monica Seles	US
6	Conchita Martinez	Spain
7	Lindsay Davenport	US
8	Anke Huber	Germany
9	Irinia Spirlea	Romania
10	Iva Majoli	Croatia

* *WTA rankings as of March 17, 1997*

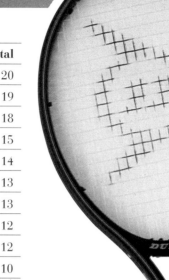

T O P 1 0

PLAYERS WITH THE MOST WIMBLEDON TITLES

	Player/country	Years	Singles	Doubles	Mixed	Total
1	Billie Jean King (US)	1961–79	6	10	4	20
2	Elizabeth Ryan (US)	1914–34	0	12	7	19
3	Martina Navratilova (Czechoslovakia/US)	1976–95	9	7	2	18
4	Suzanne Lenglen (France)	1919–25	6	6	3	15
5	William Renshaw (UK)	1880–89	7	7	0	14
6=	Louise Brough (US)	1946–55	4	5	4	13
6=	Lawrence Doherty (UK)	1897–1905	5	8	0	13
8=	Helen Wills-Moody (US)	1927–38	8	3	1	12
8=	Reginald Doherty (UK)	1897–1905	4	8	0	12
10=	Margaret Court (Australia)	1953–75	3	2	5	10
10=	Doris Hart (US)	1947–55	1	4	5	10

Billie Jean King's first and last Wimbledon titles were in the ladies' doubles. The first, in 1961, as Billie Jean Moffitt, was with Karen Hantze when they beat Jan Lehane and Margaret Smith 6–3, 6–4. When Billie Jean won her record-breaking 20th title in 1979, she partnered Martina Navratilova to victory over Betty Stove and Wendy Turnbull. Billie Jean could have increased her total in 1983 but was defeated in the mixed doubles.

T O P 1 0

PLAYERS WITH THE MOST FRENCH CHAMPIONSHIP SINGLES TITLES

	Player*	Years	Titles
1	Chris Evert-Lloyd (US)	1974–86	7
2	Björn Borg (Sweden)	1974–81	6
3=	Margaret Court (Australia)	1962–73	5
3=	Steffi Graf (Germany)	1987–96	5
4=	Henri Cochet	1926–32	4
4=	Helen Wills-Moody (US)	1928–32	4
7=	René Lacoste	1925–29	3
7=	Hilde Sperling (Germany)	1935–37	3
7=	Yvon Petra	1943–45	3
7=	Ivan Lendl (Czechoslovakia)	1984–7	3
7=	Mats Wilander (Sweden)	1982–88	3
7=	Monica Seles (Yug/US)	1990–92	3

* Players are from France unless otherwise stated

T O P 1 0

PLAYERS WITH THE MOST AUSTRALIAN CHAMPIONSHIP SINGLES TITLES

	Player*	Years	Titles
1	Margaret Court	1960–73	11
2=	Nancy Bolton	1937–51	6
2=	Roy Emerson	1961–67	6
4	Daphne Akhurst	1925–30	5
5=	Pat Wood	1914–23	4
5=	Jack Crawford	1931–35	4
5=	Ken Rosewall	1953–72	4
5=	Evonne Cawley	1974–77	4
5=	Steffi Graf (Germany)	1988–94	4
5=	Monica Seles (Yug/US)	1991–96	4

* Players are from Australia unless otherwise stated

T O P 1 0

PLAYERS WITH THE MOST US OPEN SINGLES TITLES

	Player*	Years	Titles
1	Molla Mallory	1915–26	8
2=	Richard Sears	1881–87	7
2=	William Larned	1901–11	7
2=	Bill Tilden	1920–29	7
2=	Helen Wills-Moody	1923–31	7
2=	Margaret Court (Australia)	1962–70	7
7	Chris Evert-Lloyd	1975–82	6
8=	Jimmy Connors	1974–83	5
8=	Steffi Graf (Germany)	1988–96	5
10=	Robert Wrenn	1893–97	4
10=	Elisabeth Moore	1896–1905	4
10=	Hazel Wightman	1909–19	4
10=	Helen Jacobs	1932–35	4
10=	Alice Marble	1936–40	4
10=	Pauline Betz	1942–46	4
10=	Maria Bueno (Brazil)	1959–66	4
10=	Billie Jean King	1967–74	4
10=	John McEnroe	1979–84	4
10=	Martina Navratilova	1983–87	4

* Players are from the US unless otherwise stated

SPORTS

BASEBALL

THE 10

FIRST PITCHERS TO THROW PERFECT GAMES

	Player	Game	Date
1	Lee Richmond	Worcester v Cleveland	Jun 12, 1880
2	Monte Ward	Providence v Buffalo	Jun 17, 1880
3	Cy Young	Boston v Philadelphia	May 5, 1904
4	Addie Joss	Cleveland v Chicago	Oct 2, 1908
5	Charlie Robertson	Chicago v Detroit	Apr 30, 1922
6	Don Larsen*	New York v Brooklyn	Oct 8, 1956
7	Jim Bunning	Philadelphia v New York	Jun 21, 1964
8	Sandy Koufax	Los Angeles v Chicago	Sep 9, 1965
9	Catfish Hunter	Oakland v Minnesota	May 8, 1968
10	Len Barker	Cleveland v Toronto	May 15, 1981

* Larsen's perfect game was, uniquely, in the World Series.

TOP 10

LARGEST MAJOR LEAGUE BALLPARKS*

	Stadium	Home team	Capacity
1	Anaheim Stadium	Anaheim Angels	64,593
2	Veterans Stadium	Philadelphia Phillies	62,268
3	3Com Park#	San Francisco Giants	62,000
4	Jack Murphy Stadium	San Diego Padres	59,690
5	The Kingdome	Seattle Mariners	59,158
6	Busch Stadium	St. Louis Cardinals	57,673
7	Yankee Stadium	New York Yankees	57,545
8	Dodger Stadium	Los Angeles Dodgers	56,000
9	Shea Stadium	New York Mets	55,777
10	The Astrodome	Houston Astros	54,370

* By capacity # Formerly Candlestick Park

TOP 10

TEAMS WITH THE MOST WORLD SERIES WINS

	Team*	Wins
1	New York Yankees	23
2=	St. Louis Cardinals	9
2=	Philadelphia/Kansas City/Oakland Athletics	9
4	Brooklyn/Los Angeles Dodgers	6
5=	New York/San Francisco Giants	5
5=	Boston Red Sox	5
5=	Cincinnati Reds	5
5=	Pittsburgh Pirates	5
9	Detroit Tigers	4
10=	Boston/Milwaukee/Atlanta Braves	3
10=	St. Louis/Baltimore Orioles	3
10=	Washington Senators/Minnesota Twins	3

* Teams separated by / indicate changes of franchise and are regarded as the same team for Major League record purposes.

Major League Baseball started with the forming of the National League in 1876. The rival American League was started in 1901, and two years later Pittsburgh, champions of the National League, invited American League champions Boston to take part in a best-of-nine games series to find the "real" champions. Boston won 5–3.

TOP 10

PLAYERS WITH THE MOST RUNS IN A CAREER

	Player	Runs
1	Ty Cobb	2,245
2=	Babe Ruth	2,174
2=	Hank Aaron	2,174
4	Pete Rose	2,165
5	Willie Mays	2,062
6	Stan Musial	1,949
7	Lou Gehrig	1,888
8	Tris Speaker	1,882
9	Mel Ott	1,859
10=	Rickey Henderson#	1,829
10=	Frank Robinson	1,829

TOP 10

PLAYERS WHO PLAYED THE MOST GAMES IN A CAREER

	Player	Games
1	Pete Rose	3,562
2	Carl Yastrzemski	3,308
3	Hank Aaron	3,298
4	Ty Cobb	3,034
5	Stan Musial	3,026
6	Willie Mays	2,992
7	Dave Winfield	2,973
8	Eddie Murray*	2,971
9	Rusty Staub	2,951
10	Brooks Robinson	2,896

* Still active at end of 1995–96 season

TOP 10

TEAMS WITH THE BIGGEST PAYROLLS IN MAJOR LEAGUE BASEBALL, 1997

	Team	Payroll ($)		Team	Payroll ($)
1	New York Yankees	58,499,545	6	Texas Rangers	50,112,268
2	Baltimore Orioles	55,085,778	7	Florida Marlins	47,738,000
3	Chicago White Sox	54,205,000	8	Cincinnati Reds	46,237,000
4	Cleveland Indians	54,122,460	9	Toronto Blue Jays	45,894,833
5	Atlanta Braves	50,488,500	10	St. Louis Cardinals	44,129,167

THE FIRST PLAYERS TO HIT FOUR HOME RUNS IN ONE GAME

	Player	Club	Date
1	Bobby Lowe	Boston National League	May 30, 1884
2	Ed Delahanty	Philadelphia	Jul 13, 1896
3	Lou Gehrig	New York (Yankees)	Jun 3, 1932
4	Chuck Klein	Philadelphia	Jul 10, 1936
5	Pat Seerey	Chicago	Jul 18, 1948
6	Gil Hodges	Brooklyn	Aug 31, 1950
7	Joe Adcock	Milwaukee	Jul 31, 1954
8	Rocky Colavito	Cleveland	Jun 10, 1959
9	Willie Mays	San Francisco	Apr 30, 1961
10	Mike Schmidt	Philadelphia	Apr 17, 1976

The only other players to score four homers in one game are Bob Horner, who did so for Atlanta on July 6, 1986, and Mark Whitten for St. Louis on September 7, 1993.

PLAYERS WITH THE HIGHEST CAREER BATTING AVERAGES

	Player	At bat	Hits	Average
1	Ty Cobb	11,434	4,189	.366
2	Rogers Hornsby	8,173	2,930	.358
3	Joe Jackson	4,981	1,772	.356
4	Ed Delahanty	7,505	2,597	.346
5	Tris Speaker	10,195	3,514	.345
6=	Billy Hamilton	6,268	2,158	.344
6=	Ted Williams	7,706	2,654	.344
8=	Dan Brouthers	6,711	2,296	.342
8=	Harry Heilmann	7,787	2,660	.342
8=	Babe Ruth	8,399	2,873	.342

OLDEST STADIUMS IN MAJOR LEAGUE BASEBALL

	Stadium	Home club	Year built
1=	Tiger Stadium	Detroit Tigers	1912
1=	Fenway Park	Boston Red Sox	1912
3	Wrigley Field	Chicago Cubs	1914
4	Yankee Stadium	New York Yankees	1923
5	County Stadium	Milwaukee Brewers	1953
6	3Com Park*	San Francisco Giants	1960
7	Dodger Stadium	Los Angeles Dodgers	1962
8	Shea Stadium	New York Mets	1964
9	The Astrodome	Houston Astros	1965
10=	Anaheim Stadium	Anaheim Angels	1966
10=	Busch Stadium	St. Louis Cardinals	1966
10=	Oakland-Alameda County Coliseum	Oakland Athletics	1966

* Formerly Candlestick Park

SALARIES IN MAJOR LEAGUE BASEBALL, 1997

	Player	Team	Salary($)*
1	Barry Bonds	San Francisco Giants	11,450,000#
2	Albert Belle	Chicago White Sox	11,000,000
3	Gary Sheffield	Florida Marlins	10,166,667
4	Ken Griffey Jr.	Seattle Mariners	8,500,000
5	Roger Clemens	Toronto Blue Jays	8,250,000
6	John Smoltz	Atlanta Braves	7,750,000
7	Mike Piazza	Los Angeles Dodgers	7,500,000
8	Barry Bonds	San Francisco Giants	7,291,667#
9	Frank Thomas	Chicago White Sox	7,250,000
10	Cecil Fielder	New York Yankees	7,237,500

* Figures include guaranteed income, but not income from potential incentive bonuses.
# Bonds' figure at #1 is for the 1999–2000 season, while his #8 figure refers to his existing contract for 1993–98.

FOOTBALL

T O P 1 0

BIGGEST WINNING MARGINS IN THE SUPER BOWL

	Winners	Runners-up	Year	Score	Margin
1	San Francisco 49ers	Denver Broncos	1990	55–10	45
2	Chicago Bears	New England Patriots	1986	46–10	36
3	Dallas Cowboys	Buffalo Bills	1993	52–17	35
4	Washington Redskins	Denver Broncos	1988	42–10	32
5	LA Raiders	Washington Redskins	1984	38–9	29
6	Green Bay Packers	Kansas City Chiefs	1967	35–10	25
7	San Francisco 49ers	San Diego Chargers	1995	49–26	23
8	San Francisco 49ers	Miami Dolphins	1985	38–16	22
9	Dallas Cowboys	Miami Dolphins	1972	24–3	21
10=	Green Bay Packers	Oakland Raiders	1968	33–14	19
10=	New York Giants	Denver Broncos	1987	39–20	19

T O P 1 0

PLAYERS WITH THE MOST TOUCHDOWNS IN AN NFL CAREER*

	Player	Touchdowns
1	Jerry Rice	165
2	Marcus Allen	134
3	Jim Brown	126
4	Walter Payton	125
5	John Riggins	116
6	Emmitt Smith	115
7	Lenny Moore	113
8	Don Hutson	105
9	Steve Largent	101
10	Franco Harris	100

* To end of 1996–97 season
Source: National Football League

T O P 1 0

PLAYERS WITH THE MOST PASSING YARDS IN AN NFL CAREER*

	Player	Passing yards
1	Dan Marino	51,636
2	Fran Tarkenton	47,003
3	John Elway	45,034
4	Warren Moon	43,787
5	Dan Fouts	43,040
6	Joe Montana	40,551
7	Johnny Unitas	40,239
8	Dave Krieg	37,946
9	Boomer Esiason	36,442
10	Jim Kelly	35,467

* To end of 1996–97 season

T O P 1 0

COLLEGES WITH THE MOST BOWL WINS

	College	Wins
1	Alabama	27
2	University of Southern California (USC)	24
3=	Oklahoma	20
3=	Penn State	20
3=	Tennessee	20
6=	Georgia Tech	17
6=	Texas	17
8	Nebraska	16
9=	Georgia	15
9=	Florida State	15

Source: National Football League

Bowl games are annual end-of-season college championship games, played at the end of December or the beginning of January. The "Big Four" Bowl games are: Rose Bowl, Cotton Bowl, Sugar Bowl, and Orange Bowl. The Rose Bowl, one of college football's great occasions, dates to 1902, when the leading Eastern and Western teams met at Pasadena as part of the Tournament of Roses celebration, which was first held in 1890. By the turn of the century it had become a major attraction.

T O P 1 0

MOST SUCCESSFUL COACHES IN AN NFL CAREER

	Coach	Games won
1	Don Shula	347
2	George Halas	324
3	Tom Landry	270
4	Curly Lambeau	229
5	Chuck Noll	209
6	Chuck Knox	193
7	Paul Brown	170
8	Bud Grant	168
9	Steve Owen	153
10	Dan Reeves*	149

* Still active at end of 1996–97 season

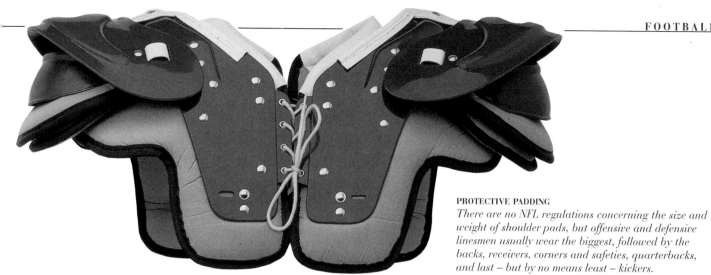

PROTECTIVE PADDING
There are no NFL regulations concerning the size and weight of shoulder pads, but offensive and defensive linesmen usually wear the biggest, followed by the backs, receivers, corners and safeties, quarterbacks, and last – but by no means least – kickers.

TOP 10

LARGEST NFL STADIUMS

	Stadium	Home team	Capacity
1	Pontiac Silverdrome	Detroit Lions	80,365
2	Rich Stadium	Buffalo Bills	80,024
3	Arrowhead Stadium	Kansas City Chiefs	79,101
4	Giants Stadium	New York Giants/Jets	77,716
5	Mile High Stadium	Denver Broncos	76,123
6	Pro Player Stadium	Miami Dolphins	74,916
7	Houlihan's Stadium	Tampa Bay Buccaneers	74,321
8	Sun Devil Stadium	Arizona Cardinals	73,273
9	Jacksonville Municipal Stadium	Jacksonville Jaguars	73,000
10	Ericsson Stadium	Carolina Panthers	72,520

Source: National Football League

TOP 10

FOOTBALL TEAMS*

	Team	Wins	Runners-up	Points
1	Dallas Cowboys	5	3	13
2=	San Francisco 49ers	5	0	10
2=	Pittsburgh Steelers	4	1	10
4	Washington Redskins	3	2	8
5	Oakland/Los Angeles Raiders	3	1	7
6	Miami Dolphins	2	3	7
7	Green Bay Packers	3	0	6
8	New York Giants	2	0	4
9=	Buffalo Bills	0	4	4
9=	Denver Broncos	0	4	4
9=	Minnesota Vikings	0	4	4

* Based on two points for a Super Bowl win, and one for runner-up

TOP 10

POINT SCORERS IN AN NFL SEASON

	Player	Team	Year	Points
1	Paul Hornung	Green Bay Packers	1960	176
2	Mark Moseley	Washington Redskins	1983	161
3	Gino Cappelletti	Boston Patriots	1964	155*
4	Emitt Smith	Dallas Cowboys	1995	150
5	Chip Lohmiller	Washington Redskins	1991	149
6	Gino Cappelletti	Boston Patriots	1961	147
7	Paul Hornung	Green Bay Packers	1961	146
8=	Jim Turner	New York Jets	1968	145
8=	John Kasay	Carolina Panthers	1996	145
10=	John Riggins	Washington Redskins	1983	144
10=	Kevin Butler#	Chicago Bears	1985	144

* Including a two-point conversion   # The only rookie in this Top 10

TOP 10

RUSHERS IN AN NFL CAREER

	Player	Total yards gained rushing
1	Walter Payton	16,726
2	Eric Dickerson	13,259
3	Tony Dorsett	12,739
4	Jim Brown	12,312
5	Franco Harris	12,120
6	Marcus Allen*	11,738
7	Barry Sanders*	11,725
8	John Riggins	11,352
9	O. J. Simpson	11,236
10	Thurman Thomas*	10,762

* Still active at end of 1996–97 season

BASKETBALL

PLAYERS WHO HAVE PLAYED MOST GAMES IN THE NBA AND THE ABA

	Player	Games played
1	Robert Parish*	1,611
2	Kareem Abdul-Jabbar	1,560
3	Moses Malone*	1,455
4	Artis Gilmore	1,329
5	Elvin Hayes	1,303
6	Caldwell Jones	1,299
7	John Havlicek	1,270
8	Buck Williams*	1,266
9	Paul Silas	1,254
10	Julius Erving	1,243

* *Still active at end of 1996–97 season*

The ABA (American Basketball Association) was established as a rival to the National Basketball Association (NBA) in 1968 and survived until 1976. Because many of the sport's top players "defected," their figures are still included in this list. During the 1995–96 season, Robert Parish moved to the top of this list by playing his 1,561st game on April 6, 1996 at the Gateway Arena in Cleveland, between the Charlotte Hornets and the Cleveland Cavaliers.

POINT SCORERS IN AN NBA CAREER*

	Player	Total points
1	Kareem Abdul-Jabbar	38,387
2	Wilt Chamberlain	31,419
3	Moses Malone#	27,409
4	Elvin Hayes	27,313
5	Michael Jordan#	26,920
6	Oscar Robertson	26,710
7	Dominique Wilkins#	26,534
8	John Havlicek	26,395
9	Alex English	25,613
10	Karl Malone#	25,574

* *Regular season games only*
# *Still active at end of 1997 season*

If points from the ABA were also considered, then Abdul-Jabbar would still be number one, with the same total. He was born Lew Alcindor but adopted a new name when he converted to the Islamic faith in 1969. The following year he turned professional, playing for Milwaukee. His career spanned 20 seasons before he retired at the end of the 1989 season. Despite scoring an NBA record 38,387 points, he could not emulate the great Wilt Chamberlain by scoring 100 points in a game, which Chamberlain achieved for Philadelphia against New York at Hershey, Pennsylvania, on March 2, 1962. Chamberlain also scored 70 points in a game six times, a feat Abdul-Jabbar never succeeded in rivaling.

HIGHEST-EARNING PLAYERS IN THE NBA, 1996–97

	Player/team	Earnings ($)*
1	Michael Jordan, Chicago Bulls	30,140,000
2	Horace Grant, Orlando Magic	14,857,000
3	Reggie Miller, Indiana Pacers	11,250,000
4	Shaquille O'Neal, Los Angeles Lakers	10,714,000
5	Gary Payton, Seattle Supersonics	10,212,000
6	David Robinson, San Antonio Spurs	9,952,000
7	Juwan Howard, Washington Bullets	9,750,000
8	Hakeem Olajuwon, Houston Rockets	9,655,000
9	Alonzo Mourning, Miami Heat	9,380,000
10	Dennis Rodman, Chicago Bulls	9,000,000

* *Salary only*

PLAYERS WITH THE MOST CAREER ASSISTS

	Player	Assists
1	John Stockton*	12,170
2	Magic Johnson	10,141
3	Oscar Robertson	9,887
4	Isiah Thomas	9,061
5	Maurice Cheeks	7,392
6	Lenny Wilkens	7,211
7	Bob Cousy	6,995
8	Guy Rodgers	6,917
9	Nate Archibald	6,476
10	John Lucas	6,454

* *Still active at end of 1996–97 season*

MOST SUCCESSFUL DIVISION 1 NCAA TEAMS

	College	Division 1 wins		College	Division 1 wins
1	Kentucky	1,677	6	Temple	1,476
2	North Carolina	1,668	7	Syracuse	1,451
3	Kansas	1,625	8	Oregon State	1,442
4	St. John's	1,532	9	Pennsylvania	1,436
5	Duke	1,515	10	Notre Dame	1,415

Based on percentage Kentucky has the best record, with 1,650 wins from 2,171 games played for a percentage of 0.760.

BIGGEST ARENAS IN THE NBA

	Arena	Location	Home team	Capacity
1	The Alamodome	San Antonio, Texas	San Antonio Spurs	25,666
2	Charlotte Coliseum	Charlotte, North Carolina	Charlotte Hornets	23,696
3	SkyDome	Toronto	Toronto Raptors	22,911
4	United Center	Chicago, Illinois	Chicago Bulls	21,500
5	The Palace of Auburn Hills	Auburn Hills, Michigan	Detroit Pistons	21,454
6	The Rose Garden	Portland, Oregon	Portland Trailblazers	21,400
7	Gund Arena	Cleveland, Ohio	Cleveland Cavaliers	20,562
8	Continental Airlines Arena	East Rutherford, New Jersey	New Jersey Nets	20,049
9	General Motors Place	Vancouver	Vancouver Grizzlies	19,193
10	Delta Center Arena	Salt Lake City, Utah	Utah Jazz	19,911

The smallest arena is the 15,200 capacity Miami Arena, home of the Miami Heat. The largest-ever NBA stadium was the Louisiana Superdome used by the New Orleans (now Utah) Jazz from 1975 to 1979, which was capable of holding crowds of 47,284.

A CENTURY OF PRO BASKETBALL

The National Basketball League (NBL), founded in 1898, was the first professional league in the world. Although similar games had been played for centuries, the modern game of basketball was invented just eight years earlier by Canadian physical education teacher Dr. James A. Naismith (1861–1939) at the International YMCA College in Springfield, Massachusetts, as a game that could be played indoors during the winter. Peach baskets were originally used but were replaced by metal rings with netting. In 1949 the NBL merged with the Basketball Association of America to create the National Basketball Association (NBA). Basketball is today reckoned to be the world's most popular indoor sport.

100 YEARS AGO • YEARS AGO • YEARS AGO •

WARRIORS BATTLE ON
Kevin Wallis is one of the more recent members of the successful Golden State Warriors. The team, formerly the Philadelphia Warriors (1946–62) and San Francisco Warriors (1962–71), won the first ever NBA title in 1947.

TEAMS WITH THE MOST NBA TITLES

	Team*	Titles
1	Boston Celtics	16
2	Minnesota/Los Angeles Lakers	11
3	Chicago Bulls	5
4=	Philadelphia/Golden State Warriors	3
4=	Syracuse Nationals/ Philadelphia 76ers	3
6=	Detroit Pistons	2
6=	Houston Rockets	2
6=	New York Knickerbockers	2
9=	Baltimore Bullets	1
9=	Houston Rockets	1
9=	Milwaukee Bucks	1
9=	Rochester Royals#	1
9=	St. Louis Hawks+	1
9=	Seattle Supersonics	1
9=	Portland Trail Blazers	1
9=	Washington Bullets	1

* *Teams separated by(/) indicate change of franchise: they have won the championship under both names*
\# *Now the Sacramento Kings*
\+ *Now the Atlanta Hawks*

ICE HOCKEY

T O P 1 0

BIGGEST NHL ARENAS

	Stadium	Home team	Capacity
1	Molson Centre, Montreal	Montreal Canadiens	21,347
2	United Center, Chicago	Chicago Blackhawks	20,500
3	Canadian Airlines Saddledome, Calgary	Calgary Flames	20,230
4=	Ice Palace, Tampa	Tampa Bay Lightning	19,500
4=	Marine Midland Arena, Buffalo	Buffalo Sabres	19,500
4=	CoreStates Center, Philadelphia	Philadelphia Flyers	19,500
7	Joe Louis Sports Arena, Detroit	Detroit Red Wings	19,275
8	Kiel Center, St. Louis	St. Louis Blues	19,260
9	General Motors Place, Vancouver	Vancouver Canucks	19,056
10	Continental Airlines Arena, East Rutherford	New Jersey Devils	19,040

T O P 1 0

POINT-SCORERS IN STANLEY CUP PLAY-OFF GAMES

	Player	Total points			Player	Total points
1	Wayne Gretzky*	382		6	Bryan Trottier	184
2	Mark Messier*	295		7	Jean Beliveau	176
3	Jari Kurri*	233		8	Denis Savard*	175
4	Glenn Anderson	214		9=	Doug Gilmour*	164
5	Paul Coffey*	195		9=	Denis Potvin	164

Still active 1996–97 season

T O P 1 0

WINNERS OF THE HART TROPHY

	Player	Years	Wins
1	Wayne Gretzky	1980–89	9
2	Gordie Howe	1952–63	6
3	Eddie Shore	1933–38	4
4=	Bobby Clarke	1973–76	3
4=	Howie Morenz	1928–32	3
4=	Bobby Orr	1970–72	3
4=	Mario Lemieux	1988–96	3
8=	Jean Beliveau	1956–64	2
8=	Bill Cowley	1941–43	2
8=	Phil Esposito	1969–74	2
8=	Bobby Hull	1965–66	2
8=	Guy Lafleur	1977–78	2
8=	Mark Messier	1990–92	2
8=	Stan Mikita	1967–68	2
8=	Nels Stewart	1926–30	2

The Hart Trophy has been awarded annually since 1924 and is presented to the player "adjudged to be the most valuable to his team during the season." The trophy is named after Cecil Hart, the former manager/coach of the Montreal Canadiens.

T O P 1 0

GOAL-SCORERS IN AN NHL SEASON

	Player/team	Season	Goals
1	Wayne Gretzky (Edmonton Oilers)	1981–82	92
2	Wayne Gretzky (Edmonton Oilers)	1983–84	87
3	Brett Hull (St. Louis Blues)	1990–91	86
4	Mario Lemieux (Pittsburgh Penguins)	1988–89	85
5=	Phil Esposito (Boston Bruins)	1970–71	76
5=	Alexander Mogilny (Buffalo Sabres)	1992–93	76
5=	Teemu Selanne (Winnipeg Jets)	1992–93	76
8	Wayne Gretzky (Edmonton Oilers)	1984–85	73
9	Brett Hull (St. Louis Blues)	1989–90	72
10=	Wayne Gretzky (Edmonton Oilers)	1982–83	71
10=	Jari Kurri (Edmonton Oilers)	1984–85	71

T O P 1 0

GOALTENDERS IN AN NHL CAREER*

	Goaltender	Seasons	Games won
1	Terry Sawchuk	21	447
2	Jacques Plante	18	434
3	Tony Esposito	16	423
4	Glenn Hall	18	407
5	Grant Fuhr#	15	359
6	Rogie Vachon	16	355
7	Andy Moog#	16	354
8	Patrick Roy#	11	349
9	Gump Worsley	21	335
10	Harry Lumley	16	333

Regular season only
Still active at end of 1996-97 season

T O P 1 0

POINT-SCORERS IN AN NHL CAREER*

	Player	Seasons	Goals	Assists	Total points
1	Wayne Gretzky#	18	862	1,843	2,705
2	Gordie Howe	26	801	1,049	1,850
3	Marcel Dionne	18	731	1,040	1,771
4	Phil Esposito	18	717	873	1,590
5	Mark Messier#	18	575	977	1,552
6	Stan Mikita	22	541	926	1,467
7	Bryan Trottier	18	524	901	1,425
8	Paul Coffey#	17	378	1058	1,436
9	Dale Hawerchuk#	16	518	891	1,409
10	Mario Lemieux#	12	613	881	1,494

* Regular season only
\# Still active at end of 1996-97 season

BEST-PAID PLAYERS IN THE NHL, 1996–97

	Player	Team	Salary ($)*
1	Mario Lemieux	Pittsburgh Penguins	11,321,429
2	Mark Messier	New York Rangers	6,000,000
3	Wayne Gretsky	New York Rangers	5,047,500
4	Pavel Bure	Vancouver Canucks	5,000,000
5	Pat Lafontaine	Buffalo Sabres	4,600,000
6	Patrick Roy	Colorado Avalanche	4,455,944
7	Brett Hull	St. Louis Blues	4,400,000
8=	Sergei Fedorov	Detroit Red Wings	4,200,000
8=	Dominik Hasek	Buffalo Sabres	4,200,000
10	Eric Lindros	Philadelphia Flyers	4,182,000

* Salaries take into account base salary and deferred payments. Signing bonuses are not included.

Source: NHL Players' Association

GOAL-SCORERS IN AN NHL CAREER*

	Player	Seasons	Goals
1	Wayne Gretzky#	18	862
2	Gordie Howe	26	801
3	Marcel Dionne	18	731
4	Phil Esposito	18	717
5	Mike Gartner#	18	696
6	Mario Lemieux#	12	613
7	Bobby Hull	16	610
8	Jari Kurri#	16	596
9	Dino Ciccarelli#	17	586
10	Mark Messier#	17	575

* Regular season only
\# Still active at end of 1996-97 season

Mario Lemieux is the only player in this list to have scored all of his goals for one team – the Pittsburgh Pirates – during a twelve-year career, which came to an end at the close of the 1996–97 season with the announcement of his retirement. The team with the most scorers on this list is the New York Rangers with five.

ASSISTS IN AN NHL CAREER*

	Player	Seasons	Assists
1	Wayne Gretzky#	18	1,883
2	Paul Coffey#	17	1,058
3	Gordie Howe	26	1,049
4	Marcel Dionne	18	1,040
5	Ray Bourque#	18	1,001
6	Mark Messier#	18	977
7	Ron Francis#	16	943
8	Stan Mikita	22	926
9	Bryan Trottier	18	901
10	Dale Hawerchuk#	16	891

* Regular season only
\# Still active at end of 1996–97 season

Gretzky heads both this list and that of top goalscorers. Of his total of 862 goals, he scored the bulk (583) during his career with the Edmonton Oilers. Following his trade to the Los Angeles Kings, he scored a further 231 goals, before moving to the New York Rangers, where he netted 48 goals.

TEAMS WITH THE MOST STANLEY CUP WINS

	Team	Wins
1	Montreal Canadiens	23
2	Toronto Maple Leafs	13
3	Detroit Red Wings	7
4=	Boston Bruins	5
4=	Edmonton Oilers	5
6=	New York Islanders	4
6=	New York Rangers	4
8	Chicago Black Hawks	3
9=	Philadelphia Flyers	2
9=	Pittsburgh Penguins	2

During his time as Governor General of Canada from 1888 to 1893, Sir Frederick Arthur Stanley (Lord Stanley of Preston and 16th Earl of Derby) became interested in what is called hockey in the United States, and ice hockey elsewhere, and in 1893 presented a trophy to be contested by the best amateur teams in Canada. The first trophy went to the Montreal Amateur Athletic Association, who won it without a challenge from any other team.

SOCCER – THE WORLD CUP

TOP 10

HIGHEST-SCORING WORLD CUP FINALS

	Year	Games	Goals	Average per game
1	1954	26	140	5.38
2	1938	18	84	4.66
3	1934	17	70	4.11
4	1950	22	88	4.00
5	1930	18	70	3.88
6	1958	35	126	3.60
7	1970	32	95	2.96
8	1982	52	146	2.81
9=	1962	32	89	2.78
9=	1966	32	89	2.78

TOP 10

HIGHEST-SCORING MATCHES IN THE FINAL STAGES OF THE WORLD CUP

	Match/year	Score
1	Austria vs. Switzerland, 1954	7–5
2=	Brazil vs. Poland, 1938	6–5
2=	Hungary vs. W. Germany, 1954	8–3
2=	Hungary vs. El Salvador, 1982	10–1
5	France vs. Paraguay, 1958	7–3
6=	Hungary vs. South Korea, 1954	9–0
6=	W. Germany vs. Turkey, 1954	7–2
6=	France vs. W. Germany, 1958	6–3
6=	Yugoslavia vs. Zaïre, 1974	9–0
10=	Italy vs. US, 1934	7–1
10=	Sweden vs. Cuba, 1938	8–0
10=	Uruguay vs. Bolivia, 1950	8–0
10=	England vs. Belgium, 1954	4–4
10=	Portugal vs. North Korea, 1966	5–3

TOP 10

GOAL SCORERS IN THE FINAL STAGES OF THE WORLD CUP

	Player/country/years	Goals
1	Gerd Müller (W. Germany), 1970–74	14
2	Just Fontaine (France), 1958	13
3	Pelé (Brazil), 1958–70	12
4	Sandor Kocsis (Hungary), 1954	11
5=	Helmut Rahn (W. Germany), 1954–58	10
5=	Teófilo Cubillas (Peru), 1970–78	10
5=	Grzegorz Lato (Poland), 1974–82	10
5=	Gary Lineker (England), 1986–90	10
9=	Leónidas da Silva (Brazil), 1934–38	9
9=	Ademir Marques de Menezes (Brazil), 1950	9
9=	Vavà (Brazil), 1958–62	9
9=	Eusébio (Portugal), 1966	9
9=	Uwe Seeler (W. Germany), 1958–70	9
9=	Jairzinho (Brazil), 1970–74	9
9=	Paolo Rossi (Italy), 1978–82	9
9=	Karl-Heinz Rummenigge (W. Germany), 1978–86	9

TOP 10

COUNTRIES THAT HAVE PLAYED THE MOST MATCHES IN THE FINAL STAGES OF THE WORLD CUP

	Country	Tournaments	Matches played
1=	Brazil	15	73
1=	Germany/West Germany	13	73
3	Italy	13	61
4	Argentina	11	52
5	England	9	41
6=	Uruguay	9	37
6=	Spain	9	37
6=	Sweden	9	37
9=	France	9	34
9=	USSR/Russia	8	34

TOP 10

HOST NATIONS IN THE WORLD CUP

	Host	Year	Final Standing
1=	Uruguay	1930	Winners
1=	Italy	1934	Winners
1=	England	1966	Winners
1=	West Germany	1974	Winners
1=	Argentina	1978	Winners
6=	Brazil	1950	Runners-up
6=	Sweden	1958	Runners-up
8=	Chile	1962	Third
8=	Italy	1990	Third
10=	France	1938	Last 8
10=	Switzerland	1954	Last 8
10=	Mexico	1970	Last 8
10=	Mexico	1986	Last 8

Spain in 1982 (last 12) and United States in 1994 (last 16) are the only two hosts not to have reached the last eight.

THE 10

LEAST-SUCCESSFUL COUNTRIES IN THE WORLD CUP

	Country	Tournaments	Matches played	won
1	Bulgaria	5	16	0
2	South Korea	4	11	0
3=	El Salvador	2	6	0
3=	Bolivia	3	6	0
5	Republic of Ireland	1	5	0
6	Egypt	2	4	0
7=	Canada	1	3	0
7=	Greece	1	3	0
7=	Haiti	1	3	0
7=	Iraq	1	3	0
7=	New Zealand	1	3	0
7=	United Arab Emirates	1	3	0
7=	Zaïre	1	3	0

THE WORLD CUP

Launched in 1930, credit for the inauguration of the tournament goes to former FIFA president Jules Rimet, who lent his name to the trophy that was first won by Uruguay on home soil. Thirteen nations competed in the first tournament, in marked contrast to the 176 countries attempting to qualify for the 1998 tournament in France. The most dominant nation has been Brazil, who won the first of their four trophies in 1958. After winning the title for the third time in 1970, they became the permanent holders of the Jules Rimet trophy, and, four years later, West Germany became the first nation to capture the new FIFA World Cup trophy.

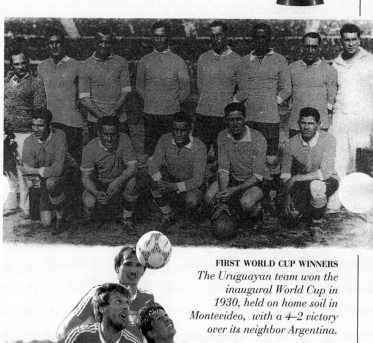

FIRST WORLD CUP WINNERS
The Uruguayan team won the inaugural World Cup in 1930, held on home soil in Montevideo, with a 4–2 victory over its neighbor Argentina.

TOP 10

COUNTRIES IN THE WORLD CUP*

	Country	Win	R/u	3rd	4th	Total
1	Germany/W. Germany	3	3	2	1	26
2	Brazil	4	1	2	1	24
3	Italy	3	2	1	1	21
4	Argentina	2	2	-	-	14
5	Uruguay	2	-	-	2	10
6	Sweden	-	1	2	1	8
7=	Czechoslovakia	-	2	-	-	6
7=	Hungary	-	2	-	-	6
7=	Netherlands	-	2	-	-	6
10=	England	1	-	-	1	5
10=	France	-	-	2	1	5

* Based on 4 pts for winning the tournament, 3 pts for runner-up, 2 pts for 3rd place, and 1 pt for 4th, up to and including 1994 World Cup

GARY'S HAT TRICK
England appeared destined to exit the 1986 World Cup finals in Mexico until Gary Lineker scored three goals against Poland.

GERMAN WIN
Victory for West Germany over Argentina in 1990 was sweet revenge for their defeat four years earlier.

PELÉ THE CONQUEROR
Pelé, considered the world's greatest player, is seen here in action in what is regarded as the greatest ever World Cup final, Brazil vs. Italy, 1970.

CYCLING

MOST SUCCESSFUL OLYMPIC CYCLING COUNTRIES

	Country	Medals gold	silver	bronze	total
1	France	32	18	21	71
2	Italy	30	15	6	51
3	Great Britain	8	21	16	45
4	Germany/W Germany	7	12	14	33
5	Holland	10	12	5	27
6	USSR/Russia	12	5	9	26
7	Belgium	6	6	9	21
8=	Denmark	6	7	7	20
8=	Australia	5	7	8	20
10=	East Germany	7	6	4	17
10=	US	4	4	9	17

Although it is the most successful country, France has not won a gold medal since Daniel Morelon won the sprint title in 1972.

LONGEST *TOURS DE FRANCE*

	Winner/nationality	Year	Stages	Distance km	miles
1	Lucien Buysse (Belgium)	1926	17	5,745	3,570
2	Firmin Lambot (Belgium)	1919	15	5,560	3,455
3	Gustave Garrigou (France)	1911	15	5,544	3,445
4	Philippe Thys (Belgium)	1920	15	5,503	3,419
5	Léon Scieur (Belgium)	1921	15	5,484	3,408
6	Ottavio Bottecchia (Italy)	1925	18	5,430	3,374
7	Ottavio Bottecchia (Italy)	1924	15	5,427	3,372
8	Philippe Thys (Belgium)	1914	15	5,414	3,364
9	Philippe Thys (Belgium)	1913	15	5,387	3,347
10	Henri Pélissier (France)	1923	15	5,386	3,347

The Tour de France is considered both the most important cycle stage race and the sporting event that attracts the largest live audience in the world. It was founded in 1903 by Henri Desgrange, a cyclist who was the first holder of the world one-hour record. He later became editor of the specialist cycling newspaper *L'Auto*, and the race was originally staged to publicize it. The first race covered 1,510 miles/2,428 km and was held over six extremely long stages, some involving riding through the night. The inaugural race was won by an Italian-born but naturalized Frenchman, a chimney sweep called Maurice Garin, who won by a remarkable 2 hours 49 minutes, the biggest ever winning margin in the race. The longest postwar race was in 1948 when Italy's Gino Bartali won the 3,058-mile/4,922-km race. The shortest ever race was the second Tour in 1904, and measured just 1,484 miles/2,388 km. The winner was Henri Cornet of France.

CYCLISTS WITH THE MOST CLASSIC RACE WINS

	Cyclist/country	Wins
1	Eddy Merckx (Belgium)	38
2	Bernard Hinault (France)	23
3	Fausto Coppi (Italy)	20
4	Kacqiues Anquetil (France)	19
5=	Alfredo Binda (Italy)	14
5=	Roger De Vlaeminck (Belgium)	14
7	Rik van Looy (Belgium)	13
8=	Gino Bartali (Italy)	12
8=	Felice Gimondi (Italy)	12
10=	Rik van Steenbergen (Belgium)	11
10=	Sean Kelly (Ireland)	11

The Classic races are the three major tours of France, Italy, and Spain, the Grand Prix des Nations, World Championship Road Race, and other prestigious road races including the Paris–Brussels, Paris–Roubaix, and Tour of Lombardy.

COUNTRIES WITH MOST *TOUR DE FRANCE* WINNERS

	Country	Winners
1	France	36
2	Belgium	18
3=	Italy	8
3=	Spain	8
5	Luxembourg	4
6	US	3
7=	Switzerland	2
7=	Holland	2
9=	Denmark	1
9=	Ireland	1

In 1991 Brazil became the 19th nation to win a stage in the tour.

T O P 1 0

TOWNS AND CITIES MOST VISITED BY CYCLISTS DURING THE *TOUR DE FRANCE*

	Town/city	No. of visits
1	Paris	78
2	Bordeaux	72
3	Pau	48
4	Luçon	47
5	Nice	34
6=	Bayon	32
6=	Perpignan	32
8	Marseilles	30
9	Briançon	29
10	Brest	28

T O P 1 0

TOUR DE FRANCE WINS

	Cyclist/country	Wins
1=	Jacques Anquetil (France)	5
1=	Eddy Merckx (Belgium)	5
1=	Bernard Hinault (France)	5
1=	Miguel Indurain (Spain)	5
5=	Philippe Thys (Belgium)	3
5=	Louison Bobet (France)	3
5=	Greg LeMond (US)	3
8=	Lucien Petit-Breton (France)	2
8=	Firmin Lambot (Belgium)	2
8=	Ottavio Bottecchia (Italy)	2
8=	Nicholas Frantz (Luxembourg)	2
8=	André Leducq (France)	2
8=	Antonin Magne (France)	2
8=	Gino Bartali (Italy)	2
8=	Sylvere Maës (Belgium)	2
8=	Fausto Coppi (Italy)	2
8=	Bernard Thevenet (France)	2
8=	Laurent Fignon (France)	2

Gino Bartali won the race in 1938 and 1948 and is the only man to win both before and after World War II.

ON YOUR BIKE

Perhaps because its introduction was gradual and informal, rather than based on a single invention, the precise origin of the mountain bike is hotly debated, but it seems probable that it dates from 1973. In that year, a group of cycling enthusiasts in Cupertino, California, began customizing road cycles to use them off-road. Shortly afterward, another group of road race devotees in Marin County, California, known as the Canyon Gang, started riding off-road in the Mt. Tamalpais area, using bicycles with balloon tires. Influenced by contact with the Cupertino group, they and other followers made further modifications to their bikes, progressively establishing the features that have since become familiar as mountain biking has become an internationally popular recreation and sport.

25 YEARS AGO · YEARS AGO · YEARS AGO ·

T O P 1 0

FASTEST AVERAGE WINNING SPEEDS IN THE *TOUR DE FRANCE*

	Winner/country/year	Average speed kph	mph
1	Bjarne Rijs (Denmark), 1996	39.969	24.841
2	Miguel Indurain (Spain), 1992	39.504	24.551
3	Miguel Indurain (Spain), 1995	39.193	24.359
4	Pedro Delgado (Spain), 1988	39.142	24.322
5	Miguel Indurain (Spain), 1991	39.021	24.247
6	Greg LeMond (US), 1990	38.933	24.192
7	Miguel Indurain (Spain), 1993	38.709	24.058
8	Miguel Indurain (Spain), 1994	38.383	23.855
9	Bernard Hinault (France), 1981	37.844	23.515
10	Greg LeMond (US), 1989	37.818	23.499

T O P 1 0

TOURS DE FRANCE WITH THE MOST FINISHERS

	Year	Starters	Finishers
1	1991	198	158
2	1990	198	156
3	1988	198	151
4	1989	198	148
5	1985	180	144
6	1993	180	136
7	1987	207	135
8	1986	210	132
9	1992	198	130
10	1996	198	129

The first time 100 riders finished the Tour was in 1970, when exactly 100 of the 150 starters reached Paris.

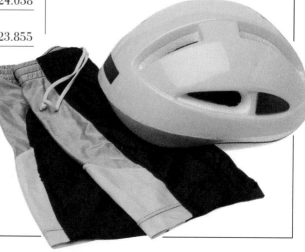

MOTOR RACING

DRIVERS WITH THE MOST GRAND PRIX WINS

	Driver/country	Years	Wins
1	Alain Prost (France)	1981–93	51
2	Ayrton Senna (Brazil)	1985–93	41
3	Nigel Mansell (UK)	1985–94	31
4	Jackie Stewart (UK)	1965–73	27
5=	Jim Clark (UK)	1962–68	25
5=	Niki Lauda (Austria)	1974–85	25
7	Juan Manuel Fangio (Argentina)	1950–57	24
8	Nelson Piquet (Brazil)	1980–91	23
9	Michael Schumacher (Germany)	1992–96	22
10	Damon Hill (UK)	1993–96	21

RACING RIVALS
At the end of the 1996 season, just one win separated the new World Champion Damon Hill (right) and Michael Schumacher (left).

DRIVERS WITH THE BEST WIN/RACE RATIO IN FORMULA ONE

	Driver (Country)	Wins	Races	Ratio
1	Juan Manuel Fangio (Argentina)	24	51	47.05
2	Alberto Ascari (Italy)	13	32	40.62
3	Jim Clark (UK)	25	72	34.72
4	Damon Hill (UK)	21	69	30.43
5	Jacques Villeneuve (Canada)	5	18	27.77
6	Jackie Stewart (UK)	27	99	27.27
7	Alain Prost (France)	51	199	25.63
8	Michael Schumacher (Germany)	22	87	25.29
9	Ayrton Senna (Brazil)	41	161	25.47
10	Stirling Moss (UK)	16	66	24.24

MANUFACTURERS WITH THE MOST WORLD TITLES

	Manufacturer	Titles
1=	Ferrari	8
1=	Williams	8
3	Lotus	7
4	McLaren	6
5=	Brabham	2
5=	Cooper	2
7=	BRM	1
7=	Matra	1
7=	Tyrrell	1
7=	Vanwall	1
7=	Benetton	1

DRIVERS WITH THE MOST GRAND PRIX POINTS

	Driver/country	Years	Points
1	Alain Prost (France)	1980–93	798.5
2	Ayrton Senna (Brazil)	1985–94	614
3	Nelson Piquet (Brazil)	1978–91	485.5
4	Nigel Mansell (UK)	1980–94	482
5	Niki Lauda (Austria)	1971–85	420.5
6	Michael Schumacher (Germany)	1991–96	361
7	Jackie Stewart (UK)	1965–73	360
8	Gerhard Berger (Austria)	1984–95	338
9	Damon Hill (UK)	1993-96	326
10	Carlos Reutemann (Argentina)	1972–82	310

DRIVERS WITH THE LONGEST FORMULA ONE CAREERS

	Driver	Career length years	months
1	Graham Hill	16	8
2	Riccardo Patrese	16	5
3	Jack Brabham	15	3
4	Nigel Mansell	14	9
5	Joe Bonnier	14	8
6	Maurice Trintignant	14	4
7	Niki Lauda	14	3
8	Andrea de Cesaris	14	1
9	Mario Andretti	13	11
10	Michele Alboreto	13	6

McLaren had their 104th win in 1993 when Ayrton Senna won at Monaco. The McLaren team was first formed in 1963 by New Zealander Bruce McLaren and ventured into Formula One in 1966. McLaren's first Grand Prix did not come until the 1968 Belgian Grand Prix. The team suffered a great loss in 1970 when McLaren was killed during a training session at Goodwood.

By coming into the list at No.9, Damon Hill has pushed his father Graham into 11th place and off the list for the first time. The World Drivers' Championship was launched in 1950, and over the years the format has changed allowing, in many cases, for only a certain number of successful drives to be taken into consideration.

The Top 10 takes into account the gap between a driver's first and last Grand Prix. Periods of "retirement" and inactivity are also included.

TOP 10

DRIVERS WITH THE MOST WORLD TITLES

	Driver/country	Titles		Driver/country	Titles
1	Juan Manuel Fangio (Argentina)	5	**3=**	Jackie Stewart (UK)	3
2	Alain Prost (France)	4	**8=**	Alberto Ascari (Italy)	2
3=	Jack Brabham (Australia)	3	**8=**	Jim Clark (UK)	2
3=	Niki Lauda (Austria)	3	**8=**	Graham Hill (UK)	2
3=	Nelson Piquet (Brazil)	3	**8=**	Emerson Fittipaldi (Brazil)	2
3=	Ayrton Senna (Brazil)	3	**8=**	Michael Schumacher (Germany)	2

TOP 10

YOUNGEST WORLD CHAMPIONS OF ALL TIME

	Driver/country	Year	Age* yrs	Age* mths
1	Emerson Fittipaldi (Brazil)	1972	25	9
2	Michael Schumacher (Germany)	1994	25	10
3	Niki Lauda (Austria)	1975	26	7
4	Jim Clark (UK)	1963	27	7
5	Jochen Rindt (Austria)	1970	28	6
6	Ayrton Senna (Brazil)	1988	28	7
7=	James Hunt (UK)	1976	29	2
7=	Nelson Piquet (Brazil)	1981	29	2
9	Mike Hawthorn (UK)	1958	29	6
10	Jody Scheckter (South Africa)	1979	29	8

* If a driver can appear twice, only his youngest age is considered

TOP 10

OLDEST WORLD CHAMPIONS OF ALL TIME

	Driver/country	Year	Age* yrs	Age* mths
1	Juan Manuel Fangio (Argentina)	1957	46	2
2	Giuseppe Farina (Italy)	1950	43	11
3	Jack Brabham (Australia)	1966	40	6
4	Graham Hill (UK)	1968	39	9
5	Mario Andretti (US)	1978	38	8
6	Alain Prost (France)	1993	38	7
7	Nigel Mansell (UK)	1992	37	11
8	Damon Hill (UK)	1996	36	1
9	Niki Lauda (Austria)	1984	35	8
10	Nelson Piquet (Brazil)	1987	35	3

* If a driver can appear twice, only his oldest age is considered

THE WORLD LAND SPEED RECORD

The first world land speed record was set on December 18, 1898, when at Achères, France, Count Gaston de Chasseloup-Laubat drove a Jeantaud to a speed of 39.24 mph/62.78 km/h. Concerned that the sales of his vehicles would be affected, Belgian car manufacturer Camille Jenatzy set about smashing the record himself, which he did on January 17, 1899, taking it to 41.42 mph/66.27 km/h. Both men each broke the record on two further occasions during 1899, and by the end of the year it had reached 65.79 mph/105.26 km/h. The record was held until 1902, when Leon Serpollet attained 75.06 mph/120.09 km/h at Nice. The psychologically important mph "barriers" were then progressively broken: 100 mph in 1904, 200 mph in 1927, 300 mph in 1935, 400 mph in 1963, 500 mph in 1964, and 600 mph in 1965. The record currently stands at 633.47 mph/1,013.47 km/h – over 16 times as fast as Chasseloup-Laubat's original achievement.

100 YEARS AGO • YEARS AGO • YEARS AGO

TOP 10

MANUFACTURERS WITH THE MOST GRAND PRIX WINS

	Manufacturer	Years	Wins
1	Ferrari	1951–96	108
2	McLaren	1968–93	104
3	Williams	1979–96	95
4	Lotus	1960–87	79
5	Brabham	1964–85	35
6	Benetton	1986–95	25
7	Tyrrell	1971–83	23
8	BRM	1959–72	17
9	Cooper	1958–67	16
10	Renault	1979–83	15

CAR RACING

T O P 1 0

FASTEST WINNING SPEEDS OF THE INDIANAPOLIS 500

	Driver*	Car	Year	Speed km/h	mph
1	Arie Luyendyk (Netherlands)	Lola-Chevrolet	1990	299.307	185.984
2	Rick Mears	Chevrolet-Lumina	1991	283.980	176.457
3	Bobby Rahal	March-Cosworth	1986	274.750	170.722
4	Emerson Fittipaldi (Brazil)	Penske-Chevrolet	1989	269.695	167.581
5	Rick Mears	March-Cosworth	1984	263.308	163.612
6	Mark Donohue	McLaren-Offenhauser	1972	262.619	162.962
7	Al Unser, Jr.	March-Cosworth	1987	260.995	162.175
8	Tom Sneva	March-Cosworth	1983	260.902	162.117
9	Gordon Johncock	Wildcat-Cosworth	1982	260.760	162.029
10	Al Unser	Lola-Cosworth	1978	259.689	161.363

* All US drivers unless otherwise stated

The first Indianapolis 500, known affectionately as the "Indy," was held on Memorial Day, May 30, 1911, and was won by Ray Harroun driving a bright yellow 447-cubic-inch six-cylinder Marmon Wasp at an average speed of 74.602 mph/120.060 km/h. The race takes place over 200 laps of the 2½-mile Indianapolis Raceway, which from 1927 to 1945 was owned by the World War I flying ace Eddie Rickenbacker. Over the years the speed has steadily increased: Harroun's race took 6 hours 42 minutes 6 seconds to complete, while Arie Luyendyk's record-breaking win was achieved in just 2 hours 18 minutes 18.248 seconds.

T O P 1 0

WINNERS OF THE INDIANAPOLIS 500 WITH THE HIGHEST STARTING POSITIONS

	Driver	Year	Starting position
1=	Ray Harroun	1911	28
1=	Louis Meyer	1936	28
3	Fred Frame	1932	27
4	Johnny Rutherford	1974	25
5=	Kelly Petillo	1935	22
5=	George Souders	1927	22
7	L.L. Corum and Joe Boyer	1924	21
8=	Frank Lockart	1926	20
8=	Tommy Milton	1921	20
8=	Al Unser, Jr.	1987	20

Of the 75 winners of the Indianapolis 500, 44 have started from a position between 1 and 5 on the starting grid. This Top 10 lists those winners who started the race from farthest back in the starting lineup.

T O P 1 0

MONEY-WINNERS AT THE INDIANAPOLIS 500 IN 1996

	Driver	Car	Total prizes ($)
1	Buddy Lazier	Reynard/Ford Cosworth	1,367,854
2	Davy Jones	Lola/Mercedes Illmor	632,503
3	Richie Hearn	Reynard/Ford Cosworth	375,203
4	Roberto Guerrero	Reynard/Ford Cosworth	315,503
5	Alessandro Zampedri	Lola/Ford Cosworth	270,853
6	Hideshi Matsuda	Lola/Ford Cosworth	233,953
7	Danny Ongais	Lola/Menard V6	228,253
8	Eliseo Salazar	Lola/Ford Cosworth	226,653
9	Scott Sharp	Lola/Ford Cosworth	202,053
10	Robbie Buhl	Lola/Ford Cosworth	195,403

Drivers are ranked here according to their prize money, which in 1996 totaled $8,114,600. Even losers can be high-earners in the Indy: Johnny Unser, who finished in 33rd and last position, earned $143,953. The only woman in the race, Lyn St. James, placed 14th in the money-winners with $182,603.

T O P 1 0

DRIVERS WITH THE MOST WINSTON CUP TITLES

	Driver	Years	Victories	Titles
1=	Richard Petty	1964–79	200	7
1=	Dale Earnhardt	1980–94	68	7
3=	Lee Petty	1954–59	54	3
3=	David Pearson	1966–69	106	3
3=	Cale Yarborough	1976–78	83	3
3=	Darrell Waltrip	1981–85	84	3
7=	Herb Thomas	1951–53	49	2
7=	Tim Flock	1952–55	40	2
7=	Buck Baker	1956–57	46	2
7=	Ned Jarrett	1961–65	50	2
7=	Joe Weatherly	1962–63	24	2

The Winston Cup is a season-long series of races organized by the National Association of Stock Car Auto Racing, Inc. (NASCAR). Races, which take place over enclosed circuits, are among the most popular car races in the US. The series started in 1949 as the Grand National series, but changed its title to the Winston Cup in 1970.

TOP 10

FASTEST WINNING SPEEDS OF THE DAYTONA 500

	Driver*	Car	Year	Speed km/h	mph
1	Buddy Baker	Oldsmobile	1980	285.823	177.602
2	Bill Elliott	Ford	1987	283.668	176.263
3	Bill Elliott	Ford	1985	277.234	172.265
4	Richard Petty	Buick	1981	273.027	169.651
5	Derrike Cope	Chevrolet	1990	266.766	165.761
6	A.J. Foyt, Jr.	Mercury	1972	259.990	161.550
7	Richard Petty	Plymouth	1966	258.504	160.627#
8	Davey Allison	Ford	1992	257.913	160.260
9	Bobby Allison	Ford	1978	257.060	159.730
10	LeeRoy Yarborough	Ford	1967	254.196	157.950

* All drivers from the US
# Race reduced to 495 miles/797 km

First held in 1959, the Daytona 500 is raced every February at the Daytona International Speedway, Daytona Beach, Florida. One of the most prestigious races of the NASCAR season, it covers 200 laps of the 2½-mile high-banked oval circuit. The race has produced its share of exciting racing, as in 1988 when Bobby Allinson, the winner in 1978 and 1982, driving a Buick, beat his son Davey Allison in a Ford into second place by a margin of just two car lengths. The fastest speed recorded in the Top 10, that of Buddy Baker in 1980, also produced the shortest full-length race time, of 2 hrs 48 min 55 secs, compared with the slowest-ever winning time of 4 hrs 30 min in 1960, when the race was won by Junior Johnson in a Chevrolet at an average speed of 124.740 mph/200.750 km/h.

THE 10

SLOWEST WINNING SPEEDS OF THE INDIANAPOLIS 500

	Winner/year	Average speed km/h	mph
1	Ray Harroun, 1911	120.060	74.602
2	Jules Goux, 1913	122.202	75.933
3	Joe Dawson, 1912	126.686	78.719
4	Rene Thomas, 1914	132.735	82.474
5	Dario Resta, 1916	135.187	84.001
6	Howard Wilcox, 1919	141.703	88.050
7	Gaston Chevrolet, 1920	142.617	88.618
8	Ralph DePalma, 1915	143.296	89.040
9	Tommy Milton, 1921	144.231	89.621
10	Tommy Milton, 1923	146.376	90.954

The speed of the Indianapolis 500 has steadily increased. The 100 mph (161 km/h) barrier was broken in 1930 by Billy Arnold, who won at an average speed of 100.448 mph (161.655 km/h).

TOP 10

NASCAR MONEY-WINNERS OF ALL TIME*

	Driver	Total prizes ($)
1	Dale Earnhardt	28,617,845
2	Bill Elliott	16,591,529
3	Darrell Waltrip	15,391,155
4	Terry Labonte	15,049,797
5	Rusty Wallace	14,788,069
6	Mark Martin	12,234,017
7	Ricky Rudd	11,871,803
8	Jeff Gordon	11,074,328
9	Geoff Bodine	10,733,939
10	Sterling Martin	9,288,581

* Up to and including April 6th, 1997 Interstate Batteries 500 race in Fort Worth, TX

Source: NASCAR (National Association of Stock Car Auto Racing, Inc.)

TOP 10

CART DRIVERS WITH THE MOST RACE WINS

	Driver/race career	Wins
1	A.J. Foyt, Jr. (1960-1981)	67
2	Mario Andretti (1965-1993)	52
3	Al Unser (1965-1987)	39
4	Bobby Unser (1966-1981)	35
5	Michael Andretti (1986-1996)	35
6	Al Unser Jr. (1984-1995)	31
7	Rick Mears (1978-1991)	29
8	Johnny Rutherford (1965-1986)	27
9	Roger Ward (1953-1966)	26
10	Gordon Johncock (1965-1983)	25

Source: Championship Auto Racing Teams

THE 10

LAST DRIVERS KILLED DURING THE INDIANAPOLIS 500

	Driver	Year
1	Swede Savage	1973
2=	Eddie Sachs	1964
2=	Dave MacDonald	1964
4	Pat O'Connor	1958
5	Bill Vukovich Sr.	1955
6	Carl Scarborough	1953
7	Shorty Cantlon	1947
8	Floyd Roberts	1939
9	Clay Weatherly	1935
10=	Mark Billman	1933
10=	Lester Spangle	1933

WINTER SPORTS

WINTER OLYMPIC MEDAL-WINNING NATIONS

	Country	G	S	B	Total
1	Russia/ Former USSR	99	71	71	241
2	Norway	73	77	64	214
3	US	53	55	39	147
4	Austria	36	48	44	128
5	West Germany/ Germany	45	43	37	125
6	Finland	36	45	42	123
7	East Germany	39	36	35	110
8	Sweden	39	26	34	99
9	Switzerland	27	29	29	85
10	Italy	25	21	21	67

The United States' first Winter Olympics gold medal was won at Chamonix in 1924 by Charles Jewtraw in the 500-meter speed skating event, the first event at the first ever Winter Olympics. Since that victory, the US has enjoyed considerable success at the Winter Olympics, especially in ice hockey. In 1960, at Squaw Valley, they took the gold medal after beating the pre-tournament favorites Canada and then defending champions the Soviet Union. Twenty years later, at Lake Placid, they beat the Soviets as they clinched their second ice hockey gold.

DOWNHILL RACER
Ski races have been held since the last century, but have developed as major Olympic and World events in the 20th century along with the international growth of interest in the sport.

ALPINE SKIING WORLD CUP TITLES – MEN

	Name/country	Years	Titles
1	Marc Girardelli (Luxembourg)	1985–93	5
2=	Gustavo Thoeni (Italy)	1971–75	4
2=	Pirmin Zurbriggen (Switzerland)	1984–90	4
4=	Ingemar Stenmark (Sweden)	1976–78	3
4=	Phil Mahre (US)	1981–83	3
6=	Jean-Claude Killy (France)	1967–68	2
6=	Karl Schranz (Austria)	1969–70	2
8=	Piero Gross (Italy)	1974	1
8=	Peter Lüscher (Switzerland)	1979	1
8=	Andreas Wenzel (Leichtenstein)	1980	1
8=	Paul Accola (Switzerland)	1992	1
8=	Kjetil Andre Aaamodt (Norway)	1994	1
8=	Alberto Tomba (Italy)	1995	1

The Alpine Skiing World Cup was launched as an annual event in 1967. Points are awarded for performances over a series of selected races during the winter months at meetings worldwide.

ALPINE SKIING WORLD CUP TITLES – WOMEN

	Name/country	Years	Titles
1	Annemarie Moser-Pröll (Austria)	1971–79	6
2=	Vreni Schneider (Switzerland)	1989–95	3
2=	Petra Kronberger (Austria)	1990–92	3
4=	Nancy Greene (Canada)	1967–68	2
4=	Hanni Wenzel (Liechtenstein)	1978–80	2
4=	Erika Hess (Switzerland)	1982–84	2
4=	Michela Figini (Switzerland)	1985–88	2
4=	Maria Walliser (Switzerland)	1986–87	2
9=	Gertrude Gabl (Austria)	1969	1
9=	Michèle Jacot (France)	1970	1
9=	Rosi Mittermeier (West Germany)	1976	1
9=	Lise-Marie Morerod (Switzerland)	1977	1
9=	Marie-Thérèse Nadig (Switzerland)	1981	1
9=	Tamara McKinney (US)	1983	1
9=	Anita Wachter (Austria)	1993	1
9=	Kajta Seizinger (Germany)	1996	1

TOP 10

WORLD AND OLYMPIC FIGURE SKATING TITLES – MEN

	Skater/country	Years	Titles
1	Ulrich Salchow (Sweden)	1901–11	11
2	Karl Schäfer (Austria)	1930–36	9
3	Dick Button (US)	1948–52	7
4	Gillis Grafstrom (Sweden)	1920–29	6
5=	Hayes Jenkins (US)	1953–56	5
5=	Scott Hamilton (US)	1981–84	5
7=	Willy Bockl (Austria)	1925–28	4
7=	David Jenkins (US)	1957–60	4
7=	Ondrej Nepela (Czechoslovakia)	1971–73	4
7=	Kurt Browning (Canada)	1989–93	4

TOP 10

WORLD AND OLYMPIC FIGURE SKATING TITLES – WOMEN

	Skater/country	Years	Titles
1	Sonja Henie (Norway)	1927–36	13
2=	Carol Heiss (US)	1956–60	6
2=	Herma Planck Szabo (Austria)	1922–26	6
2=	Katarina Witt (East Germany)	1984–88	6
5=	Lily Kronberger (Hungary)	1908–11	4
5=	Sjoukje Dijkstra (Netherlands)	1962–64	4
5=	Peggy Fleming (US)	1966–68	4
8=	Meray Horvath (Hungary)	1912–14	3
8=	Tenley Albright (US)	1953–56	3
8=	Annett Poetzsch (East Gemany)	1978–80	3
8=	Beatrix Schuba (Austria)	1971–72	3
8=	Barbara Ann Scott (Canada)	1947–48	3
8=	Kristi Yamaguchi (US)	1991–92	3
8=	Madge Sayers (UK)	1906–08	3

TOP 10

OLYMPIC BOBSLEDDING NATIONS

	Country	G	S	B	Total
1	Switzerland	9	8	8	25
2	Germany/West Germany	4	5	6	15
3	US	5	4	5	14
4	East Germany	5	6	2	13
5	Italy	3	4	3	10
6=	Austria	1	2	0	3
6=	UK	1	1	1	3
6=	Former USSR	1	0	2	3
9	Belgium	0	1	1	2
10=	Canada	1	0	0	1
10=	Romania	0	0	1	1

TOP 10

WINNERS OF WORLD ICE DANCE TITLES

	Skater/country	Years	Titles
1=	Alexsandr Gorshkov (USSR)	1970–76	6
1=	Lyudmila Pakhomova (USSR)	1970–76	6
3=	Lawrence Demmy (UK)	1951–55	5
3=	Jean Westwood (UK)	1951–55	5
5=	Courtney Jones (UK)	1957–60	4
5=	Eva Romanova (Czechoslovakia)	1962–65	4
5=	Pavel Roman (Czechoslovakia)	1963–65	4
5=	Diane Towler (UK)	1966–69	4
5=	Bernard Ford (UK)	1966–69	4
5=	Jayne Torvill (UK)	1981–84	4
5=	Christopher Dean (UK)	1981–84	4
5=	Natalya Bestemianova (USSR)	1985–88	4
5=	Andrei Bukin (USSR)	1985–88	4
5=	Oksana Gritschuk (Rus)	1994-97	4
5=	Yevgeniy Platov (Rus)	1994-97	4

TOP 10

FASTEST WINNING TIMES OF THE IDITAROD DOG SLED RACE

	Winner*/year		Time		
		day	hr	min	sec
1	Doug Swingley, 1995	9	2	42	19
2	Jeff King, 1996	9	5	43	19
3	Martin Buser, Switzerland, 1997	9	8	30	45
4	Martin Buser, 1994	10	13	02	39
5	Jeff King, 1993	10	15	38	15
6	Martin Buser, 1992	10	19	17	15
7	Susan Butcher, 1990	11	01	53	28
8	Susan Butcher, 1987	11	02	05	13
9	Joe Runyan, 1989	11	05	24	34
10	Susan Butcher, 1988	11	11	41	40

* Players are from the US unless otherwise stated

Source: Iditarod Trail Committee

This race runs from Anchorage to Nome, Alaska. Iditarod is a deserted mining village along the route, and the race commemorates an operation in 1925 to get medical supplies to Nome following a diphtheria epidemic.

ON THE WATER

T O P   1 0

FASTEST WINNING TIMES OF THE OXFORD AND CAMBRIDGE BOAT RACE

	Year	Winner	Time
1	1984	Oxford	16.45
2	1976	Oxford	16.58
3	1991	Oxford	16.59
4	1985	Oxford	17.11
5	1990	Oxford	17.15
6=	1974	Oxford	17.35
6=	1988	Oxford	17.35
8	1992	Oxford	17.48
9	1948	Cambridge	17.50
10=	1971	Cambridge	17.58
10=	1986	Cambridge	17.58

The Boat Race was first rowed at Henley in 1829. The course from Putney to Mortlake (4 miles 374 yards/6.78 km) has been used since 1843 – although the race was rowed in the opposite direction in 1846, 1856, and 1863. There were two races in 1849, and the race has been rowed annually since 1856 except during the two world wars. Cambridge has won the race 70 times and still holds the record for the longest unbroken sequence of 13 wins from 1924 to 1936. Oxford has won on 68 occasions, and there was one dead heat in 1877. The heavier crew has won the race on 79 occasions, the lighter crew has won 53 races, and the crews have weighed the same four times (1870, 1876, 1890, and 1980). Cambridge sank in 1859 and 1978 and Oxford in 1925; both crews sank in 1912, and Oxford won when the race was rowed again a week later; Oxford sank near the start in 1951, and Cambridge won the re-row two days later. The most successful Boat Race oarsman is Boris Rankov; he won six races with Oxford. C.R.W. Tottenham coxed Oxford to five successive victories.

T O P   1 0

WINNERS OF THE MOST MEN'S WORLD WATER-SKIING TITLES

	Skier/nationality	Total wins
1	Patrice Martin (Fra)	8
2	Sammy Duval (USA)	6
3=	Alfredo Mendoza (USA)	5
3=	Mike Suyderhoud (USA)	5
3=	Bob La Point (USA)	5
6=	George Athans (Can)	3
6=	Guy de Clercq (Bel)	3
6=	Wayne Grimditch (USA)	3
6=	Mike Hazelwood (GB)	3
6=	Ricky McCormick (USA)	3
6=	Billy Spencer (USA)	3
6=	Andy Mapple (GB)	3

T O P   1 0

POWERBOAT OWNERS WITH MOST RACE WINS

	Owner	Years	Wins
1	Bernie Little*	1966–97	104
2	Bill Muncey	1976–81	29
3	Joe & Lee Schoenith	1952–72	27
4	Ole Bardahl	1958–68	27
5	Dave Heerensperger	1968–82	25
6	Fran Muncey	1982–88	24
7	Willard Rhodes	1956–63	18
8	Steve Woomer*	1984–96	14
9	Bill Waggoner	1956–59	12
10	George Simon	1955–76	12

Active as of June 1, 1997

T O P   1 0

WINNERS OF THE MOST WOMEN'S WORLD WATER-SKIING TITLES

	Skier/nationality	Total
1	Liz Shetter (*née* Allen) (USA)	11
2	Willa McGuire (*née* Worthington) (USA)	8
3	Cindy Todd (USA)	7
4	Deena Mapple (*née* Brush) (USA)	6
5=	Marina Doria (Swi)	4
5=	Natalya Ponomaryeva (*née* Rumyantseva) (USSR)	4
7=	Maria Victoria Carrasco (Ven)	3
7=	Tawn Larsen (USA)	3
7=	Helena Kjellander (Swe)	3
10=	Leah Marie Rawls (USA)	2
10=	Vickie Van Hook (USA)	2
10=	Sylvie Hulseman (Lux)	2
10=	Jeanette Brown (USA)	2
10=	Jeanette Stewart-Wood (GB)	2
10=	Christy Weir (USA)	2
10=	Evie Wolford (USA)	2
10=	Kim Laskoff (USA)	2
10=	Dany Duflot (Fra)	2
10=	Ana Marie Carasco (Ven)	2
10=	Nancie Rideout (USA)	2
10=	Renate Hansluvka (Aut)	2
10=	Karen Neville (Aus)	2

Stewart-Wood is the only British woman to win a world title.

OLYMPIC YACHTING COUNTRIES

	Country	gold	Medals silver	bronze	total
1	US	15	13	11	39
2	Great Britain	15	8	8	31
3	Sweden	9	11	9	29
4	Norway	14	11	2	27
5	France	9	6	9	24
6	Denmark	8	8	3	19
7	West Germany	5	5	6	16
8	USSR	4	5	4	13
9	Holland	4	4	4	12
10=	Australia	3	1	4	8
10=	Italy	2	1	5	8
10=	Finland	1	1	6	8
10=	New Zealand	5	1	2	8

Yachting has provided one of the Olympics' most durable competitors: Paul Elvström of Denmark. The first person to win gold medals at four consecutive games (1948–60), he went on to compete in an additional four Games in 1968, 1972, 1984, and 1988, when he was partnered by his daughter in the Tornado class.

SURFERS IN THE WORLD, 1996*

1	Kelly Slater (US)
2	Shane Beschen (US)
3	Sunny Garcia (US)
4	Luke Egan (Australia)
5	Kaipo Jaquias (US)
6	Taylor Know (US)
7	Kalani Robb (US)
8	Matt Hoy (Australia)
9	Michael Rommelse (Australia)
10	Rob Machado (US)

* According to the Association of Surfing Professionals

OLYMPIC ROWING COUNTRIES

	Country	gold	Medals silver	bronze	total
1	US	30	20	15	65
2	East Germany	33	7	8	48
3	USSR	12	20	11	43
4	West Germany	17	12	12	41
5	Great Britain	16	15	6	37
6	Italy	12	10	8	30
7	France	4	13	9	26
8=	Romania	8	6	6	20
8=	Switzerland	4	7	9	20
10	Canada	3	8	8	19

A member of the winning US eights team at the 1924 Paris Olympics was Benjamin Spock, who later became famous as the "baby expert," and whose book *The Common Sense Book of Baby and Child Care* has sold more than 39,200,000 copies worldwide.

OLYMPIC CANOEING COUNTRIES

	Country	gold	Medals silver	bronze	total
1	USSR	29	13	9	51
2	Hungary	7	19	16	42
3	Germany/ West Germany	8	14	10	32
4	East Germany	14	7	9	30
5	Romania	9	9	11	29
6	Sweden	13	8	2	23
7	France	1	5	10	16
8	Austria	3	6	5	14
9	Canada	3	6	4	13
10	Bulgaria	3	3	6	12

Canoeing has been an official Olympic sport since 1936, although it was first seen as a demonstration sport 12 years earlier.

SPORTS MISCELLANY

TV AUDIENCES OF ALL TIME FOR SPORTS EVENTS IN THE US

	Program	Date	TV households total	%
1	Super Bowl XVI (San Francisco *vs.* Cincinnati)	Jan 24, 1982	40,020,000	49.1
2	Super Bowl XVII (Washington *vs.* Miami)	Jan 30, 1983	40,500,000	48.6
3	XVII Winter Olympics	Feb 23, 1994	45,690,000	48.5
4	Super Bowl XX (Chicago *vs.* New England)	Jan 26, 1986	41,490,000	48.3
5	Super Bowl XII (Dallas *vs.* Denver)	Jan 15, 1978	34,410,000	47.2
6	Super Bowl XIII (Dallas *vs.* Pittsburgh)	Jan 21, 1979	35,090,000	47.1
7=	Super Bowl XVIII (LA Raiders *vs.* Washington)	Jan 22, 1984	38,800,000	46.4
7=	Super Bowl XIX (San Francisco *vs.* Miami)	Jan 20, 1985	39,390,000	46.4
9	Super Bowl XIV (LA Rams *vs.* Pittsburgh)	Jan 20, 1980	35,330,000	46.3
10	Super Bowl XXI (Giants *vs.* Denver)	Jan 25, 1987	40,030,000	45.8

Copyright © 1997 Nielsen Media Research

"TV households" indicates the number of households with TV sets: population growth and the acquisition of sets steadily increase this figure, so recent events attract higher audiences. Super Bowl XXX on January 28, 1996 attracted the greatest number of individual viewers of any US TV program ever, but a rating of only 41.3 keeps it outside this Top 10.

HIGHEST-EARNING SPORTSMEN* IN THE WORLD

	Name	Sport	Income 1996 ($)
1	Mike Tyson	Boxing	75,000,000
2	Michael Jordan	Basketball	52,600,000
3	Michael Schumacher (Germany)	Motor racing	33,000,000
4	Shaquille O'Neal	Basketball	24,400,000
5	Emmitt Smith	Football	16,500,000
6	Evander Holyfield	Boxing	15,500,000
7	Andre Agassi	Tennis	15,200,000
8	Arnold Palmer	Golf	15,100,000
9	Dennis Rodman	Basketball	12,900,000
10	Patrick Ewing	Basketball	12,400,000

* All from the US unless otherwise stated
Used by permission of Forbes Magazine

PARTICIPATION SPORTS, GAMES, AND PHYSICAL ACTIVITIES IN THE US

	Activity	Participants*
1	Exercise walking	70,794,000
2	Swimming	60,277,000
3	Fishing	51,992,000
4	Cycling	49,818,000
5	Exercising with equipment	43,784,000
6	Camping	42,932,000
7	Bowling	37,356,000
8	Billiards/pool	34,000,000
9	Basketball	28,191,000
10	Boating	26,400,000

* On more than one occasion
Source: National Sporting Goods Association

This survey indicated that the national game of baseball as a participation sport scored relatively low, with only 15,096,000 participants.

PARTICIPATION SPORTS, GAMES, AND PHYSICAL ACTIVITIES IN THE UK

	Activity	Percentage participating females	males
1	Walking	37	45
2	Snooker, pool, and billiards	5	21
3	Swimming	16	15
4	Cycling	7	14
5=	Darts	3	9
5=	Golf	2	9
5=	Weightlifting and training	3	9
8	Soccer	0	9
9	Running, jogging, etc.	2	7
10	Fitness and yoga	17	6

Based on interviews conducted in 1993–94, the percentages represent those who had participated in the activity in question during the four weeks prior to the interview. In that period, 72 percent of men and 57 percent of women had engaged in at least one sports or physical activity.

THE 10

MOST COMMON SPORTS INJURIES

	Common name	Medical term
1	Bruise	Soft tissue contusion
2	Sprained ankle	Sprain of the lateral ligament
3	Sprained knee	Sprain of the medial collateral ligament
4	Low back strain	Lumbar joint dysfunction
5	Hamstring tear	Muscle tear of the hamstring
6	Jumper's knee	Patella tendinitis
7	Achilles tendinitis	Tendinitis of the Achilles tendon
8	Shin splints	Medial periostitis of the tibia
9	Tennis elbow	Lateral epicondylitis
10	Shoulder strain	Rotator cuff tendinitis

THE 10

WORST DISASTERS AT SPORTS VENUES IN THE 20TH CENTURY

	Location	Disaster	Date	No. killed
1	Hong Kong Jockey Club	Stand collapse and fire	Feb 26, 1918	604
2	Lenin Stadium, Moscow, Russia	Crush in soccer stadium	Oct 20, 1982	340
3	Lima, Peru	Soccer stadium riot	May 24, 1964	320
4	Sinceljo, Colombia	Bullring stand collapse	Jan 20, 1980	222
5	Hillsborough, Sheffield, UK	Crush in soccer stadium	Apr 15, 1989	96
6	Guatemala City, Guatemala	Stampede in soccer stadium	Oct 16, 1996	83
7	Le Mans, France	Racing car crash	Jun 11, 1955	82
8	Katmandu, Nepal	Stampede in soccer stadium	Mar 12, 1988	80
9	Buenos Aires, Argentina	Riot in soccer stadium	May 23, 1968	74
10	Ibrox Park, Glasgow, UK	Barrier collapse in soccer stadium	Jan 2, 1971	66

If stunt-flying is included as a "sport," the worst airshow disaster of all time occurred at the Ramstein US base, Germany, on August 28, 1988, when three fighters collided, one of them crashing into the crowd, leaving 70 dead and 150 injured. Such tragedies are not an exclusively modern phenomenon: during the reign of Roman Emperor Antoninus Pius (AD 138–161), a stand at the Circus Maximus collapsed killing 1,162 spectators.

TOP 10

CATEGORIES OF ATHLETES WITH THE LARGEST* HEARTS

1	*Tour de France* cyclists
2	Marathon runners
3	Rowers
4	Boxers
5	Sprint cyclists
6	Middle-distance runners
7	Weightlifters
8	Swimmers
9	Sprinters
10	Decathletes

* *Based on average medical measurements*

The size of the heart of a person who engages regularly in a demanding sport enlarges according to the strenuousness involved in participating in the sport.

TOP 10

MOST EFFECTIVE FITNESS ACTIVITIES

1	Swimming
2	Cycling
3	Rowing
4	Gymnastics
5	Judo
6	Dancing
7	Football
8	Jogging
9	Walking (briskly)
10	Squash

These sports and activities are the best means of building stamina and strength, and of increasing suppleness.

TOP 10

MOVIES WITH SPORTS THEMES

	Film/year	Sport
1	*Days of Thunder* (1990)	Stock car racing
2	*Rocky IV* (1985)	Boxing
3	*Rocky III* (1982)	Boxing
4	*Rocky* (1976)	Boxing
5	*A League of Their Own* (1992)	Women's baseball
6	*Rocky II* (1979)	Boxing
7	*Tin Cup* (1996)	Golf
8	*White Men Can't Jump* (1992)	Basketball
9	*Field of Dreams* (1989)	Baseball
10	*Chariots of Fire* (1983)	Tracks

Led by superstar Sylvester Stallone's *Rocky* series, the boxing ring, a natural source of drama and thrills, dominates Hollywood's most successful sports-based epics. Baseball is a popular follow-up.

THE GOOD & THE BAD

THE 10

COUNTRIES WITH THE LOWEST CRIME RATES

	Country	Reported crime rate per 100,000 population
1	Togo	11.0
2	Nepal	13.0
3	Guinea	18.4
4=	Congo	32.0
4=	Niger	32.0
6	Mali	33.0
7	Burkina Faso	41.0
8	Bangladesh	64.0
9	Côte d'Ivoire	67.0
10	Burundi	84.0

There are just 13 countries in the world with reported crime rates of fewer than 100 per 100,000 inhabitants; the other three are Burundi (87.0), Syria (89.0), and Ethiopia (94.0). It should be noted, however, that these figures are based on reported crimes. For propaganda purposes, many countries do not publish accurate figures, while in certain countries crime is so common and law enforcement so inefficient or corrupt that countless incidents are unreported.

UNDER ARREST
World crime rates reflect not only lawlessness but also police efficiency and public faith in the force's competence to deal with criminals.

THE 10

COUNTRIES WITH THE HIGHEST CRIME RATES

	Country	Reported crime rate per 100,000 population
1	Suriname	17,819
2	St. Kitts and Nevis	15,468
3	New Zealand	14,496
4	Sweden	13,750
5	Canada	13,297
6	Gibraltar	12,581
7	US Virgin Islands	10,441
8	Denmark	10,339
9	Netherlands	10,181
10	Guam	10,080
	US	*5,278*

An appearance on this list does not necessarily confirm these as the most crime-ridden countries, since (as with the comparative list of The 10 Countries with the Lowest Crime Rates) the rate of reporting relates closely to such factors as confidence in local law enforcement authorities. However, a rate of approximately 1,000 per 100,000 may be considered average, so those in the Top 10 are well above it.

THE 10

COUNTRIES WITH MOST BURGLARIES

	Country	Annual burglaries per 100,000 population
1	Netherlands	3,803.0
2	US Virgin Islands	3,183.7
3	New Zealand	2,942.3
4	England and Wales	2,401.0
5	Denmark	2,381.0
6	Germany	2,039.4
7	Antigua and Barbuda	1,984.4
8	Australia	1,962.8
9	Bermuda	1,949.2
10	Finland	1,921.9
	US	987.6

THE 10

COUNTRIES WITH MOST AUTO THEFTS

	Country	Annual thefts per 100,000 population
1	Switzerland	1,520.0*
2	Australia	1,005.5
3	England and Wales	992.8
4	US Virgin Islands	954.0
5	New Zealand	905.4
6	Sweden	748.0
7	France	648.5
8	Denmark	619.7
9	Italy	566.6
10	US	560.5

* Including motorcycles and bicycles

CAR CRIME
Although car manufacturers are using increasingly sophisticated security measures, thieves continue to view cars as easy targets, and thefts of and from cars continue to grow.

THE 10

WORST CITIES FOR MURDER IN THE US

	City	Murders*
1	New York, New York	1,182
2	Los Angeles, Calfornia	828
3	Chicago, Illinois	823
4	Detroit, Michigan	514
5	Philadelphia, Pennsylvania	404#
6	New Orleans, Louisiana	364
7	Washington, DC	360
8	Baltimore, Maryland	324
9	Houston, Texas	304
10	Dallas, Texas	276

* 1995 figures
\# 1994 figure

America's Top 10 murder capitals remain fairly consistent from year to year.

THE 10

FBI "MOST WANTED" FUGITIVES

Fugitive/crime

1 Andrew Phillip Cunanan
(b. August 31, 1969, US)

He has been charged with murder in Minnesota and implicated in other murders. Committed suicide July 23, 1997.

2 Lamen Khalifa Fhimah
(b. April 4, 1956, Libya)

He is wanted for blowing up PanAm flight 103 over Lockerbie, 1988. Up to $4,000,000 reward.

3 Victor Manuel Gerena
(b. June 24, 1958, US)

Gerena is wanted for bank and armed robbery.

4 Glen Stewart Godwin
(b. June 26, 1958, US)

Godwin escaped from Folsom State Prison.

5 Mir Aimal Kansi
(b. February 10, 1964, Pakistan)

He is wanted for the murder of two in a shooting at CIA Headquarters, Langley, Virginia.

6 Abdel Basset Ali Al-Megrahi
(b. April 1, 1952, Libya)

Al-Megrahi is wanted for the blowing up of PanAm flight 103 over Lockerbie, 1988.

7 Agustin Vasquez-Mendoza
(b. October 1, 1969, Mexico)

He is wanted for murder of a Drug Enforcement Administration special agent. $50,000 reward.

8 Thang Thanh Nguyen
(b. March 20, 1969, Vietnam)

Nguyen is wanted for murder, attempted murder, burglary, and robbery.

9 Arthur Lee Washington, Jr.
(b. November 30, 1949, US)

He is charged with the attempted murder of a state trooper.

10 Donald Eugene Webb
(b. July 14, 1931, US)

Webb is wanted for murder.

The FBI's "10 Most Wanted Fugitives" was first published on March 14, 1950. The lists are not ranked and have been given here in alphabetical order. The criteria used for selection are that the individual must have a lengthy record of committing serious crimes and/or be considered a particularly dangerous menace to society, and it must be believed that the nationwide publicity given by the program can be of assistance in apprehending the fugitive.

POLICE, COURTS & PRISONS

COUNTRIES WITH THE MOST POLICE OFFICERS

	Country	Population per police officer
1	Angola	14*
2	Kuwait	80
3	Nicaragua	90*
4	Brunei	100
5=	Nauru	110
5=	Cape Verde	110
7=	Antigua and Barbuda	120
7=	Mongolia	120
7=	Seychelles	120
10=	Iraq	140
10=	United Arab Emirates	140
	US	318

* Including civilian militia

Police manpower figures generally include only full-time paid officials, and exclude clerical and volunteer staff, but there are variations around the world as to how these categories are defined.

COUNTRIES WITH THE FEWEST POLICE OFFICERS

	Country	Population per police officer
1	Maldives	35,710
2	Canada	8,640
3	Rwanda	4,650
4	Côte d'Ivoire	4,640
5	Gambia	3,310
6	Benin	3,250
7	Madagascar	2,900
8	Central African Republic	2,740
9	Bangladesh	2,560
10	Niger	2,350

* Including paramilitary forces

The saying "there's never a policeman when you need one" is nowhere truer than in the countries appearing in this list, where the police are remarkably thin on the ground. There are various possible and contradictory explanations for these ratios: countries may be so law-abiding that there is simply no need for large numbers of police officers, or the force may be so underfunded and inefficient as to be irrelevant.

US CITIES WITH THE MOST POLICE OFFICERS

	City	Officers
1	New York, New York	37,450
2	Chicago, Illinois	13,344
3	Los Angeles, California	8,363
4	Philadelphia, Pennsylvania	6,376
5	Houston, Texas	5,170
6	Detroit, Michigan	3,819
7	Washington, D.C.	3,671
8	Baltimore, Maryland	3,110
9	Dallas, Texas	2,833
10	Phoenix, Arizona	2,183

REASONS FOR HIRING PRIVATE DETECTIVES IN THE UK

1 Tracing debtors
2 Serving legal writs
3 Locating assets
4 Assessing accident
5 Tracing missing persons
6 Insurance claims
7 Matrimonial disputes
8 Countering industrial espionage
9 Criminal cases
10 Checking personnel

THE CITY'S FINEST
New York's police force is by far the largest of any US city.

T H E 1 0

LARGEST FEDERAL CORRECTIONAL INSTITUTIONS IN THE US

	Institute	Location	Rated capacity
1	Federal Correctional Institution	Fort Dix, New Jersey	3,683
2	Federal Correctional Institution (Low and Medium Security)	Coleman, Florida	2,682
3	Federal Correctional Institution	Beaumont, Texas	1,536
4	US Penitentiary	Atlanta, Georgia	1,429
5	Federal Detention Center	Miami, Florida	1,259
6	US Penitentiary	Leavenworth, Kansas	1,201
7	Federal Correctional Institution	Beckley, West Virginia	1,152
8	Federal Medical Center	Fort Worth, Texas	1,132
9	Federal Medical Center	Lexington, Kentucky	1,106
10	Federal Correctional Institution	Milan, Michigan	1,065

Source: Bureau of Federal Prisons

T H E 1 0

US STATES WITH THE MOST PRISON INMATES, 1980/1996

	State	1980	1996
1	California	24,569	142,814
2	Texas	29,892	129,937
3	New York	21,815	68,721
4	Florida	20,735	64,332
5	Ohio	13,489	45,314
6	Michigan	15,124	41,884
7	Illinois	11,899	38,373
8	Georgia	12,178	34,808
9	Pennsylvania	8,171	33,939
10	North Carolina	15,513	30,671
	US total:	*329,821*	*1,112,448*

In mid-1996 there were 1,019,281 prisoners in state prisons and 93,167 in federal institutions in the US. At the time of this census, an additional 518,492 prisoners were held in local jails. The state with the fewest prisoners over the same period was North Dakota, with 253 in 1980 and 640 in 1996. The nationwide prison population in 1991 was more than three times greater than that in 1980, but that of certain states increased to an even greater extent: California's, for example, grew more than fivefold. The rate of incarceration in 1996 is equivalent to 615 prisoners for every 100,000 of the US population – in 1980 the rate was 146 per 100,000. Extrapolating from these figures, and keeping in mind population projections for the coming decades, readers may wish to indulge in the mathematical exercise of calculating the year in which the entire US population will be in jail.

T H E 1 0

US STATES WITH THE HIGHEST RATE OF PRISON INCARCERATION

	State	Prisoners per 100,000 mid-1996*
1	Texas	659
2	Louisiana	611
3	Oklahoma	580
4	South Carolina	540
5	Nevada	493
6	Alabama	487
7	Mississippi	486
8	Arizona	481
9	Georgia	468
10	Florida	448

* *Prisoners with a sentence of more than one year per 100,000 residents*

The rate for the District of Columbia is 1,444 per 100,000, but is distorted by the fact that the DC prison and local jail systems are integrated. The state with the lowest rate is North Dakota, with 640 prisoners in total, equivalent to a rate of 90 per 100,000 residents.

T H E 1 0

MOST OVERCROWDED STATE PRISONS*

	State prison	Overcrowding (% above highest capacity)
1	California	189
2	Ohio	171
3=	Iowa	164
3=	New Jersey	164
5	Pennsylvania	154
6	Virginia	149
7	Wisconsin	145
8	Illinois	138
9	Massachusetts	137
10	Oklahoma	128

* *As at December 31, 1995*
Source: Department of Justice

MASS MURDER

Serial killers are mass murderers who kill repeatedly, often over long periods, in contrast to the so-called "spree killers" who have been responsible for single occasion massacres, usually with guns, and other perpetrators of single outrages, often by means of bombs, resulting in multiple deaths. Because of the time spans involved and the secrecy surrounding the horrific crimes of multiple killers, it is almost impossible to calculate the precise numbers of their victims. This is especially true of poisoners in the years before forensic science was developed, since establishing the cause of death was so imprecise. The tallies of murders attributed to the criminals listed here should therefore be taken as "best estimates" based on the most reliable evidence available, but such is the magnitude of the crimes of some of these killers that some of the figures may be underestimates.

THE 10

MOST PROLIFIC POISONERS IN THE WORLD*

	Poisoner	Victims
1	Susannah Olah	up to 100
2	Gesina Margaretha Gottfried	at least 30
3	Hélène Jegado	23
4	Mary Ann Cotton	20
5=	Dr. William Palmer	14
5=	Sadamichi Hirasawa	14
7=	Johann Otto Hoch	at least 12
7=	Marie Becker	12
9	Lydia Sherman	at least 11
10=	Amy Archer-Gilligan	at least 5
10=	Dr. Thomas Neill Cream	5
10=	Herman Billik	5

* Prior to 1950 and excluding poisoners where evidence is so confused with legend (such as that surrounding the Borgia family) as to be unreliable

THE 10

MOST PROLIFIC MURDERESSES IN THE WORLD

	Murderess	Victims
1	Countess Erszébet Báthory	up to 650

In the period up to 1610 in Hungary, Báthory (1560–1614), known as "Countess Dracula" – later the title of a 1970 Hammer horror film about her life and crimes – was alleged to have murdered between 300 and 650 girls (her personal list of 610 victims was described at her trial) in the belief that drinking their blood would prevent her from aging. She was eventually arrested in 1611. Tried and found guilty, she died on August 21, 1614, walled up in her own castle at Csejthe.

	Murderess	Victims
2	Susannah Olah	up to 100

At the age of 40, Susi Olah, a 40-year-old nurse and midwife, arrived at Nagzrev, a Hungarian village. Over the next few years she "predicted" the demise of anything up to 100 people, who subsequently met their deaths as a result of arsenic poisoning. Many inhabitants believed the woman who came to be nicknamed the "Angel-maker" had prophetic powers, but her victims ranged from newborn and handicapped children to elderly people and the husbands of many of the local women – in most cases with the full complicity of their relatives. When the law finally caught up with her in 1929, she committed suicide.

	Murderess	Victims
3	Delfina and Maria de Jesús Gonzales	at least 91

After abducting girls to work in their Mexican brothel, Rancho El Angel, as many as 80 of them, and an unknown number of their customers, were murdered and buried in the grounds by the Gonzales sisters, who in 1964 were sentenced to 40 years imprisonment.

	Murderess	Victims
4	Bella Poulsdatter Sorensen Gunness	42

Bella or Belle Gunness (1859–1908?), a Norwegian-born immigrant to the US, is believed to have murdered her husband Peter Gunness for his life insurance (she claimed that an ax had fallen from a shelf and onto his head). After this she lured between 16 and 28 suitors through "lonely hearts" advertisements, as well as numerous others – a total of as many as 42 – to her Laporte, Indiana, farm, where she murdered them. On April 28, 1908 her farm was burned to the ground. A headless corpse found in the ruins was declared to be Gunness, killed along with her three children by her accomplice Ray Lamphere, but it seems probable that she faked her own death and disappeared.

	Murderess	Victims
5	Gesina Margaretha Gottfried	at least 30

Having poisoned her first husband and two children with arsenic in 1815, German murderess Gesina Mittenberg killed both her parents by the same method and then her next husband, Gottfried, whom she married on his deathbed, thereby inheriting his fortune. As her income dwindled, she carried out an extensive series of murders, including those of her brother, a creditor, and most of the family of a Bremen wheelwright called Rumf, for whom she worked as a housekeeper. Rumf himself became suspicious, and in 1828 Gottfried was arrested. After a trial at which she admitted to more than 30 murders, she was executed.

	Murderess	Victims
6	Jane Toppan	30

Boston-born Nora Kelley, also known as Jane Toppan (1854–1938), was the daughter of Peter Kelley, who ended his days in an insane asylum, and she herself was almost certainly insane. She trained as a nurse, and within a few years, after numerous patients in her care had died, their bodies were exhumed and revealed traces of morphine and atropine poisoning. It seems probable, according to both evidence and her own confession, that she killed as many as 30 victims. She died in an asylum on August 17, 1938, at the age of 84.

	Murderess	Victims
7	Hélène Jegado	23

Jegado was a French housemaid who was believed to have committed some 23 murders by arsenic. She was tried at Rennes in 1851, found guilty, and guillotined in 1852.

	Murderess	Victims
8	Genene Jones	21

In 1984 Jones was found guilty of killing a baby at the San Antonio, Texas, hospital at which she worked as a nurse, by administering the drug succinylcholine. She was sentenced to 99 years in prison. Jones had been dismissed from the previous hospital at which she had worked after up to 20 babies in her care had died of suspicious, and some authorities linked her with as many as 42 deaths.

	Murderess	Victims
9	Mary Ann Cotton	20

Cotton (1832–73), a one-time nurse, is generally held to be Britain's worst mass murderer. Over a 20-year period, it seems probable that she disposed of 14–20 victims, including two husbands, children, and stepchildren, by arsenic poisoning. She was hanged at Durham Prison on March 24, 1873, five days after giving birth.

	Murderess	Victims
10	Waltraud Wagner	15

Wagner was the ringleader but only one of four nurses found guilty of causing numerous deaths through deliberate drug overdoses and other means at the Lainz hospital, Vienna, in the late 1980s – between 42 and possibly as many as several hundred patients became the victims of the Wagner "death squad," for which she was sentenced to life imprisonment on charges that included 15 counts of murder and 17 of attempted murder.

THE 10

MOST PROLIFIC SERIAL KILLERS* OF THE 20th CENTURY

Serial killer	Victims
1 Pedro Alonzo (or Armando) López	over 300

Following his 1980 capture López, known as the "Monster of the Andes," led police to 53 graves, but probably murdered more than 300 young girls in Columbia, Ecuador, and Peru. He was sentenced to life imprisonment.

2 Henry Lee Lucas	over 200

The subject of the film, Henry, Portrait of a Serial Killer, Lucas (b. 1937) may have committed 200 or more murders, many of them in partnership with Ottis Toole. He admitted in 1983 to 360 and was convicted of 11, and is currently on Death Row in Huntsville, Texas.

3 Delfina and Maria de Jesús Gonzales	at least 91

(See The 10 Most Prolific Murderesses in the World, No. 3.)

Serial killer	Victims
4 Bruno Lüdke	86

Lüdke (b. 1909) was a German who confessed to murdering 86 women between 1928 and January 29, 1943. Declared insane, he was incarcerated in a Vienna hospital where he was subjected to medical experiments, apparently dying on April 8, 1944, after a lethal injection.

5 Daniel Camargo Barbosa	71

Coincidentally, eight years after the arrest of Pedro López in Ecuador, Barbosa was captured following a similar series of horrific murders of children – a probable total of 71 victims, for which he was sentenced to just 16 years.

6 Kampatimar Shankariya	70

Caught after a two-year spree during which he killed as many as 70 times, Shankariya was hanged in Jaipur, India, on May 16, 1979.

Serial killer	Victims
7 Randolph Kraft	67

From 1972 until his arrest on May 14, 1983, Kraft is thought to have murdered 67 men.

8 Dr. Marcel André Henri Félix Petiot	63

Dr. Marcel Petiot admitted to 63 murders during World War II. It is probable that they were wealthy Jews whom he robbed.

9 Donald Harvey	58

Working in hospitals, Harvey is believed to have murdered some 58 patients.

10 Andrei Chikatilo	52

Russia's worst serial killer was convicted in Rostov-on-Don in 1992 of killing 52 women and children between 1978 and 1990.

* Including only individual and partnership murderers

THE 10

WORST GUN MASSACRES* OF ALL TIME

Perpetrator/location/date	Victims
1 Woo Bum Kong, Sang-Namdo, South Korea, April 28, 1982	57

Off-duty policeman Woo Bum Kong (or Wou Bom-Kon), 27, went on a drunken rampage with rifles and hand grenades, killing 57 and injuring 38 before blowing himself up.

2 Martin Bryant, Port Arthur, Tasmania, Australia, April 28, 1996	35

Bryant used a rifle in a horrific spree that began in a restaurant and ended with a siege in a guesthouse which he set on fire before being captured by police.

3 Baruch Goldstein, Hebron, Occupied West Bank, Israel, February 25, 1994	29

Goldstein, a 42-year-old US immigrant doctor, carried out a gun massacre of Palestinians at prayer at the Tomb of the Patriarchs before being beaten to death by the crowd.

4= James Oliver Huberty, San Ysidro, California, July 18, 1984	22

Huberty opened fire in a McDonald's, killing 21 before being shot dead by a SWAT marksman. 19 more were wounded, including one who died the following day.

Perpetrator/location/date	Victims
4= George Jo Hennard, Killeen, Texas, October 16, 1991	22

Hennard drove his pickup truck through the window of Luby's Cafeteria and, in 11 minutes, killed 22 with semiautomatic pistols.

6 Thomas Hamilton, Dunblane, Stirling, Scotland March 13, 1996	17

Hamilton, 43, shot 16 children and a teacher in Dunblane Primary School before killing himself in the UK's worst shooting incident.

7= Charles Joseph Whitman, Austin, Texas, July 31 – August 1, 1966	16

Whitman killed his mother and wife on July 31, 1996. The following day he ascended to the observation deck of the campus tower at the University of Texas, from where he shot 14 and wounded 34 before being shot dead by police officer Romero Martinez.

7= Michael Ryan, Hungerford, Berkshire, England August 19, 1987	16

Ryan, 26, shot 14 dead and wounded 16 others (two of whom later died) before shooting himself.

Perpetrator/location/date	Victims
7= Ronald Gene Simmons, Russellville, Arkansas, December 28, 1987	16

Simmons' total included 14 family members.

10= Wagner von Degerloch, Muehlhausen, Germany, September 3–4, 1913	14

Wagner von Degerloch murdered his wife and children before embarking on a shooting spree.

10= Patrick Henry Sherrill, Edmond, Oklahoma, August 20, 1986	14

Sherrill, age 44, shot 14 dead and wounded six others at the post office where he worked.

10= Christian Dornier, Luxiol, Doubs, France, July 12, 1989	14

Dornier went on a rampage leaving 14 dead.

10= Marc Lépine, Université de Montreal, Quebec, Canada, December 6, 1989	14

Lépine went on a rampage, firing only at women, then shot himself.

* By individuals, excluding terrorist and military actions; totals exclude perpetrator

MURDER FILE

COUNTRIES WITH THE HIGHEST MURDER RATES

	Country	Murders p.a. per 100,000 population
1	Swaziland	87.8
2	Lesotho	51.1
3	Colombia	40.5
4	Sudan	30.5
5	Philippines	30.1
6	Guatemala	27.4
7	French Guiana	27.2
8	Nauru	25.0
9	Aruba	24.9
10	Puerto Rico	24.1
	US	9.0

The incidence of murder is affected by intertribal conflicts in Africa and by drug-related killings in Colombia.

MURDER BY NUMBERS

As the lists on these pages indicate, there are countries with worse murder rates (numbers of victims as a ratio of population) than the US, but nowhere in the world has as many murders each year. This has not always been so: in 1900 there were just 230 murders, a rate of 1.2 per 100,000 inhabitants. The number grew steadily, first exceeding 1,000 in 1906, when there were 1,310 cases, and first topping 10,000 in 1930 (10,331). By 1933 gangland violence pushed the figure up to an all-time peak of 12,124 and a rate of 9.7 per 100,000. This number was not exceeded until 1967, when 13,425 murders were recorded, but continuing increases since then mean that in 1994 there were 23,305 murders in the US, a rate of 9.0 per 100,000.

MOST COMMON MURDER WEAPONS AND METHODS IN THE US

	Weapon/method	Victims 1995
1	Handguns	11,198
2	Knives or cutting instruments	2,538
3	"Personal weapons" (hands, feet, fists, etc.)	1,182
4	Shotguns	917
5	Blunt objects (hammers, clubs, etc.)	904
6	Firearms (type not stated)	892
7	Rifles	637
8	Strangulation	232
9	Explosives	190
10	Fire	166

In 1995 "other weapons or weapons not stated" were used in 960 murders. The number of deaths from explosives increased dramatically from the 10 incidents recorded in the previous year. This was a consequence of the bombing of the Federal Building, Oklahoma City, on April 19, 1995, in which 169 people were killed. Relatively less common methods included asphyxiation (135 cases), drowning (29), and poisoning (12). The total number of murders for the year amounted to 20,043 – equivalent to one person in every 13,162. The total number of murders committed has escalated dramatically during the 20th century, although the order of the weapons has not changed much in recent years. Perhaps most surprisingly, the proportion of killings involving firearms has scarcely changed at all – and has even gone down compared with the figures for the early years of the century.

MOST COMMON MURDER WEAPONS AND METHODS IN ENGLAND AND WALES

	Weapon/method	Victims 1995
1	Sharp instrument	251
2	Hitting and kicking	113
3	Blunt instrument	85
4	Strangulation and asphyxiation	84
5	Shooting	70
6	Burning	38
7	Poison and drugs	20
8	Motor vehicle	7
9	Drowning	3
10	Explosives	1

According to Home Office statistics, there were 699 homicides in 1995 in England and Wales (474 male and 225 female victims). In addition to those in the list, the apparent method in another 17 incidents is described as "other," and in 10 cases as "unknown." This represents a nine percent increase over the previous year (from 639), although it should be noted that some offenses first recorded as homicides were later reclassified. The number of victims first exceeded the 400 mark in 1952; there were 500 in 1974, and 600 in 1979. The use of certain types of weapon has also varied disproportionately. Contrary to press reports suggesting the contrary, killings involving guns have actually declined from a 1987 peak of 78, while homicides caused by sharp instruments have become more widespread, in 1995 accounting for 36 percent of all killings. Based on the 1995 statistic, however, England and Wales (Scotland classifies its homicides according to a different system, which makes it misleading to compare the numbers) are still relatively safe countries: the odds of being murdered in England and Wales are one in 73,589. One is almost six times as likely to be a victim in the US.

THE 10
WORST STATES FOR MURDER IN THE US

	State	Firearms used	Total murders
1	California	2,593	3,531
2	Texas	1,143	1,642
3	New York	1,012	1,522
4	Florida	615	1,037
5	Illinois*	601	810
6	Michigan	559	791
7	Louisiana	568	715
8	Pennsylvania	476	677
9	North Carolina	448	671
10	Georgia	454	649

* Provisional figures

THE 10
WORST CITIES FOR MURDER IN THE US

	City	Murders (1996)*
1	New York, New York	507
2	Chicago, Illinois	383
3	Los Angeles, California	370
4	Philadelphia, Pennsylvania	209
5	Detroit, Michigan	201
6	Washington, DC	199
7	Baltimore, Maryland	165
8	New Orleans, Louisiana	155
9	Houston, Texas	134
10	Dallas, Texas	114

* Provisional figures

TOP 10
RELATIONSHIPS OF MURDER VICTIMS TO PRINCIPAL SUSPECTS IN THE US

	Relationship	Victims
1	Acquaintance	6,125
2	Stranger	2,888
3	Wife	823
4	Friend	733
5	Girlfriend	525
6	Husband	346
7	Son	326
8	Boyfriend	228
9	Daughter	212
10	Neighbor	173

THE 10
WORST METROPOLITAN AREAS FOR VIOLENT CRIME* (1995)

	Metro Area	Violent crimes per 1,000 people
1	Miami-Dade, FL	18.9
2 =	Los Angeles-Long Beach, CA	14.2
2 =	Gainesville, GA	14.2
4 =	New York, NY	13.9
4 =	Baton Rouge, LA	13.9
6	Baltimore, MD	13.4
7 =	New Orleans, LA	13.3
7 =	Lawton, OK	13.3
9	Sioux City, IA	12.7
10	Memphis, TN	12.5

* Murder, rape, aggravated assault, and robbery

THE 10
COUNTRIES WITH THE LOWEST MURDER RATES

	Country	Murders p.a. per 100,000 population
1 =	Argentina	0.1
1 =	Brunei	0.1
3 =	Burkina Faso	0.2
3 =	Niger	0.2
5 =	Guinea	0.5
5 =	Guinea-Bissau	0.5
5 =	Iran	0.5
8 =	Finland	0.6
8 =	Saudi Arabia	0.6
10 =	Cameroon	0.7
10 =	Ireland	0.7
10 =	Mongolia	0.7

Among countries that report to international monitoring organizations, some 18, which include Japan, record murder rates of fewer than one per 100,000.

THE 10
WORST YEARS FOR GUN MURDERS IN THE US

	Year	Victims
1	1993	16,136
2	1994	15,546
3	1992	15,489
4	1991	14,373
5	1980	13,650
6	1990	13,035
7	1981	12,523
8	1974	12,474
9	1975	12,061
10	1989	11,832

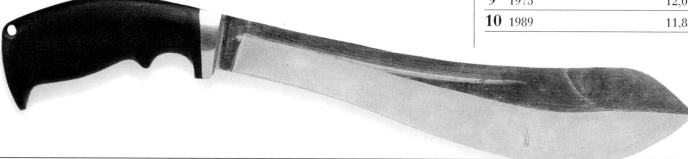

CAPITAL PUNISHMENT

INSTRUMENT OF EXECUTION
*Harold P. Brown and electrical pioneer
Thomas Alva Edison's chief electrician
Dr. A.E. Kennelly jointly take the credit for
inventing the electric chair, first used to
execute murderer William Kemmler in 1890.*

THE 10

FIRST COUNTRIES TO ABOLISH CAPITAL PUNISHMENT

	Country	Abolished
1	Russia	1826
2	Venezuela	1863
3	Portugal	1867
4=	Brazil	1882
4=	Costa Rica	1882
6	Ecuador	1897
7	Panama	1903
8	Norway	1905
9	Uruguay	1907
10	Colombia	1910

Some countries abolished capital punishment in peacetime only, or for all crimes except treason, although several countries later reinstated the penalty.

10 US EXECUTION FIRSTS

1 First to be hanged

John Billington, for the shooting murder of John Newcomin in Plymouth, Massachusetts, September 30, 1630.

2 First to be hanged for witchcraft

Achsah Young, in Massachusetts on May 27, 1647. Eighty-year-old Giles Cory became the last man to be pressed to death (for refusing to plead on charges of witchcraft) in Salem, Massachusetts, on September 19, 1692; the last executions for witchcraft (of eight women) also took place at Salem on September 22, 1692.

3 First to be hanged for treason

Jacob Leisler, for insurrection against New York Governor Francis Nicholson, in City Hall Park, New York, May 16, 1691.

4 First to be hanged for slave trading

Captain Nathaniel Gordon (technically hanged for piracy, which included slave trading) was executed at the Tombs Prison, New York, February 21, 1862.

5 First civilian to be hanged for treason

William Bruce Mumford, for tearing down the Union flag in New Orleans, June 7, 1862.

6 First man to be electrocuted

William Kemmler (alias John Hart), for murder, at Auburn Prison, New York, August 6, 1890.

7 First woman to be electrocuted

Martha M. Place, for murder, at Sing Sing Prison, New York, March 20, 1899.

8 First to be executed in the gas chamber

Gee Jon, for murder, in Carson City, Nevada, February 8, 1924.

9 First to be electrocuted for treason

Julius and Ethel Rosenberg, at Sing Sing Prison, New York, June 19, 1953.

10 First to be executed by lethal injection

Charles Brooks, for murder, at the Department of Corrections, Huntsville, Texas, December 6, 1982.

THE 10

LAST PEOPLE EXECUTED AT THE TOWER OF LONDON

1 Wilhelm Johannes Roos   Jul 30, 1915

Roos was a Dutchman who posed as a cigar salesman and sent coded messages to a company in Holland detailing ship movements in British ports. Roos was the 3rd spy of World War I to be executed at the Tower of London. He was shot.

2 Haike Marinus Petrus Janssen
Jul 30, 1915

An accomplice of Roos who used the same methods. The two were tried together and executed the same day. Janssen was shot 10 minutes after Roos, at 6:10am.

3 Ernst Waldemar Melin   Sep 10, 1915

A German spy who was shot after general court martial during World War I.

4 Agusto Alfredo Roggen   Sep 17, 1915

A German who attempted to escape the death penalty by claiming to be Uruguayan. He was found guilty of spying on the trials of a new torpedo at Loch Lomond, then sending the information in invisible ink.

5 Fernando Buschman   Oct 19, 1915

Posing as a Dutch violinist, he spied while offering entertainment at Royal Navy bases.

6 Georg T. Breeckow   Oct 26, 1915

Posing as an American (Reginald Rowland), with a forged passport, he was caught when he sent a parcel containing secret messages, but addressed in German style, with country and town name preceding that of the street.

7 Irving Guy Ries   Oct 27, 1915

A German traveling salesman who was sentenced to death on spying charges.

8 Albert Meyer   Dec 2, 1915

Like Ries, Meyer was a German spy posing as a traveling salesman.

9 Y.L. Zender-Hurwitz   Apr 11, 1916

A spy of Peruvian descent charged with sending information to Germany about British troop movements, for which he received a salary of $150 a month.

10 Josef Jakobs   Aug 15, 1941

A German army sergeant who was caught when he parachuted into England wearing civilian clothes and carrying an identification card in the name of James Rymer. Following general court martial, he was shot at 7:15am – the only spy executed at the Tower during the course of World War II.

T H E 1 0

US STATES WITH THE MOST PRISONERS ON DEATH ROW

	State	Prisoners under death sentence
1	California	420
2	Texas	404
3	Florida	362
4	Pennsylvania	196
5	Ohio	155
6	Illinois	154
7	Alabama	143
8	North Carolina	139
9	Oklahoma	129
10	Arizona	117

* As of December 31, 1995
Source: Department of Justice

T H E 1 0

US STATES WITH THE MOST WOMEN ON DEATH ROW

	State	No. under death sentence*
1	California	7
2	Texas	6
3=	Florida	5
3=	Oklahoma	5
5=	Alabama	4
5=	Illinois	4
5=	Pennsylvania	4
8=	Missouri	2
8=	North Carolina	2
10=	Arizona	1
10=	Idaho	1
10=	Louisiana	1
10=	Mississippi	1
10=	Nevada	1
10=	Tennessee	1

* As of May 14, 1996

T H E 1 0

US STATES WITH THE MOST EXECUTIONS

	State	Method now in force	Executed 1930–94
1	Texas	Lethal injection	401
2	Georgia	Electrocution	386
3	New York	Lethal injection	329
4	California	Lethal gas	294
5	North Carolina	Lethal gas or injection	271
6	Florida	Electrocution	206
7	Ohio	Electrocution	172
8	South Carolina	Electrocution	167
9	Mississippi	Lethal injection*	158
10	Louisiana	Lethal injection	155

* Lethal gas if sentenced prior to July 1, 1984
Source: Department of Justice

T H E 1 0

FIRST ELECTROCUTIONS AT SING-SING PRISON, NEW YORK

	Name	Electrocuted
1	Harris A. Smiler	Jul 7, 1891
2	James Slocum	Jul 7, 1891
3	Joseph Wood	Jul 7, 1891
4	Schihick Judigo	Jul 7, 1891
5	Martin D. Loppy	Dec 7, 1891
6	Charles McElvaine	Feb 8, 1892
7	Jeremiah Cotte	Mar 28, 1892
8	Fred McGuire	Dec 19, 1892
9	James L. Hamilton	Apr 3, 1893
10	Carlyle Harris	May 8, 1893

The electric chair was installed in Sing-Sing Prison, New York, in 1891, just a year after it was first used to execute William Kemmler at Auburn Prison, also in New York State. By the end of the 19th century, 29 inmates had been executed by this means (including the first female, 44-year-old Martha M. Place, on March 20, 1899).

T H E 1 0

YEARS WITH THE MOST EXECUTIONS IN THE US*

	Year	Executions
1	1935	199
2	1936	195
3	1938	190
4	1934	168
5=	1933	160
5=	1939	160
7	1930	155
8=	1931	153
8=	1947	153
10	1937	147

* All offenses, 1930 to 1995

The total number of executions in the US fell below three figures for the first time this century in 1952, when 82 prisoners were executed, and below double figures in 1965, with seven executions. Only one prisoner was executed in 1966, in 1977 (when Gary Gilmore became the first for 10 years to receive the death penalty), and 1981. There were no executions at all between 1968 and 1976, but double figures were recorded again in 1984 (21 executions) and in all subsequent years.

T H E 1 0

NAZI WAR CRIMINALS HANGED AT NUREMBERG

1	Joachim von Ribbentrop
2	Field Marshal Wilhelm von Keitel
3	General Ernst Kaltenbrunner
4	Reichsminister Alfred Rosenburg
5	Reichsminister Hans Frank
6	Reichsminister Wilhelm Frick
7	Gauleiter Julius Streicher
8	Reichsminister Fritz Sauckel
9	Colonel-General Alfred Jodl
10	Gauleiter Artur von Seyss-Inquart

WORLD WAR I

TOP 10

LARGEST ARMED FORCES OF WORLD WAR I

	Country	Personnel*
1	Russia	12,000,000
2	Germany	11,000,000
3	British Empire#	8,904,467
4	France	8,410,000
5	Austria–Hungary	7,800,000
6	Italy	5,615,000
7	US	4,355,000
8	Turkey	2,850,000
9	Bulgaria	1,200,000
10	Japan	800,000

* Total at peak strength
\# Including Australia, Canada, India, New Zealand, South Africa, and other countries in the Commonwealth

THE 10

COUNTRIES SUFFERING THE GREATEST MILITARY LOSSES IN WORLD WAR I

	Country	Killed
1	Germany	1,773,700
2	Russia	1,700,000
3	France	1,357,800
4	Austria–Hungary	1,200,000
5	British Empire	908,371
6	Italy	650,000
7	Romania	335,706
8	Turkey	325,000
9	US	116,516
10	Bulgaria	87,500

The number of battle fatalities and deaths from other causes among military personnel varied enormously: Romania's death rate was highest at 45 percent and Japan's 0.04 percent among the lowest.

WAR DEAD
The carnage of trench warfare in particular resulted in as many as 8,545,800 military casualties in World War I.

FIGHTING FORCE
More Russian troops served in World War I than those of any other nation, with one in seven killed and one in five taken prisoner.

THE 10

COUNTRIES SUFFERING THE GREATEST MERCHANT SHIPPING LOSSES IN WORLD WAR I

	Country	Vessels sunk number	tonnage
1	UK	2,038	6,797,802
2	Italy	228	720,064
3	France	213	651,583
4	US	93	372,892
5	Germany	188	319,552
6	Greece	115	304,992
7	Denmark	126	205,002
8	Netherlands	74	194,483
9	Sweden	124	192,807
10	Spain	70	160,383

THE 10

COUNTRIES WITH THE MOST PRISONERS OF WAR, 1914–18

	Country	Prisoners			Country	Prisoners
1	Russia	2,500,000		6	Turkey	250,000
2	Austria–Hungary	2,200,000		7	British Empire	191,652
3	Germany	1,152,800		8	Serbia	152,958
4	Italy	600,000		9	Romania	80,000
5	France	537,000		10	Belgium	34,659

AMERICA'S TOP AIR ACE DIES

Edward ("Eddie") Rickenbacker first established his reputation in the US as a champion auto-racing driver. A visit to England in 1917 encouraged his interest in flying, and, when the US entered World War I, he enlisted and trained as a pilot. On March 19, 1918 Rickenbacker took part in the first-ever US patrol over enemy lines, and on April 29 shot down his first aircraft. A month later, with five kills to his credit, he became an acknowledged "ace," eventually achieving a total of 26 kills and winning the US Medal of Honor. Rickenbacker also served in World War II. He died in Zurich, Switzerland, on July 23, 1973 at the age of 82.

TOP 10

BRITISH AND COMMONWEALTH AIR ACES OF WORLD WAR I

	Pilot	Nationality	Kills claimed
1	Edward Mannock	British	73
2	William Avery Bishop	Canadian	72
3	Raymond Collishaw	Canadian	62
4	James Thomas Byford McCudden	British	57
5=	Anthony Wetherby Beauchamp-Proctor	South African	54
5=	Donald MacLaren	Canadian	54
7=	William George Barker	Canadian	52
7=	Philip Fletcher Fullard	British	52
9	R.S. Dallas	Australian	51
10	George Edward Henry McElroy	Irish	49

TOP 10

US AIR ACES OF WORLD WAR I

	Pilot*	Kills claimed
1	Edward Vernon Rickenbacker	26
2	William C. Lambert	22
3=	August T. Iaccaci	18
3=	Frank Luke, Jr.	18
5=	Frederick W. Gillet	17
5=	Gervais Raoul Lufbery	17
7=	Howard A. Kuhlberg	16
7=	Oren J. Rose	16
9	Clive W. Warman	15
10=	David Endicott Putnam	13
10=	George Augustus Vaughan, Jr.	13

Includes American pilots flying with RAF and French flying service

The term "ace" was first used during World War I for a pilot who had brought down at least five enemy aircraft. The first-ever reference in print to an air "ace" appeared in an article in *The Times* (September 14, 1917), which described Raoul Lufbery as "the 'ace' of the American Lafayette Flying Squadron." The names of French pilots who achieved this feat were recorded in official communiqués, but although US and other pilots followed the same system, the British definition of an "ace" varied from three to ten aircraft and was never officially approved, remaining an informal concept during both World Wars.

TOP 10

GERMAN AIR ACES OF WORLD WAR I

	Pilot	Kills claimed
1	Manfred von Richthofen	80
2	Ernst Udet	62
3	Erich Loewenhardt	53
4	Werner Voss	48
5=	Bruno Loerzer	45
5=	Fritz Rumey	45
7	Rudolph Berthold	44
8	Paul Bäumer	43
9	Josef Jacobs	41
10=	Oswald Boelcke	40
10=	Franz Büchner	40
10=	Lothar Freiherr von Richthofen	40

The claims of top World War I ace Rittmeister Manfred, Baron von Richthofen of 80 kills has been disputed, since only 60 of them have been completely confirmed. Richthofen, known as the "Red Baron" and leader of the so-called "Flying Circus" (because the aircraft were painted in distinctive bright colors), shot down 21 Allied fighters in the month of April 1917.

TOP 10

FRENCH AIR ACES OF WORLD WAR I

	Pilot	Kills claimed
1	Capitaine René P. Fonck	75
2	Capitaine George M.L.J. Guynemer	54
3	Lieutenant Charles E.J.M. Nungesser	45
4	Capitaine Georges F. Madon	41
5	Lieutenant Maurice Boyau	35
6	Lieutenant Jean-Pierre L. Bourjade	28
7	Capitaine Armand Pinsard	27
8=	Sous-Lieutenant René Dorme	23
8=	Lieutenant Gabriel Guérnin	23
8=	Sous-Lieutenant Claude M. Haegelen	23

154 WORLD WAR II

THE 10

FIRST COUNTRIES TO DECLARE WAR IN WORLD WAR II

	Declaration	Date
1=	UK on Germany	Sep 3, 1939
1=	Australia on Germany	Sep 3, 1939
1=	New Zealand on Germany	Sep 3, 1939
1=	France on Germany	Sep 3, 1939
5	South Africa on Germany	Sep 6, 1939
6	Canada on Germany	Sep 9, 1939
7	Italy on UK and France	Jun 10, 1940
8	France on Italy	Jun 11, 1940
9=	Japan on US, UK, Australia, Canada, New Zealand, and South Africa	Dec 7, 1941
9=	UK on Finland, Hungary, and Romania	Dec 7, 1941

The last of these declarations took place on the day of the Japanese attack on Pearl Harbor, as a result of which the US (as well as the UK and Free France) declared war on Japan the next day. On December 11, 1941, Germany and Italy declared war on the US, followed the same day by a counter-declaration by the US. Further declarations followed right up to 1945, some even in the closing months of the war. Italy, for example, declared war on Japan as late as July 14, 1945.

SHIP OF STATE
One of the largest battleships in service during World War II, the 887-ft/270-m USS New Jersey last saw action in the Gulf War of 1990.

THE 10

COUNTRIES SUFFERING THE GREATEST MILITARY LOSSES IN WORLD WAR II

	Country	Killed
1	USSR	13,600,000
2	Germany	3,300,000
3	China	1,324,516
4	Japan	1,140,429
5	British Empire (of which UK	357,116 264,000)
6	Romania	350,000
7	Poland	320,000
8	Yugoslavia	305,000
9	US	292,131
10	Italy	279,800

THE 10

COUNTRIES SUFFERING THE GREATEST CIVILIAN LOSSES IN WORLD WAR II

	Country	Killed
1	China	8,000,000
2	USSR	6,500,000
3	Poland	5,300,000
4	Germany	2,350,000
5	Yugoslavia	1,500,000
6	France	470,000
7	Greece	415,000
8	Japan	393,400
9	Romania	340,000
10	Hungary	300,000

TOP 10

LARGEST ARMED FORCES OF WORLD WAR II

	Country	Personnel			Country	Personnel
1	USSR	12,500,000		**6**	UK	4,683,000
2	US	12,364,000		**7**	Italy	4,500,000
3	Germany	10,000,000		**8**	China	3,800,000
4	Japan	6,095,000		**9**	India	2,150,000
5	France	5,700,000		**10**	Poland	1,000,000

TOP 10

LARGEST BATTLESHIPS OF WORLD WAR II

	Battleship	Country	Status	Length m	ft	Tonnage
1=	*Musashi*	Japan	Sunk Oct 25, 1944	263	862	72,809
1=	*Yamato*	Japan	Sunk Apr 7, 1945	263	862	72,809
3=	*Iowa*	US	Decommissioned Oct 26, 1990	270	887	55,710
3=	*Missouri*	US	Decommissioned Mar 31, 1992	270	887	55,710
3=	*New Jersey*	US	Decommissioned Feb 8, 1991	270	887	55,710
3=	*Wisconsin*	US	Decommissioned Sep 30, 1991	270	887	55,710
7=	*Bismarck*	Germany	Sunk May 27, 1941	251	823	50,153
7=	*Tirpitz*	Germany	Sunk Nov 12, 1944	251	823	50,153
9=	*Jean Bart*	France	Survived war, later scrapped	247	812	47,500
9=	*Richelieu*	France	Survived war, later scrapped	247	812	47,500

FAST AND FURIOUS
*More than 20,000 of the fast and
highly maneuverable Spitfire fighter planes
were built during the course of World War II.*

T O P 1 0
FASTEST FIGHTER AIRCRAFT OF WORLD WAR II

	Aircraft	Country	Maximum speed km/h	mph
1	Messerschmitt *Me 163*	Germany	959	596
2	Messerschmitt *Me 262*	Germany	901	560
3	Heinkel *He 162A*	Germany	890	553
4	*P-51-H Mustang*	US	784	487
5	Lavochkin *La11*	USSR	740	460
6	*Spitfire XIV*	UK	721	448
7	Yakolev *Yak-3*	USSR	719	447
8	*P-51-D Mustang*	US	708	440
9	*Tempest VI*	UK	705	438
10	Focke-Wulf *Fw 190D*	Germany	700	435

T H E 1 0
MOST HEAVILY BLITZED CITIES IN THE UK

	City	Major raids	Tonnage of high explosive
1	London	85	23,949
2	Liverpool/Birkenhead	8	1,957
3	Birmingham	8	1,852
4	Glasgow/Clydeside	5	1,329
5	Plymouth/Devonport	8	1,228
6	Bristol/Avonmouth	6	919
7	Coventry	2	818
8	Portsmouth	3	687
9	Southampton	4	647
10	Hull	3	593

T O P 1 0
US AIR ACES OF WORLD WAR II

	Pilot	Kills claimed
1	Richard I. Bong	40
2	Thomas B. McGuire	38
3	David S. McCampbell	34
4=	Francis S. Gabreski	28
4=	Gregory "Pappy" Boyington	28*
6=	Robert S. Johnson	27
6=	Charles H. MacDonald	27
8=	George E. Preddy	26
8=	Joseph J. Foss	26
10	Robert M. Hanson	25

* Also 6.5 kills in the Korean War

T O P 1 0
BRITISH AND COMMONWEALTH AIR ACES OF WORLD WAR II

	Pilot	Nationality	Kills claimed
1	Marmaduke Thomas St. John Pattle	South African	over 40
2	James Edgar "Johnny" Johnson	British	33.91
3	Brendan "Paddy" Finucane	Irish	32
4	George Frederick Beurling	Canadian	31.33
5	John Randall Daniel Braham	British	29
6	Adolf Gysbert "Sailor" Malan	South African	28.66
7	Clive Robert Caldwell	Australian	28.5
8	James Harry "Ginger" Lacey	British	28
9	Neville Frederick Duke	British	27.83
10	Colin F. Gray	New Zealander	27.7

156 BATTLES & MEDALS

THE AMERICAN CIVIL WAR
More than 50,000 were killed, wounded, captured, or missing in the Battle of Gettysburg, Pennsylvania, on July 1–3, 1863, the site of which is now preserved as a National Battlefield. The action was the bloodiest of the Civil War, itself the second worst in US history.

THE 10

LONGEST WARS OF ALL TIME

	War	Combatants	Dates	Duration (years)
1	Hundred Years War	France *vs.* England	1338–1453	115
2=	Wars of the Roses	Lancaster *vs.* York	1455–85	30
2=	Thirty Years War	Catholic *vs.* Protestant	1618–48	30
4	Peloponnesian War	Peloponnesian League (Sparta, Corinth, etc.) *vs.* Delian League (Athens, etc.)	431–404 BC	27
5=	First Punic War	Rome *vs.* Carthage	264–241 BC	23
5=	Napoleonic Wars	France *vs.* other European countries	1792–1815	23
7=	Greco-Persian Wars	Greece *vs.* Persia	499–478 BC	21
7=	Second Great Northern War	Russia *vs.* Sweden and Baltic states	1700–21	21
9	Vietnam War	South Vietnam (with US support) *vs.* North Vietnam and Viet Cong	1957–75	18
10	Second Punic War	Rome *vs.* Carthage	218–201 BC	17

It may be argued that the total period of the Crusades (Christianity *vs.* Islam) constitutes one long single conflict spanning a total of 195 years from 1096 to 1291, rather than a series of nine short ones, in which case it ranks as the longest war ever. Similarly, if all the Punic Wars between 264 and 146 BC are taken as one, they would rank second at 118 years. The War of the Spanish Succession (1701–14) is the only other major conflict to have lasted more than 10 years, with the War of the Austrian Succession (1740–48), the American War of Independence (1775–83), and Chinese-Japanese War (1937–45) each lasting eight years.

THE 10

FIRST NATIONAL BATTLEFIELDS IN THE US

	National Battlefield/ battle	Established
1	Chickamauga and Chattanooga, Georgia/ Tennessee, Sep 19–20, 1863	Aug 19, 1890
2	Antietam, Maryland, Sep 17, 1862	Aug 30, 1890
3	Shiloh, Tennessee, Apr 6–7, 1862	Dec 27, 1894
4	Gettysburg, Pennsylvania, Jul 1–3, 1863	Feb 11, 1895
5	Vicksburg, Mississippi, Jan 9–Jul 4, 1863	Feb 21, 1899
6	Big Hole, Montana, Aug 9, 1877	Jun 23, 1910
7	Guilford Courthouse, North Carolina, Mar 15, 1781	Mar 2, 1917
8	Kennesaw Mountain, Georgia, Jun 20–Jul 2, 1864	Apr 22, 1917
9	Moores Creek, North Carolina, Feb 27, 1776	Jun 2, 1926
10	Petersburg, Virginia, Jun 15, 1864– Apr 3, 1865	Jul 3, 1926

* *Dates include those for locations originally assigned other designations but later authorized as National Battlefields, National Battlefield Parks, and National Military Parks*

There are in all 24 National Battlefields, National Battlefield Parks, and National Military Parks, but just one National Battlefield Site, Brices Cross Roads, Mississippi (the scene of a Civil War engagement on June 10, 1864; the site was established on February 21, 1929). The earliest battle to be so commemorated is Fort Necessity, Pennsylvania (July 3, 1754; National Battlefield established March 4, 1931), the site of the opening hostility in the French and Indian War, in which the militia led by George Washington, then a 22-year-old Lt. Colonel, was defeated and captured.

T O P 1 0

US MEDAL OF HONOR CAMPAIGNS

	Campaign	Years	Medals awarded
1	Civil War	1861–65	1,520
2	World War II	1941–45	433
3	Indian Wars	1861–98	428
4	Vietnam War	1965–73	238
5	Korean War	1950–53	131
6	World War I	1917–18	123
7	Spanish–American War	1898	109
8	Philippines/Samoa	1899–1913	91
9	Boxer Rebellion	1900	59
10	Veracruz	1914	55

The Medal of Honor, the US's highest military award, was first issued in 1863. In addition to the medal itself, recipients receive such benefits as a $400 per month pension for life, free air travel, and the right to be buried in the Arlington National Cemetery. Past winners of the award include William "Buffalo Bill" Cody, who received it in 1872. His medal was revoked in 1917 when a new ruling stipulated that recipients had to have been serving members of the military, but it was reinstated in 1989.

T H E 1 0

20TH-CENTURY WARS WITH THE MOST MILITARY FATALITIES

	War/years	Approximate no. of fatalities
1	World War II (1939–45)	15,843,000
2	World War I (1914–18)	8,545,800
3	Korean War (1950–53)	1,893,100
4=	Sino-Japanese War (1937–41)	1,000,000
4=	Biafra–Nigeria Civil War (1967–70)	1,000,000
6	Spanish Civil War (1936–39)	611,000
7	Vietnam War (1965–73)	546,000
8=	India–Pakistan War (1947)	200,000
8=	Soviet invasion of Afghanistan (1979–89)	200,000
8=	Iran–Iraq War (1980–88)	200,000

The statistics of warfare have always been an imperfect science. Not only are battle deaths seldom recorded accurately, but figures are often deliberately inflated by both sides in a conflict. For political reasons and to maintain morale, each is anxious to enhance reports of its military success and low casualty figures, so that often quite contradictory reports of the same battle may be issued. These figures thus represent military historians' "best guesses."

T H E 1 0

WORST US CIVIL WAR BATTLES

	Battle/date	Casualties*
1	Gettysburg, Jul 1–3, 1863	51,116
2	Seven Days Battles, Jun 25–Jul 1, 1862	36,463
3	Chickamauga, Sep 19–20, 1863	34,624
4	Chancellorsville/ Fredericksburg, May 1–4, 1863	29,609
5	Wilderness#, May 5–7, 1862	25,416
6	Manassas/Chantilly, Aug 27–Sep 2, 1862	25,340
7	Stone's River, Dec 31, 1862–Jan 1, 1863	24,645
8	Shiloh, Apr 6–7, 1862	23,741
9	Antietam, Sep 17, 1862	22,726
10	Fredericksburg, Dec 13, 1862	17,962

* Killed, missing, and wounded
\# Confederate totals estimated

T H E 1 0

WARS WITH MOST US MILITARY FATALITIES

	War/years	Military fatalities
1	World War II, 1941–46	292,131
2	Civil War, 1861–65	140,414*
3	World War I, 1917–18	53,513
4	Vietnam War, 1965–73	47,369
5	Korean War, 1950–53	33,651
6	Revolutionary War, 1775–83	4,435
7	War of 1812, 1812–15	2,260
8	Mexican War, 1846–48	1,733
9	Spanish-American War, 1898	385
10	Gulf War, 1990–91	148

* Union only; Confederate deaths estimated 74,524, but data incomplete

WAR WOUNDED
Innumerable civilians have also been killed or injured. More than 30 million military fatalities have resulted from 20th-century conflicts.

MODERN MILITARY

COUNTRIES WITH THE LARGEST DEFENSE BUDGETS

	Country	Budget ($)
1	US	267,900,000,000
2	Russia	48,000,000,000
3	Japan	46,800,000,000
4	France	37,200,000,000
5	Germany	33,600,000,000
6	UK	33,200,000,000
7	Italy	20,000,000,000
8	South Korea	15,600,000,000
9	Saudi Arabia	13,900,000,000
10=	China	8,400,000,000
10=	India	8,400,000,000
	Canada	*7,200,000,000*

The so-called "peace dividend" – the savings made as a consequence of the end of the Cold War between the West and the former Soviet Union – means that both the numbers of personnel and the defense budgets of many countries have been cut. That of the US has gone down from its 1989 peak of $303.6 billion.

LARGEST ARMED FORCES IN THE WORLD

	Country	Army	Estimated active forces Navy	Air Force	Total
1	China	2,200,000	265,000	470,000	2,935,000
2	US	495,000	426,700	388,200	1,880,600 *
3	Russia	460,000	190,000	145,000	1,270,000 #
4	India	980,000	110,000	55,000	1,145,000
5	North Korea	923,000	46,000	85,000	1,054,000
6	South Korea	548,000	60,000	52,000	660,000
7	Turkey	525,000	51,000	63,000	639,000
8	Pakistan	520,000	22,000	45,000	587,000
9	Vietnam	500,000	42,000	15,000	572,000
10	Iran	345,000	18,000	30,000	513,000 +

* Includes 173,900 Marine Corps and 499,800 members of the National Guard
 # Includes Strategic Deterrent Forces, Paramilitary, National Guard, etc
+ Includes 120,000 Revolutionary Guards

In addition to the active forces listed here, many of the world's foremost military powers have considerable reserves on standby. South Korea's has been estimated at some 4,500,000, Vietnam's at 3–4,000,000, and China's 1,200,000. Russia's has steadily dwindled as a result both of the end of the Cold War and its current economic problems. China is also notable for having a massive arsenal of military equipment at its disposal, including some 8,000 tanks, 4,600 fighter aircraft, and 1,225 bombers and ground attack aircraft.

COUNTRIES WITH THE HIGHEST PER CAPITA DEFENSE EXPENDITURE

	Country	Expenditure per capita, 1995 ($)
1	Kuwait	2,091
2	Singapore	1,349
3	Israel	1,279
4	US	1,056
5	United Arab Emirates	1,044
6	Oman	978
7	Brunei	909
8	Norway	863
9	France	826
10	Switzerland	720

ARMS IMPORTERS IN THE WORLD

	Country	Annual imports ($)
1	Saudi Arabia	5,200,000,000
2	Libya	1,800,000,000
3	Egypt	1,500,000,000
4	US	1,100,000,000
5=	Israel	1,000,000,000
5=	South Korea	1,000,000,000
7	Turkey	950,000,000
8	Japan	650,000,000
9	Angola	600,000,000
10	Spain	525,000,000

COUNTRIES WITH THE HIGHEST MILITARY/ CIVILIAN RATIO

	Country	Military personnel per 10,000 population
1	Russia	833
2	North Korea	435
3	United Arab Emirates	357
4	Israel	303
5	Syria	286
6	Jordan	217
7	Qatar	213
8	Bahrein	189
9	Iraq	175
10	Armenia	167
	US	*56*

T O P   1 0

RANKS OF THE US NAVY, ARMY, AND AIR FORCE

	Navy	Army	Air Force
1	Fleet Admiral	General	General
2	Admiral	Lieutenant General	Lieutenant General
3	Vice Admiral	Major General	Major General
4	Rear Admiral (Upper Half)	Brigadier General	Brigadier General
5	Rear Admiral (Lower Half)	Colonel	Colonel
6	Captain	Lieutenant Colonel	Lieutenant Colonel
7	Commodore	Major	Major
8	Lieutenant Commander	Captain	Captain
9	Lieutenant	First Lieutenant	First Lieutenant
10	Lieutenant (Junior Grade)	Second Lieutenant	Second Lieutenant

STORMIN' NORMAN'S DESERT VICTORY
General Norman Schwarzkopf acknowledges applause during a special meeting of the US Congress after his return from the Gulf War. He declared, "It's a great day to be a soldier and a great day to be an American."

T O P   1 0

RANKS OF THE ROYAL NAVY, ARMY, AND ROYAL AIR FORCE

	Royal Navy	Army	Royal Air Force
1	Admiral	General	Air Chief Marshal
2	Vice-Admiral	Lieutenant-General	Air Marshal
3	Rear-Admiral	Major-General	Air Vice-Marshal
4	Commodore	Brigadier	Air Commodore
5	Captain	Colonel	Group Captain
6	Commander	Lieutenant-Colonel	Wing Commander
7	Lieutenant-Commander	Major	Squadron Leader
8	Lieutenant	Captain	Flight Lieutenant
9	Sub-Lieutenant	Lieutenant	Flying Officer
10	Acting Sub-Lieutenant	Second Lieutenant	Pilot Officer

T O P   1 0

COUNTRIES WITH THE LARGEST UN PEACEKEEPING FORCES*

	Country	Troops
1	Pakistan	1,725
2	Bangladesh	1,155
3	Russian Federation	1,114
4	Jordan	1,101
5	Poland	1,094
6	India	1,082
7	Canada	1,067
8	Brazil	1,014
9	Finland	910
10	Austria	865

* As of March 31, 1997

United Nations peacekeeping forces are established by the UN Security Council. Although most UN member states provide troops, they are most frequently drawn from neutral or nonaligned members.

In February 1996 the three most senior ranks in all three services – Admiral of the Fleet, Field Marshal, and Marshal of the Royal Air Force – were abolished, in the cases of the first two ending a tradition that dates back several centuries. The names given to some ranks date back to Medieval times – in the case of Admiral of the Fleet, for example, its earliest use in English has been dated to *c.* 1425, while Admiral was used even earlier to mean a prince or other military ruler in the service of a Sultan. The first recorded use of General was in 1576, and it appeared in Shakespeare's plays soon afterwards. The term Brigadier dates from 1678, and Field Marshall first appeared in print in 1736, when the Duke of Argyll and the Earl of Orkney were both appointed as Field Marshalls of the British army. Some terms have parallels in the US military, but with certain differences: in the Royal Navy, for example, the rank of Commodore, first recorded in 1695, is a temporary one applied to senior officers in command of detached squadrons, and is divided into two classes, the upper of which receives pay equivalent to that of a Rear-Admiral and has a captain under him, while the second class does not. Since 1862, in the US navy, a commodore may command a naval division or station, or a first-class warship.

WORLD RELIGIONS

THE WAY OF BUDDHA
*Originating in India in the 6th century BC,
Buddhism's quest for enlightenment and its
espousal of peace and tolerance have contributed
to its appeal throughout Asia and beyond.*

TOP 10

ORGANIZED RELIGIONS IN THE WORLD

	Religion	Members
1	Christianity	1,927,953,000
2	Islam	1,099,634,000
3	Hinduism	780,547,000
4	Buddhism	323,894,000
5	Sikhism	19,161,000
6	Judaism	14,117,000
7	Confucianism	5,254,000
8	Baha'ism	6,104,000
9	Jainism	4,886,000
10	Shintoism	2,844,000

This list excludes the followers of various
tribal and folk religions, new religions, and
shamanism, which together total almost
500,000,000. There are also perhaps more
than 800,000,000 people who may be
classified as "nonreligious" (having no
interest in religion of any persuasion), and
a further 220,000,000 atheists (opposed to
religion of any kind, or followers of
alternative, nonreligious philosophies).

TOP 10

LARGEST BUDDHIST POPULATIONS IN THE WORLD

	Location	Total Buddhist population
1	China	102,000,000
2	Japan	89,650,000*
3	Thailand	55,480,000
4	Vietnam	49,690,000
5	Myanmar	41,610,000
6	Sri Lanka	12,540,000
7	South Korea	10,920,000
8	Taiwan	9,150,000
9	Cambodia	9,130,000
10	India	7,000,000

* Including many who also practice Shintoism

TOP 10

LARGEST JEWISH POPULATIONS IN THE WORLD

	Location	Total Jewish population
1	US	5,602,000
2	Israel	4,390,000
3	Russia	1,450,000
4	France	640,000
5	Canada	350,000
6	UK	320,000
7	Argentina	250,000
8	Brazil	150,000
9	Australia	92,000
10	South Africa	70,000

The Diaspora, or scattering of Jewish
people, has been in progress for
nearly 2,000 years, and as a
result Jewish communities
are found in virtually every
country in the world.

TOP 10

LARGEST CHRISTIAN POPULATIONS IN THE WORLD

	Location	Total Christian population
1	US	224,457,000
2	Brazil	139,000,000
3	Mexico	86,210,000
4	Germany	67,170,000
5	Philippines	63,470,000
6	UK	51,060,000
7	Italy	47,690,000
8	France	44,150,000
9	Nigeria	38,180,000
10	Russia	37,400,000

It is difficult to put a precise figure on
nominal membership of a religion (declared
religious persuasion) rather than active
participation (regular attendance at a place of
worship). It was claimed, for example, that
out of the total US population of
248,709,873 (according to the 1990 Census),
62.86 percent were active members of a
religious organization including
non-Christian groups, whereas this Top 10
asserts a nominal figure for Christians alone
that is equivalent to almost 90 percent of
the country's current population.

PRACTICING THE JEWISH FAITH
*The prayer shawl (tallith), skull cap
(yarmulke), branched candlestick (menorah),
and Hebrew Bible are important in the
practice of Judaism.*

THE BLUE MOSQUE
The superbly decorated Blue Mosque in Istanbul, Turkey, is one of the great centers of the Muslim faith. Islam, the world's fastest-growing religion, has almost 800 million followers in the Top 10 countries alone.

T O P 1 0

LARGEST MUSLIM POPULATIONS IN THE WORLD

	Location	Total Muslim population
1	Indonesia	170,310,000
2	Pakistan	136,000,000
3	Bangladesh	106,050,000
4	India	103,000,000
5	Turkey	62,410,000
6	Iran	60,790,000
7	Egypt	53,730,000
8	Nigeria	47,720,000
9	Algeria	27,910,000
10	Morocco	26,900,000

Historically, Islam spread as a result of both missionary activity and through contact with Muslim traders. In countries such as Indonesia, where Islam was introduced as early as the 14th century, its appeal lay partly in its opposition to Western colonial influences, which, along with the concept of Islamic community and other tenets, has attracted followers worldwide. The global Muslim population is now thought to be in the region of 1,126,325,000.

T O P 1 0

LARGEST HINDU POPULATIONS IN THE WORLD

	Location	Total Hindu population
1	India	751,000,000
2	Nepal	17,380,000
3	Bangladesh	12,630,000
4	Sri Lanka	2,800,000
5	Pakistan	2,120,000

	Location	Total Hindu population
6	Malaysia	1,400,000
7	US	910,000
8	Mauritius	570,000
9	South Africa	420,000
10	UK	410,000

T O P 1 0

RELIGIOUS AFFILIATIONS IN THE US

	Affiliation	Members
1	Protestant	85,500,000
2	Roman Catholic	59,450,000
3	African-American Christian	34,800,000
4	Orthodox Christian	5,631,000
5	Jewish	5,602,000
6	Muslim	3,767,000
7	Episcopalian	2,350,000
8	Buddhist	1,864,000
9	Hindu	795,000
10	Baha'i	683,000

T O P 1 0

FASTEST GROWING RELIGIOUS AFFILIATIONS IN THE US*

	Affiliation	Members 1970	1995	percent growth
1	Sikh	1,000	190,000	18,900.0
2	Hindu	100,000	910,000	810.0
3	Muslim	800,000	5,100,000	537.5
4	Buddhist	200,000	780,000	290.0
5	Baha'i	138,000	300,000	117.4
6	Evangelical Christian	50,688,000	72,363,000	42.8
7	Orthodox Christian	4,387,000	5,631,000	28.4
8	Roman Catholic	48,391,000	55,259,000	14.2
9	Jewish	6,700,000	5,602,000	-16.4
10	Episcopalian	3,234,000	2,350,000	-27.3

Based on increases/decreases in membership between 1970 and 1995

THE BIBLE

NAMES MOST MENTIONED IN THE BIBLE

	Name	OT*	NT*	Total
1	Jesus (984)/ Christ (576)	0	1,560	1,560
2	David	1,005	59	1,064
3	Moses	767	80	847
4	Jacob	350	27	377
5	Aaron	347	5	352
6	Solomon	293	12	305
7=	Joseph	215	35	250
7=	Abraham	176	74	250
9	Ephraim	182	1	183
10	Benjamin	162	2	166

* Occurrences in verses in the King James Bible (Old and New Testaments), including possessive uses, such as "John's"

In addition to these personal names, "God" is referred to on 4,105 occasions (2,749 Old Testament; 1,356 New Testament). The name Judah also appears 816 times, but the total includes references to the territory as well as the individual with that name. At the other end of the scale, there are many names that – perhaps fortunately – appear only once or twice, among them Berodach-baladan and Tilgath-pilneser. The most mentioned place names produce few surprises, with Israel heading the list (2,600 references), followed by Jerusalem (814), Egypt (736), Babylon (298), and Assyria (141). Heaven is referred to 440 times in both the Old and New Testaments.

ANIMALS MOST MENTIONED IN THE BIBLE

	Animal	OT*	NT*	Total
1	Sheep	155	45	200
2	Lamb	153	35	188
3	Lion	167	9	176
4	Ox	156	10	166
5	Ram	165	0	165
6	Horse	137	27	164
7	Bullock	152	0	152
8	Ass	142	8	150
9	Goat	131	7	138
10	Camel	56	6	62

* Occurrences in verses in the King James Bible (Old and New Testaments), including plurals

The sheep are sorted from the goats in this Top 10, in a menagerie of the animals considered most significant in biblical times, either economically or symbolically (as in the many references to the lion's strength). A number of generic terms are also found in abundance: beast (a total of 337 references), cattle (153), fowl (90), fish (56), and bird (41). Some creatures are mentioned only once, in *Leviticus* 11, which contains a list of animals that are considered "unclean" – the weasel, chameleon, and tortoise, for example – and are never referred to again. Though Egypt may have suffered a plague of frogs, just 14 appear in the Bible, along with just three spiders and two mice.

LONGEST WORDS IN THE BIBLE

	Word*	Letters
1=	covenantbreakers (NT only)	16
1=	evilfavouredness	16
1=	lovingkindnesses	16
1=	unprofitableness	16
1=	unrightreousness (and NT)	16
1=	uprightreousness	16
7=	acknowledgement	15
7=	administrations (NT only)	15
7=	bloodyguiltness	15
7=	confectionaries	15
7=	fellowdisciples (NT only)	15
7=	fellowlabourers (NT only)	15
7=	interpretations	15
7=	kneadingtroughs	15
7=	notwithstanding (and NT)	15
7=	prognosticators	15
7=	righteousnesses	15
7=	stumblingblocks	15
7=	threshingfloors	15

* All Old Testament only (King James version) unless otherwise stated

GIDEONS INTERNATIONAL

If you have ever wondered where the bibles that are found in hotel rooms the world over came from, the answer dates back to 1898, when traveling salesman John H. Nicholson and his colleague Sam Hill stayed at the Central Hotel Boscobel, Wisconsin, and there decided to establish an association of Christian businessmen. Their avowed aim was to "put the word of God into the hands of the unconverted," which they proposed to achieve by placing bibles in hotel rooms, hospitals, prisons, and other locations. A century on, Gideons International continues to distribute a total of more than 16,000,000 bibles a year the world over.

YEARS AGO • YEARS AGO • 100 • YEARS AGO

T O P   1 0

LONGEST NAMES OF PEOPLE AND PLACES IN THE BIBLE

	Name	Letters
1	Mahershalalhashbaz (Isaiah's son)	18
2=	Bashanhavothjair (alternative name of Argob)	16
2=	Chepharhaammonai (Ammonite settlement)	16
2=	Chusharishathaim (king of Mesopotamia)	16
2=	Kibrothhattaavah (desert encampment of Israelites)	16
2=	Selahammahlekoth (stronghold in Maon)	16
7=	Abelbethmaachah (town near Damascus)	15
7=	Almondiblathaim (stopping-place of Israelites)	15
7=	Apharsathchites (Assyrian nomadic group)	15
7=	Berodachbaladan/Merodachbaladan (king of Babylon)	15
7=	Helkathhazzurim (a battlefield)	15
7=	Ramathaimzophin (town where Samuel was born)	15
7=	Tilgathpilneser (king of Assyria)	15
7=	Zaphnathpaaneah (name given to Joseph by Pharaoh)	15

T O P   1 0

WORDS MOST MENTIONED IN THE BIBLE

	Word	OT*	NT*	Total
1	The	52,948	10,976	63,924
2	And	40,975	10,721	51,696
3	Of	28,518	6,099	34,617
4	To	10,207	3,355	13,562
5	That	9,152	3,761	12,913
6	In	9,767	2,900	12,667
7	He	7,348	3,072	10,420
8	For	6,690	2,281	8,971
9	I	6,669	2,185	8,854
10	His	7,036	1,437	8,473

* *Occurrences in verses in the King James Bible (Old and New Testaments)*

A century before computers were invented, Thomas Hartwell Horne (1780–1862), a dogged biblical researcher, undertook a manual search of biblical word frequencies and concluded that "and" appeared a total of 35,543 times in the Old Testament and 10,684 times in the New Testament. He was fairly close on the latter – but he clearly missed quite a few in the Old Testament, as a recent computer search of the King James Bible indicates.

T H E   1 0

CHAPTERS OF THE BIBLE WITH MOST VERSES

	Chapter	Verses		Chapter	Verses
1	Psalms	2,461	6	Ezekiel	1,273
2	Genesis	1,533	7	Exodus	1,213
3	Jeremiah	1,364	8	Luke	1,151
4	Isaiah	1,292	9	Matthew	1,071
5	Numbers	1,288	10	Job	1,070

There are 31,102 verses in the bible (King James Version), 23,145 in the Old Testament and 7,957 in the New. *Psalms* not only contains the greatest number of verses, but also the most words – a total of 42,732 (though *Jeremiah* runs only three behind, with 42,729). *The Second Epistle of John* contains the fewest verses – just 13. The longest verse in the bible is *Esther* 8:9, which comprises 90 words, and the shortest is *John* 11:35, which consists of the two words, "Jesus wept."

T O P   1 0

CROPS MOST MENTIONED IN THE BIBLE

	Crop	OT*	NT*	Total
1	Corn	86	11	97
2	Fig	45	21	66
3	Olive	42	19	61
4	Wheat	40	12	52
5	Grape	46	3	49
6	Barley	43	3	46
7	Pomegranate	33	0	33
8	Raisin	9	7	16
9	Apple	11	0	11
10	Bean	6	0	6

* *Occurrences in verses in the King James Bible (Old and New Testaments), including plurals*

DISASTERS

RAIL DISASTERS **164**

ROAD TRANSPORTATION

DISASTERS **166**

MARINE DISASTERS **168**

AIR DISASTERS **170**

MAN-MADE & OTHER

DISASTERS **172**

NATURAL DISASTERS **174**

T H E 1 0

WORST RAIL DISASTERS IN THE WORLD

Location/date/incident	No. killed
1 Bagmati River, India, June 6, 1981	c. 800

The carriages of a train traveling from Samastipur to Banmukhi in Bihar plunged off a bridge over the Bagmati River near Mansi when the driver braked, apparently to avoid hitting a sacred cow. Although the official death toll was said to have been 268, many authorities have claimed that the train was so massively overcrowded that the actual figure was in excess of 800, making it probably the worst rail disaster of all time.

2 Chelyabinsk, Russia, June 3, 1989	up to 800

Two Trans-Siberian passenger trains, going to and from the Black Sea, were destroyed when liquid gas from a nearby pipeline exploded.

3 Guadalajara, Mexico, January 18, 1915	over 600

A train derailed on a steep incline, but political strife in the country meant that full details of the disaster were suppressed.

4 Modane, France, December 12, 1917	573

A troop-carrying train ran out of control and was derailed. It was probably overloaded, and as many as 1,000 people may have died.

5 Balvano, Italy, March 2, 1944	521

A heavily-laden train stalled in the Armi Tunnel, and many passengers asphyxiated.

6 Torre, Spain, January 3, 1944	over 500

A double collision and fire in a tunnel resulted in many deaths. Like the disaster at Balvano two months later, wartime secrecy prevented full details from being published.

Location/date/incident	No. killed
7 Awash, Ethiopia, January 13, 1985	428

A derailment hurled a train into a ravine.

8 Cireau, Romania, January 7, 1917	374

An overcrowded passenger train crashed into a military train and was derailed.

9 Quipungo, Angola, May 31, 1993	355

A train was derailed by UNITA guerrilla action.

10 Sangi, Pakistan, January 4, 1990	306

A diverted train resulted in a fatal collision.

Casualty figures for rail accidents are often extremely imprecise, especially during wartime – and no fewer than half of the 10 worst disasters occurred during the two World Wars. Other vague incidents, such as one at Kalish, Poland, in December 1914, for example, with "400 dead," one in November 1918 at Norrköpping, Sweden, alleged to have killed 300, and certain other similarly uncertain cases have been omitted.

SCENE OF THE ACCIDENT
Some of the worst rail accidents in both the US and UK occurred when signaling and safety equipment was less sophisticated than it is today.

THE 10

WORST RAIL DISASTERS IN THE US

	Location/date/incident	No. killed
1	Nashville, Tennessee, July 9, 1918	101

On the Nashville, Chattanooga, and St. Louis Railroad, a head-on collision resulted in a death toll that remains the worst in US history, with 171 injured.

2	Brooklyn, New York, November 2, 1918	97

A subway train was derailed in the Malbone Street tunnel.

3=	Eden, Colorado, August 7, 1904	96

A bridge washed away during a flood smashed Steele's Hollow Bridge as the "World's Fair Express" was crossing.

3=	Wellington, Washington, March 1, 1910	96

An avalanche swept two trains into a canyon.

5	Bolivar, Texas, September 8, 1900	85

A train traveling from Beaumont encountered the hurricane that destroyed Galveston killing 6,000. Attempts to load the train onto a ferry were abandoned, and when it tried to return it was destroyed by the storm.

6	Woodbridge, New Jersey, February 6, 1951	84

A Pennsylvania Railroad train crashed while speeding through a sharply curving detour.

7	Chatsworth, Illinois, August 10, 1887	82

A trestle bridge caught fire and collapsed as the Toledo, Peoria & Western train was crossing. As many as 372 were injured.

8	Ashtabula, Ohio, December 29, 1876	80

A bridge collapsed in a snow storm, and the Lake Shore train fell into the Ashtabula river. The death toll may have been as high as 92.

9=	Frankford Junction, Pennsylvania, September 6, 1943	79

This was Pennsylvania's worst railroad accident since that at Camp Hill on July 17, 1856, which resulted in the deaths of 66 school children on a church picnic outing.

9=	Richmond Hill, New York, November 22, 1950	79

A Long Island Railroad commuter train rammed into the rear of another, leaving 79 dead and 363 injured.

THE 10

WORST RAIL DISASTERS IN THE UK

	Location/date/incident	No. killed
1	Quintinshill near Gretna Green, May 22, 1915	227

A troop train carrying 500 members of the 7th Royal Scots Regiment collided head on with a passenger train. Barely a minute later, the Scottish express, drawn by two engines and weighing a total of 600 tons, plowed into the wreckage. The 15 coaches of the troop train, 640 yards/195 m long, were so crushed that they ended up just 200 ft/61 m long. The gas-lit troop train then caught fire. Since their records were destroyed in the blaze, the actual number of soldiers killed was never established. It was probably 215, as well as two members of the train's crew, eight in the express, and two in the local train – a total of 227 killed and 246 injured, many very seriously. An inquest established that the accident was caused by the negligence of the signalmen, George Meakin and James Tinsley, who were convicted of manslaughter and jailed.

2	Harrow and Wealdstone Station, October 8, 1952	122

In patchy fog Robert Jones, the relief driver of the Perth to Euston sleeping car express, pulled by the City of Glasgow, failed to see a series of signal lights warning him of danger, and at 8:19am collided with the waiting Watford to Euston train. Seconds later, the Euston to Liverpool and Manchester express hit the wreckage of the two trains. The casualties were 112 killed instantly, 10 who died later, and 349 injured.

3	Lewisham, South London, December 4, 1957	90

A steam and an electric train collided in fog. The disaster was made worse by the collapse of a bridge onto the wreckage.

4	Tay Bridge, Scotland, December 28, 1879	80

As the North British mail train passed over it during a storm, the bridge collapsed, killing all 75 passengers and the crew of five. The bridge – the longest in the world at that time – had only been opened on May 31 the previous year, and Queen Victoria had crossed it in a train soon afterward. The locomotive was salvaged from the bed of the Tay several months later. It had surprisingly little damage and was repaired. It continued in service until 1919.

5	Armagh, Northern Ireland, June 12, 1889	78

A Sunday school excursion train with 940 passengers stalled on a hill. When 10 coaches were uncoupled, they ran backward and collided with a passenger train, killing 78 (claims of 300 deaths have not been substantiated) and leaving 250 injured.

6	Hither Green, South London, November 5, 1967	49

The Hastings to Charing Cross train was derailed by a broken track. As well as those killed, 78 were injured, 27 of them seriously.

7=	Bourne End, Hertfordshire, September 30, 1945	43

Traveling at about 50 mph, the Perth to Euston express sped through a crossover with a 20 mph speed restriction imposed during engineering works, and was derailed. Its coaches plunged down an embankment.

7=	Moorgate Station, London, February 28, 1975	43

A subway train ran into the wall at the end of the tunnel, killing 43 and injuring 74 in London Transport's worst rail disaster.

9	Castlecary, Scotland, December 10, 1937	35

The Edinburgh to Glasgow train ran into a stationary train and rode over the top of it.

10=	Shipton near Oxford, 24 December 1874	34

The Paddington to Birkenhead train plunged over the embankment after a coach wheel broke, killing 34 and badly injuring 65.

10=	Clapham Junction, London, December 12, 1988	34

The 7:18 Basingstoke to Waterloo train, carrying 906 passengers, stopped at signals outside Clapham Junction; the 6:30 train from Bournemouth ran into its rear, and an empty train from Waterloo hit the wreckage, leaving 33 dead (and one who died later) and 111 injured.

OFF THE RAILS

Rail passengers are not always as lucky as those who miraculously escaped when this carriage failed to plunge over a viaduct.

ROAD TRANSPORTATION DISASTERS

THE 10

WORST MOTOR VEHICLE AND ROAD DISASTERS IN THE WORLD

	Location/date/incident	No. killed
1	Afghanistan, November 3, 1982	2,000+

Following a collision with a Soviet army truck, a gasoline tanker exploded in the 1.7-mile/2.7-km long Salang Tunnel. Some authorities estimate that the death toll could be as high as 3,000.

2	Colombia, August 7, 1956	1,200

Seven army ammunition trucks exploded at night in the center of the city of Cali, destroying eight city blocks.

3	Thailand, February 15, 1990	150+

A dynamite truck exploded.

4	Nepal, November 23, 1974	148

Hindu pilgrims were killed when a suspension bridge over the Mahahali River collapsed.

5	Egypt, August 9, 1973	127

A bus drove into an irrigation canal.

6	Togo, December 6, 1965	125+

Two trucks collided with a group of dancers during a festival at Sotouboua.

7	Spain, July 11, 1978	120+

A liquid-gas tanker exploded in a camping site at San Carlos de la Rapita.

8	South Korea, April 28, 1995	110

An underground explosion destroyed vehicles and caused about 100 cars and buses to plunge into the pit it created.

9	Gambia, November 12, 1992	c. 100

A bus full of passengers plunged into a river when its brakes failed.

10	Kenya, early December 1992	nearly 100

A bus carrying 112 passengers skidded, hit a bridge, and plunged into a river.

The worst-ever motor racing accident occurred on June 13, 1955, at Le Mans, France, when French driver Pierre Levegh's Mercedes-Benz 300 SLR went out of control, hit a wall, and exploded in mid-air, showering wreckage into the crowd and killing a total of 82 people.

TOP 10

"SAFEST" CAR COLORS

	Color	Light reflection percent
1	White	84.0
2	Cream	68.8
3	Ivory	66.7
4	Light pink	66.5
5	Yellow	57.0
6	Flesh	51.6
7	Buff	51.5
8	Light gray	51.5
9	Light green	45.2
10	Aluminum gray	41.0

Source: Mansell Color Company, Inc., published by the National Safety Council

There is little agreement as to what car color is "safest," but some authorities claim that those that reflect the most light are the most visble, and hence safer than darker colors.

THE 10

WORST YEARS FOR FATAL MOTOR VEHICLE ACCIDENTS IN THE US

	Year	Fatalities per 100,000,000 VMT*	Total deaths#
1	1972	4.3	54,589
2	1973	4.1	54,052
3	1969	5.0	53,543
4	1968	5.2	52,725
5	1970	4.7	52,627
6	1971	4.5	52,542
7	1979	3.3	51,093
8	1980	3.3	51,091
9	1966	5.5	50,894
10	1967	5.3	50,724

* Vehicle Miles of Travel
 # Traffic fatalities occurring within 30 days of accident

THE 10

MOST VULNERABLE AGES FOR ROAD FATALITIES IN THE US

	Age group	Deaths (1995)	Deaths per 1,000,000
1	16–20	5,686	319
2	21–24	4,266	298
3	74+	3,873	262
4	25–34	7,907	193
5	65–74	3,118	166
6	35–44	6,416	151
7	55–64	2,937	139
8	45–54	4,163	134
9	10–15	1,637	72
10	5–9	856	45

THE 10

MOST COMMON FACTORS IN FATAL CRASHES IN THE US, 1995

	Cause	Deaths	%
1	Failure to keep in proper lane or running off road	15,873	28.3
2	Driving too fast for conditions or in excess of posted speed limit	11,656	20.8
3	Failure to yield right of way	4,868	8.7
4	Inattention (talking, eating, etc.)	3,323	5.9
5	Failure to obey traffic signs, signals, or officer	3,189	5.7
6	Operating vehicle in erratic, reckless, careless, or negligent manner	2,850	5.1
7	Swerving or avoiding due to wind, slippery surface, vehicle, object, nonmotorist in street, etc.	1,926	3.4
8	Drowsiness, sleep, fatigue, illness, or blackout	1,816	3.2
9	Driving wrong way on one-way street or on wrong side of road	1,387	2.5
10	Overcorrecting/ oversteering	1,328	2.4

DEATH ON THE ROAD

As the number of vehicles on the world's roads has increased, so have fatalities resulting from traffic accidents. Based on total numbers of deaths, the US tops the list, but not because American drivers are any less careful than those of other countries: the US has far more vehicles that collectively travel greater distances than any other country on Earth, and when these factors are considered, the rate of fatal accidents is actually much lower than in many countries. On the basis of deaths per 100 million vehicle miles, the US has just 1.8, while South Korea, for example, has a rate of 46.9, or 26 times as many, implying that driving habits and road conditions play more significant roles.

FLAG OF INCONVENIENCE
Until 1896 British drivers had to warn of their presence by waving a red flag.

THE 10

COUNTRIES WITH THE HIGHEST NUMBER OF ROAD DEATHS

	Country	Total deaths*
1	US	41,465
2	Thailand	15,176
3	Japan	10,649
4	South Korea	10,087
5	Germany	9,814
6	France	8,533
7	Brazil	6,759
8	Poland	6,744
9	Italy	6,578
10	Spain	6,378

* In latest year for which figures are available

SCENE OF THE ACCIDENT
Car crashes in the US kill more than 40,000 people every year.

AFTER THE EVENT
Firefighters are called in to rescue crash victims and to clear up after road accidents.

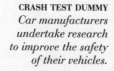

CRASH TEST DUMMY
Car manufacturers undertake research to improve the safety of their vehicles.

MARINE DISASTERS

WORST MARINE DISASTERS
OF THE 20TH CENTURY

	Vessel	Date	Approx. no. killed
1	Wilhelm Gustloff	January 30, 1945	up to 7,700

This German liner, laden with refugees, was torpedoed off Danzig by a Soviet submarine, S-13. The precise death toll remains uncertain, but it is thought to be in the range of 5,348–7,700.

2	Goya	April 16, 1945	6,500

A German ship carrying evacuees from Danzig was torpedoed in the Baltic near Cape Rixhöft.

3	Unknown vessel	November 1947	over 6,000

An unidentified Chinese troopship carrying Nationalist soldiers from Manchuria sank off Yingkow. The exact date is unknown.

4	Cap Arcona	May 3, 1945	4,650

A German ship carrying concentration camp survivors was bombed and sunk by British aircraft in Lübeck harbor.

5	Lancastria	June 17, 1940	4,000

A British troopship sank off St. Nazaire.

6	Yamato	April 7, 1945	3,033

The Japanese battleship sank off Kyushu Island.

7	Dona Paz	December 20, 1987	up to 3,000

The ferry Dona Paz was struck by oil tanker MV Victor in the Tabias Strait, Philippines.

8	Kiangya	December 3, 1948	over 2,750

An overloaded steamship carrying refugees struck a Japanese mine off Woosung, China.

9	Thielbeck	May 3, 1945	2,750

A refugee ship sank during the British bombardment of Lübeck harbor in the closing weeks of World War II.

10	Arisan Maru	October 24, 1944	1,790

A Japanese vessel carrying American prisoners of war was torpedoed by a US submarine in the South China Sea.

Due to a reassessment of the death tolls in some World War II marine disasters, the most famous of all, the sinking of the *Titanic* (the British liner that struck an iceberg in the North Atlantic on April 15, 1912 and went down with the loss of 1,517 lives), no longer ranks in this list. However, the *Titanic* tragedy remains one of the worst-ever peacetime disasters, along with such notable incidents as that involving the *General Slocum*, an excursion liner that caught fire in the port of New York on June 15, 1904, with the loss of 1,021. Among other disasters occurring during wartime are the sinking of the British cruiser *HMS Hood* by the German battleship *Bismarck* in the Denmark Strait on May 24, 1941, with 1,418 killed; the torpedoing by German submarine *U-20* of the British passenger liner *Lusitania* on May 7, 1915, with the loss of 1,198 civilians; and the accidental sinking by a US submarine of *Rakuyo Maru*, a Japanese troopship carrying Allied prisoners of war, on September 12, 1944, killing some 1,141.

WORST SUBMARINE DISASTERS OF ALL TIME
(Excluding those as a result of military action)

	Submarine	Date	No. killed
1	Le Surcourf	February 18, 1942	159

The French submarine was accidentally rammed by a US merchant ship.

2	Thresher	April 10, 1963	129

The three-year-old US nuclear submarine, worth $45,000,000, sank in the North Atlantic, 220 miles/350 km east of Boston, Mass.

3	I-12	January 1945	114

The Japanese submarine sank in the Pacific in unknown circumstances.

4	I-174	3 April 1944	107

A Japanese submarine sank in the Pacific in unknown circumstances.

5	I-26	October 1944	105

This Japanese submarine sank east of Leyte, cause and date unknown.

6	I-169	April 4, 1944	103

A Japanese submarine flooded and sank while in harbor at Truk.

7	I-22	October 1942	100

A Japanese submarine sank off the Solomon Islands, exact date unknown.

8=	Seawolf	October 3, 1944	99

A US submarine was sunk in error by USS Rowell off Morotai.

8=	Thetis	March 13, 1943	99

The British submarine sank on June 1, 1939 during trials in Liverpool Bay, with civilians on board. Her captain and three crew members escaped. Thetis was later salvaged and renamed Thunderbolt. She was sunk by an Italian ship with the loss of 63 lives.

8=	Scorpion	May 21, 1968	99

This US nuclear submarine was lost in the North Atlantic, south west of the Azores. The wreck was located on October 31 of that year.

The loss of the *Thresher* is the worst accident ever involving a nuclear submarine. It sank while undertaking tests off the US coast and was located by the bathyscaphe *Trieste*. The remains of the submarine were scattered over the ocean floor at a depth of 8,400 ft/2,560 m. The cause of the disaster remains a military secret.

CLEANING UP
As well as major oil spills, an average of two million tons is spilled into the world's seas every year, causing widespread environmental damage.

THE 10

WORST PASSENGER FERRY DISASTERS OF THE 20TH CENTURY

	Ferry/location/date	Approx. no. killed
1	*Dona Paz*, Philippines, December 20, 1987	up to 3,000
2	*Neptune*, Haiti, February 17, 1992	1,800
3	*Toya Maru*, Japan, September 26, 1954	1,172
4	*Don Juan*, Philippines, April 22, 1980	over 1,000
5	*Estonia*, Baltic Sea, September 28, 1994	909
6	*Samia*, Bangladesh, May 25, 1986	600
7	*MV Bukoba*, Tanzania, May 21, 1996	549
8	*Salem Express*, Egypt, December 14, 1991	480
9	*Tampomas II*, Indonesia, January 27, 1981	431
10	*Nam Yung Ho*, South Korea, December 15, 1970	323

THE 10

WORST OIL TANKER SPILLS OF ALL TIME

	Tanker	Location	Date	Approx. spillage (tons)
1	*Atlantic Empress* and *Aegean Captain*	Trinidad	July 19, 1979	331,000
2	*Castillio de Bellver*	Cape Town, South Africa	August 6, 1983	281,000
3	*Olympic Bravery*	Ushant, France	January 24, 1976	276,000
4	*Showa-Maru*	Malacca, Malaya	June 7, 1975	261,000
5	*Amoco Cadiz*	Finistère, France	March 16, 1978	246,000
6	*Odyssey*	Atlantic, off Canada	November 10, 1988	154,000
7	*Torrey Canyon*	Scilly Isles, UK	March 18, 1967	132,000
8	*Sea Star*	Gulf of Oman	December 19, 1972	127,000
9	*Irenes Serenada*	Pilos, Greece	February 23, 1980	112,000
10	*Urquiola*	Corunna, Spain	May 12, 1976	111,000

The grounding of the *Exxon Valdez* in Prince William Sound, Alaska, on March 24, 1989 ranks outside the 10 worst spills at about 38,500 tons of oil spilled, but resulted in major ecological damage. All the accidents in this Top 10 were caused by collision, grounding, fire, or explosion, but worse tanker oil spills have been caused by military action. Between January and June 1942, for example, German U-boats torpedoed a number of tankers off the east coast of the US with a loss of some 661,000 tons of oil, and in 1991, during the Gulf War, various tankers were sunk in the Persian Gulf, spilling a total of more than 1,100,000 tons of oil.

THE SINKING OF *LA BOURGOGNE*

One of the 10 worst marine disasters of the 19th century occurred on July 4, 1898, when *La Bourgogne*, a French steam liner, collided with the British sailing vessel *Cromartyshire* off Sable Island, Nova Scotia. *La Bourgogne* had set out from New York the previous day, heading for Le Havre, France. Despite dense fog, the ship maintained a high speed and was sailing off course when she was struck. The rule of "women and children first" was ignored as crew members pushed passengers overboard as they scrambled into lifeboats, with the result that 560 lives were lost. Of the 165 survivors, some 100 were French.

100 YEARS AGO · YEARS AGO · YEARS AGO

AIR DISASTERS

T H E 1 0

WORST AIR DISASTERS IN THE WORLD

Incident	Killed
1 March 27, 1977, Tenerife, Canary Islands	583

Two Boeing 747s (Pan Am and KLM, carrying 364 passengers with 16 crew, and 230 passengers with 11 crew, respectively) collided and caught fire on the runway of Los Rodeos airport after the pilots received incorrect control tower instructions.

2 August 12, 1985, Mt. Ogura, Japan	520

A JAL Boeing 747 on a domestic flight from Tokyo to Osaka crashed, killing all but four on board in the worst-ever disaster involving a single aircraft.

3 November 12, 1996, Charkhi Dadrio, India	349

Soon after taking off from New Delhi's Indira Gandhi International Airport, a Saudi Airways Boeing 747 collided with a Kazakh Airlines Ilyushin IL-76 cargo aircraft on its descent and exploded, killing all 312 on the Boeing and 37 on the Ilyushin in the world's worst midair crash.

4 March 3, 1974, Paris, France	346

A Turkish Airlines DC-10 crashed at Ermenonville, north of Paris, immediately after takeoff for London, with many English rugby supporters among the dead.

5 June 23, 1985, off the Irish coast	329

An Air India Boeing 747, on a flight from Vancouver to Delhi, exploded in midair, perhaps as a result of a terrorist bomb.

6 August 19, 1980, Riyadh, Saudi Arabia	301

A Saudia (Saudi Arabian) Airlines Lockheed TriStar caught fire during an emergency landing.

7 January 8, 1996, Kinshasa, Zaïre	300

A Zaïrean Antonov-32 cargo plane crashed shortly after takeoff, killing shoppers in a city-center market in Kinshasa. The final death toll has not yet been officially announced.

8 July 3, 1988, off the Iranian coast	290

An Iran Air A300 Airbus was shot down in error by a missile fired by the USS Vincennes.

9 May 25, 1979, Chicago, Illinois	273

The worst air disaster in the US occurred when an engine fell off a DC-10 as it took off from Chicago's O'Hare airport. The aircraft plunged out of control, killing all 271 on board and two on the ground.

10 December 21, 1988, Lockerbie, Scotland, UK	270

Pan Am Flight 103 from London Heathrow to New York exploded in midair as a result of a terrorist bomb, killing 243 passengers, 16 crew, and 11 on the ground in the UK's worst-ever air disaster.

Five other air disasters have resulted in the deaths of more than 250 people: on September 1, 1983, a Korean Air Lines Boeing 747 that had strayed into Soviet airspace was shot down with the loss of 269 lives; on April 26, 1994, a China Airlines Airbus A300-600 crashed while landing, killing 264; on July 11, 1991, at Jeddah, Saudi Arabia, a DC-8 crashed on takeoff killing 261; on November 28, 1979, a DC-10 crashed killing 257 passengers and crew; and on December 12, 1985 a DC-8 crashed killing all 256 on board.

T H E 1 0

WORST AIR COLLISIONS IN THE WORLD

Incident	Killed
1 November 12, 1996, Charkhi Dadrio, India	349

(See The 10 Worst Air Disasters in the World, No. 3.)

2 September 10, 1976, Near Gaj, Yugoslavia	177

A British Airways Trident and a Yugoslav DC-9 collided, killing all 176 on board and a woman on the ground.

3 August 11, 1979, Near Dneprodzerzhinsk, Ukraine, USSR	173

Two Soviet Tupolev-134 Aeroflot airliners collided in midair.

4 July 30, 1971, Morioka, Japan	162

An air collision occurred between an All Nippon Boeing 727 and Japanese Air Force F-86F. The student pilot and instructor in the fighter survived, but were both were found guilty of negligence and jailed.

5 December 22, 1992, near Souq as-Sabt, Libya	157

A Libyan Boeing 747 and a Libyan air force MiG-23 fighter collided. The fighter crew reportedly ejected to safety, but all passengers and crew on the airliner were killed.

6 September 25, 1978, San Diego, California	144

A Pacific Southwest Boeing 727 collided in the air with a Cessna 172 light aircraft with a student pilot, killing 135 in the airliner, two in the Cessna, and seven on the ground.

7 December 16, 1960, New York, New York	135

A United Airlines DC-8, with 77 passengers and a crew of seven, and a TWA Super Constellation, with 39 passengers and four crew, collided in a snowstorm. The DC-8 crashed in Brooklyn killing eight on the ground; the Super Constellation crashed in Staten Island, killing all passengers and crew on board.

8 February 8, 1993, Tehran, Iran	132

As it took off, a passenger aircraft carrying pilgrims was struck by a military aircraft, causing it to crash and killing all on board.

9 June 30, 1956, Grand Canyon, Arizona	128

A United Airlines DC-7 and a TWA Super Constellation collided in the air, killing all passengers and crew on board both airliners, in the worst civil aviation disaster to that date, and the first ever commercial aviation accident with more than 100 fatalities.

10 February 1, 1963, Ankara, Turkey	104

A Middle East Airlines Viscount 754 and a Turkish Air Force C-47 collided and plunged onto the city. All 14 on the airliner, three in the fighter, and 87 on the ground were killed by the crash and fire that followed.

The first air collision resulting in the deaths of more than 50 people occurred on November 1, 1949, when a Bolivian Air Force P-38 fighter collided with an Eastern Air Lines DC-4 as they came in to land at Washington, DC. In the collision the pilot of the P-38 and all 55 on board the airliner were killed, making this the worst air disaster in the US up to that date. Although air traffic control, radar, and communications equipment have greatly improved since that disaster, the volume of air traffic has vastly increased, and the midair collision of two aircraft remains one of the major hazards of modern aviation.

T H E 1 0
WORST AIRSHIP DISASTERS IN THE WORLD

	Incident	Killed
1	April 4, 1933, off the US Atlantic coast	73

US Navy airship Akron *crashed into the sea in a storm, leaving only three survivors in the world's worst airship tragedy.*

2	December 21, 1923, over the Mediterranean	52

French airship Dixmude *is assumed to have been struck by lightning, broken up, and crashed into the sea. Wreckage believed to be from the airship was found off Sicily 10 years later.*

3	October 5, 1930, near Beauvais, France	50

British airship R101 *crashed into a hillside, leaving 48 dead, with two dying later, and six saved.*

4	August 24, 1921, off the coast near Hull, UK	44

Airship R38, *sold by the British Government to the US and renamed USN ZR-2, broke in two on a training and test flight.*

5	May 6, 1937, Lakehurst, New Jersey	36

German Zeppelin Hindenburg *caught fire when mooring.*

6	February 21, 1922, Hampton Roads, Virginia	34

Roma, an Italian airship bought by the US Army, crashed killing all but 11 people on board.

7	October 17, 1913, Berlin, Germany	28

German airship LZ18 *crashed after engine failure during a test flight at Berlin-Johannisthal.*

8	March 30, 1917, Baltic Sea	23

German airship SL9 *was struck by lightning on a flight from Seerappen to Seddin and crashed into the sea.*

9	September 3, 1915, mouth of the River Elbe, Germany	19

German airship L10 *was struck by lightning and plunged into the sea.*

10=	September 9, 1913, off Heligoland	14

German Navy airship L1 *crashed into the sea, leaving six survivors out of the 20 on board.*

10=	September 3, 1925, Caldwell, Ohio	14

US dirigible Shenandoah, *the first airship built in the US and the first to use safe helium instead of inflammable hydrogen, broke up in a storm, scattering sections over many miles of the Ohio countryside.*

From its earliest years, the history of the airship has been a mixture of triumphs and disasters. Following a series of accidents in the 1920s, the world's largest airship, the 777-ft/237-m British-built *R101*, crashed in France, broke in two, and burst into flames. Britain's interest in airships promptly ended, as did that of the US after the loss of the *Akron* less than three years later. Germany's enthusiasm lasted until 1937, when the 803.8-ft/245-m *Hindenburg* arrived at Lakehurst, New Jersey, after a three-day trip from Frankfurt. As she moored, she caught fire and turned into an inferno, the last moments of which remain among the most haunting sights ever captured on newsreel, with commentator Herb Morrison describing the horrific scene through floods of tears.

T H E 1 0
WORST AVIATION DISASTERS WITH GROUND FATALITIES

	Incident	Ground fatalities
1	January 8, 1996, Kinshasa, Zaïre	300

(See The 10 Worst Air Disasters in the World, No. 7.)

2	December 24, 1966, Da Nang, South Vietnam	107

A Canadair CL-44 crash-landed onto a village.

3	February 1, 1963, Ankara, Turkey	87

A Vickers Viscount 754 and a Turkish Air Force Douglas C-47 collided and fell into the city.

4	March 16, 1969, Maracaibo, Venezuela	71

A DC-9 crashed onto the city after hitting power lines.

5	October 4, 1992, Amsterdam, Netherlands	70

An El Al cargo plane crashed into a suburban apartment house.

6	August 28, 1988, Ramstein US base, Germany	67

Three fighters in an Italian aerobatic team collided, one of them crashing into the crowd, leaving 70 dead (including the three pilots) and 150 spectators injured.

7	July 24, 1938, Campo de Marte, Bogota, Colombia	53

A low-flying stunt plane crashed into a stand, broke up, and hurled blazing wreckage into the crowd.

8	August 23, 1944, Freckelton, Lancashire, UK	51

A B-24 bomber crashed onto a school.

9	September 3, 1989, Near Havana, Cuba	34

An Ilyushin Il-62M crashed and exploded on takeoff.

10	October 22, 1996, Manta, Ecuador	30

A Boeing 707 crashed into a residential area.

DOWN IN FLAMES *Overweight and unstable, British airship* R101 *crashed en route for India and was engulfed in a fireball when its 5,000,000 cu ft/ 141,585 cu m of hydrogen exploded, killing all but six on board.*

MAN-MADE & OTHER DISASTERS

T H E 1 0

WORST MINING DISASTERS IN THE WORLD

	Location/date	Killed
1	Hinkeiko, China, April 26, 1942	1,549
2	Courrières, France, March 10, 1906	1,060
3	Omuta, Japan, November 9, 1963	447
4	Senghenydd, UK, October 14, 1913	439
5	Coalbrook, South Africa, January 21, 1960	437
6	Wankie, Rhodesia, June 6, 1972	427
7	Dharbad, India, May 28, 1965	375
8	Chasnala, India, December 27, 1975	372
9	Monongah, WV, December 6, 1907	362
10	Barnsley, UK, December 12, 1866	361 *

* *Including 27 killed the following day while searching for survivors*

A mining disaster at the Fushun mines, Manchuria, China, in February 1931 may have resulted in up to 3,000 deaths, but information was suppressed by the Chinese government. Soviet security was also responsible for obscuring details of an explosion at the East German Johanngeorgendstadt uranium mine on November 29, 1949, when as many as 3,700 may have died. The two worst disasters both resulted from underground explosions, and the large numbers of deaths among mine workers resulted from that cause, and from asphyxiation by poisonous gases. Among the most tragic disasters of this century, that at Aberfan, Wales, on October 20, 1966, was a mine disaster that affected the community rather than the miners. Waste from the local mine had been building up for many years to become a heap some 800ft/244m in height. Weakened by the presence of a spring, a huge volume of slurry suddenly flowed down and engulfed the local school, killing 144, of whom 116 were children.

WORST COMMERCIAL AND INDUSTRIAL DISASTERS*

	Location/incident	Date	Killed
1	Bhopal, India (methyl isocyanate gas escape at Union Carbide plant)	December 3, 1984	over 2,500
2	Seoul, Korea (collapse of department store)	June 29, 1995	640
3	Oppau, Germany (explosion at chemical plant)	September 21, 1921	561
4	Mexico City, Mexico (explosion at PEMEX gas plant)	November 20, 1984	540
5	Brussels, Belgium (fire in L'Innovation department store)	May 22, 1967	322
6	Guadalajara, Mexico (explosions after gas leak into sewers)	April 22, 1992	230
7	São Paulo, Brazil (fire in Joelma bank and office building)	February 1, 1974	227
8	Bangkok, Thailand (fire engulfed a four-story doll factory)	May 10, 1993	187
9	North Sea (Piper Alpha oil rig explosion and fire)	July 6, 1988	173
10	New York City (fire in Triangle Shirtwaist Factory)	March 25, 1911	145

* *Including industrial sites, factories, offices, and stores; excluding military, mining, marine, and other transportation disasters*

Officially, the meltdown of the nuclear reactor at Chernobyl, Ukraine, on April 26, 1986 caused the immediate death of 31 people. However, it has been suggested that by 1992 some 6,000 to 8,000 people had died as a direct result of radioactive contamination, a toll that will continue to increase for many years to come.

WORST FIRES IN THE WORLD*

	Location/incident	Date	Killed
1	Kwanto, Japan (following earthquake)	September 1, 1923	60,000
2	Cairo (city fire)	1824	4,000
3	London, UK (London Bridge)	July 1212	3,000
4	Peshtigo, Wisconsin (forest)	October 8, 1871	2,682
5	Santiago, Chile (church of La Compañía)	December 8, 1863	2,500 #
6	Chungking, China (docks)	September 2, 1949	1,700
7	Constantinople, Turkey (city fire)	June 5, 1870	900
8	Cloquet, Minnesota (forest)	October 12, 1918	800
9	Mandi Dabwali, India (school tent)	December 23, 1995	over 500
10	Hinckley, Minnesota (forest)	September 1, 1894	480

* *Excluding sports and entertainment venues, mining disasters, and the results of military action*
# *Burned, crushed, and drowned in ensuing panic*

Historically, city fires have caused the greatest loss of life – in 1212, about 3,000 are thought to have died when London Bridge caught fire. However, while the Great Fire of London of 1666 resulted in great material damage, there were just eight fatalities.

THE 10

WORST EXPLOSIONS IN THE WORLD*

	Location/incident	Date	Killed#
1	Lanchow, China (arsenal)	October 26, 1935	2,000
2	Halifax, Nova Scotia (ammunition ship *Mont Blanc*)	December 6, 1917	1,635
3	Memphis, Tennessee (*Sultana* boiler explosion)	April 27, 1865	1,547
4	Bombay, India (ammunition ship *Fort Stikine*)	April 14, 1944	1,376
5	Cali, Colombia (ammunition trucks)	August 7, 1956	1,200
6	Salang Tunnel, Afghanistan (gasoline tanker collision)	November 2, 1982	over 1,100
7	Chelyabinsk, USSR (liquid gas beside railroad)	June 3, 1989	up to 800
8	Texas City, Texas (ammonium nitrate on *Grandcamp* freighter)	April 16, 1947	752
9	Oppau, Germany (chemical plant)	September 21, 1921	561
10	Mexico City, Mexico (PEMEX gas plant)	November 20, 1984	540

* *Excluding mining disasters, and terrorist and military bombs*
\# *All these "best estimate" figures should be treated with caution, since – as with fires and shipwrecks – body counts are notoriously unreliable*

MEXICO CITY GAS EXPLOSION
The PEMEX gas plant explosion of November 20, 1984 in Mexico City, Mexico, which left 540 dead, is not only one of the worst industrial disasters but also one of the worst explosions of modern times.

THE 10

WORST DISASTERS AT THEATER AND ENTERTAINMENT VENUES*

	Location/date	No. killed
1	Canton, China (theater), May 25, 1845	1,670
2	Shanghai, China (theater) (precise date unknown), June 1871	900
3	Lehmann Circus, St. Petersburg, Russia, February 14, 1836	800
4	Antoung, China (movie house), February 13, 1937	658
5	Ring Theater, Vienna, December 8, 1881	620
6	Iroquois Theater, Chicago, December 30, 1903	591
7	Cocoanut Grove Night Club, Boston, November 28, 1942	491
8	Abadan, Iran (theater), August 20, 1978	422
9	Niteroi, Brazil (circus), December 17, 1961	323
10	Brooklyn Theater, New York, December 5, 1876	295

* *Nineteenth and twentieth centuries, excluding sports stadiums and race tracks*

All the worst theater disasters have been caused by fire. The figure given for the first entry in this list is a conservative estimate, some sources putting the figure as high as 2,500, but, even in recent times, reports from China are often unreliable. The figure for the Ring Theater fire also varies greatly according to source, some claiming it to be as high as 850. The US's worst circus fire (which precipitated a stampede) occurred at Ringling Brothers' Circus, Hartford, Connecticut, on July 6, 1944 when 168 lives were lost and 480 people were injured.

NATURAL DISASTERS

WORST AVALANCHES AND LANDSLIDES OF THE 20th CENTURY*

	Location	Incident	Date	Estimated no. killed
1	Yungay, Peru	Landslide	May 31, 1970	17,500
2	Italian Alps	Avalanche	December 13, 1916	10,000
3	Huarás, Peru	Avalanche	December 13, 1941	5,000
4	Nevada Huascaran, Peru	Avalanche	January 10, 1962	3,500
5	Medellin, Colombia	Landslide	September 27, 1987	683
6	Chungar, Peru	Avalanche	March 19, 1971	600
7	Rio de Janeiro, Brazil	Landslide	January 11, 1966	550
8=	Northern Assam, India	Landslide	February 15, 1949	500
8=	Grand Rivière du Nord, Haiti	Landslide	November 13/14, 1963	500
10	Blons, Austria	Avalanche	January 11, 1954	411

* Excluding those where most deaths resulted from flooding, earthquakes, etc. associated with landslides

The worst incident of all, the destruction of Yungay, Peru, in May 1970, was only part of a much larger cataclysm that left a total of up to 70,000 dead. Following an earthquake and flooding, the town was wiped out by an avalanche that left just 2,500 survivors out of a population of 20,000. Similar incidents, in which the avalanche was a contributor in a series of disasters, include that at Kansu, China, on December 16, 1920, when a total of 180,000 were killed from the combined effects of earthquake, a massive landslide, and winter weather after their homes were destroyed.

THE WRATH OF THE VOLCANO
There are perhaps more than 500 currently active volcanoes in the world, with as many as 2,500 that have been active in recorded history. Fortunately, most do not endanger human life, but the attractions of farming on rich volcanic soil mean that settlements have sometimes fallen victim to major eruptions.

WORST TSUNAMIS OF THE 20th CENTURY

	Locations affected/date	Estimated no. killed
1	Agadir, Morocco,* Feb 29, 1960	12,000
2=	Philippines, Aug 17, 1976	5,000
2=	Chile/Pacific islands/Japan, May 22, 1960	5,000
4	Japan/Hawaii, Mar 2, 1933	3,000
5	Japan,* Dec 21, 1946	1,088
6	Kü, Japan, 1944	998
7	Colombia, Dec 12, 1979	500
8	Lomblem Island, Indonesia, Jul 22, 1979	700
9	Hawaii/Aleutians/California, Apr 1, 1946	173
10	Alaska/Aleutians/California,* Mar 27, 1964	122

* Combined effect of earthquake and tsunamis

Tsunamis (from the Japanese *tsu* [port] and *nami* [wave]), are powerful waves caused by undersea disturbances such as earthquakes or volcanic eruptions. Tsunamis can be so intense that they frequently cross entire oceans, devastating islands and coastal regions in their paths.

WORST FLOODS AND STORMS OF THE 20th CENTURY

	Location	Date	Estimated no. killed
1	Huang Ho River, China	August 1931	3,700,000
2	Bangladesh	November 13, 1970	300–500,000
3	Henan, China	1939	more than 200,000
4	Chang Jiang River, China	September 1911	100,000
5	Bengal, India	November 15–16, 1942	40,000
6	Bangladesh	June 1–2, 1965	30,000
7	Bangladesh	May 28–29, 1963	22,000
8	Bangladesh	May 11–12, 1965	17,000
9	Morvi, India	August 11, 1979	5,000–15,000
10	Hong Kong	September 18, 1906	10,000

THE AFTERMATH OF AN EARTHQUAKE
Even though instruments can now detect impending seismic activity, there is rarely sufficient time for inhabitants of areas prone to earthquakes to evacuate their homes. Caught unawares in increasingly densely populated cities, many catastrophes have occurred during the 20th century.

THE 10

WORST EARTHQUAKES OF THE 20th CENTURY

	Location	Date	Estimated no. killed
1	Tang-shan, China	July 28, 1976	242,419
2	Nanshan, China	May 22, 1927	200,000
3	Kansu, China	December 16, 1920	180,000
4	Messina, Italy	December 28, 1908	160,000
5	Tokyo/Yokohama, Japan	September 1, 1923	142,807
6	Kansu, China	December 25, 1932	70,000
7	Callejon de Huaylas, Peru	May 31, 1970	66,800
8	Quetta, India*	May 30, 1935	50–60,000
9	Armenia	December 7, 1988	over 55,000
10	Iran	June 21, 1990	over 40,000

* Now Pakistan

There are some discrepancies between the "official" death tolls in many of the world's worst earthquakes and the estimates of other authorities: a figure of 750,000 is sometimes quoted for the Tang-shan earthquake of 1976, for example, and totals ranging from 58,000 to 250,000 are given for the quake that devastated Messina in 1908. Several other earthquakes in China and Turkey have resulted in deaths of 10,000 or more.

THE 10

WORST VOLCANIC ERUPTIONS OF THE 20th CENTURY

	Location/date	Estimated no. killed
1	Mt. Pelée, Martinique, May 8, 1902	up to 40,000

After lying dormant for centuries, Mt. Pelée began to erupt in April 1902. Assured that there was no danger, the 30,000 residents of the main city, St. Pierre, stayed in their homes and were there on May 8, when the volcano burst apart at 7:30am and showered the port with molten lava, ash, and gas, destroying all life and property.

2	Nevado del Ruiz, Colombia, November 13, 1985	22,940

The Andean volcano gave warning signs of erupting, but by the time it was decided to evacuate the local inhabitants, it was too late. The hot steam, rocks, and ash ejected from Nevado del Ruiz melted its ice cap, resulting in a mudslide that completely engulfed the town of Armero.

3	Keluit, Java, May 19, 1919	5,110

One of the most remarkable of all volcanic eruptions on record, Keluit's crater lake was ejected and drowned inhabitants on its lower slopes.

4	Santa Maria, Guatemala, October 24, 1902	4,500

Some 1,500 died as a direct consequence of the volcanic eruption, and an additional 3,000 as a result of its aftereffects.

5	Mt. Lamington, New Guinea, January 21, 1951	2,942

Mt. Lamington erupted with hardly any warning, with a huge explosion that was heard up to 200 miles/320 km away.

6	El Chichón, Mexico, March 29, 1982	1,879

Of these, 1,755 people were reported missing and 124 confirmed killed.

7	Lake Nyos, Cameroon, August 21, 1986	more than 1,700

A volcano erupted beneath the lake, and gases killed sleeping villagers.

8	La Soufrière, St. Vincent, May 7–8, 1902	1,565

The day before the cataclysmic eruption of Mt. Pelée (No. 1), La Soufrière erupted and engulfed the local inhabitants in ash flows.

9	Merapi, Java, December 18, 1931	1,369

In addition to the human casualties, 2,140 cattle were killed.

10	Taal, Philippines, January 30, 1911	1,335

Taal has erupted frequently, with the 1911 incident the worst of several during this century.

SPITTING FIRE AND BRIMSTONE
Red hot lava (liquid rock) shoots out of a volcano in a curtain of fire. Severe volcanic eruptions in the past have destroyed entire communities and killed thousands of people.

CULTURE & LEARNING

TOP 10

COUNTRIES WITH MOST CHILDREN AT PRIMARY SCHOOL

	Country	Primary-school children*
1	China	154,529,000
2	India	109,043,663
3	US	33,410,000
4	Brazil	30,520,748
5	Indonesia	29,598,790
6	Pakistan	16,722,000
7	Nigeria	16,191,000
8	Mexico	14,468,700
9	Bangladesh	14,202,000
10	Philippines	10,731,453

* In latest year for which information is available

Absentees from this list include such countries as Japan: even though its population is greater than Mexico's, its low birth rate means that it has little more than half as many children at primary school.

TOP 10

COUNTRIES WITH MOST SECONDARY-SCHOOL STUDENTS

	Country	Secondary-school students*
1	India	56,615,000
2	China	49,817,000
3	US	17,390,000
4	Indonesia	9,435,000
5	Japan	9,296,000
6	Iran	6,684,000
7	France	5,737,000
8	Pakistan	5,610,000
9	Germany	5,532,000
10	Spain	4,734,000

* In latest year for which information is available

Certain countries, such as Russia, do not provide data for primary and secondary school enrollments separately. Russia's total of 21,600,000 is however presumed to comprise mainly secondary students, since its low birth rate means that primary numbers are low.

TOP 10

COUNTRIES WITH THE HIGHEST RATIO OF UNIVERSITY STUDENTS

	Country	University students per 100,000
1	Canada	7,197
2	US	5,653
3	New Zealand	4,232
4	South Korea	4,208
5	Puerto Rico	4,091
6	Norway	3,883
7	Finland	3,757
8	Peru	3,465
9	France	3,414
10	Spain	3,335

T O P 1 0

LARGEST UNIVERSITIES
IN THE US

University*/location	Enrollment (1995–96)
1 Ohio State University, Columbus, Ohio	48,676
2 University of Texas, Austin, Texas	47,905
3 Arizona State University, Tempe, Arizona	42,040
4 Texas A&M University, College Station, Texas	41,790
5 Michigan State University, East Lansing, Michigan	40,647
6 Penn State University, University Park, Pennsylvania	39,646
7 University of Florida, Gainesville, Florida	39,439
8 University of Wisconsin, Madison, Wisconsin	37,890
9 University of Minnesota, Minneapolis, Minnesota	36,995
10 University of Michigan, Ann Arbor, Michigan	36,687

* *Four-year colleges only*

Source: National Center For Education Statistics, US Department of Education

T O P 1 0

COUNTRIES WITH THE
LONGEST SCHOOL YEARS

Country	School year (days)
1 China	251
2 Japan	243
3 Korea	220
4 Israel	215
5= Germany	210
5= Russia	210
7 Switzerland	207
8= Netherlands	200
8= Scotland	200
8= Thailand	200

T O P 1 0

LARGEST UNIVERSITIES
IN THE WORLD

University	Students
1 University of Paris, France	308,904
2 University of Calcutta, India	300,000
3 University of Bombay, India	262,350
4 University of Mexico, Mexico	261,693
5 University of Guadalajara, Mexico	214,986
6 University of Buenos Aires, Argentina	206,658
7 University of Rome, Italy	184,000
8 University of Rajasthan, India	175,000
9 University of Wisconsin, US	154,620
10 State University of New York, US	146,873

The huge number of university institutions in India reflects not only the country's population and the high value placed on education in Indian culture but also the inclusion of many "Affiliating and Teaching" colleges attached to universities.

GRADUATION DAY
Education to university level for a high proportion of a country's population has long been the goal of most industrialized countries, and is increasingly the aspiration of developing countries.

T H E 1 0

COUNTRIES WITH THE
LOWEST LITERACY RATES
IN THE WORLD

Country	Literacy %
1 Niger	13.6
2 Burkina Faso	19.2
3 Eritrea	20.0
4 Mali	31.0
5 Sierra Leone	31.4
6 Afghanistan	31.5
7 Senegal	33.1
8 Burundi	35.3
9 Ethiopia	35.5
10 Guinea	35.9

* *Total of males and females age 15 and over who can read*

While most Western countries report literacy rates of virtually 100 percent, this list represents 10 countries where, on average, fewer than one person in three is able to read. Even within countries with these low levels of literacy, there are disparities between males and females, with the females often receiving inferior education. In Niger, for example, as few as 6.6 percent, or one woman in 15, are regarded as literate.

LIBRARIES OF THE WORLD

TOP 10

LARGEST REFERENCE LIBRARIES IN THE WORLD

	Library	Location	Founded	Books
1	Library of Congress	Washington, DC	1800	29,000,000
2	British Library	London, UK	1753*	20,303,000
3	Harvard University Library	Cambridge, Masachusetts	1638	13,369,855
4	New York Public Library	New York City	1848#	12.485,183+
5	Russian State Library★	Moscow, Russia	1862	11,750,000
6	Yale University Library	New Haven, Connecticut	1701	9,758,341
7	Biblioteca Academiei Romane	Bucharest, Romania	1867	9,397,260
8	Bibliothèque Nationale	Paris, France	1480	9,000,000
9	University of Illinois	Urbana, Illinois	1867	8,840,362
10	University of Califonia	Berkeley, Califonia	1868	8,462,123

* *Founded as part of the British Museum 1753; became an independent body 1973*
\# *Astor Library founded February 1, 1848; consolidated with Lenox Library and Tilden Trust to form New York Public Library in 1895*
\+ *Reference holdings only, excluding books in lending library branches*
★ *Founded as Rumyantsev Library; formerly State V.I. Lenin Library*

RUSSIAN STATE LIBRARY
Formerly the Lenin Library, this huge building, designed by V.A. Shchuko and V.G. Gel'freytch, was begun in 1928 and completed in the 1950s.

THE 10

COUNTRIES WITH MOST PUBLIC LIBRARIES

	Country	Libraries
1	Russia	33,200
2	UK	23,678
3	Germany	20,448
4	US	9,097
5	Czech Republic	8,398
6	Romania	7,181
7	Bulgaria	5,591
8	Hungary	4,765
9	Brazil	3,600
10	China	2,406

The very high figure reported by UNESCO for the former Soviet Union's public libraries may owe more to the propaganda value attached to cultural status than to reality. National literary traditions play a major role in determining the ratio of libraries to population. The people of Japan, for example, do not customarily borrow books, and consequently the country has only 1,107 public libraries, whereas Finland, which has a population of little over one twenty-fifth that of Japan, has 461 libraries.

THE 10

FIRST 10 PUBLIC LIBRARIES IN THE US

	Library	Founded
1	Peterboro Public Library, Peterboro, New Hampshire	1833
2	New Orleans Public Library, New Orleans, Louisiana	1843
3	Boston Public Library, Boston, Massachusetts	1852
4	Public Library of Cincinnati and Hamilton County, Cincinnati, Ohio	1853
5	Springfield City Library, Springfield, Massachusetts	1857
6	Worcester Public Library, Worcester, Massachusets	1859
7	County Library, Portland, Oregon	1864
8=	Detroit Public Library, Detroit, Michigan	1865
8=	St. Louis Public Library, St. Louis, Missouri	1865
10	Atlanta-Fulton Public Library, Atlanta, Georgia	1867

TOP 10

LARGEST PUBLIC LIBRARIES IN THE US

	Library/no. of branches	Location	Founded	Books
1	New York Public Library (The Branch Libraries) (82)	New York City	1895*	11,661,064#
2	Public Library of Cincinnati and Hamilton County (41)	Cincinnati, Ohio	1853	8,268,543
3	Queens Borough Public Library (62)	Queens, New York	1896	7,963,171
4	Free Library of Philadelphia (52)	Philadelphia, Pennsylvania	1891	7,881,335
5	Chicago Public Library (81)	Chicago, Illinois	1872	7,095,735
6	Boston Public Library (26)	Boston, Massachusetts	1852	6,704,883
7	Houston Public Library (37)	Houston, Texas	1901	6,551,173
8	Carnegie Library of Pittsburgh (18)	Pittsburgh, Pennsylvania	1895	6,526,198
9	County of Los Angeles Public Library (147)	Los Angeles, California	1872	6,404,353
10	Brooklyn Public Library (59)	Brooklyn, New York	1896	6,134,045

* *Astor Library founded February 1, 1848; consolidated with Lenox Library and Tilden Trust to form New York Public Library in 1895*
\# *Lending library and reference library holdings available for loan*

STUDENT IN UNIVERSITY LIBRARY

TOP 10

LARGEST REFERENCE LIBRARIES IN THE UK*

	Library	Location	Founded	Books
1	British Library	London	1753	20,303,000
2	National Library of Scotland	Edinburgh	1682	6,979,000
3	Bodleian Library	Oxford	1602	5,900,000
4	University of Cambridge Library	Cambridge	c.1400	4,728,419
5	National Library of Wales	Aberystwyth	1907	3,678,000
6	John Rylands University Library of Manchester	Manchester	1972*	3,600,000
7	University of Leeds	Leeds	1904	2,501,770
8	University of Edinburgh	Edinburgh	1583	2,324,648
9	University of Birmingham	Birmingham	1900	2,055,000
10	University of Liverpool	Liverpool	1903	1,401,108

* *In 1972 the John Rylands Library (founded 1900) was amalgamated with Manchester University Library (1851)*

In addition to the books held by these libraries, many have substantial holdings of manuscripts, periodicals, and other printed material. The annual growth of five of the institutions listed here is enhanced by the law under which one copy of every book that is published must be deposited within a month of publication with each of five "copyright deposit libraries": the British Library, National Library of Scotland, Bodleian Library, University of Cambridge, and National Library of Wales, together with Trinity College, Dublin.

THE 10

FIRST PUBLIC LIBRARIES IN THE UK

	Library	Founded
1	Manchester Free Library	1852
2	Liverpool	1852
3	Sheffield	1856
4	Birmingham	1860
5	Cardiff	1862
6	Nottinghamshire	1868
7	Dundee	1869
8	Glasgow (Mitchell Library)	1874
9	Aberdeen	1884
10	Edinburgh	1890

Various special institutions, such as theological libraries, existed in Britain as early as the 17th century and were joined in the 19th by others that charged a small fee. Following the 1850 Public Libraries Act, the Manchester Free Library was the country's first free municipally supported lending library open to the public.

WORD POWER

TOP 10

LONGEST WORDS IN THE OXFORD ENGLISH DICTIONARY

	Word (first used)	Letters
1	Pneumonoultramicroscopicsilico-volcanoconiosis (1936)	45
2	Supercalifragilisticexpialidocious (1964)	34
3	Pseudopseudohypoparathyroidism (1952)	30
4=	Floccinaucinihilipilification (1741)	29
4=	Triethylsulphonemethylmethane (19??)	29
6=	Antidisestablishmentarianism (1923)	28
6=	Hepaticocholangiogastrostomy (1933)	28
6=	Octamethylcyclotetrasiloxane (1946)	28
6=	Tetrachlorodibenzoparadioxin (1959)	28
9=	Radioimmunoelectrophoresis (1962)	26
9=	Radioimmunoelectrophoretic (1962)	26

Words that are hyphenated, including such compound words as "transformational-generative" and "tristhio-dimethyl-benzaldehyde," have not been included. Only one unhyphenated word did not quite make it into the Top 10, the 25-letter psychophysicotherapeutics. After this, there is a surprisingly large number of words containing 20 to 24 letters (pneumonoence-phalographic, pneumonoventriculography, psychoneuroendocrinology, radioimmuno-precipitation, spectrophotofluorometric, thyroparathyroidectomize, hypergamma-globulinaemia, hypergammaglobulinaemic, roentgenkymographically, tribothermo-luminescence, photomorphogenetically, honorificabilitudinity, and immuno-sympathectomized, for example) – few of which are ever used by anyone except scientists and crossword compilers. Supercalifragilisticexpialidocious was popularized by the song in the movie *Mary Poppins* (1964) where it is used to mean "wonderful." It originally appeared in 1949 in an unpublished song in which it was spelled "supercalafajalistickespialadojus" – which has 32 letters.

TOP 10

MOST COMMON WORDS IN ENGLISH

	Spoken English	Written English
1	the	the
2	and	of
3	I	to
4	to	in
5	of	and
6	a	a
7	you	for
8	that	was
9	in	is
10	it	that

Various surveys have been conducted to establish the most common words in spoken English of various types, from telephone conversations to broadcast commentaries.

TOP 10

MOST QUOTED AUTHORS IN THE *OXFORD ENGLISH DICTIONARY*

	Author	Number of references*
1	William Shakespeare (1564–1616)	33,303
2	Sir Walter Scott (1771–1832)	16,628
3	John Milton (1608–74)	12,464
4	John Wyclif (c.1330–84)	11,962
5	Geoffrey Chaucer (c.1343–1400)	11,901
6	William Caxton (c.1422–91)	10,324
7	John Dryden (1631–1700)	9,123
8	Charles Dickens (1812–70)	8,536
9	Philemon Holland (1552–1637)	8,401
10	Alfred, Lord Tennyson (1809–92)	6,943

* These figures may not be absolutely precise because of variations in the way in which sources are quoted, where there is more than one example from the same author, etc.

TOP 10

MOST USED LETTERS IN WRITTEN ENGLISH

	i	ii
1	e	e
2	t	t
3	a	a
4	o	i
5	i	n
6	n	o
7	s	s
8	r	h
9	h	r
10	l	d

Column i is the order as indicated by a survey of approximately 1,000,000 words appearing in a wide variety of printed texts, ranging from newspapers to novels. Column ii is the order estimated by Samuel Morse, the inventor in the 1830s of Morse Code, based on his calculations of the respective quantities òf type used by a printer. The number of letters in the printer's type trays ranged from 12,000 for "e" to 4,400 for "d," with only 200 pieces of type for "z."

TOP 10

WORDS WITH MOST MEANINGS IN THE OXFORD ENGLISH DICTIONARY

	Word	Meanings
1	set	464
2	run	396
3	go	368
4	take	343
5	stand	334
6	get	289
7	turn	288
8	put	268
9	fall	264
10	strike	250

TOP 10

MOST WIDELY SPOKEN LANGUAGES IN THE WORLD

	Language	Approx. no. of speakers
1	Chinese (Mandarin)	975,000,000
2	English	478,000,000
3	Hindustani	437,000,000
4	Spanish	392,000,000
5	Russian	284,000,000
6	Arabic	225,000,000
7	Bengali	200,000,000
8	Portuguese	184,000,000
9	Malay-Indonesian	159,000,000
10	Japanese	126,000,000

According to 1995 estimates by Sidney S. Culbert of the University of Washington, in addition to those languages appearing in the Top 10, there are only three other languages that are spoken by more than 100,000,000 individuals: French (125,000,000), German (123,000,000), and Urdu (103,000,000). A further 14 languages are spoken by between 50,000,000 and 100,000,000 people.

TOP 10

COUNTRIES WITH THE MOST ENGLISH-LANGUAGE SPEAKERS

	Country	Approx. no. of speakers
1	US	228,770,000
2	UK	57,190,000
3	Canada	18,112,000
4	Australia	15,538,000
5	South Africa	3,800,000
6	Irish Republic	3,540,000
7	New Zealand	3,290,000
8	Jamaica	2,390,000
9	Trinidad and Tobago	1,189,000
10	Guyana	692,000

TOP 10

MOST WIDELY SPOKEN LANGUAGES IN US HOMES

	Language	Approx. no. of speakers*
1	English	198,601,000
2	Spanish	17,339,000
3	French	1,702,000
4	German	1,547,000
5	Italian	1,309,000
6	Chinese (Mandarin)	1,249,000
7	Tagalog	843,000
8	Polish	723,000
9	Korean	626,000
10	Vietnamese	507,000

* Based on most recent Census (1990)

TOP 10

MOST STUDIED FOREIGN LANGUAGES IN THE US*

	Language	Registrations
1	Spanish	606,286
2	French	205,351
3	German	96,263
4	Japanese	44,723
5	Italian	43,760
6	Chinese	26,471
7	Latin	25,897
8	Russian	24,729
9	Ancient Greek	16,272#
10	Hebrew	13,127

* In US Institutions of Higher Education

 # Comprises 5,648 registrations in Biblical Hebrew and 7,479 in Modern Hebrew

TOP 10

MOST WIDELY SPOKEN LANGUAGES IN THE EUROPEAN COMMUNITY

	Language	Approx. no. of speakers*
1	German	86,562,000
2	English	59,735,000
3	French	58,084,000
4	Italian	55,320,000
5	Spanish (Castilian)	31,398,000
6	Dutch	20,711,000
7	Portuguese	10,622,000
8	Greek	10,411,000
9	Swedish	8,207,000
10	Catalan	5,120,000

* As a "first language," including speakers resident in EC countries other than those where it is the main language, such as German-speakers living in France

TOP 10

MOST STUDIED FOREIGN LANGUAGES IN THE UK

1	French
2	Spanish
3	Arabic
4	Chinese (Mandarin)
5	German
6	Italian
7	Russian
8	Japanese
9	Dutch
10	Portuguese

This ranking is based on language courses studied by students at the School of Languages at the University of Westminster (formerly the Polytechnic of Central London), which is the largest single source of language teaching in the state sector throughout the whole of Europe. The school offers courses in 28 different languages.

BOOKS & READERS

TOP 10

MOST ANTHOLOGIZED ENGLISH-LANGUAGE POEMS

Poem/poet	Appearances*
1 *The Tyger*, William Blake (1757–1827)	62
2 *Dover Beach*, Matthew Arnold (1822–88)	61
3 *Kubla Khan*, Samuel Taylor Coleridge (1722–1834)	58
4 *La belle dame sans merci*, John Keats (1795–1821)	52
5 *To Autumn*, John Keats	50
6 *Pied Beauty*, Gerard Manley Hopkins (1844–89)	49
7 *Sir Patrick Spens*, Unknown (early Scottish)	48
8 *Stopping by Woods on a Snowy Evening*, Robert Frost (1874–1963)	56
9 *To the Virgins, to Make Much of Time*, Robert Herrick (1591–1674)	55
10 *That Time of Year Thou Mayst in Me Behold*, William Shakespeare (1564–1616)	51

* *In anthologies listed in* Granger's Index to Poetry

TOP 10

MOST TRANSLATED AUTHORS IN THE WORLD

Author	Translations
1 V.I. Lenin (1870–1924)	3,842
2 Agatha Christie (1890–1976)	1,904
3 Jules Verne (1828–1905)	1,856
4 William Shakespeare (1564–1616)	1,689
5 Enid Blyton (1897–1968)	1,582
6= Leo Tolstoy (1828–1910)	1,429
6= Charles Perrault (1628–1703)	1,429
8 Georges Simenon (1903–89)	1,392
9 Karl Marx (1818–83)	1,312
10 Fyodor Dostoevski (1821–81)	1,202

TOP 10

MOST POPULAR ENGLISH-LANGUAGE POEMS IN THE UK*

Poem/poet		Poem/poet
1 *If*, Rudyard Kipling (1865–1936)		**6** *To Autumn*, John Keats (1795–1821)
2 *The Lady of Shallot*, Alfred, Lord Tennyson (1809–92)		**7** *The Lake Isle of Innisfree*, W.B. Yeats (1864–1939)
3 *The Listener*, Walter de la Mare (1873–1956)		**8** *Dulce et Decorum*, Wilfred Owen (1893–1918)
4 *Not Waving but Drowning*, Stevie Smith (1902–71)		**9** *Ode to a Nightingale*, John Keats
5 *Daffodils*, William Wordsworth (1770–1850)		**10** *He Wishes for the Cloths of Heaven*, W.B. Yeats (1865–1939)

* *Based on a survey conducted in the UK on National Poetry Day, 1995*

During a six-day survey conducted by telephone during the six days leading up to the UK's National Poetry Day on October 12, 1995, more than 1,000 poems by over 200 authors were nominated. Bookmakers Ladbrokes had laid odds of two to one that Shakespeare's *Sonnet XVIII* ("Shall I compare thee to a summer's day?") would win, but in the event the Bard, along with other favorites such as William Blake's *The Tyger*, failed even to make the Top 10, while several votes were cast for poets that the organizers could not identify – perhaps attempts at poll-rigging by the poets themselves. A survey conducted by the BBC between October 2–10, 1996, which invited people to nominate only postwar poems, identified Jenny Joseph's *Warning* as the nation's favorite.

TOP 10

MOST PUBLISHED AUTHORS OF ALL TIME

Author	Nationality	Author	Nationality
1 William Shakespeare (1564–1616)	British	**8** Mark Twain (1835–1910)	American
2 Charles Dickens (1812–70)	British	**9** M. Tullius Cicero (106–43 BC)	Roman
3 Sir Walter Scott (1771–1832)	British	**10** Honoré de Balzac (1799–1850)	French
4 Johann Goethe (1749–1832)	German		
5 Aristotle (384–322 BC)	Greek		
6 Alexandre Dumas (*père*) (1802–70)	French		
7 Robert Louis Stevenson (1850–94)	British		

This Top 10 is based on a search of a major US library computer database. Citations, which include books by and about the author, total more than 15,000 for Shakespeare.

THE BIRDS OF AMERICA
John James Audubon's sumptious collection of over 400 large colored engravings was sold for $3,600,000 in 1989.

TOP 10

BOOK-PRODUCING COUNTRIES IN THE WORLD

	Country	Titles published*
1	UK	101,504
2	China	73,923
3	Germany	62,277
4	US	49,276
5	France	45,379
6	Japan	42,245
7	Spain	37,325
8	Italy	26,620
9	South Korea	25,017
10	Russia	22,028

* Total of new titles, new editions, and reprints in latest year for which figures are available

TOP 10

BOOK MARKETS IN THE WORLD

	Country	Annual book sales ($)
1	US	25,490,000,000
2	Japan	10,467,000,000
3	Germany	9,962,000,000
4	UK	3,651,000,000
5	France	3,380,000,000
6	Spain	2,992,000,000
7	South Korea	2,805,000,000
8	Brazil	2,526,000,000
9	Italy	2,246,000,000
10	China	1,760,000,000

Source: Euromonitor

TOP 10

MOST EXPENSIVE BOOKS AND MANUSCRIPTS EVER SOLD AT AUCTION

	Book/manuscript/sale	Price ($)*
1	*The Codex Hammer,* Christie's, New York, November 11, 1994	30,800,000

This is one of Leonardo da Vinci's notebooks, which includes many scientific drawings and diagrams. It was purchased by Bill Gates, the billionaire founder of Microsoft.

2	*The Gospels of Henry the Lion, c.* 1173–75, Sotheby's, London, December 6, 1983	10,841,000

At the time of its sale, it became the most expensive manuscript, book, or work of art other than a painting ever sold.

3	*The Gutenberg Bible,* 1455, Christie's, New York, October 22, 1987	5,390,000

One of the first books ever printed, by Johann Gutenberg and Johann Fust in 1455, it holds the record for the most expensive printed book.

4	*The Northumberland Bestiary, c.* 1250–60, Sotheby's, London, November 29, 1990	5,049,000

The highest price ever paid for an English manuscript.

5	Autographed manuscript of nine symphonies by Wolfgang Amadeus Mozart, *c.* 1773–74, Sotheby's, London, May 22, 1987	3,854,000

The record for a music manuscript.

	Book/manuscript/sale	Price ($)*
6	John James Audubon's *The Birds of America,* 1827–38, Sotheby's, New York, June 6, 1989	3,600,000

The record for any natural history book. A facsimile reprint of Audubon's The Birds of America *published in 1985 by Abbeville Press, New York, is listed at $30,000/£15,000, making it the most expensive book ever published.*

7	*The Bible in Hebrew,* Sotheby's, London, December 5, 1989	2,932,000

A manuscript written in Iraq, Syria, or Babylon in the ninth or tenth century, it holds the record for any Hebrew manuscript.

8	*The Monypenny Breviary,* illuminated manuscript, *c.* 1490–95, Sotheby's, London, June 19, 1989	2,639,000

The record for any French manuscript.

9	*The Hours and Psalter of Elizabeth de Bohun, Countess of Northampton, c.* 1340–45, Sotheby's, London, June 21, 1988	2,530,000

10	*Biblia Pauperum,* Christie's, New York, October 22, 1987	2,200,000

A block-book bible printed in the Netherlands in c.1460.

* Excluding premiums

WORLD BEST-SELLERS

ESSENTIAL READING
Popularly known as "The Thoughts of Chairman Mao" and the "Little Red Book," this work by Chinese Communist Party leader Mao Zedong (1893–1976) was a summary of the strict doctrine through which China was controlled for many years. Since its possession was mandatory during the so-called Cultural Revolution that began in 1966, it inevitably became a best-seller, while photographs and films of frenzied crowds brandishing copies remain vivid images of the political fervor of that era.

DID YOU KNOW

BIRTH OF THE BLURB

American humorist Frank Gelett Burgess (1866–1951), best known as the author of the nonsense poem, "I Never Saw a Purple Cow," was also the inventor of the word "blurb," the effusive text used on book jackets to describe the book within. Special promotional copies of Burgess's *Are You a Bromide?* were claimed to have been written by a Miss Belinda Blurb, whose work was said to be the "sensation of the year." "Blurb" is what this sort of writing has been called ever since.

TOP 10

BEST-SELLING BOOKS OF ALL TIME

Title	No. sold
1 The Bible	6,000,000,000

No one really knows how many copies of the Bible have been printed, sold, or distributed. The Bible Society's attempt to calculate the number printed between 1816 and 1975 produced the figure of 2,458,000,000. A more recent survey, for the years up to 1992, put it closer to 6,000,000,000 in more than 2,000 languages and dialects.

2 *Quotations from Chairman Mao Tse-Tung (Little Red Book)*	800,000,000

Chairman Mao's Little Red Book *could scarcely fail to become a best-seller: between the years 1966 and 1971 it was compulsory for every Chinese adult to own a copy. It was both sold and distributed to the people of China – although what proportion voluntarily bought it must remain open to question. Some 100,000,000 copies of his* Poems *were also disseminated.*

3 American Spelling Book by Noah Webster	100,000,000

First published in 1783, this reference book by the American man of letters Noah Webster (1758–1843) remained a best-seller in the US throughout the 19th century.

4 The Guinness Book of Records	79,000,000 *

First published in 1955, The Guinness Book of Records *stands out as the greatest contemporary publishing achievement. There have now been 40 editions in the UK alone.*

5 The McGuffey Readers by William Holmes McGuffey	60,000,000

Published in numerous editions from 1853 on, some authorities have put the total sales of these educational textbooks as high as 122,000,000.

6 A Message to Garcia by Elbert Hubbard	40–50,000,000

Now forgotten, Hubbard's polemic on the subject of labor relations was published in 1899 and within a few years had achieved these phenomenal sales, largely because many American employers purchased bulk supplies to distribute to their employees.

7 World Almanac	over 40,000,000 *

Having been published annually since 1868 (with a break from 1876 to 1886), this wide-ranging reference book has remained a constant best-seller ever since.

8 The Common Sense Book of Baby and Child Care by Dr. Benjamin Spock	over 39,200,000

Dr. Spock's 1946 manual became the bible of infant care for subsequent generations of parents. Most of the sales have been of the paperback edition of the book.

9 The Valley of the Dolls by Jacqueline Susann	30,000,000

This tale of sex, violence, and drugs by Jacqueline Susann (1921–74), first published in 1966, is perhaps surprisingly the world's best-selling novel.

10 In His Steps: "What Would Jesus Do?" by Rev. Charles Monroe Sheldon	28,500,000

Although virtually unknown today, American clergyman Charles Sheldon (1857–1946) achieved fame and fortune with this 1896 instructive religious treatise on moral dilemmas.

* Aggregate sales of annual publication

It is extremely difficult to establish precise sales of contemporary books and virtually impossible to do so with books published long ago. How many copies of the complete works of Shakespeare or Arthur Conan Doyle's Sherlock Holmes books have been sold in countless editions? The publication of variant editions, translations, and pirated copies all affect the global picture, and few publishers or authors are willing to expose their royalty statements to public scrutiny. As a result, this Top 10 list offers no more than the "best guess" at the great best-sellers of the past, and it may well be that there are many other books with a valid claim to a place on it.

THE BEST-SELLING CHILDREN'S AUTHORS IN THE WORLD

René Goscinny and Albert Uderzo

René Goscinny (1926–77) and Albert Uderzo (b. 1927) created the comic-strip character Astérix the Gaul in 1959. They produced 30 books with total sales of some 250,000,000 copies.

Hergé

Georges Rémi (1907–83), the Belgian author-illustrator who wrote under the pen name Hergé, created the comic-strip character Tintin in 1929. Tintin appeared in book form from 1948 onward. He achieved worldwide popularity, and the books have been translated into about 45 languages and dialects. Total sales are believed to be at least 160,000,000.

Enid Blyton

With sales of her Noddy books exceeding 60,000,000 copies, and with more than 700 children's books to her name (UNESCO calculated that there were 974 translations of her works in the 1960s alone), total sales of her works are believed to be over 100,000,000, making her the best-selling English language author of the 20th century.

Dr. Seuss

His books in the US Top 10 alone total about 30,000,000 copies. To this must be added those titles that have sold fewer than 5,000,000 in the US and all foreign editions of all his books, suggesting total sales of more than 100,000,000.

Beatrix Potter

The Tale of Peter Rabbit (1902) was one of a series of books, the cumulative total sales of which probably exceed 50,000,000.

Lewis Carroll

Total world sales of all editions of Carroll's two classic children's books, Alice's Adventures in Wonderland and Alice Through the Looking Glass, are incalculable. However, just these two books probably place Lewis Carroll among the 20 best-selling children's authors of all time.

Rev. W. (Wilbert Vere) Awdry

Collectively, the various Thomas the Tank Engine books which the Rev. Awdry began writing in 1946 have sold over 50,000,000 copies. Sales of the books have been enhanced in recent years, along with the popularity of videos of the stories and associated products.

Mark Twain

Book sales in the US were not accurately recorded prior to 1895, but it is probable that Twain's The Adventures of Tom Sawyer and The Adventures of Huckleberry Finn may each have sold more than 20,000,000 copies.

Judy Blume

Several of American author Judy Blume's novels, including Are You There God, It's Me, Margaret, *and* Tales of a Fourth-Grade Nothing *have sold more than 5,000,000 copies in the US alone, implying substantial cumulative sales of her many popular books.*

Roald Dahl

British writer Roald Dahl has been popular the world over since James and the Giant Peach *was first published in 1961. Sales of that novel, and others, including* Charlie and the Chocolate Factory, The B.F.G., *and* Matilda *have been further enhanced through the release of animated and live-action films.*

It is impossible to make a definitive list of the best-selling children's books in the world. However, based on total sales of their entire output, the authors above have produced titles that have been best-sellers – especially those in numerous translations – over a long period of time.

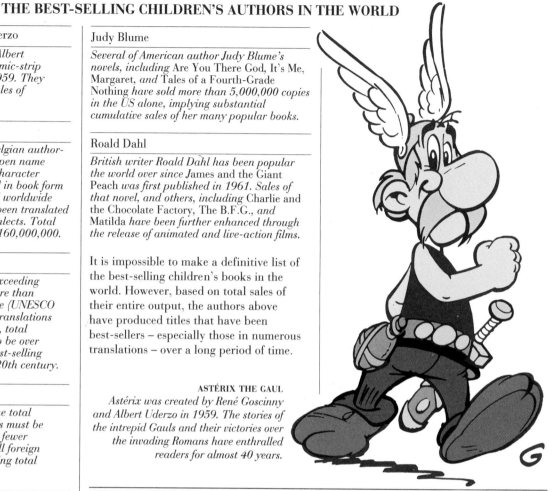

ASTÉRIX THE GAUL
Astérix was created by René Goscinny and Albert Uderzo in 1959. The stories of the intrepid Gauls and their victories over the invading Romans have enthralled readers for almost 40 years.

THE WORLD'S BEST-SELLING FICTION

Author	Title
Richard Bach	*Jonathan Livingstone Seagull*
William Blatty	*The Exorcist*
Peter Benchley	*Jaws*
Erskine Caldwell	*God's Little Acre*
Harper Lee	*To Kill a Mockingbird*
Colleen McCullough	*The Thorn Birds*
Grace Metalious	*Peyton Place*
Margaret Mitchell	*Gone with the Wind*
George Orwell	*Animal Farm*
Mario Puzo	*The Godfather*
J.D. Salinger	*The Catcher in the Rye*
Erich Segal	*Love Story*
Jacqueline Susann	*Valley of the Dolls*
J.R.R. Tolkein	*The Hobbit*

As with the best-selling books of all time, it is virtually impossible to arrive at a definitive list of fiction best-sellers that encompasses all permutations including hardback and paperback editions, book club sales, and translations, and takes account of the innumerable editions of earlier classics such as *Robinson Crusoe* or the works of Jane Austen, Charles Dickens, or popular foreign authors such as Jules Verne. Although only Jacqueline Susann's *The Valley of the Dolls* appears in the all-time list, and publishers' precise sales data remains tantalizingly elusive (it has been said that the most widely published fiction is publishers' own sales figures), there are many other novels that must be close contenders for this list. It seems certain that all the titles in this list have sold in excess of 10,000,000 copies in hardback and paperback worldwide.

ENGLISH LANGUAGE BEST-SELLERS

T O P 1 0
CHILDREN'S HARDBACKS IN THE US, 1996

	Title/author	Sales
1	*Falling Up*, Shel Silverstein	[confidential]
2	*The Hunchback of Notre Dame* (Classic), Disney/Mouse Works	1,204,600
3	*Disney's Hunchback of Notre Dame*, Justine Korman	603,600
4	*My Many Colored Days*, Dr. Seuss	496,833
5	*Disney's Hunchback of Notre Dame: Quasimodo the Hero*, Barbara Bazaldua	485,100
6	*Disney's 101 Dalmatians: Snow Puppies*, Barbara Bazaldua	455,555
7	*Disney's Winnie the Pooh: The Sweetest Christmas*, Ann Braybrooks	441,200
8	*Guess How Much I Love You* (Board book), Sam McBratney	434,018
9	*Oh, the Places You'll Go!*, Dr. Seuss	395,594
10	*Guess How Much I Love You*, Sam McBratney	384,016

Source: Publishers Weekly

T O P 1 0
HARDBACK NONFICTION BEST-SELLERS OF 1996 IN THE US

	Title/author	Sales
1	*Make the Connection*, Oprah Winfrey & Bob Greene	2,302,697
2	*Men Are From Mars, Women Are From Venus*, John Gray	1,485,089
3	*The Dilbert Principle*, Scott Adams	1,319,507
4	*Simple Abundance*, Sarah Ban Breathnach	1,087,149
5	*The Zone*, Barry Sears with Bill Lawren	930,311
6	*Bad As I Wanna Be*, Dennis Rodman	800,000
7	*In Contempt*, Christopher Darden	752,648
8	*A Reporter's Life*, Walter Cronkite	673,591
9	*Dogbert's Top Secret Management Handbook* Scott Adams	652,085
10	*My Sergei: A Love Story*, Ekaterina Gordeeva with E.M. Swift	563,567

Source: Publishers Weekly

T O P 1 0
HARDBACK FICTION BEST-SELLERS OF 1996 IN THE US

	Title/author	Sales
1	*The Runaway Jury*, John Grisham	2,775,000
2	*Executive Orders*, Tom Clancy	2,371,602
3	*Desperation*, Stephen King	1,542,077
4	*Airframe*, Michael Crichton	1,487,494
5	*The Regulators*, Richard Bachman	1,200,000
6=	*Malice*, Danielle Steel	1,150,000
6=	*Silent Honor*, Danielle Steel	1,150,000
8	*Primary Colors*, Anonymous (Joe Klein)	972,385
9	*Cause of Death*, Patricia Cornwell	920,403
10	*The Tenth Insight*, James Redfield	892,687

Source: Publishers Weekly

T O P 1 0
CHILDREN'S PAPERBACKS IN THE US, 1996

	Title/author	Sales
1	*Say Cheese and Die ... Again*, R. L. Stine	2,140,000
2	*Ghost Camp*, R. L. Stine	1,741,000
3	*How to Kill a Monster*, R. L. Stine	1,734,000
4	*Night of the Living Dummy*, R. L. Stine	1,633,000
5	*Egg Monsters from Mars*, R. L. Stine	1,631,000
6	*Bad Hare Day*, R. L. Stine	1,579,000
7	*Legend of the Lost Legend*, R. L. Stine	1,466,000
8	*The Beast from the East*, R. L. Stine	1,460,000
9	*Attack of the Jack-o'-Lanterns*, R. L. Stine	1,418,000
10	*Vampire Breath*, R. L. Stine	1,070,000

Source: Publishers Weekly

TOP 10
US ALMANACS, ATLASES, AND ANNUALS OF 1996

	Title	Sales
1	*The World Almanac and Book of Facts, 1997*	1,812,877
2	*The Universal Almanac, 1997*	536,154
3	*The World Almanac for Kids, 1997*	327,506
4	*What Color is Your Parachute 1996*	320,000
5	*The World Almanac and Book of Facts, 1996*	271,318
6	*Old Farmer's Almanac*	189,538
7	*Birnbaum's Walt Disney World: The Official 1997 Guide*	184,660
8	*Birnbaum's Walt Disney World: The Official 1996 Guide*	123,479
9	*1997 Sports Illustrated Almanac*	115,893
10	*Let's Go Europe 1996*	109,433

Source: Publishers Weekly

TOP 10
US TRADE PAPERBACK BEST-SELLERS OF 1996

	Title/author	Sales
1	*A 3rd Serving of Chicken Soup for the Soul,* Jack Canfield & Mark Victor Hansen	1,602,439
2	*Snow Falling On Cedars,* David Guterson	1,490,590
3	*It's A Magical World: A Calvin and Hobbes Collection,* Bill Watterson	1,250,000
4	*There's Treasure Everywhere: A Calvin and Hobbes Collection,* Bill Watterson	1,100,000
5	*Chicken Soup for the Woman's Soul,* Jack Canfield, Mark Victor Hansen, Jennifer Read Hawthorne, and Marci Shimoff	1,069,402
6	*A Journal of Daily Renewal: The Companion to Make the Connection,* Bob Greene and Oprah Winfrey	1,034,160
7	*Windows95 for Dummies,* Andy Rathbone	1,000,000
8	*Fugitive from the Cubicle Police: A Dilbert Book,* Scott Adams	663,123
9	*The Last Chapter and Worse: A Far Side Collection,* Gary Larson	605,000
10	*The English Patient,* Michael Ondaatje	575,630

Source: Publishers Weekly

TOP 10
FICTION BEST-SELLERS OF 1948 IN THE US

1	Lloyd C. Douglas, *The Big Fisherman*
2	Norman Mailer *The Naked and the Dead*
3	Frances Parkinson Keynes, *Dinner at Antoine's*
4	Agnes Sligh Turnbull, *The Bishop's Mantle*
5	Betty Smith, *Tomorrow Will Be Better*
6	Frank Yerby, *The Golden Hawk*
7	Ross Lockridge Jr., *Raintree Country*
8	A. J. Cronin *Shannon's Way*
9	Elizabeth Goudge, *Pilgrim's Inn*
10	Irwin Shaw, *The Young Lions*

The No. 1 best-seller fifty years ago, Lloyd C. Douglas's *The Big Fisherman*, also held the No. 2 position during the following year.

MICHAEL CRICHTON
Michael Crichton's success as a novelist is matched by the success of his books on screen. Jurassic Park *became the highest-grossing film of all time.*

TOP 10
FICTION BEST-SELLERS OF 1973 IN THE US

1	Richard Bach, *Jonathan Livingston Seagull*
2	Jacqueline Susann, *Once is Not Enough*
3	Kurt Vonnegut, *Breakfast of Champions*
4	Frederick Forsyth, *The Odessa File*
5	Gore Vidal, *Burr*
6	Mary Stewart, *The Hollow Hills*
7	Irwin Shaw, *Evening in Byzantium*
8	Robert Ludlum, *The Matlock Paper*
9	Paul E. Erdman, *The Billion Dollar Sure Thing*
10	Graham Greene, *The Honorary Consul*

The US fiction best seller list of a quarter of a century ago represents an eclectic mix of popular novels.

LITERARY PRIZES

THE 10

LATEST WINNERS OF THE PULITZER PRIZE FOR FICTION

	Author/novel	Year
1	Richard Ford, *Independence Day*	1996
2	Carol Shields, *The Stone Diaries*	1995
3	E. Annie Proulx, *The Shipping News*	1994
4	Robert Olen Butler, *A Good Scent from a Strange Mountain: Stories*	1993
5	Jane Smiley, *A Thousand Acres*	1992
6	John Updike, *Rabbit at Rest*	1991
7	Oscar Hijuelos, *The Mambo Kings Play*	1990
8	Anne Tyler, *Breathing Lessons*	1989
9	Toni Morrison, *Beloved*	1988
10	Peter Taylor, *A Summons to Memphis*	1987

THE 10

LATEST BOOKER PRIZE WINNERS

	Author/novel	Year
1	Graham Swift, *Last Orders*	1996
2	Pat Barker, *The Ghost Road*	1995
3	James Kelman, *How Late It Was, How Late*	1994
4	Roddy Doyle, *Paddy Clarke Ha Ha Ha*	1993
5=	Michael Ondaatje, *The English Patient*	1992
5=	Barry Unsworth, *Sacred Hunger*	1992
7	Ben Okri, *Famished Road*	1991
8	A.S. Byatt, *Possession: A Romance*	1990
9	Kazuo Ishiguro, *The Remains of the Day*	1989
10	Peter Carey, *Oscar and Lucinda*	1988

THE 10

LATEST WINNERS OF THE NATIONAL BOOK AWARD FOR FICTION

1996	Andrea Barrett, *Ship Fever and Other Stories*	
1995	Philip Roth, *Sabbath's Theater*	
1994	William Gaddis, *A Frolic of His Own*	
1993	E. Annie Proulx, *The Shipping News*	
1992	Cormac McCarthy, *All the Pretty Horses*	
1991	Norman Rush, *Mating*	
1990	Charles Johnson, *Middle Passage*	
1989	John Casey, *Spartina*	
1988	Pete Dexter, *Paris Trout*	
1987	Larry Heinemann, *Paco's Story*	

The National Book Award is presented by the National Book Foundation as part of its program to foster reading in the United States through such activities as author events and fund-raising for literacy campaigns. Award winners are announced each November and receive $10,000. Past recipients include many books that are now regarded as modern classics, some of which have since been filmed, among them William Styron's *Sophie's Choice*, John Irving's *The World According to Garp*, and Alice Walker's *The Color Purple*.

THE 10

LATEST WINNERS OF THE NATIONAL BOOK CRITICS CIRCLE AWARD FOR FICTION

1996	Gina Berricault, *Women In Their Beds*	
1995	Stanley Elkin, *Mrs. Ted Bliss*	
1994	Carol Shields, *The Stone Diaries*	
1993	Ernest J. Gaines, *A Lesson Before Dying*	
1992	Cormac McCarthy, *All The Pretty Horses*	
1991	Jane Smiley, *A Thousand Acres*	
1990	John Updike, *Rabbit at Rest*	
1989	E. L. Doctorow, *Billy Bathgate*	
1988	Bharati Mukherjee, *The Middleman and Other Stories*	
1987	Philip Roth, *The Counterlife*	

The National Book Critics Circle was founded in 1974 and consists of almost 700 active reviewers. The Circle presents annual awards in five categories: fiction, general nonfiction, biography, and autobiography, poetry, and criticism. Awards are made in March, and winners receive a scroll and citation. E.L. Doctorow won the first fiction Award in 1975 for his novel *Ragtime*.

THE 10

LATEST WINNERS OF HUGO AWARDS FOR BEST SCIENCE FICTION NOVEL

	Author/novel	Year
1	Lois McMaster Bujold, *Mirror Dance*	1995
2	Kim Stanley Robinson, *Green Mars*	1994
3	Vernor Vinge, *A Fire Upon the Deep*	1993
4	Connie Willis, *Doomsday Book*	1993
5	Lois McMaster Bujold, *Barrayar*	1992
6	Lois McMaster Bujold, *The Vor Game*	1991
7	Dan Simmons, *Hyperion*	1990
8	C.J. Cherryh, *Cyteen*	1989
9	David Brin, *The Uplift War*	1988
10	Orson Scott Card, *Speaker for the Dead*	1987

Hugo Awards for science fiction novels, short stories, and other fiction and nonfiction works are presented by the World Science Fiction Society. They were established in 1953 as "Science Fiction Achievement Awards for the best science fiction writing." The prize in the Awards' inaugural year was presented to Alfred Bester for *The Demolished Man*.

T O P 1 0

FIRST WINNERS OF THE "ODDEST TITLE AT THE FRANKFURT BOOK FAIR" COMPETITION

	Title	Year
1	*Proceedings of the Second International Workshop on Nude Mice*	1978
2	*The Madam as Entrepreneur: Career Management in House Prostitution*	1979
3	*The Joy of Chickens*	1980
4	*Last Chance at Love – Terminal Romances*	1981
5	Judges split between *Population and Other Problems* and *Braces Owners Manual*	1982
6	*The Theory of Lengthwise Rolling*	1983
7	*The Book of Marmalade: Its Antecedents, Its History and Its Role in the World Today*	1984
8	*Natural Bust Enlargement with Total Mind Power: How to Use the Other 90 Percent of Your Mind to Increase the Size of Your Breasts*	1985
9	*Oral Sadism and the Vegetarian Personality*	1986
10	*Versailles: The View From Sweden*	1988

Every year since 1978 the Diagram Group and *The Bookseller* have organized a competition for the book title spotted at the Frankfurt Book Fair that "most outrageously exceeds all bounds of credibility." In 1987 the judges did not consider that the standard was sufficiently high, and no award was presented.

T H E 1 0

LATEST WINNERS OF THE JOHN NEWBERY MEDAL

	Title	Year
1	E.L. Konigsburg, *The View from Saturday*	1997
2	Karen Cushman, *The Midwife's Apprentice*	1996
3	Sharon Creech, *Walk Two Moons*	1995
4	Lois Lowry, *The Giver*	1994
5	Cynthia Rylant, *Missing May*	1993
6	Phyllis Reynolds Naylor, *Shiloh*	1992
7	Jerry Spinelli, *Maniac Magee*	1991
8	Lois Lowry, *Number The Stars*	1990
9	Paul Fleischman, *Joyful Noise*	1989
10	Walter Myers, *Scorpions*	1989

The John Newbery Medal is awarded annually for "the most distinguished contribution to American literature for children."

T H E 1 0

LATEST RANDOLPH CALDECOTT MEDAL WINNERS

	Author/title	Year
1	David Wisniewski, *Golem*	1997
2	Peggy Rathman, *Officer Buckle and Gloria*	1996
3	Eve Bunting (illustrated by David Diaz), *Smoky Night*	1995
4	Allen Say, *Grandfather's Journey*	1994
5	Emily McCully Honor, *Mirette on High Wire*	1993
6	David Weisner, *Tuesday*	1992
7	David Macauley, *Black & White*	1991
8	Ed Young, *Lon Po Po*	1990
9	Stephen Gammell, *Song & Dance Man*	1989
10	Jane Yolen (illustrated by John Schoenherr), *Owl Moon*	1988

The Randolph Caldecott Medal, named after the English illustrator (1846–86), has been awarded annually since 1938 "to the artist of the most distinguished American picture book for children published in the United States during the preceding year."

T H E 1 0

LATEST KATE GREENAWAY MEDAL WINNERS

	Artist/author/title	Year
1	Helen Cooper, *The Baby Who Wouldn't Go to Bed*	1996
2	P.J. Lynch (text Susan Wojciechowski), *The Christmas Miracle of Jonathan Toomey*	1995
3	Gregory Rogers (text Libby Hathorn), *The Way Home*	1994
4	Alan Lee (text Rosemary Sutcliff), *Black Ships Before Troy*	1993
5	Anthony Browne, *Zoo*	1992
6	Janet Ahlberg (text Allan Ahlberg), *The Jolly Christmas Postman*	1991
7	Gary Blythe (text Dyan Sheldon), *The Whales' Song*	1990
8	Michael Foreman, *War Boy: A Country Childhood*	1989
9	Barbara Firth (text Martin Waddell), *Can't You Sleep, Little Bear?*	1988
10	Adrienne Kennaway (text Mwenye Hadithi), *Crafty Chameleon*	1987

The Kate Greenaway Medal, named after the English illustrator (1846–1901), has been awarded annually since 1956 for the most distinguished work in the illustration of children's books published in the United Kingdom.

THE PRESS

T O P 1 0

COUNTRIES WITH THE MOST DAILY NEWSPAPERS

	Country	No. of daily newspapers
1	India	2,300
2	US	1,586
3	Turkey	399
4	Brazil	373
5	Germany	355
6	Russia	339
7	Mexico	292
8	Pakistan	274
9	Argentina	190
10	Spain	148

Certain countries have large numbers of newspapers, each serving relatively small areas and therefore with restricted circulations. The US is the most notable example with 1,586 daily newspapers, but only four of them with average daily sales of more than 1,000,000. The UK, with fewer individual newspapers, has five with circulations of over 1,000,000. If the table is arranged by total sales of daily newspapers per 1,000 inhabitants, the result – as seen below – is somewhat different:

	Country	Sales per 1,000 inhabitants
1	Hong Kong	822
2	Norway	607
3	Japan	577
4	Iceland	519
5	Finland	512
6	Sweden	511
7	Macau	510
8	South Korea	412
9	Austria	398
10	Russia	387
	US	240

THE DAILY NEWS
Reading the newspaper has been an important part of everyday life for several hundred years.

T O P 1 0

ENGLISH-LANGUAGE DAILY NEWSPAPERS IN THE WORLD

	Newspaper/ founded/country	Average daily circulation
1	*The Sun,* September 15, 1964, UK	3,935,312
2	*The Mirror,* November 2, 1903, UK	2,370,891
3	*Daily Mail,* May 4, 1896, UK	2,126,637
4	*Wall Street Journal,* July 8, 1889, US	1,837,194
5	*USA Today,* September 15, 1982, US	1,662,060
6	*Daily Express,* April 24, 1900, UK	1,207,851
7	*Daily Telegraph,* June 29, 1855, UK	1,126,479
8	*New York Times,* September 18, 1851, US	1,107,168
9	*Los Angeles Times,* December 4, 1881, US	1,068,812
10	*Washington Post,* December 6, 1877, US	818,231

Several long-established English-language dailies fail to make this Top 10: in the UK *The Times* has been published since January 1, 1785, while the *New York Post*, first published on November 16, 1801, holds the record as America's longest-running daily (the *Hartford Courant* was first issued as a weekly on October 29, 1764 but was not a daily until 1836).

T O P 1 0

DAILY NEWSPAPERS IN THE US

	Newspaper	Average daily circulation *
1	*Wall Street Journal*	1,837,194
2	*USA Today*	1,662,060
3	*New York Times*	1,107,168
4	*Los Angeles Times*	1,068,812
5	*Washington Post*	818,231
6	*New York Daily News*	728,107
7	*Chicago Tribune*	664,586
8	*Long Island Newsday*	559,233
9	*Houston Chronicle*	549,856
10	*San Francisco Chronicle/ Examiner*	494,093

* Through March 31, 1997
Source: Audit Bureau of Circulations

Apart from the *Wall Street Journal*, which focuses mainly on financial news, *USA Today* remains the United States' only real national daily newspaper.

T O P 1 0

SUNDAY NEWSPAPERS IN THE US

	Newspaper	Average Sunday circulation*
1	*New York Times*	1,644,128
2	*Los Angeles Times*	1,361,988
3	*Washington Post*	1,123,305
4	*Chicago Tribune*	1,045,756
5	*Philadelphia Inquirer*	865,989
6	*New York News*	854,815
7	*Dallas News*	800,306
8	*Detroit Free Press*	787,133
9	*Boston Globe*	751,377
10	*Houston Chronicle*	740,952

* Through March 31, 1997
Source: Audit Bureau of Circulations

T O P 1 0

MOST VALUABLE COMICS IN THE US

	Comic	Value ($)*
1	*Action Comics No.1*	105,000

Published in June 1938, the first issue of Action Comics marked the original appearance of Superman.

2	*Detective Comics No.27*	96,000

Issued in May 1939, it is prized as the first comic book to feature Batman.

3	*Marvel Comics No.1*	75,000

The Human Torch and other heroes were first introduced in the issue dated October 1939.

4	*Superman No.1*	72,000

The first comic book devoted to Superman, reprinting the original Action Comics story, was published in summer 1939.

5	*Detective Comics No.1*	51,000

Published in March 1937, it was the first in a longrunning series.

* For example in "Near Mint" condition.

	Comic	Value ($)*
6	*Whiz Comics No.1*	44,000

Published in February 1940 – and confusingly numbered "2" – it was the first comic book to feature Captain Marvel.

7	*All American Comics No.16*	39,000

The Green Lantern made his debut in the issue dated July 1940.

8=	*Batman No.1*	38,000

Published in spring 1940, this was the first comic book devoted to Batman.

8=	*Captain America Comics*	38,000

Published in March 1941, this was the original comic book in which Captain America appeared.

10	*New Fun Comics No.1*	36,000

Its February 1935 publication was notable as the first-ever DC comic book.

Source: © Overstreet Publications Inc.

HOT OFF THE PRESS
Huge quantities of newsprint are consumed to satisfy global demand, but increasingly large amounts are recycled.

T O P 1 0

MAGAZINES IN THE US

	Magazine/ no. of issues a year	Circulation*
1	*NRTA/AARP Bulletin* (10)	20,716,609
2	*Modern Maturity* (36)	20,673,063
3	*Reader's Digest* (12)	15,150,822
4	*TV Guide* (52)	13,076,790
5	*National Geographic Magazine* (12)	9,184,878
6	*Better Homes and Gardens* (12)	7,616,270
7	*Good Housekeeping* (12)	5,032,901
8	*Family Circle* (17)	5,003,227
9	*Ladies Home Journal* (12)	4,705,020
10	*Woman's Day* (17)	4,501,612

* Average for first six months of 1996
Source: Magazine Publishers of America

National Geographic, the official publication of the National Geographic Society, was first published as a monthly magazine in 1896.

DID YOU KNOW

BACK ISSUES

The oldest journal in print in the UK is the *Philosophical Transactions of the Royal Society*, which was first issued on March 6, 1665. *The Scots Magazine* (1739), *Archaeologia* (the journal of the Society of Antiquaries, 1770), and *Curtis's Botanical Magazine* (1787) have also all been published for more than 200 years. The medical journal *The Lancet* (1823) is the oldest British weekly publication. The oldest-established magazine in the US is the *Saturday Evening Post*, which was started in Philadelphia in 1821 by Samuel C. Atkinson and Charles Alexander (the often-stated claim that it was published as early as 1728 is unfounded). *Scientific American* began publication in New York on August 28, 1845, *Town & Country* in 1846, and *Harper's Magazine* in 1850 (then named *Harper's Monthly*). *Harper's Bazar* was first issued in 1867. After William Randolph Hearst bought it in 1913, he subtly changed its name by spelling *Bazaar* with a double "a."

T O P 1 0

CONSUMERS OF NEWSPRINT

	Country	Consumption per inhabitant		
		kg	lb	oz
1	Sweden	54.32	119	12
2	US	47.633	105	0
3	Austria	46.271	102	0
4	Switzerland	46.235	101	15
5	Norway	42.654	94	1
6	Denmark	42.226	93	1
7	Australia	37.395	82	7
8	Hong Kong	36.500	80	8
9	Singapore	36.367	80	3
10	UK	32.243	71	1

National consumption of newsprint provides a measure of the extent of the newspaper sales in the Top 10 countries above.

ART AT AUCTION

TOP 10

MOST EXPENSIVE PAINTINGS BY ANDY WARHOL

Work/sale	Price ($)
1 *Marilyn X 100,* Sotheby's, New York, November 17, 1992	3,400,000
2 *Shot Red Marilyn,* Christie's, New York, May 3, 1989	3,700,000
3 *Marilyn Monroe, Twenty Times,* Sotheby's, New York, November 10, 1988	3,600,000
4 *Shot Red Marilyn,* Christie's, New York, November 2, 1994	3,300,000
5 *Liz,* Christie's, New York, November 7, 1989	2,050,000
6 *Triple Elvis,* Sotheby's, New York, November 8, 1989	2,000,000
7 *210 Coca-Cola bottles,* Christie's, New York, May 5, 1992	1,900,000
8 *Ladies and Gentlemen, 1975,* Binoche et Godeau, Paris, November 30, 1989	1,607,000
9= *The Last Supper,* Sotheby's, New York, November 8, 1989	1,600,000
9= *Race Riot,* Christie's, New York, November 7, 1989	1,600,000

Born Andrew Warhola, Andy Warhol (1926–87) became one of the most famous American artists of all time through his leadership of the Pop Art movement. He typically featured images derived from popular culture, among them familiar brands, such as Campbell's soup cans, and portraits – often multiple images – of well-known celebrities from Marilyn Monroe to Mao Tse-Tung. He also produced graphic designs, including album covers for the Rolling Stones and others, and was a filmmaker and magazine publisher.

TOP 10

MOST EXPENSIVE PAINTINGS BY PABLO PICASSO

Work/sale	Price ($)
1 *Les Noces de Pierrette,* Binoche et Godeau, Paris, November 30, 1989	51,671,920
2 *Self Portrait: Yo Picasso,* Sotheby's, New York, May 9, 1989	43,500,000
3 *Au Lapin Agile,* Sotheby's, New York, November 15, 1989	37,000,000
4 *Acrobate et Jeune Arlequin,* Christie's, London, November 28, 1988	35,530,000
5 *Angel Fernandez de Soto,* Sotheby's, New York, May 8, 1995	28,152,500
6 *Le Miroir,* Sotheby's, New York, November 15, 1989	24,000,000
7 *Maternité,* Christie's, New York, June 14, 1988	22,500,000
8 *Les Tuileries,* Christie's, London, June 25, 1990	22,000,000
9 *Le Miroir,* Christie's, New York, November 7, 1995	18,200,000
10 *Mère et Enfant,* Sotheby's, New York, November 15, 1989	17,000,000

By the late 1950s the Spanish painter Pablo Picasso (1881–1973) was already being hailed as the foremost artist of the 20th century. This was progressively reflected in the salesroom: when *Mère et Enfant* (*Mother and Child*) was sold in 1957 for $185,000, it was the highest price ever paid for a painting during an artist's lifetime. The upward spiral continued with *Woman and Child at the Seashore,* sold in 1962 for $304,000.
In 1981 Picasso's *Self Portrait: Yo Picasso* made $5,300,000 – a level considered astonishing at the time. The May 8, 1995 sale of the painting *Angel Fernandez De Soto* achieved the highest price for any painting sold at auction since 1990.

THE 10

FIRST PAINTINGS AUCTIONED FOR OVER $3M

Work/artist/price	Sale date
1 *Portrait of Juan de Pareja,* Diego Rodriguez de Silva y Velásquez (Spanish; 1599–1660), Christie's, London, $5,524,000	Nov 27, 1970
2 *The Death of Actaeon,* Titian (Italian; c. 1488–1576), Christie's, London, $4,036,000	Jun 25, 1971
3 *The Resurrection,* Dirk Bouts (Dutch; 1400–75), Sotheby's, London, $3,740,000	Apr 16, 1980
4 *Saltimbanque Seated with Arms Crossed,* Pablo Picasso (Spanish; 1881–1973), Sotheby's, New York, $3,000,000	May 12, 1980
5 *Paysan en Blouse Bleu,* Paul Cézanne (French; 1839–1906), Christie's, New York, $3,900,000	May 13, 1980
6 *Le Jardin du Poète, Arles,* Vincent van Gogh (Dutch; 1853–80), Christie's, New York, $5,200,000	May 13, 1980
7 *Juliet and Her Nurse,* J.M.W. Turner (British; 1775–1851), Sotheby's, New York, $6,400,000	May 29, 1980
8 *Samson and Delilah,* Sir Peter Paul Rubens (Flemish; 1577–1640), Christie's, London, $5,474,000	Jul 11, 1980
9 *The Holy Family with Saints and Putti,* Nicolas Poussin (French; 1594–1665), Christie's, London, $3,564,000	Apr 10, 1981
10 *Self Portrait: Yo Picasso,* Pablo Picasso, Sotheby's, New York, $5,300,000	May 21, 1981

TOP 10

MOST EXPENSIVE PAINTINGS EVER SOLD AT AUCTION

Work/artist/sale	Price ($)
1 *Portrait of Dr. Gachet*, Vincent van Gogh (Dutch; 1853–80), Christie's, New York, May 15, 1990	75,000,000

Both this painting and the one in the No. 2 position were bought by Ryoei Saito, head of Japanese Daishowa Paper Manufacturing.

2 *Au Moulin de la Galette*, Pierre-Auguste Renoir (French; 1841–1919), Sotheby's, New York, May 17, 1990	71,000,000
3 *Les Noces de Pierrette*, Pablo Picasso (Spanish; 1881–1973), Binoche et Godeau, Paris, November 30, 1989	51,671,920

The painting was sold by Swedish financier Fredrik Roos to Tomonori Tsurumaki, a property developer, who bid for it by telephone from Tokyo.

4 *Irises*, Vincent van Gogh, Sotheby's, New York, November 11, 1987	49,000,000

After much speculation, its purchaser was confirmed as businessman Alan Bond. However, he was unable to pay for it in full, so its former status as the world's most expensive work of art has been disputed.

5 *Self Portrait: Yo Picasso*, Pablo Picasso, Sotheby's, New York, May 9, 1989	43,500,000

Work/artist/sale	Price ($)
6 *Au Lapin Agile*, Pablo Picasso, Sotheby's, New York, November 15, 1989	37,000,000

The painting depicts Picasso as a harlequin at the bar of the café Lapin.

7 *Sunflowers*, Vincent van Gogh, Christie's, London, March 30, 1987	36,225,000

At the time this was the most expensive picture ever sold.

8 *Acrobate et Jeune Arlequin*, Pablo Picasso, Christie's, London, November 28, 1988	35,000,000

Until the sale of Yo Picasso, this held the world record for a 20th-century painting. It was bought by Mitsukoshi, a Japanese department store (in Japan, many major stores have important art galleries).

9 *Portrait of Duke Cosimo I de Medici*, Jacopo da Carucci (Pontormo) (Italy; 1494–1556/7), Christie's, New York, May 31, 1989	32,000,000

This is the record price paid for an Old Master – and the only one in this Top 10. It was bought by the J. Paul Getty Museum, Malibu, CA.

10 *Angel Fernandez De Soto*, Pablo Picasso, Sotheby's, New York, May 8, 1995	28,152,500

This painting was sold by one Greek shipowner, George Embiricos, and bought by another, Stavros Niarchos.

TOP 10

MOST EXPENSIVE PAINTINGS BY WOMEN ARTISTS

Work/artist/sale	Price ($)
1 *The Conversation*, Mary Cassatt (American; 1844–1926), Christie's, New York, May 11, 1988	4,100,000
2 *In the Box*, Mary Cassatt (American; 1844–1926), Christie's, New York, May 23, 1988	3,700,000
3 *Mother, Sara, and the Baby*, Mary Cassatt, Christie's, New York, May 10, 1989	3,500,000
4 *Autoretrato con chango y loro*, Frida Kahlo (Mexican; 1907–54), Sotheby's, New York, May 17, 1995	2,900,000
5 *Augusta Reading to Her Daughter*, Mary Cassatt, Sotheby's, New York, May 9, 1989	2,800,000
6 *Sara Holding Her Dog*, Mary Cassatt, Sotheby's, New York, November 11, 1988	2,500,000
7 *Young Lady in a Loge, Gazing to the Right*, Mary Cassatt, Sotheby's, New York, November 10, 1992	2,300,000
8 *Madame H. de Fleury and Her Child*, Mary Cassatt, Sotheby's, New York, May 25, 1988	1,900,000
9= *Adam et Eve*, Tamara de Lempicka (Polish; 1898–1980), Christie's, New York, March 3, 1994	1,800,000
9= *Black Hollyhocks with Blue Larkspur*, Georgia O'Keeffe (American; 1887–1986), Sotheby's, New York, December 3, 1987	1,800,000

RISING SUNFLOWERS
When it was sold in 1987 for $36,225,000, Vincent van Gogh's Sunflowers (1888) almost tripled the world record price for a painting. One of several works in a series, its price is equivalent to $3,000,000 per sunflower.

COLLECTIBLES

TOP 10

MOST EXPENSIVE PIECES OF FURNITURE EVER SOLD AT AUCTION

Item/auction	Price ($)
1 18th-century "Badminton Cabinet," Christie's, London, July 5, 1990	16,070,340
2 1760s mahogany desk by John Goddard, Christie's, New York, June 3, 1989	12,100,000
3 Porcelain-mounted jewel coffer by Martin Carlin, Ader Picard & Tajan, Paris, November 7, 1991	4,349,650
4 Louis XIV bureau plate by A-C Boulle, Christie's, Monaco, December 4, 1993	3,217,549
5 Pair of Louis XV porphyry and gilt-bronze two-handled vases, Christie's, London, December 8, 1994	2,976,057
6 Louis XVI Weisweiler ormolu-mounted ebony and Japanese lacquer commode à vantaux and companion secretaire à abbatant, Sotheby's, New York, December 6, 1991	2,860,000
7 Porcelain-mounted commode by Martin Carlin, Ader Picard & Tajan, Paris, November 7, 1991	2,811,173
8 Louis XVI console table by Riesener for Marie-Antoinette's cabinet interieur, Versailles, Sotheby's, London, November 24, 1988	2,767,050
9 Le mobilier Crozat, a suite of Regence seat furniture, Christie's, Monaco, December 7, 1987	2,723,108
10 Louis XIV ebony and tortoiseshell coffres de toilette (marriage) by A-C Boulle, Christie's, London, December 8, 1994	2,381,309

TOP 10

MOST COLLECTED POSTCARD THEMES

1 Street scenes (especially busy, turn-of-the-century subjects)

2 Social history

3 Greetings

4 Photographic nudes

5= Glamour (especially from Art Nouveau and Art Deco periods)

5= The *Titanic*

7 Cat illustrations (especially turn-of-the-century by Louis Wain and other artists)

8 Novelty subjects

9 World War I

10 Miscellaneous modern subjects

The first postcards appeared in Great Britain in 1870, but Post Office regulations meant that they were not illustrated until 1894, and it was another eight years before they were issued with the now familiar "divided back" so that the message and address could appear on the same side with a picture on the other. After this, the fashion for sending picture postcards took off and cartophily – postcard collecting – is today an internationally popular hobby, with rare and early examples often changing hands for considerable amounts.

TOP 10

MOST EXPENSIVE SCULPTURES BY AUGUSTE RODIN EVER SOLD AT AUCTION

Sculpture/sale	Price ($)
1 *Les Bourgeois de Calais grands modèles – Pierre de Wiessant Vetu*, Sotheby's, New York, May 17, 1990	3,900,000
2 *Psyche regardant l'amour*, Sotheby's, New York, November 8, 1995	1,800,000
3 *La fauness*, Christie's, New York, May 11, 1995	1,200,000
4 *Le penseur*, Sotheby's, New York, May 17, 1990	1,050,000
5 *Le penseur*, Sotheby's, New York, November 13, 1990	1,100,000
6 *Eve*, Sotheby's, New York, November 8, 1994	925,000
7 *Le penseur*, Christie's, New York, May 10, 1994	900,000
8 *Le penseur*, Sotheby's, New York, November 15, 1989	825,000
9 *Le penseur*, Sotheby's, New York, November 8, 1995	780,000
10 *Le baiser*, Christie's, New York, May 11, 1995	775,000

Auguste Rodin (1840–1917) was the foremost French sculptor of his day. He achieved international fame through such creations as *The Thinker* and *The Kiss*, which was commissioned by American connoisseur Edward Perry Warren and kept at his house in Lewes, England, until it was sold to the Tate Gallery, London. Bronze casts of Rodin's works mean that multiple copies exist of a number of them, including *The Burghers of Calais*, one of his most celebrated sculptures. A version of this sculpture heads this list, but it can also be seen in Calais and in Victoria Tower Gardens in London.

TOP 10

BEST-SELLING POSTCARDS IN THE NATIONAL GALLERY, LONDON

1 Vincent van Gogh, *Sunflowers*, 1888

2 Vincent van Gogh, *A Cornfield, with Cypresses*, 1889

3 J. M. W. Turner, *The Fighting Téméraire Tugged to her Last Berth to be Broken Up*, before 1839

4 Claude Monet, *The Thames Below Westminster*, 1871

5 Georges Pierre Seurat, *Bathers, Asnières*, 1884

6 Pierre-Auguste Renoir, *The Umbrellas, c.* 1881–86

7 Henri Rousseau, *Tropical Storm with a Tiger*, 1891

8 Jan van Eyck, *The Marriage of Giovanni(?) Arnolfini and Giovanna Cenami (?)*, 1434

9 Claude Monet, *The Water-Lily Pond*, 1899

10 J. M. W. Turner, *Rain, Steam, and Speed – The Great Western Railway*, before 1844

TOP 10

MOST VALUABLE VANITY FAIR CARICATURES

	Subject	Profession	Caption	Date	Value ($)
1=	Lord Hawke	Cricketer	"Yorkshire Cricket"	Sep 24, 1892	2,500
1=	Jack Hobbs	Cricketer	"A Tested Centurion"	Aug 7, 1912	2,500
1=	Frederick Spofforth	Cricketer	"The Demon Bowler"	Jul 13, 1878	2,500
4	Lord Harris	Cricketer	"Kent"	Jul 16, 1881	2,425
5	Winston Churchill	Politician	"Winnie"	Mar 8, 1911	2,250
6	Winston Churchill	Politician	"Winston"	Sep 27, 1900	2,000
7=	W.S. Gilbert	Dramatist	"Patience"	May 21, 1881	1,500
7=	Tod Sloane	Jockey	"An American Jockey"	May 25, 1899	1,500
9=	William Gillette	Actor	"Sherlock Holmes"	Feb 27, 1907	1,375
9=	Oscar Wilde	Writer	"Oscar"	May 24, 1884	1,375

When Vanity Fair magazine was first published 1865 it contained popular colored caricatures of men of the day, from sportsmen and soldiers to artists and royalty. They were produced initially by an Italian-born aristocrat Carlo Pellegrini, working under the pseudonym "Ape." He was briefly succeeded by James Tissot (pseudonym Coïdé), and then by Sir Leslie Ward, working under the name "Spy," whose caricatures appeared over a long period (1877–1909). Other contributors included Jean de Paleologu ("Pal"), Adriano Cecioni, Walter Sickert ("Sic"), and Max Beerbohm ("Max"). The individual elongated style of the Vanity Fair caricatures made them instantly recognizable, and they have become highly collectible. There is scarcely a lawyer's office in the UK that does not display one of an eminent judge or barrister. Cricketers are especially popular – outside this Top 10, W.G. Grace is much sought after.

TOP 10

MOST EXPENSIVE SCIENTIFIC INSTRUMENTS EVER SOLD AT AUCTION BY CHRISTIE'S, UK

	Item/sale	Price ($)
1	Pair of globes, terrestrial and celestial, attributed to Gerard Mercator, 1579, October 30, 1991	1,723,755
2	Ptolemaic armillary sphere, *c.* 1579, April 9, 1997	1,252,145
3	Astrolabe by Ersamus Habermel, *c.* 1590, October 11, 1995	838,350
4	Astrolabe by Walter Arsenius, 1559, September 29, 1988	645,645
5	The Regiomontanus Astrolabe, 1462, September 28, 1989	324,786
6	Astrolabe quadrant by Christopher Schissler, 1576, September 28, 1989	290,598
7	Universal rectilinear dial by Erasmus Habermel, *c.* 1590, September 27, 1990	288,442
8	Section of Difference Engine No.1 by Charles and Henry Prevost Babbage, November 16, 1995	274,404
9	Arithmometre (mechanical calculator) by Thomas de Colmar, 1848, April 9, 1997	270,230
10	Astrolabe by George Hartman, 1581, March 2, 1995	137,784

ASTROLABE
This Flemish brass astrolabe, made by Walter Arsenius in 1559, held the world record for the highest price paid for a scientific instrument when it was sold in 1988 for $645,645.

MUSIC

T O P 1 0

SINGLES OF ALL TIME WORLDWIDE

Title/artist	Sales exceed
1 *White Christmas,* Bing Crosby	30,000,000
2 *Rock Around the Clock,* Bill Haley & His Comets	17,000,000
3 *I Want to Hold Your Hand,* The Beatles	12,000,000
4= *It's Now or Never,* Elvis Presley	10,000,000
4= *I Will Always Love You,* Whitney Houston	10,000,000
6= *Hound Dog/Don't Be Cruel,* Elvis Presley	9,000,000
6= *Diana,* Paul Anka	9,000,000
8= *Hey Jude,* The Beatles	8,000,000
8= *I'm a Believer,* The Monkees	8,000,000
8= *(Everything I Do) I Do It For You,* Bryan Adams	8,000,000

Global sales are notoriously difficult to calculate, since for many decades little statistical research on record sales was done in a large part of the world. "Worldwide" is thus usually taken to mean the known minimum "Western World" sales.

T O P 1 0

SINGLES OF ALL TIME IN THE US

Title/artist	Year
1 *White Christmas,* Bing Crosby	1942
2 *I Want to Hold Your Hand,* The Beatles	1964
3 *Hound Dog/Don't Be Cruel,* Elvis Presley	1956
4 *It's Now or Never,* Elvis Presley	1960
5 *I Will Always Love You,* Whitney Houston	1992
6 *Hey Jude,* The Beatles	1968
7 *We Are the World,* USA For Africa	1985
8 *Whoomp! There It Is,* Tag Team	1993
9 *Everything I Do (I Do It for You),* Bryan Adams	1991
10 *Macarena,* Los Del Rio	1995

T O P 1 0

SINGLES WITH MOST CONSECUTIVE WEEKS ON THE US CHARTS

Title/artist	Weeks
1 Macarena, *Los Del Rio (Bayside Boys Mix)*	54 *
2 *Run-Around,* Blues Traveler	49
3= *Whoomp! (There It Is),* Tag Team	45
3= *Another Night,* Real McCoy	45
3= *100% Pure Love,* Crystal Waters	45
6= *You Gotta Be,* Des'ree	44
6= *Come To My Window,* Melissa Etheridge	44
6= *Missing,* Everything But The Girl	44
6= *As I Lay Me Down,* Sophie Hawkins	44
6= *Hold My Hand,* Hootie & the Blowfish	44

* *The Four Seasons' December 1963 (Oh, What A Night) also spent 54 weeks on the chart, but in two different chart runs; all the songs listed charted since 1994*

BAND AID
George Michael, Bono, Freddie Mercury, and other international stars contributed to make Band Aid's 1984 single the UK's all-time best-seller.

I WANT TO HOLD YOUR HAND
The Beatles' smash hit became the bestselling record of the 1960s in the US, and the world's third most successful single ever.

T O P 1 0

SINGLES OF THE 1960s IN THE US

	Title/artist	Year
1	*I Want To Hold Your Hand,* The Beatles	1964
2	*It's Now Or Never,* Elvis Presley	1960
3	*Hey Jude,* The Beatles	1968
4	*The Ballad Of The Green Berets,* S/Sgt Barry Sadler	1966
5	*Love Is Blue,* Paul Mauriat	1968
6	*I'm A Believer,* The Monkees	1966
7	*Can't Buy Me Love,* The Beatles	1964
8	*She Loves You,* The Beatles	1964
9	*Sugar Sugar,* The Archies	1969
10	*The Twist,* Chubby Checker	1960

T O P 1 0

SINGLES OF THE 1980s IN THE US

	Title/artist	Year
1	*We Are the World,* USA for Africa	1985
2	*Physical,* Olivia Newton-John	1981
3	*Endless Love,* Diana Ross and Lionel Richie	1981
4	*Eye of the Tiger,* Survivor	1982
5	*I Love Rock 'n' Roll,* Joan Jett & the Blackhearts	1982
6	*When Doves Cry,* Prince	1984
7	*Celebration,* Kool & the Gang	1981
8	*Another One Bites the Dust,* Queen	1980
9	*Wild Thing,* Tone Loc	1989
10	*Islands in the Stream,* Kenny Rogers and Dolly Parton	1983

America's top-selling single of the 1980s was, rather fittingly, a record that included contributions from many of those artists who had become the recording elite during the decade – the charity single for Africa's famine victims, *We Are The World.* Meanwhile, three of the close runners-up, *Endless Love* (same movie), *Eye Of The Tiger* (from *Rocky III*), and *When Doves Cry* (from Prince's *Purple Rain*) were all taken from movies.

T O P 1 0

SINGLES OF THE 1990s IN THE US TO DATE*

	Title/artist	Year
1	*I Will Always Love You,* Whitney Houston	1992
2	*Whoomp! There It Is,* Tag Team	1993
3	*Macarena,* Los Del Rio	1995
4	*Everything I Do (I Do It for You),* Bryan Adams	1991
5	*Gangsta's Paradise,* Coolio featuring LV	1995
6	*Tha Crossroads,* Bone Thugs 'N Harmony	1996
7	*Fantasy,* Mariah Carey	1995
8	*Jump,* Kris Kross	1992
9	*Vogue,* Madonna	1990
10	*How Do U Want It/ California Love,* 2 Pac featuring Dr. Dre & Roger Troutman	1996

* *Up to December 31, 1996*

T O P 1 0

ARTISTS WITH LONGEST CAREER RUNS IN THE US, 1955–97*

	Artist(s)	Career run	Years
1	Elton John	1970–97	28
2	Stevie Wonder	1963–88	26
3=	Elvis Presley	1955–77	24
3=	Rod Stewart	1971–94	24
5	James Brown	1958–77	20
6	Neil Diamond	1966–84	19
7	Prince	1978–95	18
8=	Ray Charles	1957–73	17
8=	Miracles	1959–75	17
8=	Andy Williams	1956–72	17
8=	Luther Vandross	1981–97	17

* *Based on chart success in consecutive years*
Source : The Popular Music Database

THE GLITZ AND HITS OF 1973

The Watergate hearings, the oil crisis, and the ceasefire in Vietnam were all more momentous than events in the world of pop music during 1973, although the second-biggest single of the year, Dawn's *Tie a Yellow Ribbon Round the Ole Oak Tree,* was a "coming home" song that probably struck a chord with some returning servicemen and their families. It was outsold only by Roberta Flack's *Killing Me Softly With His Song,* one of several quality ballads to make No. 1 during the year – others included Paul McCartney and Wings' *My Love,* Charlie Rich's *The Most Beautiful Girl,* and, most poignant of all, the philosophical *Time in a Bottle* by Jim Croce. This was a posthumous release.

25 YEARS AGO

CHART TOPPERS

FIRST AMERICAN GROUPS TO HAVE
A NO. 1 HIT IN THE UK

	Artist	Title	Date at No. 1
1	Bill Haley & His Comets	*Rock around the Clock*	Nov 12, '55
2	Dream Weavers	*It's Almost Tomorrow*	Mar 17, '56
3	The Teenagers	*Why Do Fools Fall in Love?*	Jul 21, '56
4	Buddy Holly & the Crickets	*That'll Be the Day*	Nov 2, '57
5	Johnny Otis Show	*Ma, He's Making Eyes At Me*	Jan 4, '58
6	The Platters	*Smoke Gets In Your Eyes*	Mar 14, '59
7	The Marcels	*Blue Moon*	May 6, '61
8	Highwaymen	*Michael*	Oct 7, '61
9	B.Bumble & The Stingers	*Nut Rocker*	May 12, '62
10	The Supremes	*Baby Love*	Nov 14, '64

Numbers two, three, five, and nine all scored higher on the UK chart than in their native country. Note that it took until the mid-1960s for an all-female US group to top the British charts.

FIRST FEMALE SINGERS TO HAVE
A NO. 1 HIT IN THE US

	Artist	Title	Date at No. 1
1	Dinah Shore	*I'll Walk Alone*	Oct 5, '44
2	Betty Hutton	*Doctor, Lawyer, Indian Chief*	Feb 21, '46
3	Peggy Lee	*Mañana*	Mar 5, '48
4	Margaret Whiting	*A Tree in the Meadow*	Oct 1, '48
5	Evelyn Knight	*A Little Bird Told Me*	Jan 14, '49
6	Teresa Brewer	*Music! Music! Music!*	Mar 10, '50
7	Eileen Barton	*If I Knew You Were Comin', I'd Have Baked a Cake*	Apr 7, '50
8	Patti Page	*The Tennessee Waltz*	Dec 22, '50
9	Rosemary Clooney	*Come On-A My House*	Jul 20, '51
10	Kay Starr	*Wheel of Fortune*	Mar 7, '52

The American singles chart was inaugurated in 1940, so it can be seen that it took four years before a record by a female soloist headed it, and well over a decade before the ranks of distaff chart-toppers swelled to double figures. All the above ladies were Americans, as was Doris Day, who would be the 11th in this particular line, but the 12th female singer to hit the top in the US was to be a British export in the shape of Vera Lynn, who dominated the US chart for nine weeks in mid-1952 with *Auf Weiderseh'n Sweetheart*.

FIRST BRITISH GROUPS TO HAVE
A NO. 1 HIT IN THE US

	Artist	Title	Date at No. 1
1	The Tornados	*Telstar*	Dec 22, '62
2	The Beatles	*I Want to Hold Your Hand*	Feb 1, '64
3	The Animals	*House of the Rising Sun*	Sep 5, '64
4	Manfred Mann	*Do Wah Diddy Diddy*	Oct 17, '64
5	Freddie & The Dreamers	*I'm Telling You Now*	Apr 10, '65
6	Wayne Fontana & The Mindbenders	*The Game of Love*	Apr 24, '65
7	Herman's Hermits	*Mrs. Brown You've Got a Lovely Daughter*	May 1, '65
8	The Rolling Stones	*(I Can't Get No) Satisfaction*	Jul 10, '65
9	Dave Clark Five	*Over and Over*	Dec 25, '65
10	The Troggs	*Wild Thing*	Jul 30, '66

It was not until 1977, when Manfred Mann's Earthband hit US No. 1 with *Blinded By The Light*, that the number of British groups to top the American survey reached 20.

ALBUMS THAT STAYED LONGEST AT NO. 1
IN THE US CHARTS*

	Album/artist	Year	Weeks at No. 1
1	*Thriller*, Michael Jackson	1982	37
2=	*Calypso*, Harry Belafonte	1956	31
2=	*Rumours*, Fleetwood Mac	1977	31
4=	*Saturday Night Fever* (Soundtrack)	1978	24
4=	*Purple Rain* (Soundtrack), Prince	1984	24
6	*Please Hammer Don't Hurt'Em*, MC Hammer	1990	21
7=	*The Bodyguard* (Soundtrack), Whitney Houston	1992	20
7=	*Blue Hawaii* (Soundtrack), Elvis Presley	1962	20
9=	*More Of The Monkees*, Monkees	1967	18
9=	*Dirty Dancing* (Soundtrack)	1988	18
9=	*Ropin' The Wind*, Garth Brooks	1991	18

* *Based on Billboard charts, up to December 31, 1996*

Some sources identify the soundtrack album of *West Side Story* (1962) as the longest No. 1 resident of the Billboard chart, but its 57-week stay was in a chart exclusively for stereo albums – then a relatively new phenomenon.

BOYZ II MEN
Boyz II Men, a Philadelphia R&B vocal quartet, have been Motown's biggest-selling act of the 1990s by far, scoring three platinum singles within 18 months.

T O P 1 0

SINGLES WITH MOST WEEKS AT NO. 1 IN THE US

	Title/artist	Year	Weeks at No. 1
1	*One Sweet Day*, Maria Carey and Boyz II Men	1995	16
2=	*I Will Always Love You*, Whitney Houston	1992	14
2=	*I'll Make Love to You*, Boyz II Men	1994	14
2=	*Macarena (Bayside Boys Mix)*, Los Del Rios	1995	14
5	*End of the Road*, Boyz II Men	1992	13
6=	*Don't Be Cruel/Hound Dog*, Elvis Presley	1956	11
6=	*I Swear*, All-4-One	1994	11
6=	*Cherry Pink and Apple Blossom White*, Perez Prado	1955	10
6=	*You Light Up My Life*, Debby Boone	1977	10
6=	*Physical*, Olivia Newton-John	1981	10

* *Based on* Billboard *charts*

This listing covers the period from 1955 when *Billboard's* US Top 100 was inaugurated for singles. Long No. 1 runs were actually more commonplace in the pre-Rock 'n' Roll days of the 1940s and early 1950s, when the market was generally slower moving. Oddly enough, 1981 holds the record for the greatest number of singles (three) having runs of two months or more.

T O P 1 0

YOUNGEST SINGERS TO HAVE A NO. 1 SINGLE IN THE US*

	Artist/title	Age yrs	mths
1	Jimmy Boyd, *I Saw Mommy Kissing Santa Claus*	12	11
2	Stevie Wonder, *Fingertips*	13	2
3	Donny Osmond, *Go Away Little Girl*	13	9
4	Michael Jackson, *Ben*	13	11
5	Laurie London, *He's Got the Whole World in His Hands*	14	3
6	Little Peggy March, *I Will Follow Him*	15	1
7	Brenda Lee, *I'm Sorry*	15	7
8=	Paul Anka, *Diana*	16	1
8=	Tiffany, *I Think We're Alone Now*	16	1
10=	Little Eva, *The Loco-Motion*	17	1
10=	Lesley Gore, *It's My Party*	17	1

* *To December 31, 1996*

T O P 1 0

ARTISTS WITH THE MOST CONSECUTIVE NO. 1 SINGLES IN THE US

	Artist	Consecutive No. 1 singles
1	Elvis Presley (1956–58)	10
2	Whitney Houston (1985–88)	7
3=	The Beatles (1964–66)	6
3=	The Bee Gees (1977–79)	6
3=	Paula Abdul (1988–91)	6
6=	Michael Jackson (1987–88)	5
6=	The Supremes (1964–65)	5
6=	Mariah Carey (1990–91)	5
9=	The Jackson 5 (1970)	4
9=	George Michael (1987–88)	4
9=	Mariah Carey (1993–94)	4

Source : The Popular Music Database

T O P 1 0

ARTISTS WITH THE MOST NO. 1 SINGLES IN THE US

	Artist	No 1 singles
1	The Beatles	20
2	Elvis Presley	18
3	Michael Jackson	13
4	The Supremes	12
5=	Mariah Carey	11*
5=	Whitney Houston	11
5=	Madonna	11
8=	Stevie Wonder	10
8=	George Michael/Wham!	10
10=	Paul McCartney/Wings	9
10=	Bee Gees	9

* *Includes a duet with Boyz II Men*
Source : The Popular Music Database

Three of George Michael's No. 1 hits were as half of Wham! If discounted, both Elton John and the Rolling Stones join the list, with eight US No. 1 singles each.

GOLD & PLATINUM ALBUMS

TOP 10
ARTISTS WITH MOST PLATINUM ALBUMS IN THE US

	Artist	Platinum albums
1	Barbra Streisand	22
2	The Beatles	20
3	Elton John	19
4=	Alabama	18
4=	Neil Diamond	18
4=	Elvis Presley	18
4=	The Rolling Stones	18
4=	George Strait	18
9	Chicago	17
10=	Willie Nelson	14
10=	Prince	14

Source: RIAA, February 1997

This award, made by the Recording Industry Association of America (RIAA), the trade association of record companies in the US, confirms a minimum sale of 1,000,000 copies of an album.

TOP 10
ARTISTS WITH THE MOST GOLD ALBUMS IN THE US

	Artist	Gold albums
1	Elvis Presley	46
2	The Rolling Stones	36
3=	Neil Diamond	32
3=	Barbra Streisand	32
5	Elton John	31
6	The Beatles	29
7=	Bob Dylan	22
7=	Kenny Rogers	22
7=	Frank Sinatra	22
7=	Willie Nelson	22

Source: RIAA, February 1997

This award confirms a minimum sale of 500,000 copies of an album. The RIAA began certification for gold records in 1958, when the *Oklahoma Original Soundtrack* was awarded the first such honor.

THE BIRTH OF THE LONG-PLAYER

A team of engineers at Columbia Records, led by Dr. Peter Goldmark (the inventor who had developed the first color TV in 1940), developed the "long-player," a 12-inch microgroove disc of unbreakable vinyl, which was launched in 1948. It reproduced a clearer sound, turned at 33⅓ revolutions per minute, and could accommodate up to 23 minutes per side of recording (compared with a maximum of 4 minutes per side on a 78-rpm record). It was unveiled to the trade in Atlantic City on June 21, and then to the public on July 21, at the Waldorf-Astoria Hotel, New York City. The following year, RCA Victor introduced the smaller, five-minute 45-rpm vinyl record as hardware manufacturers began producing multispeed turntables that could facilitate all three speeds. The initialization "LP" was the common term for the extended format, but "album" had usurped this role by the late 1970s.

TOP 10
GROUPS WITH THE MOST PLATINUM ALBUMS IN THE US

	Group	Platinum albums
1	The Beatles	20
2=	Alabama	18
2=	The Rolling Stones	18
4	Chicago	17
5=	Aerosmith	13
5=	Rush	13
7=	AC/DC	12
7=	Pink Floyd	12
9=	Kiss	11
9=	Led Zeppelin	11
9=	Van Halen	11

Source: RIAA; to February 1997

The official RIAA platinum certification, signifying one million US sales of an album, was introduced in 1976 in response to ever-increasing LP sales, though awards were also made retrospectively where appropriate – as here to 1960s albums by the Beatles, the Rolling Stones, and Led Zeppelin. The odd men out among the enduring rock bands in this list are clearly country music quartet Alabama, whose album career did not take off until 1980, but who have been consistently huge sellers in the country market ever since.

TOP 10
GROUPS WITH THE MOST GOLD ALBUMS IN THE US

	Group	Gold albums
1	The Rolling Stones	36
2	The Beatles	29
3=	Kiss	21
3=	Rush	21
5=	Alabama	20
5=	Chicago	20
7	Jefferson Airplane/Starship*	18
8	The Beach Boys	17
9=	AC/DC	16
9=	Pink Floyd	16

* *Includes awards for Jefferson Airplane, Jefferson Starship, and Starship (the evolution of the band's name)*

Source: RIAA; to February 1997

The RIAA introduced its gold certification for albums in 1958, originally awarding it to releases which generated a million dollars' worth of sales. When inflation eventually began to devalue this approach, the criteria were changed to instead recognize US sales of half a million, and this is still the basis on which these awards are made in the late 1990s. Naturally, every platinum album also receives a gold award when its sales pass the appropriate level.

T O P 1 0

MALE ARTISTS WITH THE MOST PLATINUM ALBUMS IN THE US

	Artist	Platinum albums
1	Elton John	19
2=	Neil Diamond	18
2=	Elvis Presley	18
2=	George Strait	18
5=	Willie Nelson	14
5=	Prince	14
7	Billy Joel	13
8=	Bruce Springsteen	12
8=	Rod Stewart	12
10	Kenny Rogers	11

Source: RIAA; to February 1997

T O P 1 0

MALE ARTISTS WITH THE MOST GOLD ALBUMS IN THE US

	Artist	Gold albums
1	Elvis Presley	46
2	Neil Diamond	32
3	Elton John	31
4=	Bob Dylan	22
4=	Willie Nelson	22
4=	Kenny Rogers	22
4=	Frank Sinatra	22
8=	John Denver	19
8=	Prince	19
10=	Rod Stewart	18
10=	George Strait	18

Source: RIAA; to February 1997

ELTON JOHN
Britain's most successful solo artist ever in the US, Elton scored his first American Top 10 hit in 1970, and followed it with 15 No. 1 records and 40 million-sellers over the next 25 years.

T O P 1 0

FEMALE ARTISTS WITH THE MOST PLATINUM ALBUMS IN THE US

	Artist	Platinum albums
1	Barbra Streisand	22
2	Reba McEntire	13
3	Linda Ronstadt	12
4	Madonna	11
5	Gloria Estefan	10
6	Amy Grant	7
7=	Pat Benatar	6
7=	Olivia Newton-John	6
9=	Mariah Carey	5
9=	Whitney Houston	5
9=	Bette Midler	5
9=	Sade	5

Source: RIAA; to February 1997

Most of the acts in this top 10 have appeared on the scene during the 1980s and '90s, with only Barbra Streisand's platinum career stretching back to the 1960s. Her first million-selling album was *My Name Is Barbra, Two* in 1965.

T O P 1 0

FEMALE ARTISTS WITH THE MOST GOLD ALBUMS IN THE US

	Artist	Gold albums
1	Barbra Streisand	32
2	Reba McEntire	17
3	Linda Ronstadt	16
4	Olivia Newton-John	13
5	Gloria Estefan	12
6=	Natalie Cole	11
6=	Aretha Franklin	11
6=	Madonna	11
6=	Anne Murray	11
6=	Donna Summer	11

Source: RIAA; to February 1997

As in the platinum certifications, Barbra Streisand, with a hit-making career of more than a third of a century behind her, leads the female ranks of gold album awardees by a huge margin, having first had a "million dollar sale" LP in 1963, with her Grammy-winning debut set *The Barbra Streisand Album*. By contrast, second-placed country singer Reba McEntire did not make her first gold album until the 1980s.

T H E 1 0

FIRST SINGLES TO SELL A MILLION IN THE US

	Single/artist	Date
1	*Catch a Falling Star*, Perry Como	Mar 14, 1958
2	*He's Got the Whole World in His Hands*, Laurie London	July 8, 1958
3	*Hard Headed Woman*, Elvis Presley	Aug 11, 1958
4	*Patricia*, Perez Prado	Aug 18, 1958
5	*Tom Dooley*, Kingston Trio	Jan 21, 1959
6	*Calcutta*, Lawrence Welk	Feb 14, 1961
7	*Big Bad John*, Jimmy Dean	Dec 14, 1961
8	*The Lion Sleeps Tonight*, The Tokens	Jan 9, 1962
9	*Can't Help Falling in Love*, Elvis Presley	Mar 30, 1962
10	*I Can't Stop Loving You*, Ray Charles	July 19, 1962

Source : RIAA

STAR SINGLES

T O P 1 0

ROLLING STONES SINGLES IN THE US

1	*(I Can't Get No) Satisfaction*	1965
2	*Miss You*	1978
3	*Honky Tonk Women*	1969
4	*Get Off Of My Cloud*	1965
5	*Ruby Tuesday*	1967
6	*Angie*	1973
7	*Brown Sugar*	1971
8	*Paint It Black*	1966
9	*19th Nervous Breakdown*	1966
10	*Jumpin' Jack Flash*	1968

Unlike in the UK, where the Stones' Top 10 sellers all occurred before 1970, the group's US successes have been more evenly spread over their career, with second-placed *Miss You* perhaps benefiting from being released during the period in 1978 when American singles sales were at their all-time high.

T O P 1 0

ELVIS PRESLEY SINGLES IN THE US

1	*Don't Be Cruel/Hound Dog*	1956
2	*It's Now Or Never*	1960
3	*Love Me Tender*	1956
4	*Heartbreak Hotel*	1956
5	*Jailhouse Rock*	1957
6	*All Shook Up*	1957
7	*(Let Me Be Your) Teddy Bear*	1957
8	*Are You Lonesome Tonight?*	1960
9	*Don't*	1958
10	*Too Much*	1957

Elvis had dozens of million-selling singles, scattered throughout his career, but most of his absolute monsters were during his 1950s heyday when he was the spearhead of rock 'n' roll music. The inspired coupling of *Don't Be Cruel* and *Hound Dog*, which held the number one spot for almost a quarter of 1956, sold some 6,000,000 copies in the US alone. *It's Now Or Never*, the biggest of his post-Army successes, sold in the region of 5,000,000.

THE ROLLING STONES IN CONCERT
One of the leading groups of the 1960s, the Rolling Stones still attract a huge following today. Their most recent "Voodoo Lounge World Tour" consisted of 123 concerts played worldwide on four continents. The tour grossed a total of $320 million and is still the most successful tour by a rock band to date.

T O P 1 0

BEATLES SINGLES IN THE US

	Title/label	Cat. no.
1	*My Bonnie/The Saints* (with Tony Sheridan), Decca	31382
2	*Please Please Me/Ask Me Why*, Vee Jay	498
3	*From Me To You/ Thank You Girl*, Vee Jay	522
4	*She Loves You/I'll Get You*, Swan	4152
5	*I Want To Hold Your Hand/ I Saw Her Standing There*, Capitol	5112
6	*Please Please Me/ From Me To You*, Vee Jay	581
7	*My Bonnie/The Saints* (with Tony Sheridan), MGM	13213
8	*Twist And Shout/ There's A Place*, Tollie	9001
9	*Can't Buy Me Love/ You Can't Do That*, Capitol	5150
10	*Do You Want To Know A Secret/ Thank You Girl*, Vee Jay	587

The first Beatles single to show any American sales activity was the first issue of *From Me To You*, which "bubbled under" the top 100 at No.116 in August 1963.

T O P 1 0

BOB DYLAN SINGLES IN THE US

1	*Like A Rolling Stone*	1965
2	*Rainy Day Women, Nos. 12 & 35*	1966
3	*Positively 4th Street*	1965
4	*Lay Lady Lay*	1969
5	*Knockin' On Heaven's Door*	1973
6	*I Want You*	1966
7	*Just Like A Woman*	1966
8	*Gotta Serve Somebody*	1979
9	*Hurricane*	1976
10	*Subterranean Homesick Blues*	1965

Bob Dylan's core audience has always been album rather than singles buyers, but particularly during the mid- and late-1960s, when he was one of rock music's pacemakers, the successful albums often spun off big commercial singles too. The top two in this chart were both million sellers, but since 1979 and *Gotta Serve Somebody*, Dylan has not even had a US top 40 single.

TOP 10

MADONNA SINGLES IN THE US

1	*Like a Virgin*	1984
2	*Vogue*	1990
3	*Like A Prayer*	1989
4	*Crazy For You*	1985
5	*Justify My Love*	1990
6	*This Used To Be My Playground*	1992
7	*Papa Don't Preach*	1986
8	*Open Your Heart*	1986
9	*Live To Tell*	1986
10	*Who's That Girl*	1987

Of these US #1 hits, the first five of which were 1,000,000-plus sellers, *Crazy For You* came from the film soundtrack to *Vision Quest*, *This Used To Be My Playground* was featured in *A League Of Their Own*, *Live To Tell* was the theme to the movie *At Close Range*, and *Who's That Girl* was the title cut from the film of that name.

TOP 10

PRINCE SINGLES IN THE US

1	*When Doves Cry*	1984
2	*Kiss*	1986
3	*Let's Go Crazy*	1984
4	*Purple Rain*	1984
5	*Batdance*	1989
6	*Cream*	1991
7	*U Got The Look*	1987
8	*Raspberry Beret*	1985
9	*The Most Beautiful Girl In The World*	1994
10	*Little Red Corvette*	1983

When Doves Cry is the only Prince single to sell over 2,000,000 units in the US, and was featured in his most successful film project, *Purple Rain*, the soundtrack of which also spawned the 1,000,000-plus selling singles at #3 and 4.

TOP 10

MICHAEL JACKSON SINGLES IN THE US

1	*Billie Jean*	1983
2	*Rock With You*	1980
3	*Beat It*	1983
4	*Don't Stop 'Til You Get Enough*	1979
5	*Say Say Say**	1983
6	*I Just Can't Stop Loving You*	1987
7	*Black Or White*	1990
8	*The Girl Is Mine**	1982
9	*Bad*	1987
10	*Man In The Mirror*	1988

* *Duet with Paul McCartney*

The first eight of the Top 10 titles here sold over 1,000,000 copies each in the US alone, and all the singles in the list reached #1 on the Hot 100.

TOP 10

DIANA ROSS SINGLES IN THE US

1	*Endless Love* (duet with Lionel Richie)	1981
2	*Upside Down*	1980
3	*Ain't No Mountain High Enough*	1970
4	*Love Hangover*	1976
5	*Theme From "Mahogany" (Do You Know Where You're Going To?)*	1976
6	*Touch Me In The Morning*	1973
7	*I'm Coming Out*	1980
8	*Why Do Fools Fall In Love?*	1981
9	*It's My Turn*	1980
10	*Missing You*	1985

This Top 10 does not include records on which Diana Ross sang as lead vocalist of the Supremes in the 1960s, but if it did, numbers 5 to 10 in the list above would all be ousted by Supremes' hits. *Endless Love*, the theme from the film of the same title, was one of Motown's all-time biggest singles, topping 2,000,000 US sales.

TOP 10

BEACH BOYS SINGLES IN THE US

1	*Kokomo*	1988
2	*Good Vibrations*	1966
3	*I Get Around*	1964
4	*Surfin' USA*	1963
5	*Help Me, Rhonda*	1965
6	*Barbara Ann*	1966
7	*California Girls*	1965
8	*Sloop John B*	1966
9	*Fun Fun Fun*	1964
10	*Surfer Girl/Little Deuce Coupe*	1963

Ironically, for a group whose sound and image are so evocative of the 1960s, the Beach Boys' all-time US best-selling single *Kokomo*, written for the movie *Cocktail*, came in 1988, almost a quarter-century after their surfin' heyday. *Good Vibrations* and *I Get Around*, their only two US No.1 singles of the 60s, are also the group's only other certified US million sellers.

TOP 10

BRUCE SPRINGSTEEN SINGLES IN THE US

1	*Dancing In The Dark*	1984
2	*Hungry Heart*	1980
3	*Glory Days*	1985
4	*Brilliant Disguise*	1987
5	*I'm On Fire*	1985
6	*Cover Me*	1984
7	*My Hometown*	1985
8	*Born In The USA*	1984
9	*Streets Of Philadelphia*	1994
10	*Tunnel Of Love*	1987

Springsteen has never been a prolific singles seller (his major commercial success has come from album sales), and has never scored a #1 hit in the US, *Dancing In The Dark* being his only #2. His hit theme *Streets Of Philadelphia* from the 1993 film *Philadelphia*, was the Boss's first Top 10 hit of the 1990s, and also gained him his first "Best Song" Oscar.

WOMEN IN THE CHARTS

FEMALE SINGERS WITH THE MOST TOP 10 HITS IN THE US*

	Singer	Top 10 hits
1	Madonna	29
2	Janet Jackson (including one duet with Michael Jackson)	21
3	Whitney Houston (including one duet with CeCe Winans)	18
4	Aretha Franklin (including one duet with George Michael)	17
5	Connie Francis	16
6=	Mariah Carey (including one duet with Boyz II Men and one with Luther Vandross)	15
6=	Olivia Newton-John (including two duets with John Travolta and one with ELO)	15
7	Donna Summer	14
9=	Brenda Lee	12
9=	Diana Ross (including one duet each with Marvin Gaye and Lionel Richie)	12
9=	Dionne Warwick (including one duet with Detroit Spinners and one with "Friends" Stevie Wonder, Gladys Knight, and Elton John)	12

* To December 31, 1996

FEMALE GROUPS OF ALL TIME IN THE US*

	Group	No. 1	Top 10	Top 20
1	Supremes	12	20	24
2	Pointer Sisters	–	7	13
3	Expose	1	8	9
4=	McGuire Sisters	2	4	9
4=	Shirelles	2	6	7
6	TLC	–	7	7
7=	Bangles	2	5	6
7=	Martha & the Vandellas	–	6	7
9	Fontane Sisters	2	2	8
10	En Vogue	–	5	6

* To December 31, 1996; ranked according to total number of Top 20 singles

Source: The Popular Music Database

FEMALE GROUPS OF ALL TIME IN THE UK*

	Group	No. 1	Top 10	Top 20
1	Supremes	1	13	18
2	Bananarama	—	10	15
3	Eternal	–	10	12
4	Three Degrees	1	5	7
5	Sister Sledge	1	4	7
6	Nolans	—	3	7
7	Salt-n-Pepa	–	4	5
8	Bangles	1	3	5
9	Pointer Sisters	—	2	5
10	Spice Girls	4	4	4

* To March 31, 1997; ranked according to total number of Top 20 singles

The Supremes also had three other Top 20 hits, not included here, in partnership with Motown male groups the Four Tops and Temptations. However, Bananarama's charity revival of Help!, shared with comedians Dawn French and Jennifer Saunders, has been included because all the participants are female.

SINGLES BY FEMALE VOCALISTS IN THE US

	Single/vocalist
1	I Will Always Love You, Whitney Houston,
2	Fantasy, Mariah Carey
3	Vogue, Madonna
4	Mr. Big Stuff, Jean Knight
5	You Light Up My Life, Debby Boone
6	Physical, Olivia Newton-John
7	I Will Survive, Gloria Gaynor
8	Hot Stuff, Donna Summer
9	Emotion, Samantha Sang
10	Mickey, Toni Basil

Source: The Popular Music Database

Among these blockbusters, all of them platinum sellers, Whitney Houston's multiplatinum success from The Bodyguard Original Soundtrack was written by a woman – Dolly Parton – another superstar.

SINGLES BY FEMALE VOCALISTS IN THE UK

	Single/vocalist	Year
1	I Will Always Love You, Whitney Houston	1992
2	The Power of Love, Jennifer Rush	1985
3	Think Twice, Celine Dion	1994
4	Don't Cry for Me Argentina, Julie Covington	1977
5	Fame, Irene Cara	1982
6	Anyone Who Had a Heart, Cilla Black	1964
7	Feels Like I'm in Love, Kelly Marie	1980
8	Woman in Love, Barbra Streisand	1980
9	Nothing Compares 2 U, Sinead O'Connor	1990
10	Oooh Aah ... Just a Little Bit, Gina G	1996

TOP 10

OLDEST FEMALE SINGERS TO HAVE A NO. 1 SINGLE IN THE US

	Singer	years	months	Age days
1	Tina Turner	45	9	5
2	Bette Midler	44	8	24
3	Kim Carnes	35	9	26
4	Dolly Parton	35	1	2
5	Georgie Gibbs	34	8	18
6	Deniece Williams	33	11	23
7	Kay Starr	33	6	15
8	Anne Murray	33	4	15
9	Roberta Flack	33	2	5
10	Petula Clark	32	2	8

Source : The Popular Music Database

TOP 10

ALBUMS BY FEMALE SINGERS IN THE US

	Album/singer	Estimated copies sold
1=	*Jagged Little Pill*, Alanis Morissette	15,000,000
1=	*The Bodyguard (Soundtrack)*, Whitney Houston	15,000,000
3	*Whitney Houston*, Whitney Houston	12,000,000
4	*Tapestry*, Carole King	10,000,000
5=	*Music Box*, Mariah Carey	9,000,000
5=	*Whitney*, Whitney Houston	9,000,000
5=	*Like a Virgin*, Madonna	9,000,000
5=	*The Woman In Me*, Shania Twain	9,000,000
6=	*Toni Braxton*, Toni Braxton	8,000,000
6=	*Daydream*, Mariah Carey	8,000,000
6=	*Mariah Carey*, Mariah Carey	8,000,000
6=	*Falling Into You*, Celine Dion	8,000,000

Source: The Popular Music Database

TOP 10

YOUNGEST FEMALE SINGERS TO HAVE A NO. 1 SINGLE IN THE US

	Singer	years	Age months	days
1	Little Peggy March	15	1	20
2	Brenda Lee	15	7	7
3	Tiffany	16	1	5
4	Lesley Gore	17	0	30
5	Little Eva	17	1	27
6	Shelley Fabares	18	2	19
7	Debbie Gibson	18	6	4
8	Joan Weber	18	?	?*
9	Lulu	19	11	18
10	Martika	20	2	4

* *Birthdate unknown but was between 18 years and 6 months and 19 years*

Source: The Popular Music Database

TOP 10

ALBUMS BY FEMALE GROUPS IN THE UK

	Album/group	Year
1	*Spice*, Spice Girls	1996
2	*Always And Forever*, Eternal	1993
3	*Power of a Woman*, Eternal	1995
4	*Different Light*, Bangles	1986
5	*20 Golden Greats*, Supremes	1977
6	*The Greatest Hits Collection*, Bananarama,	1988
7	*Greatest Hits*, Bangles	1980
8	*Everything*, Bangles	1980
9	*We Are Family*, Sister Sledge	1979
10	*Break Out*, Pointer Sisters	1984

All of these albums were released within the last two decades, and the three biggest sellers of all within the last four years. Three of these groups – the Spice Girls, Eternal, and Bananarama – are British, the other four being American. Only the Bangles also played instruments while performing, all the other outfits being purely vocal groups.

TOP 10

SINGLES BY FEMALE GROUPS IN THE US

	Single/singer
1	*Don't Let Go*, En Vogue
2	*Hold On*, En Vogue
3	*Whatta Man*, Salt N Pepa
4	*Expressions*, Salt N Pepa
5	*Push It*, Salt N Pepa
6	*Waterfall*, TLC
7	*Creep*, TLC
8	*Weak*, SWV
9	*Baby, Baby, Baby*, TLC
10	*Red Light Special*, TLC

Source: The Popular Music Database

TOP 10

SINGLES BY FEMALE GROUPS IN THE UK*

	Single/singer	Year
1	*Wannabe*, Spice Girls	1996
2	*Say You'll Be There*, Spice Girls	1996
3	*2 Become 1*, Spice Girls	1996
4	*Frankie*, Sister Sledge	1985
5	*When Will I See You Again*, Three Degrees	1974
6	*Baby Love*, Supremes	1964
7	*I'm in the Mood for Dancing*, Nolans	1980
8	*Eternal Flame*, Bangles	1989
9	*Who Do You Think You Are/ Mama*, Spice Girls	1997
10	*Then He Kissed Me*, Crystals	1963

* *To March 31, 1997*

Such has been the Spice Girls' impact on popular music that they have totally re-written the record book as far as successful girl-group singles are concerned, snatching the three all-time biggest sellers with their first three releases. The fourth, already the all-time No. 9, was still a Top 3 seller as this list was being compiled.

CHRISTMAS HITS

T O P 1 0
CHRISTMAS SINGLES OF ALL TIME IN THE US

	Single/artist	Year
1	*White Christmas*, Bing Crosby	1942
2	*Silent Night/Adeste Fideles*, Bing Crosby	1942
3	*The Chipmunk Song (Christmas Don't Be Late)*, The Chipmunks	1958
4	*Rudolph the Red-Nosed Reindeer*, Gene Autry	1949
5	*I Saw Mommy Kissing Santa Claus*, Jimmy Boyd	1952
6	*The Little Drummer Boy*, Harry Simeone Chorale	1958
7	*Jingle Bell Rock*, Jimmy Helms	1957
8	*Do They Know It's Christmas*, Band Aid	1984
9	*Rockin' Around the Christmas Tree*, Brenda Lee	1960
10	*Blue Christmas*, Elvis Presley	1964

Most of America's biggest-selling Christmas singles are of extreme vintage. By and large, it is still these ancient favorites that re-surface on the radio in December and chalk up yet another appearance in Billboard's Christmas Music charts. Multimillion sales are claimed for the top five titles on the list.

T O P 1 0
CHRISTMAS HITS OF THE 1950s IN THE US

	Single/artist	Year
1	*The Chipmunk Song (Christmas Don't Be Late)*, Chipmunks	1958
2	*I Saw Mommy Kissing Santa Claus*, Jimmy Boyd	1952
3	*The Little Drummer Boy*, Harry Simeone Chorale	1958
4	*Jingle Bell Rock*, Jimmy Helms	1957
5	*Nuttin' For Christmas*, Barry Gordon	1955
6	*White Christmas*, Bing Crosby	1951–59
7	*Mary's Boy Child*, Harry Belafonte	1956
8	*Silent Night*, Bing Crosby	1951–59
9	*Home For the Holidays*, Perry Como	1955
10	*Nuttin' For Christmas*, Joe Ward	1955

T O P 1 0
CHRISTMAS HITS OF THE 1970s IN THE US

	Single/artist	Year
1	*Please Come Home for Christmas*, Eagles	1978
2	*Merry Christmas Darling*, Carpenters	1970–73
3	*Santa Claus Is Coming To Town*, Jackson 5	1970–73
4	*Happy Christmas (War Is Over)*, John Lennon	1971–72
5	*If We Make it Through December*, Merle Haggard	1973
6	*Step into Christmas*, Elton John	1973
7	*Christmas for Cowboys*, John Denver	1975
8	*Please Daddy*, John Denver	1973
9	*Mary's Boy Child/Oh My Lord*, Boney M	1978
10	*The Little Drummer Boy*, Moonlion	1975

T O P 1 0
CHRISTMAS HITS OF THE 1960s IN THE US

	Single/artist	Year
1	*Rockin' Around the Christmas Tree*, Brenda Lee	1960–69
2	*Blue Christmas*, Elvis Presley	1964–69
3	*Pretty Paper*, Roy Orbison	1963–64
4	*Please Come Home for Christmas*, Charles Brown	1961–69
5	*Rudolph the Red-Nosed Reindeer*, Chipmunks	1960–66
6	*Snoopy's Christmas*, Royal Guardsmen	1967
7	*The Little Drummer Boy*, Harry Simeone Chorale	1960–69
8	*White Christmas*, Bing Crosby	1960–69
9	*Jingle Bell Rock*, Bobby Rydell & Chubby Checker	1961
10	*Merry Christmas Baby*, Charles Brown	1964–69

T O P 1 0
CHRISTMAS HITS OF THE 1980s IN THE US

	Single/artist	Year
1	*Do They Know It's Christmas?*, Band Aid	1984
2	*Grandma Got Run Over by A Reindeer*, Elmo & Patsy	1983–89
3	*This One's for the Children*, New Kids On The Block	1989
4	*Santa Claus Is Coming to Town*, Bruce Springsteen	1985
5	*What Can You Get a Wookie for Christmas (When He Already Owns a Comb?)*, Meco	1980
6	*The Greatest Gift of All*, Kenny Rogers & Dolly Parton	1984
7	*Merry Christmas in the NFL*, Buckner & Garcia	1980
8	*Christmas in Dixie*, Alabama	1983
9	*Christmas Time*, Bryan Adams	1985
10	*Another Lonely Christmas*, Prince	1984

TOP 10

CHRISTMAS ALBUMS OF ALL TIME IN THE US

	Album/artist
1	*Miracles – The Holiday Album*, Kenny G
2	*Sing We Now of Christmas*, Harry Simeone Chorale
3	*Christmas*, Mannheim Steamroller
4	*A Fresh Aire Christmas*, Mannheim Steamroller
5	*Elvis' Christmas Album*, Elvis Presley
6	*A Christmas Album*, Barbra Streisand
7	*Merry Christmas*, Mariah Carey
8	*Beyond the Season*, Garth Brooks
9	*Christmas in the Aire*, Mannheim Steamroller
10	*A Very Special Christmas*, Various

TOP 10

CHRISTMAS SINGLES OF ALL TIME IN THE UK

	Single/artist	Year
1	*Do They Know It's Christmas?*, Band Aid	1984
2	*Bohemian Rhapsody*, Queen	1975/1991
3	*Mull of Kintyre*, Wings	1977
4	*Mary's Boy Child/Oh My Lord*, Boney M	1978
5	*I Want to Hold Your Hand*, The Beatles	1963
6	*Don't You Want Me*, The Human League	1981
7	*Last Christmas*, Wham!	1984
8	*I Feel Fine*, The Beatles	1964
9	*We Can Work it Out/Day Tripper*, The Beatles	1965
10	*It's Now or Never*, Elvis Presley	1960

With Christmas being the traditional high-point of the year for UK record sales, it is not surprising that these 10 singles rank among Britain's top 30 sellers of all time. All were No. 1 hits at the time, apart from Wham's *Last Christmas*, which despite its enormous sales, was held at No. 2 in Christmas week of 1984 by the still bigger Band Aid single.

TOP 10

CHRISTMAS ALBUMS OF ALL TIME IN THE UK

	Album/artist		Album/artist
1	*Now! – The Christmas Album*, Various	6	*Phil Spector's Christmas Album*, Various
2	*It's Christmas*, Various	7	*The No. 1 Christmas Album*, Various
3	*The Best Christmas Album in the World...Ever!*, Various	8	*12 Songs of Christmas*, Jim Reeves
4	*It's Christmas Time*, Various	9	*Together with Cliff Richard*, Cliff Richard
5	*Elvis' Christmas Album*, Elvis Presley	10	*Special Olympics – A Very Special Christmas*, Various

By comparison with the US market, British record buyers simply show no interest in Christmas albums – unless they are TV-advertised packages gathering together a familar selection of Christmas hit singles, which Nos. 1, 2, 3, 4, and 7 in this Top 10 are, sharing the same repertoire to a great extent. The hardy perennials are the Elvis, Phil Spector, and Jim Reeves albums, which have sold steadily, through innumerable reissues and repackagings, since, respectively, 1957, 1963, and 1964.

"BEST SONG" OSCARS

"BEST SONG" OSCAR WINNERS OF THE 1940s

	Song	Movie
1940	When You Wish Upon a Star	Pinocchio
1941	The Last Time I Saw Paris	Lady Be Good
1942	White Christmas	Holiday Inn
1943	You'll Never Know	Hello, Frisco, Hello
1944	Swinging on a Star	Going My Way
1945	It Might as Well Be Spring	State Fair
1946	On the Atchison, Topeka and the Santa Fe	The Harvey Girls
1947	Zip-A-Dee-Doo-Dah	Song of the South
1948	Buttons and Bows	The Paleface
1949	Baby, It's Cold Outside	Neptune's Daughter

The first "Best Song" Oscar was won in 1934 by *The Continental* from the movie *The Gay Divorcée*.

"BEST SONG" OSCAR WINNERS OF THE 1950s

	Song	Movie
1950	Mona Lisa	Captain Carey
1951	In the Cool, Cool, Cool of the Evening	Here Comes the Groom
1952	High Noon (Do Not Forsake Me, Oh My Darling)	High Noon
1953	Secret Love	Calamity Jane
1954	Three Coins in the Fountain	Three Coins in the Fountain
1955	Love Is a Many Splendored Thing	Love Is a Many Splendored Thing
1956	Whatever Will Be, Will Be (Que Sera, Sera)	The Man Who Knew Too Much
1957	All the Way	The Joker Is Wild
1958	Gigi	Gigi
1959	High Hopes	A Hole in the Head

"BEST SONG" OSCAR WINNERS OF THE 1960s

	Song	Movie
1960	Never on Sunday	Never on Sunday
1961	Moon River	Breakfast at Tiffany's
1962	Days of Wine and Roses	Days of Wine and Roses
1963	Call Me Irresponsible	Papa's Delicate Condition
1964	Chim Chim Cheree	Mary Poppins
1965	The Shadow of Your Smile	The Sandpiper
1966	Born Free	Born Free
1967	Talk to the Animals	Dr. Doolittle
1968	The Windmills of Your Mind	The Thomas Crown Affair
1969	Raindrops Keep Fallin' on My Head	Butch Cassidy and the Sundance Kid

"BEST SONG" OSCAR WINNERS OF THE 1970s

	Song	Movie
1970	For All We Know	Lovers and Other Strangers
1971	Theme from Shaft	Shaft
1972	The Morning After	The Poseidon Adventure
1973	The Way We Were	The Way We Were
1974	We May Never Love Like This Again	The Towering Inferno
1975	I'm Easy	Nashville
1976	Evergreen	A Star Is Born
1977	You Light Up My Life	You Light Up My Life
1978	Last Dance	Thank God It's Friday
1979	It Goes Like It Goes	Norma Rae

Barbra Streisand became the first artist since Frank Sinatra to win two Oscar song awards in the same decade. Her two award-winners were *The Way We Were* and *Evergreen*, both of which went on to become huge international hits.

"BEST SONG" OSCAR WINNERS OF THE 1980s

	Song	Movie
1980	Fame	Fame
1981	Up Where We Belong	An Officer and a Gentleman
1982	Arthur's Theme (Best That You Can Do)	Arthur
1983	Flashdance	Flashdance
1984	I Just Called to Say I Love You	The Woman in Red
1985	Say You, Say Me	White Nights
1986	Take My Breath Away	Top Gun
1987	(I've Had) The Time of My Life	Dirty Dancing
1988	Let the River Run	Working Girl
1989	Under the Sea	The Little Mermaid

Award winners of the 1990s are: 1990, *Sooner or Later (I Always Get My Man)* from *Dick Tracy*; 1991, *Beauty and the Beast*; 1992, *Whole New World* from *Aladdin*; 1993, *Streets of Philadelphia* from *Philadelphia*; 1994, *Can You Feel the Love Tonight* from *The Lion King*; 1995, *Colors of the Wind* from *Pocahontas*; and 1996, *You Must Love Me* from *Evita*.

THE BEST AND WORST

Although the first Oscars were presented during the last days of silent movies, since 1934 the writers of lyrics and music have been honored at the annual Academy Awards ceremony with Oscars for "Best Song." This accolade has sometimes coincided with a song's commercial success – Debbie Boone's recording of the 1977 winner *You*

Light Up My Life was also the best-selling single of the year in the US. However, a number of winners have been perversely at odds with the musical taste of the period: the whimsical *Talk to the Animals* (from the 1967 film *Doctor Dolittle*) not only failed to achieve chart success, but was honored at a time when The Beatles were dominating the charts.

SAMMY CAHN
Lyricist Sammy Cahn (1913–93) won his first Oscar in 1954 for Three Coins in the Fountain.

TOP 10

ARTISTS WITH MOST "BEST SONG" OSCAR NOMINATIONS

	Artist	Wins	Years	Nominations
1	Sammy Cahn	4	1942–75	26
2	Johnny Mercer	4	1938–71	18
3=	Paul Francis Webster	3	1944–76	16
3=	Alan and Marilyn Bergman	2	1968–95	16
5	James Van Heusen	4	1944–68	14
6=	Henry Warren	3	1935–57	11
6=	Henry Mancini	2	1961–86	11
6=	Ned Washington	1	1940–61	11
9=	Sammy Fain	2	1937–77	10
9=	Leo Robin	1	1934–53	10
9=	Jule Styne	1	1940–68	10

It was not until the 7th year of the Awards, in 1934, that the category of "Best Song" was added to the other accolades bestowed on the previous year's movies.

MOON RIVER
Henry Mancini wrote the award-winning music for Moon River *(from* Breakfast at Tiffany's*).*

THOROUGHLY MODERN MILLIE
The 1967 addition to the tally of nominations achieved by Sammy Cahn and James Van Heusen.

THE THOMAS CROWN AFFAIR
The Windmills of Your Mind *from the 1968 Steve McQueen film won the Bergmans their debut Oscar.*

BARBRA STREISAND
Barbra Streisand had a hit in 1973 with the Bergman's Oscar-winning The Way We Were.

MUSIC AWARDS

TOP 10
ARTISTS WITH MOST GRAMMY AWARDS

	Artist	Awards
1	Sir George Solti	31
2	Quincy Jones	26
3	Vladimir Horowitz	25
4=	Henry Mancini	20
4=	Stevie Wonder	20
6	Pierre Boulez	17
7=	Leonard Bernstein	16
7=	John T. Williams	16
9=	Aretha Franklin	15
9=	Itzhak Perlman	15

The Grammy Awards ceremony has been held annually in the US since its inauguration on May 4, 1959, and the awards are considered to be the most prestigious in the music industry. The proliferation of classical artists in this Top 10 is largely attributable to the large number of classical award categories at the Grammys, which have lately been overshadowed by the rise of pop and rock.

THE 10
LAST GRAMMY RECORDS OF THE YEAR

Year	Record/artist
1997	*Change The World*, Eric Clapton
1996	*Kiss From A Rose*, Seal
1995	*All I Wanna Do*, Sheryl Crow
1994	*I Will Always Love You*, Whitney Houston
1993	*Tears In Heaven*, Eric Clapton
1992	*Unforgettable*, Natalie Cole with Nat "King" Cole
1991	*Another Day In Paradise*, Phil Collins
1990	*The Wind Beneath My Wings*, Bette Midler
1989	*Don't Worry Be Happy*, Bobby McFerrin
1988	*Graceland*, Paul Simon

TOP 10
ARTISTS WITH MOST BRIT AWARDS

	Artist	Awards
1	Annie Lennox	7
2=	Phil Collins	6
2=	Prince	6
4=	Michael Jackson	5
4=	George Michael	5
6=	Blur	4
6=	Oasis	4
6=	Take That	4
9=	Dire Straits	3
9=	Trevor Horn	3
9=	R.E.M.	3
9=	Seal	3
9=	Lisa Stansfield	3
9=	David A. Stewart	3
9=	Paul Young	3

The Brits, organized annually by the British Phonographic Industry, celebrated their 10th anniversary in 1992.

THE 10
FIRST RECIPIENTS OF THE GRAMMYS' LIFETIME ACHIEVEMENT AWARD

	Artist	Type	Year
1	Bing Crosby	vocalist	1962
2	Frank Sinatra	vocalist	1965
3	Duke Ellington	jazz musician	1966
4	Ella Fitzgerald	jazz vocalist	1967
5	Irving Berlin	composer	1968
6	Elvis Presley	vocalist	1971
7=	Louis Armstrong*	jazz musician	1972
7=	Mahalia Jackson*	gospel vocalist	1972
9=	Chuck Berry	composer/performer	1984
9=	Charlie Parker*	jazz musician	1984

* *Presented posthumously*

This most prestigious of Grammy Awards is not awarded annually and is presented to artists who have made "creative contributions of outstanding significance to the field of recordings."

THE 10
FIRST GRAMMY RECORDS OF THE YEAR

	Record	Artist	Year
1	*Nel Blu Dipinto di Blu (Volare)*	Domenico Modugno	1958
2	*Mack the Knife*	Bobby Darin	1959
3	*Theme From a Summer Place*	Percy Faith	1960
4	*Moon River*	Henry Mancini	1961
5	*I Left My Heart in San Francisco*	Tony Bennett	1962
6	*The Days of Wine and Roses*	Henry Mancini	1963
7	*The Girl from Ipanema*	Stan Getz & Astrud Gilberto	1964
8	*A Taste of Honey*	Herb Alpert & the Tijuana Brass	1965
9	*Strangers in the Night*	Frank Sinatra	1966
10	*Up Up and Away*	5th Dimension	1967

THE 10

FIRST INDUCTEES INTO THE ROCK 'N' ROLL HALL OF FAME

1 Chuck Berry
2 James Brown
3 Ray Charles
4 Sam Cooke
5 Fats Domino
6 The Everly Brothers
7 Buddy Holly
8 Jerry Lee Lewis
9 Elvis Presley
10 Little Richard

These seminal artists were all inducted at the first ceremony, which took place on January 23, 1986 at the Waldorf-Astoria Hotel, New York. While only 10 performing artists were inducted, two nonperforming Rock 'n' Roll pioneers were also recipients: DJ Alan Freed and Sun record label owner Sam Phillips. Three official "Early Influence" inductions were also confirmed at this inaugural dinner: Robert Johnson, Jimmie Rodgers, and Jimmy Yancey.

THE 10

LATEST INDUCTEES INTO THE ROCK 'N' ROLL HALL OF FAME

1 Bee Gees
2 Buffalo Springfield
3 Crosby Stills & Nash
4 Jackson 5
5 Joni Mitchell
6 Parliament/Funkadelic
7 (Young) Rascals
8 Mahalia Jackson (Early Influences)
9 Bill Monroe (Early Influences)
10 Syd Nathan (Non-performer)

The latest inductees into the Rock and 'n' Roll Hall of Fame received the accolade on May 15, 1997 at the museum in Cleveland, Ohio.

THE 10

FIRST INDUCTEES INTO THE COUNTRY MUSIC HALL OF FAME

	Artist	Born	Died	Year inducted
1	Jimmie Rodgers	Sep 8, 1897	May 26, 1933	1961
2	Fred Rose	Aug 24, 1897	Dec 1, 1954	1961
3	Hank Williams	Sep 17, 1923	Jan 1, 1953	1961
4	Roy Acuff	Sep 15, 1903	Nov 23, 1992	1962
5	Tex Ritter	Jan 12, 1907	Jan 2, 1974	1964
6	Ernest Tubb	Feb 9, 1914	Sep 6, 1984	1965
7	Eddy Arnold	May 15, 1918	–	1966
8	James R. Denny	Feb 28, 1911	Aug 27, 1963	1966
9	George D. Hay	Nov 9, 1895	May 8, 1968	1966
10	Uncle Dave Macon	Oct 7, 1870	Mar 22, 1952	1966

Founded in 1961 by the Country Music Association in Nashville, the Country Music Hall of Fame recognizes outstanding contributions to the world of Country Music. Decided by a series of three ballots, the Hall of Fame inducted 54 members between 1961 and 1992.

TOP 10

COUNTRY MUSIC AWARDS WINNERS

	Artist	Awards
1	Vince Gill	15
2	Roy Clark	10
3=	Alabama	9
3=	Chet Atkins	9
3=	Garth Brooks	9
3=	Judds	9
7=	Loretta Lynn	8
7=	Ronnie Milsap	8
7=	Willie Nelson	8
7=	Dolly Parton	8
7=	Ricky Skaggs	8

The Country Music Awards are the most prestigious Country awards, held as an annual ceremony since 1967. Veteran Country instrumentalist Roy Clark netted the Instrumentalist of the Year award for seven consecutive years between 1974 and 1980.

TOP 10

AMERICAN MUSIC AWARDS WINNERS

	Artist	Awards
1	Whitney Houston	21
2	Kenny Rogers	19
3	Alabama	18
4	Michael Jackson	17
5	Lionel Richie	15
6	Reba McEntire	13
7	Willie Nelson	12
8	Stevie Wonder	11
9=	Garth Brooks	10
9=	Randy Travis	10

The only "populist" music awards in the United States based on voting by the American public, the AMAs have been held annually since their February 19, 1974 inaugural ceremony, which took place at the Aquarius Theater, Hollywood.

MUSIC IN THE SALESROOM

MOST EXPENSIVE MUSIC MANUSCRIPTS EVER SOLD AT AUCTION

	Manuscript/sale	Price ($)*
1	Nine symphonies by Wolfgang Amadeus Mozart, Sotheby's, London, May 22, 1987	3,854,000
2	Schumann's *Second Symphony*, Sotheby's, London, December 1, 1994	2,085,000
3	Ludwig van Beethoven's *Piano Sonata in E Minor*, Opus 90, Sotheby's, London, December 6, 1991	1,690,000
4	Wolfgang Amadeus Mozart's *Fantasia in C Minor* and *Sonata in C Minor*, Sotheby's, London, November 21, 1990	1,496,000
5	Robert Schumann's *Piano Concerto in A Minor*, Opus 54, Sotheby's, London, November 22, 1989	1,240,000
6	Joseph Haydn's *Four String Quartets*, Opus 50, Sotheby's, London, May 18, 1995	950,000
7	Ludwig van Beethoven's first movement of the *Sonata for Violoncello and Piano in A Major*, Opus 69, Sotheby's, London, May 17, 1990	897,000
8	Johann Sebastian Bach's *Cantata No. 2* Sotheby's, London, May 15, 1996	679,000
9	Johann Sebastian Bach's *Cantata No. 128* Sotheby's, London, November 22, 1989	604,500
10	Igor Stravinsky's *Rite of Spring*, Sotheby's, London, November 11, 1982	570,000

* *"Hammer prices," excluding premiums*

MOST EXPENSIVE MUSICAL INSTRUMENTS EVER SOLD AT AUCTION

	Instrument/sale	Price ($)*
1	"Mendelssohn" Stradivarius violin, Christie's, London, November 21, 1990	1,686,740
2	"Cholmondley" Stradivarius violoncello, Sotheby's, London, June 22, 1988	1,145,760
3	Steinway grand piano, decorated by Lawrence Alma-Tadema and Edward Poynter for Henry Marquand, 1884–87, Sotheby Parke Bernet, New York, March 26, 1980	390,000
4	Jimi Hendrix's Fender Stratocaster electric guitar, Sotheby's, London, April 25, 1990	370,260
5	Acoustic guitar owned by David Bowie, Paul McCartney, and George Michael, Christie's, London, May 18, 1994	341,000
6	Verne Powell platinum flute, Christie's, New York, October 18, 1986	187,000
7	Flemish single-manual harpsichord by Johan Daniel Dulken of Antwerp, 1755, Sotheby's, London, March 27, 1990	153,865
8	Charlie Parker's Grafton Saxophone, Christie's, London, September 8, 1994	144,925
9	Two-manual harpsichord by Andreas Ruckers of Antwerp, 1623, Sotheby's, London, November 8, 1995	138,725
10	One-keyed ebony "Quantz" flute made for Frederick the Great of Prussia, c. 1750, Sotheby's, Baden-Baden, October 10, 1995	89,280

* *Including 10 percent buyer's premium, where appropriate*

MOST EXPENSIVE ITEMS OF ROCK STARS' CLOTHING EVER SOLD AT AUCTION IN THE UK

	Item/sale	Price ($)*
1	Jimi Hendrix's orange floral velvet jacket, Bonham's, London, August 18, 1994	58,900
2	Elvis Presley's one-piece "Shooting Star" stage outfit, c. 1972, Phillips, London, August 24, 1988	48,000
3	John Lennon's black leather jacket, c. 1960–62, Christie's, London, May 7, 1992	47,916
4	Jimi Hendrix's peacock feather vest, 1967–68, Sotheby's, London, September 13, 1995	37,433
5	Jimi Hendrix's striped wool jacket, Bonham's, London, August 18, 1994	35,650
6	John Lennon's tan suede jacket, 1965, worn for the Beatles' *Rubber Soul* album cover, Christie's, London, May 25, 1995	31,388
7	Four "super hero"-style costumes worn by glam rock group Kiss in the film *Kiss Meets the Phantom* (1978), Christie's, London, May 14, 1993	31,350#
8	Jimi Hendrix's psychedelic "poppy" jacket, Bonham's, London, August 18, 1994	31,000
9	Jimi Hendrix's green velvet double-breasted jacket, Bonham's, London, August 18, 1994	29,450
10	John Lennon's "Happi" coat, 1966, given to him by Japanese Airlines during the Beatles' trip to Japan, Christie's, London, September 7, 1995	27,900#

* *Including 10 percent buyer's premium unless otherwise noted*
# *Including 12.5 percent buyer's premium*

JOHN LENNON'S ROCK 'N' ROLLS ROYCE
*The former Beatle's multicolored Phantom V became
the most expensive used car ever sold when it was acquired
by Jim Pattison, Chairman of the Expo '86 World Fair.*

TOP 10

MOST EXPENSIVE ITEMS OF POP MEMORABILIA EVER SOLD AT AUCTION*

	Item/sale	Price ($)#
1	John Lennon's 1965 Rolls-Royce Phantom V touring limousine, finished in psychedelic paintwork, Sotheby's, New York, June 29, 1985	2,299,000
2	Jimi Hendrix's Fender *Stratocaster* electric guitar, Sotheby's, London, April 25, 1990	370,260
3	Acoustic guitar owned by David Bowie, Paul McCartney, and George Michael, Christie's, London, May18, 1994	341,000
4	Paul McCartney's handwritten lyrics for *Getting Better*, 1967, Sotheby's, London, September 14, 1995	251,643
5	Buddy Holly's Gibson acoustic guitar, c. 1945, in a tooled leather case made by Holly, Sotheby's, New York, June 23, 1990	242,000
6	John Lennon's 1970 Mercedes-Benz 600 Pullman four-door limousine, Christie's, London, April 27, 1989	213,125
7	Elvis Presley's 1942 Martin D-18 guitar (used to record his first singles, 1954–56), Red Baron Antiques, Atlanta, Georgia, October 3, 1991	180,000
	The same guitar was resold by Christie's, London, May14, 1993	148,500
8	Elvis Presley's 1963 Rolls-Royce Phantom V touring limousine, Sotheby's, London, August 28, 1986	162,800
9	Charlie Parker's Grafton saxophone, Christie's, London, September 8, 1994	144,925
10	Recording of 16-year-old John Lennon singing at a 1957 church fair in Liverpool, Sotheby's, London, September 15, 1994	121,675

* *Excluding rock stars' clothing – see opposite*
# *Including 10 percent buyer's premium, where appropriate*

Pioneered particularly by Sotheby's in London, pop memorabilia has become big business – especially if it involves personal association with megastars such as the Beatles. A Rickenbacker guitar autographed by all four members was sold by Bonhams Tokyo on March 22, 1997 for $118,788 and would be in 10th place if Charlie Parker's saxophone is eliminated as belonging to the jazz, rather than "pop," genre. The painted bass drumskin featured on the album sleeve of *Sgt. Pepper's Lonely Hearts Club Band* made $80,755 at Sotheby's, London, on September 15, 1994, and even such items as the Liverpool birthplace of Ringo Starr, the barber's shop mentioned in the Beatles song "Penny Lane," and a door from John Lennon's house have been offered for sale as artifacts from the archaeology of the Beatles.Lastly, items associated with Buddy Holly have become similarly collectable – his Fender Stratocaster electric guitar was sold at Sotheby's, New York, on June 23, 1990 for $110,000, and his glasses at the same sale for $45,100. In some instances items have been reauctioned by a sequence of celebrity owners to raise money for charities (the guitar at No. 2 is in this category). Beyond the Top 10, high prices have also been paid for other musical instruments once owned by notable rock stars, such as a guitar belonging to John Entwistle of The Who and pianos that were formerly owned by Paul McCartney and John Lennon.

CLASSICAL & OPERA

WOLFGANG AMADEUS MOZART
Considered by many the greatest musical genius of all time, Mozart died at the age of just 35 after a lifetime devoted to composing and performing.

T O P 1 0

MOST PROLIFIC CLASSICAL COMPOSERS*

	Composer/nationality	Hours
1	Joseph Haydn (1732–1809), Austrian	340
2	George Handel (1685–1759), German/English	303
3	Wolfgang Amadeus Mozart (1656–91), Austrian	202
4	Johann Sebastian Bach (1685–1750), German	175
5	Franz Schubert (1797–1828), German	134
6	Ludwig van Beethoven (1770–1827), German	120
7	Henry Purcell (1659–95), English	116
8	Giuseppe Verdi (1813–1901), Italian	87
9	Antonín Dvořák (1841–1904), Czech	79
10=	Franz Liszt (1811–86), Hungarian	76
10=	Peter Tchaikovsky (1840–93), Russian	76

* Based on a survey conducted by Classical Music *magazine*

T O P 1 0

LARGEST OPERA HOUSES IN THE WORLD

	Opera house	Location	seating	Capacity standing	Total
1	The Metropolitan Opera	New York, NY	3,800	265	4,065
2	Cincinnati Opera	Cincinnati, OH	3,630	–	3,630
3	Lyric Opera of Chicago	Chicago, IL	3,563	–	3,563
4	San Francisco Opera	San Francisco, CA	3,176	300	3,476
5	The Dallas Opera	Dallas, TX	3,420	–	3,420
6	Canadian Opera Company	Toronto, Canada	3,167	–	3,167
7	Los Angeles Music Center Opera	Los Angeles, CA	3,098	–	3,098
8	San Diego Opera	San Diego, CA	2,992	84	3,076
9	Seattle Opera	Seattle, WA	3,017	–	3,017
10	L'Opéra de Montréal	Montreal, Canada	2,874	–	2,874

T O P 1 0

OPERAS MOST FREQUENTLY PERFORMED AT THE METROPOLITAN OPERA HOUSE, NEW YORK

	Opera	Composer	Performances
1	*La Bohème*	Giacomo Puccini	728
2	*Aïda*	Giuseppi Verdi	709
3	*La Traviata*	Giuseppi Verdi	579
4	*Tosca*	Giacomo Puccini	559
5	*Carmen*	Georges Bizet	548
6	*Madama Butterfly*	Giacomo Puccini	517
7	*Rigoletto*	Giuseppi Verdi	510
8	*Pagliacci*	Ruggero Leoncavallo	460
9	*Faust*	Charles Gounod	436
10	*Cavalleria Rusticana*	Pietro Mascagni	428

The first Metropolitan Opera House opened on October 22, 1883, with a performance of Charles Gounod's *Faust*. Such is the universality of opera that no fewer than eight of the Met's top operas also appear (although in a different order) in the Top 10 performed at London's principal venue, the Royal Opera House, Covent Garden, where *La Bohème* similarly tops the lists of "most performed," having been staged on 493 occasions since its October 2, 1897 premiere.

THE SYDNEY OPERA HOUSE

Plans to put Sydney on the world opera map began in 1957 when Danish architect Jørn Utzon won a competition. Although he later resigned from the project, the building was eventually constructed on Bennelong Point, Sydney Harbour. The first performance (of Prokofiev's *War and Peace*) took place on September 28, 1973, but the Opera House was officially opened by Queen Elizabeth on October 20, 1973. The art complex's distinctive sail-like roofs consist of 2,194 precast concrete sections weighing 30,015 tons, covered with 1,056,000 tiles. Although considered controversial at the time, within a quarter of a century the Opera House has become the internationally recognized symbol of the city of Sydney.

YEARS AGO • 25 • YEARS AGO

T H E 1 0

MOST RECENT WINNERS OF THE "BEST CLASSICAL ALBUM" GRAMMY AWARD

Year	Composer/title/conductor/orchestra
1997	Corigliano, *Of Rage And Remembrance*, Leonard Slatkin, National Symphony Orchestra
1996	Claude Debussy, *La Mer*, Pierre Boulez, Cleveland Orchestra
1995	Béla Bartók, *Concerto for Orchestra*; *Four Orchestral Pieces, Op. 12*, Pierre Boulez, Chicago Symphony Orchestra
1994	Béla Bartók, *The Wooden Prince*, Pierre Boulez, Chicago Symphony Orchestra and Chorus
1993	Gustav Mahler, *Symphony No. 9*, Leonard Bernstein, Berlin Philharmonic Orchestra
1992	Leonard Bernstein, *Candide*, Leonard Bernstein, London Symphony Orchestra
1991	Charles Ives, *Symphony No. 2 (and Three Short Works)*, Leonard Bernstein, New York Philharmonic Orchestra
1990	Béla Bartók, *Six String Quartets*, Emerson String Quartet
1989	Giuseppi Verdi, *Requiem and Operatic Choruses*, Robert Shaw, Atlanta Symphony Orchestra
1988	*Horowitz In Moscow*, Vladimir Horowitz

T O P 1 0

CLASSICAL ALBUMS OF ALL TIME IN THE US

	Artist/album	Year
1	Van Cliburn, *Tchaikovsky: Piano Concerto No. 1*	1958
2	Carreras, Domingo, Pavarotti, *The Three Tenors Concert*	1990
3	Soundtrack (Philadelphia Orchestra), *Fantasia (50th Anniversary Edition)*	1990
4	Placido Domingo, *Perhaps Love*	1981
5	Antal Dorati/Minneapolis Symphony Orchestra, *Tchaikovsky: 1812 Overture/Capriccio Italien*	1959
6	Mantovani, *Strauss Waltzes*	1958
7	Walter Carlos, *Switched-On Bach*	1969
8	Soundtrack (Berlin Philharmonic Orchestra), *2001: A Space Odyssey*	1968
9	Luciano Pavarotti, *O Sole Mio*	1979
10	Van Cliburn, *Rachmaninoff: Piano Concerto No. 3*	1959

T H E 1 0

MOST RECENT WINNERS OF THE "BEST OPERA RECORDING" GRAMMY AWARD

Year	Composer/title/principal soloists
1997	Benjamin Britten, *Peter Grimes*, Philip Langridge, Alan Opie, Janice Watson
1996	Hector Berlioz, *Les Troyens*, Charles Dutoit
1995	Carlisle Floyd, *Susannah*, Jerry Hadley, Samuel Ramey, Cheryl Studer, Kenn Chester
1994	George Handel, *Semele*, Kathleen Battle, Marilyn Horne, Samuel Ramey, Sylvia McNair, Michael Chance
1993	Richard Strauss, *Die Frau Ohne Schatten*, Placido Domingo, Jose Van Dam, Hildegard Behrens
1992	Richard Wagner, *Götterdämmerung*, Hildegard Behrens, Ekkehard Wlashiha
1991	Richard Wagner, *Das Rheingold*, James Morris, Kurt Moll, Christa Ludwig
1990	Richard Wagner, *Die Walküre*, Gary Lakes, Jessye Norman, Kurt Moll
1989	Richard Wagner, *Lohengrin*, Placido Domingo, Jessye Norman, Eva Randova
1988	Richard Strauss, *Ariadne Auf Naxos*, Anna Tomowa-Sintow, Kathleen Battle, Agnes Baltsa, Gary Lakes

STAGE, SCREEN & BROADCASTING

TOP 10

LONGEST-RUNNING SHOWS ON BROADWAY

	Show	Performances
1	A Chorus Line (1975–90)	6,137
2	Cats (1982–)	6,081*
3	Oh! Calcutta! (1976–89)	5,959
4	Les Misérables (1987–)	4,183*
5	The Phantom of the Opera (1988–)	3,889*
6	42nd Street (1980–89)	3,486
7	Grease (1972–80)	3,388
8	Fiddler on the Roof (1964–72)	3,242
9	Life with Father (1939–47)	3,224
10	Tobacco Road (1933–41)	3,182

* Still running; total at April 30, 1997

TOP 10

LONGEST-RUNNING CURRENT PRODUCTIONS ON BROADWAY*

	Show	Opening night
1	Cats	Oct 7, 1982
2	Les Misérables	Mar 12, 1987
3	The Phantom of the Opera	Jan 26, 1988
4	Miss Saigon	Apr 11, 1991
5	Beauty and The Beast	Apr 18, 1994
6	Grease	May 11, 1994
7	Defending the Caveman	Mar 26, 1995
8	Victor/Victoria	Oct 25, 1995
9	Master Class	Nov 5, 1995
10	Bring in 'Da Noise, Bring in 'Da Funk	Apr 9, 1996

* Still running April 30, 1997

TOP 10

LONGEST-RUNNING COMEDIES OF ALL TIME OF BROADWAY

	Show	Performances
1	Life With Father (1939–47)	3,224
2	Abie's Irish Rose (1922–27)	2,327
3	Gemini (1977–81)	1,788
4	Harvey (1944–49)	1,775
5	Born Yesterday (1946–49)	1,642
6	Mary, Mary (1961–64)	1,572
7	Voice of the Turtle (1943–48)	1,558
8	Barefoot in the Park (1963–67)	1,532
9	Same Time Next Year (1975–78)	1,444
10	Brighton Beach Memoirs (1983–86)	1,299

TOP 10

LONGEST-RUNNING MUSICALS ON BROADWAY

	Show	Performances
1	*A Chorus Line* (1975–90)	6,137
2	*Cats* (1982–)	6,081 *
3	*Les Misérables* (1987–)	4,183 *
4	*The Phantom of the Opera* (1988–)	3,889 *
5	*42nd Street* (1980–89)	3,486
6	*Grease* (1972–80)	3,388
7	*Fiddler on the Roof* (1964–72)	3,242
8	*Hello Dolly!* (1964–71)	2,844
9	*My Fair Lady* (1956–62)	2,717
10	*Annie* (1977–83)	2,377

* As of April 30, 1997

TOP 10

LONGEST-RUNNING MUSICALS IN THE UK

	Show	Performances
1	*Cats* (1981–)	6,664 *
2	*Starlight Express* (1984–)	5,458 *
3	*Les Misérables* (1985–)	4,736 *
4	*The Phantom of the Opera* (1986–)	4,381 *
5	*Oliver!* (1960–69)	4,125
6	*Jesus Christ, Superstar* (1972–80)	3,357
7	*Miss Saigon* (1989–)	3,220 *
8	*Evita* (1978–86)	2,900
9	*The Sound of Music* (1961–67)	2,386
10	*Salad Days* (1954–60)	2,283

* Still running; total at April 30, 1997

On May 12, 1989 *Cats* became the longest continuously running musical in British theater history, and on January 26, 1996, with its 6,138th performance, became the longest-running musical of all time either in the West End or on Broadway, beating the previous record holder, *A Chorus Line*, which closed on Broadway in 1990 after a total of 6,137 performances.

LORD OF THE MUSICAL

As the lists on these pages testify, Andrew Lloyd Webber, who was born on March 22, 1948, has come to dominate the London and New York stages with some of the most successful and longest-running musicals of all time. His first was *Joseph and the Amazing Technicolor Dreamcoat*, which had its debut in 1968. This was followed by a dozen more productions, with *Cats*, *Starlight Express*, *The Phantom of the Opera*, *Jesus Christ, Superstar*, and *Evita* being numbered among the Top 10 musicals of all time in London, while he became the first person ever to have three musicals running simultaneously on both sides of the Atlantic. In 1997 he became a peer with the title Lord Lloyd-Webber of Sydmonton.

50 YEARS AGO • YEARS AGO • YEARS AGO

TOP 10

LONGEST-RUNNING NONMUSICALS ON BROADWAY

	Show	Performances
1	*Oh! Calcutta!* (1976–89)	5,959
2	*Life with Father* (1939–47)	3,224
3	*Tobacco Road* (1933–41)	3,182
4	*Abie's Irish Rose* (1922–27)	2,327
5	*Deathtrap* (1978–82)	1,792
6	*Gemini* (1977–81)	1,788
7	*Harvey* (1944–49)	1,775
8	*Born Yesterday* (1946–49)	1,642
9	*Mary, Mary* (1961–64)	1,572
10	*Voice of the Turtle* (1943–48)	1,558

Several of the longest-running non-musical shows on Broadway began their runs before World War II, while others date from the period up to the 1970s, before the long-running musical dominated the Broadway stage. Off Broadway, these records have all been broken by *The Drunkard*, which was performed at the Mart Theater, Los Angeles, from July 6, 1933 to September 6, 1953, and then reopened with a musical adapation and continued its run from September 7, 1953 until October 17, 1959.

TOP 10

LONGEST-RUNNING NONMUSICALS IN THE UK

	Show	Performances
1	*The Mousetrap* (1952–)	18,494 *
2	*No Sex, Please – We're British* (1971–80; 1982–86; 1986–87)	6,761
3	*Oh! Calcutta!* (1970–80)	3,918
4	*Run for Your Wife* (1983–91)	2,638
5	*There's a Girl in My Soup* (1966–69; 1969–72)	2,547
6	*Pyjama Tops* (1969–75)	2,498
7	*Sleuth* (1970–75)	2,359
8	*Worm's Eye View* (1945–51)	2,245
9	*Boeing Boeing* (1962–63; 1965–67)	2,035
10	*Blithe Spirit* (1941–42; 1942; 1942–46)	1,997

* Still running; total at April 30, 1997

ANDREW LLOYD WEBBER
In a career spanning 30 years, originally in partnership with lyricist Tim Rice, Andrew Lloyd Webber has composed the music for and produced some of the most successful shows in theater history.

THE IMMORTAL BARD

FIRST PLAYS BY SHAKESPEARE

	Play	Approx. year written
1	*Titus Andronicus*	1588–90
2	*Love's Labour's Lost*	1590
3	*Henry VI, Parts I–III*	1590–91
4=	*The Comedy of Errors*	1591
4=	*Richard III*	1591
4=	*Romeo and Juliet*	1591
7	*The Two Gentlemen of Verona*	1592–93
8	*A Midsummer Night's Dream*	1593–94
9	*Richard II*	1594
10	*King John*	1595

Precise dating of Shakespeare's plays is difficult. Contemporary records of early performances are rare, and only half the plays were published before Shakespeare died in 1616. Even these were much altered from the originals. It was only after 1623, when the "Folios" were published, that the complete works of Shakespeare were published progressively.

MOST DEMANDING SHAKESPEAREAN ROLES

	Role	Play	Lines
1	Hamlet	*Hamlet*	1,422
2	Falstaff	*Henry IV, Parts I and II*	1,178
3	Richard III	*Richard III*	1,124
4	Iago	*Othello*	1,097
5	Henry V	*Henry V*	1,025
6	Othello	*Othello*	860
7	Vincentio	*Measure for Measure*	820
8	Coriolanus	*Coriolanus*	809
9	Timon	*Timon of Athens*	795
10	Antony	*Antony and Cleopatra*	766

Hamlet's role consists of 11,610 words – over 36 percent of the total number of lines spoken in the play, but if multiple plays are considered he is beaten by Falstaff, who, as well as appearing in *Henry IV, Parts I and II*, also appears in *The Merry Wives of Windsor*, in which he has 436 lines. His total of 1,614 lines would thus make him the most talkative of all Shakespeare's characters.

WORDS MOST USED BY SHAKESPEARE

	Word	Frequency
1	the	27,457
2	and	26,285
3	I	21,206
4	to	19,938
5	of	17,079
6	a	14,675
7	you	14,326
8	my	13,075
9	that	11,725
10	in	11,511

In his complete works, William Shakespeare wrote a total of 884,647 words – 118,406 lines comprising 31,959 separate speeches. He used a total vocabulary of 29,066 different words, some – such as "America" – appearing only once (*The Comedy of Errors*, III.ii). At the other end of the scale, this Top 10 accounts for all those words that he used on more than 10,000 occasions. Perhaps surprisingly, their relative frequency is not dissimilar to what we might encounter in modern usage.

10 ACTORS WHO HAVE PLAYED HAMLET

1 Sarah Bernhardt

French actress, appeared as Hamlet at the Adelphi Theatre, London, in 1899, and in a French silent film version in 1900.

2 Edwin Booth

American actor, opened as Hamlet in the US in 1864 for a record run.

3 Kenneth Brannagh

Brannagh took the title role as well as directing the 1996 movie of the play.

4 Richard Burton

British actor, appeared in the role at the Old Vic in 1953 and on film in 1964.

5 Richard Chamberlain

American actor previously best known for his TV role as Dr. Kildare, appeared in a television version of Hamlet in 1970.

6 Mel Gibson

American movie actor, appeared in the 1991 film directed by Franco Zeffirelli.

7 Stacy Keach

American film actor, made his stage debut in 1964 in a New York production of Hamlet.

8 Laurence Olivier

British actor, appeared in both the title role and directed the 1948 film, the first British production to win a "Best Picture" Oscar.

9 Innokenti Smoktunovski

Russian actor, starred in a 1964 Soviet film of Hamlet, translated by Doctor Zhivago author Boris Pasternak.

10 Nicol Williamson

British actor, starred in the 1969 film, with pop singer Marianne Faithfull as Ophelia.

MOST PRODUCED PLAYS BY SHAKESPEARE*

	Play	Productions
1	*Twelfth Night*	74
2	*Hamlet*	73
3=	*As You Like It*	72
3=	*The Taming of the Shrew*	72
5	*Much Ado about Nothing*	68
6	*The Merchant of Venice*	67
7	*A Midsummer Night's Dream*	66
8	*Macbeth*	60
9	*The Merry Wives of Windsor*	58
10	*Romeo and Juliet*	55

* *At Stratford-Upon-Avon, UK, from December 31, 1878 through January 1, 1997*

T O P 1 0

MOST FILMED SHAKESPEARE PLAYS

1	*Hamlet*
2	*Romeo and Juliet*
3	*Macbeth*
4	*A Midsummer Night's Dream*
5	*Julius Caesar*
6	*Othello*
7	*Richard III*
8	*Henry V*
9	*The Merchant of Venice*
10	*Antony and Cleopatra*

Counting modern versions, including those in foreign languages, but discounting made-for-TV movies, parodies, and stories derived from the plays, it appears that *Hamlet* is the most filmed of all Shakespeare's works, with some 70 releases to date, while *Romeo and Juliet* has been remade on at least 40 occasions.

T O P 1 0

MOVIES OF SHAKESPEARE'S PLAYS

1	*Romeo and Juliet*	1996
2	*Romeo and Juliet*	1968
3	*Much Ado About Nothing*	1993
4	*Hamlet*	1990
5	*Henry V*	1989
6	*Hamlet*	1996
7	*Richard III*	1995
8	*Othello*	1995
9	*The Taming of the Shrew*	1967
10	*Hamlet*	1948

The romantic appeal of *Romeo and Juliet* has insured its place as first and second among the most successful movies of Shakespeare's plays, with, respectively, those directed by Baz Luhrmann and Franco Zeffirelli. If all the movies of his plays are considered, William Shakespeare could be regarded as the most prolific movie writer of all time.

T O P 1 0

LONGEST PLAYS BY SHAKESPEARE

	Play	Lines
1	*Hamlet*	3,901
2	*Richard III*	3,886
3	*Coriolanus*	3,820
4	*Cymbeline*	3,813
5	*Othello*	3,672
6	*Antony and Cleopatra*	3,630
7	*Troilus and Cressida*	3,576
8	*Henry VIII*	3,450
9	*Henry V*	3,368
10	*The Winter's Tale*	3,354

TO BE OR NOT TO BE, THAT IS THE QUESTION *Mel Gibson, of* Mad Max *and* Lethal Weapon *fame, surprised his fans and critics alike with his masterful portrayal of Hamlet in the 1990 big-screen version of William Shakespeare's longest play. Hamlet is the most demanding of Shakespearean roles for an actor.*

MOVIE HITS & MISSES

In previous editions of The Top Ten of Everything, *the relative success of the movies that appear in the lists was measured by the rental income earned by the US and Canadian distributors. However, while this remains a valid way of comparing the success of movies over long periods of time, movies have become an international medium, and nowadays many Hollywood movies earn more outside the US than within it. The decision has therefore been taken to base the movie lists on worldwide box-office income. This revision means that certain movies that have gone on to achieve greater global than domestic success will appear at a higher ranking than in previous editions of* The Top Ten of Everything.

TOP 10
HIGHEST-GROSSING MOVIES OF ALL TIME

	Movie	Year	US	Overseas	World
1	Jurassic Park	1993	356,839,725	556,000,000	912,839,725
2	Independence Day	1996	306,153,456	491,800,000	797,953,456
3	The Lion King	1994	312,855,561	459,000,000	771,855,561
4	Star Wars	1977/97	459,095,451	281,000,000	740,095,451
5	E.T.: The Extra-Terrestrial	1982	399,804,539	301,600,000	701,404,539
6	Forrest Gump	1994	329,690,974	344,100,000	673,790,974
7	Home Alone	1990	285,016,000	248,000,000	533,016,000
8	Terminator 2: Judgement Day	1991	204,446,562	310,000,000	514,446,562
9	Ghost	1990	217,631,306	290,000,000	507,631,306
10	The Empire Strikes Back	1980/97	288,801,028	206,800,000	495,601,028

Total gross ($)

TOP 10
MOVIE SEQUELS OF ALL TIME

	Movie series	Years
1	Star Wars/The Empire Strikes Back/Return of the Jedi	1977–97
2	Raiders of the Lost Ark/Indiana Jones and the Temple of Doom/Indiana Jones and the Last Crusade	1981–89
3	Batman /Batman Returns/Batman Forever	1989–95
4	Home Alone 1–2	1990–92
5	Star Trek I–VI/Generations/First Contact	1979–96
6	Jaws I–IV	1975–87
7	Beverly Hills Cop I–III	1984–94
8	Back to the Future I–III	1985–90
9	Die Hard 1–2/Die Hard: With a Vengeance	1988–95
10	Terminator/Terminator 2: Judgment Day	1984–91

Based on total earnings of the original movie and all its sequels up to 1997, the *Star Wars* trilogy stands head and shoulders above the rest, having grossed more than $1.6 billion around the world. All the other movies in the Top 10 have achieved global earnings of more than $500,000,000 each, and have made almost $9 billion between them.

TOP 10
MOVIE OPENINGS OF ALL TIME IN THE US

	Movie	Release	Opening weekend gross ($)
1	The Lost World	May 23, 1997	72,133,000
2	Batman Forever	Jun 16, 1995	52,784,000
3	Independence Day	Jul 3, 1996	50,228,000
4	Jurassic Park	Jun 12, 1993	47,059,000
5	Mission: Impossible	May 22, 1996	45,437,000
6	Batman Returns	Jun 19, 1992	42,706,000
7	Twister	May 10, 1996	41,059,000
8	The Lion King	Jun 15, 1994	40,888,000
9	Batman	Jun 23, 1989	40,506,000
10	Ace Ventura: When Nature Calls	Nov 10, 1995	37,804,000

MOVIE BLOCKBUSTERS OF 1973

Based on worldwide box office income, *The Exorcist* was the most successful movie of 1973. This influential horror movie was nominated for "Best Picture" Oscar, but the award was won by the second commercial success of the year, *The Sting* – for his role in which Robert Redford was nominated as "Best Actor." *Live and Let Die*, the ninth James Bond movie, was the third highest earning movie of the year, principally from its popularity outside the US. The movie ranked fourth among the year's high earners was George Lucas's *American Graffiti*, in which Harrison Ford made an early career appearance, heralding the beginning of the partnership that was to produce the successful *Star Wars* and *Indiana Jones* trilogies.

T O P 1 0

HIGHEST-GROSSING MOVIES OF 1996 IN THE US

	Movie	Box office gross ($)
1	Independence Day	306,153,456
2	Twister	241,717,524
3	Mission: Impossible	180,943,675
4	The Rock	134,067,443
5	The Nutty Professor	128,810,418

	Movie	Box office gross ($)
6	Ransom	124,641,941
7	The Birdcage	123,939,840
8	A Time to Kill	108,706,165
9	Phenomenon	104,464,977
10	101 Dalmatians	104,111,652

T O P 1 0

MOVIE SEQUELS THAT EARNED THE GREATEST AMOUNT MORE THAN THE ORIGINAL*

	Original	Outearned by
1	Terminator	Terminator 2
2	First Blood	Rambo: First Blood Part II / Rambo III
3	Die Hard	Die Hard With a Vengeance
4	Ace Ventura: Pet Detective	Ace Ventura: When Nature Calls
5	Raiders of the Lost Ark	Indiana Jones and the Last Crusade
6	Lethal Weapon	Lethal Weapon 2 / 3
7	Star Trek: The Motion Picture	Star Trek IV / VI / Star Trek: First Contact
8	Patriot Games	Clear and Present Danger
9	The Karate Kid	The Karate Kid, Part II
10	A Nightmare on Elm Street	A Nightmare Elm Street 3 / 4 / 5

* Ranked by greatest differential between original and highest-earning sequel

WATERWORLD

T O P 1 0

MOST EXPENSIVE MOVIES EVER MADE

	Movie*	Year	Estimated cost ($)
1	Waterworld	1995	160,000,000
2	True Lies	1994	110,000,000
3	Cutthroat Island	1996	105,000,000
4	Inchon (US/South Korea)	1981	102,000,000
5	War and Peace (USSR)	1967	100,000,000
6	Terminator 2: Judgment Day	1991	95,000,000
7	Total Recall	1990	85,000,000
8	The Last Action Hero	1993	82,500,000
9=	Batman Returns	1992	80,000,000
9=	Superman II	1980	80,000,000

* All US-made unless otherwise stated

T O P 1 0

BIGGEST MOVIE FLOPS OF ALL TIME

	Movie	Year	Estimated loss ($)
1	Cutthroat Island	1995	94,000,000
2	The Adventures of Baron Münchhausen	1988	48,100,000
3	Ishtar	1987	47,300,000
4	Hudson Hawk	1991	47,000,000
5	Inchon	1981	44,100,000
6	The Cotton Club	1984	38,100,000
7	Santa Claus – The Movie	1985	37,000,000
8	Heaven's Gate	1980	34,200,000
9	Billy Bathgate	1991	33,000,000
10	Pirates	1986	30,300,000

MOVIES OF THE DECADES

TOP 10
MOVIES OF THE 1930s

1	Gone With the Wind*	1939
2	Snow White and the Seven Dwarfs	1937
3	The Wizard of Oz	1939
4	The Woman in Red	1935
5	King Kong	1933
6	San Francisco	1936
7=	Mr. Smith Goes to Washington	1939
7=	Lost Horizon	1937
7=	Hell's Angels	1930
10	Maytime	1937

* Winner of "Best Picture" Academy Award

Both *Gone With the Wind* and *Snow White and the Seven Dwarfs* have generated more income than any other pre-war movie. However, if the income of *Gone With the Wind* were adjusted to allow for inflation in the period since its release, it could be regarded as the most successful movie ever.

THE WONDERFUL WIZARD OF OZ
Although held to an honorable third place by blockbusters
Gone With the Wind *and* Snow White and the Seven Dwarfs,
The Wizard of Oz *was one of the most popular films of the 1930s.*

TOP 10
MOVIES OF THE 1940s

1	Bambi	1942
2	Pinocchio	1940
3	Fantasia	1940
4	Cinderella	1949
5	Song of the South	1946
6	The Best Years of Our Lives*	1946
7	The Bells of St. Mary's	1945
8	Duel in the Sun	1946
9	Mom and Dad	1944
10	Samson and Delilah	1949

* Winner of "Best Picture" Academy Award

With the top four movies of the decade classic Disney cartoons, the 1940s may truly be regarded as the "golden age" of the animated movie. The genre was especially appealing in this era as colorful escapism after the drabness of the war years. The cumulative income of a selection of the Disney cartoons has increased as a result of their systematic re-release in theaters and on video.

TOP 10
MOVIES OF THE 1950s

1	Lady and the Tramp	1955
2	Peter Pan	1953
3	Ben-Hur*	1959
4	The Ten Commandments	1956
5	Sleeping Beauty	1959
6	Around the World in 80 Days*	1956
7=	The Robe	1953
7=	The Greatest Show on Earth*	1952
9	The Bridge on the River Kwai*	1957
10	Peyton Place	1957

* Winner of "Best Picture" Academy Award

While the popularity of animated movies continued with *Lady and the Tramp*, *Peter Pan*, and *Sleeping Beauty*, the 1950s was outstanding as the decade of the "big" picture: not only were many of the most successful films enormous in terms of cast and scale, but also the magnitude of the subjects they tackled: three of these were major biblical epics.

TOP 10
MOVIES OF THE 1960s

1	101 Dalmatians	1961
2	The Jungle Book	1967
3	The Sound of Music*	1965
4	Thunderball	1965
5	Goldfinger	1964
6	Doctor Zhivago	1965
7	You Only Live Twice	1967
8	The Graduate	1968
9	Mary Poppins	1964
10	Butch Cassidy and the Sundance Kid	1969

* Winner of "Best Picture" Academy Award

During the 1960s the growth in popularity of soundtrack record albums and featured singles often matched the commercial success of the movies from which they were derived. Four of these Top 10 films of the decade were avowed musicals, while all – with the possible exception of *Thunderball* – had a high musical content.

TOP 10
MOVIES OF THE 1970s

1	Star Wars	1977
2	Jaws	1975
3	Close Encounters of the Third Kind	1977/80
4	Moonraker	1979
5	The Spy Who Loved Me	1977
6	The Exorcist	1973
7	The Sting*	1973
8	Grease	1978
9	The Godfather*	1972
10	Saturday Night Fever	1977

Winner of "Best Picture" Academy Award

In the 1970s the arrival of the two prodigies Steven Spielberg and George Lucas set the scene for the high-adventure blockbusters whose domination in movies has continued ever since. Lucas directed his first science-fiction film, *THX 1138*, in 1970 and went on to write and direct *Star Wars*. Spielberg directed *Jaws* and wrote and directed *Close Encounters of the Third Kind*.

TOP 10
MOVIES OF THE 1980s

1	E.T.: The Extra-Terrestrial	1982
2	Indiana Jones and the Last Crusade	1989
3	Batman	1989
4	Rain Man	1988
5	Return of the Jedi	1983
6	Raiders of the Lost Ark	1981
7	The Empire Strikes Back	1980
8	Who Framed Roger Rabbit?	1988
9	Back to the Future	1985
10	Top Gun	1986

The 1980s was clearly the decade of the adventure movie, with George Lucas and Steven Spielberg continuing to assert their control of Hollywood, dominating this Top 10 between them, with Lucas as producer of 5 and 7 and Spielberg director of 1, 2, 6, 8, and 9. Paradoxically, despite their colossal box office success, they consistently failed to match this with an Academy Award for "Best Picture."

TOP 10
MOVIES OF THE 1990s TO DATE

1	Jurassic Park	1993
2	Independence Day	1996
3	The Lion King	1994
4	Forrest Gump*	1994
5	Home Alone	1990
6	Terminator 2: Judgement Day	1991
7	Ghost	1990
8	Twister	1996
9	Aladdin	1992
10	Pretty Woman	1990

Winner of "Best Picture" Academy Award

All 10 of these movies of the present decade have earned more than $400,000,000 each around the world, as have four other movies, *Mission: Impossible*, *Dances with Wolves*, *The Bodyguard*, and *Mrs. Doubtfire*. *Jurassic Park* has earned more than $900,000,000 at the box office.

ALMOST A VICTORY
The colossal success of Independence Day, *in which Earth's conquest by aliens is averted, makes it a close second to the 1990s' top earner,* Jurassic Park.

MOVIE GENRES

TOP 10

COP MOVIES

1	*Die Hard with a Vengeance*	1995
2	*The Fugitive*	1993
3	*Basic Instinct*	1992
4	*Seven*	1995
5	*Beverly Hills Cop*	1984
6	*Beverly Hills Cop II*	1987
7	*Speed*	1994
8	*Heat*	1995
9	*Lethal Weapon 2*	1989
10	*Lethal Weapon 3*	1993

Although movies in which one of the central characters is a policeman have never been among the most successful films of all time, many have earned respectable amounts at the box office. Both within and outside this Top 10, they are divided between those with a comic slant, such as the two *Beverly Hills Cop* films, and darker police thrillers, such as *Basic Instinct*. Films featuring FBI and CIA agents have been excluded from the reckoning, hence eliminating blockbusters such as *The Silence of the Lambs*.

TOP 10

SCIENCE-FICTION AND FANTASY MOVIES

1	*Jurassic Park*	1993
2	*Independence Day*	1996
3	*Star Wars*	1977
4	*E.T.: The Extra-Terrestrial*	1982
5	*Terminator 2: Judgement Day*	1991
6	*Ghost*	1990
7	*The Empire Strikes Back*	1980
8	*Return of the Jedi*	1983
9	*Batman*	1989
10	*Back to the Future*	1985

The first seven movies are also the all-time Top 10, and all 10 among the 33 most successful movies ever, having earned over $348,000,000 each from worldwide box office income. Four other movies in this genre have each earned more than $200,000,000: *Batman Forever* (1995), *Close Encounters of the Third Kind* (1977/80), *Ghostbusters* (1984), and *Batman Returns* (1992).

TOP 10

WAR MOVIES

1	*Schindler's List*	1993
2	*Platoon*	1986
3	*Good Morning, Vietnam*	1987
4	*Apocalypse Now*	1979
5	*M*A*S*H*	1970
6	*Patton*	1970
7	*The Deer Hunter*	1978
8	*Full Metal Jacket*	1987
9	*Midway*	1976
10	*The Dirty Dozen*	1967

This list excludes movies with military, rather than war, themes, such as *A Few Good Men* (1992), *The Hunt for Red October* (1990), *Crimson Tide* (1995), and *An Officer and a Gentleman* (1982), which would have been in the top five; and *Top Gun* (1986), which would top the list, just beating *Rambo: First Blood 2* (1985).

TOP 10

COMEDY MOVIES

1	*Forrest Gump*	1994
2	*Home Alone*	1990
3	*Ghost*	1990
4	*Pretty Woman*	1990
5	*Mrs. Doubtfire*	1993
6	*The Flintstones*	1995
7	*Who Framed Roger Rabbit?*	1988
8	*Beverly Hills Cop*	1984
9	*Beverly Hills Cop II*	1987
10	*Look Who's Talking*	1989

Forrest Gump accelerated to the head of this list as the most succesful comedy of all time. The two *Beverly Hills Cop* films are regarded by some as "action thrillers" rather than comedies. If they are excluded, Nos. 9 and 10 become *Coming to America* (1988) and *Home Alone 2: Lost in New York* (1992)

TOP 10

DISASTER MOVIES

1	*Twister*	1996
2	*Die Hard with a Vengeance*	1995
3	*Apollo 13*	1995
4	*Outbreak*	1995
5	*Die Hard*	1988
6	*Die Hard 2*	1990
7	*The Towering Inferno*	1975
9	*Airport*	1970
9	*The Poseidon Adventure*	1972
10	*Earthquake*	1974

Disasters involving blazing buildings, natural disasters such as earthquakes, tidal waves, train and air crashes, sinking ships, and terrorist attacks have long been a staple of Hollywood films – and now, with *Twister*, *Apollo 13*, and *Outbreak*, tornadoes, exploding space capsules, and killer viruses may be added to the genre.

TOP 10

MOVIES IN WHICH THE STAR WEARS DRAG

	Film/year	Star
1	*Mrs. Doubtfire* (1994)	Robin Williams
2	*The Bird Cage* (1996)	Nathan Lane
3	*Tootsie* (1983)	Dustin Hoffman
4	*Under Siege* (1992)	Gary Busey
5	*The Rocky Horror Picture Show* (1974)	Tim Curry
6	*The Crying Game* (1993)	Jaye Davidson
7	*Psycho* (1960)	Anthony Perkins
8	*Dressed to Kill* (1980)	Michael Caine
9	*Some Like It Hot* (1959)	Tony Curtis/ Jack Lemmon
10	*La Cage aux Folles* (1979)	Michel Serrault

TOP 10

WESTERN MOVIES

1	*Dances with Wolves*	1990
2	*Maverick*	1994
3	*Unforgiven*	1992
4	*Butch Cassidy and the Sundance Kid*	1969
5	*Jeremiah Johnson*	1972
6	*How the West Was Won*	1962
7	*Young Guns*	1988
8	*Young Guns II*	1990
9	*Pale Rider*	1985
10=	*Bronco Billy*	1980
10=	*Little Big Man*	1970

Clint Eastwood is in the unusual position of directing and starring in a movie that has forced another of his own movies out of this Top 10, since the success of *Unforgiven* has ejected *The Outlaw Josey Wales* (1976). Although it has a Western setting, *Back to the Future, Part III* (1990) is essentially a science-fiction film; if included, it would be in 5th position. According to some criteria, *The Last of the Mohicans* (1992) qualifies as a Western; if included, it would be at No. 6.

TOP 10

HORROR MOVIES

1	*Jurassic Park*	1993
2	*Jaws*	1975
3	*The Lost World*	1997
4	*Interview With the Vampire*	1994
5	*Jaws II*	1978
6	*Bram Stoker's Dracula*	1992
7	*The Exorcist*	1973
8	*Mary Shelley's Frankenstein*	1994
9	*The Amityville Horror*	1979
10	*Aliens*	1986

THE BOND DYNASTY
Pierce Brosnan (right) is the sixth, and current, actor to play James Bond on film. Sean Connery in Dr. No was the first, followed by David Niven in Casino Royale. George Lazenby played Bond only once, in On Her Majesty's Secret Service. He was followed by Roger Moore, who played Bond in seven films before handing over to Timothy Dalton in 1987.

TOP 10

JAMES BOND MOVIES

	Film/year	Bond actor
1	*Goldeneye* (1995)	Pierce Brosnan
2	*Moonraker* (1979)	Roger Moore
3	*Never Say Never Again* (1983)	Sean Connery
4	*For Your Eyes Only* (1981)	Roger Moore
5	*The Living Daylights* (1987)	Timothy Dalton
6	*The Spy Who Loved Me* (1977)	Roger Moore
7	*Octopussy* (1983)	Roger Moore
8	*License to Kill* (1990)	Timothy Dalton
9	*A View to a Kill* (1985)	Roger Moore
10	*Thunderball* (1965)	Sean Connery

OSCAR WINNERS – MOVIES

GOLDEN IDOL
*Standing 13½-in
(34-cm) high,
the gold-plated
"Oscar" was
reputedly named
for his resemblance
to a film librarian's
Uncle Oscar.*

T O P 1 0
MOVIES NOMINATED FOR THE MOST OSCARS

(Oscar® is a registered trade mark of the Academy of Motion Picture Arts and Sciences)

	Movie	Year	Awards	Nominations
1	*All About Eve*	1950	6	14
2=	*Gone With the Wind*	1939	8*	13
2=	*From Here to Eternity*	1953	8	13
2=	*Mary Poppins*	1964	5	13
2=	*Who's Afraid of Virginia Woolf?*	1966	5	13
2=	*Forrest Gump*	1994	6	13
7=	*Mrs. Miniver*	1942	6	12
7=	*The Song of Bernadette*	1943	4	12
7=	*Johnny Belinda*	1948	1	12
7=	*A Streetcar Named Desire*	1951	4	12
7=	*On the Waterfront*	1954	8	12
7=	*Ben-Hur*	1959	11	12
7=	*Becket*	1964	1	12
7=	*My Fair Lady*	1964	8	12
7=	*Reds*	1981	3	12
7=	*Dances with Wolves*	1990	7	12
7=	*Schindler's List*	1993	7	12
7=	*The English Patient*	1996	9	12

* Plus two special awards

T O P 1 0
MOVIES TO WIN MOST OSCARS

	Movie	Year	Awards
1	*Ben-Hur*	1959	11
2	*West Side Story*	1961	10
3=	*Gigi*	1958	9
3=	*The Last Emperor*	1987	9
3=	*The English Patient*	1996	9
6=	*Gone With the Wind*	1939	8
6=	*From Here to Eternity*	1953	8
6=	*On the Waterfront*	1954	8
6=	*My Fair Lady*	1964	8
6=	*Cabaret*	1972	8
6=	*Gandhi*	1982	8
6=	*Amadeus*	1984	8

DID YOU KNOW
THE STORY OF "OSCAR"

The Academy of Motion Picture Arts and Sciences, founded May 4, 1927, proposed improving the image of the film industry by issuing "awards for merit or distinction." The award took the form of a statuette – a gold-plated, nude male figure clutching a sword and standing on a reel of film with five holes, each representing a branch of the Academy. It was simply called "the statuette" until 1931, when Academy librarian Margaret Herrick commented, "It looks like my Uncle Oscar!" The name stuck as a universally recognized symbol of excellence in filmmaking.

T O P 1 0
HIGHEST-EARNING "BEST PICTURE" OSCAR WINNERS

	Movie	Year
1	*Forrest Gump*	1994
2	*Dances with Wolves*	1990
3	*Rain Man*	1988
4	*Schindler's List*	1993
5	*Braveheart*	1995
6	*Gone with the Wind*	1939
7	*The Sound of Music*	1965
8	*The Sting*	1973
9	*The Godfather*	1972
10	*Platoon*	1986

THE 10

"BEST PICTURE" OSCAR WINNERS OF THE 1930s

1930	*All Quiet on the Western Front*
1931	*Cimarron*
1932	*Grand Hotel*
1933	*Cavalcade*
1934	*It Happened One Night**
1935	*Mutiny on the Bounty*
1936	*The Great Ziegfeld*
1937	*The Life of Emile Zola*
1938	*You Can't Take It with You*
1939	*Gone with the Wind*

* *Winner of Oscars for "Best Director," "Best Actor," "Best Actress," and "Best Screenplay"*

The first Academy Awards, now popularly known as the Oscars, were presented at a ceremony at the Hollywood Roosevelt Hotel on May 16, 1929, and were for movies released in the period 1927–28. A second ceremony held at the Ambassador Hotel on October 31, of the same year was for movies released in the period 1928–29, and was won by *Broadway Melody* (MGM), the first talkie and the first musical to win an Oscar.

THE 10

"BEST PICTURE" OSCAR WINNERS OF THE 1960s

1960	*The Apartment*
1961	*West Side Story*
1962	*Lawrence of Arabia*
1963	*Tom Jones*
1964	*My Fair Lady*
1965	*The Sound of Music*
1966	*A Man for All Seasons*
1967	*In the Heat of the Night*
1968	*Oliver!*
1969	*Midnight Cowboy*

The Apartment (1960) was the last black-and-white movie to receive a "Best Picture" Oscar until Steven Spielberg's *Schindler's List* in 1993, which won seven Oscars.

THE 10

"BEST PICTURE" OSCAR WINNERS OF THE 1940s

1940	*Rebecca*
1941	*How Green Was My Valley*
1942	*Mrs. Miniver*
1943	*Casablanca*
1944	*Going My Way*
1945	*The Lost Weekend*
1946	*The Best Years of Our Lives*
1947	*Gentleman's Agreement*
1948	*Hamlet*
1949	*All the King's Men*

Several of the "Best Picture" winners are now regarded as movie classics, many critics numbering *Casablanca* among the greatest movies of all time. *Mrs. Miniver* (which won a total of six Oscars) and *The Best Years of Our Lives* (seven Oscars) were both directed by William Wyler and reflected the concerns of wartime and post-war life respectively. *How Green Was My Valley* and *Going My Way* each won five Oscars. *Rebecca* and *Hamlet* both starred Laurence Olivier, who also directed the latter, winning not only the "Best Picture" award but also that for "Best Actor."

THE 10

"BEST PICTURE" OSCAR WINNERS OF THE 1970s

1970	*Patton*
1971	*The French Connection*
1972	*The Godfather*
1973	*The Sting*
1974	*The Godfather, Part II*
1975	*One Flew over the Cuckoo's Nest**
1976	*Rocky*
1977	*Annie Hall*
1978	*The Deer Hunter*
1979	*Kramer vs. Kramer*

* *Winner of Oscars for "Best Director," "Best Actor," "Best Actress," and "Best Screenplay"*

THE 10

"BEST PICTURE" OSCAR WINNERS OF THE 1950s

1950	*All About Eve*
1951	*An American in Paris*
1952	*The Greatest Show on Earth*
1953	*From Here to Eternity*
1954	*On the Waterfront*
1955	*Marty*
1956	*Around the World in 80 Days*
1957	*The Bridge on the River Kwai*
1958	*Gigi*
1959	*Ben-Hur*

The first movie of the 1950s, *All about Eve*, received the most nominations (14), while the last, *Ben-Hur*, won the most (11).

THE 10

"BEST PICTURE" OSCAR WINNERS OF THE 1980s

1980	*Ordinary People*
1981	*Chariots of Fire*
1982	*Gandhi*
1983	*Terms of Endearment*
1984	*Amadeus*
1985	*Out of Africa*
1986	*Platoon*
1987	*The Last Emperor*
1988	*Rain Man*
1989	*Driving Miss Daisy*

The winners of "Best Picture" Oscars during the 1990s are: 1990, *Dances with Wolves*; 1991, *The Silence of the Lambs* – which also won Oscars for "Best Director," "Best Actor," "Best Actress," and "Best Screenplay;" 1992, *Unforgiven*; 1993, *Schindler's List* – which also won Oscars for "Best Director," "Best Adapted Screenplay," "Best Film Editing," "Best Art Direction," "Best Cinematography," and "Best Original Score;" 1994, *Forrest Gump*; which also won Oscars in a total of five other categories; 1995, *Braveheart*; and 1996, *The English Patient*.

OSCAR WINNERS – STARS

THE 10

"BEST ACTOR IN A SUPPORTING ROLE" OSCAR WINNERS OF THE 1980s

Year	Actor	Movie
1980	Timothy Hutton	*Ordinary People*
1981	John Gielgud	*Arthur*
1982	Louis Gossett, Jr.	*An Officer and a Gentleman*
1983	Jack Nicholson	*Terms of Endearment*
1984	Haing S. Ngor	*The Killing Fields*
1985	Don Ameche	*Cocoon*
1986	Michael Caine	*Hannah and Her Sisters*
1987	Sean Connery	*The Untouchables*
1988	Kevin Kline	*A Fish Called Wanda*
1989	Denzel Washington	*Glory*

There have only ever been three occasions when the same movie has received three nominations for "Best Supporting Actor": *On the Waterfront*, *The Godfather*, and *The Godfather, Part II*.

TOP 10

OLDEST OSCAR-WINNING ACTORS

	Actor/actress	Award/movie	Year	Age*
1	Jessica Tandy	"Best Actress" (*Driving Miss Daisy*)	1989	80
2	George Burns	"Best Supporting Actor" (*The Sunshine Boys*)	1975	80
3	Melvyn Douglas	"Best Supporting Actor" (*Being There*)	1979	79
4	John Gielgud	"Best Supporting Actor" (*Arthur*)	1981	77
5	Don Ameche	"Best Supporting Actor" (*Cocoon*)	1985	77
6	Peggy Ashcroft	"Best Supporting Actress" (*A Passage to India*)	1984	77
7	Henry Fonda	"Best Actor" (*On Golden Pond*)	1981	76
8	Katharine Hepburn	"Best Actress" (*On Golden Pond*)	1981	74
9	Edmund Gwenn	"Best Supporting Actor" (*Miracle on 34th Street*)	1947	72
10	Ruth Gordon	"Best Supporting Actress" (*Rosemary's Baby*)	1968	72

* *At time of Award ceremony; those of apparently identical age have been ranked according to their precise age in days at the time of the ceremony*

Among those senior citizens who received nominations but did not win Oscars is Ralph Richardson, who was nominated as "Best Supporting Actor" for his role in *Greystoke: The Legend of Tarzan* (1984) at the age of 82. Eva Le Gallienne was the same age when she was nominated as "Best Supporting Actress" for her part in *Resurrection* (1980). Outside the four acting categories, the oldest director to be nominated for a "Best Director" Oscar was John Huston, aged 79 at the time of his nomination for *Prizzi's Honor* (1985), and the oldest winner was George Cukor for *My Fair Lady* (1964), when he was 65.

THE 10

"BEST ACTRESS IN A SUPPORTING ROLE" OSCAR WINNERS OF THE 1980s

Year	Actress	Movie	Year	Actress	Movie
1980	Mary Steenburgen	*Melvin and Howard*	1985	Anjelica Huston	*Prizzi's Honor*
1981	Maureen Stapleton	*Reds*	1986	Diane Wiest	*Hannah and Her Sisters*
1982	Jessica Lange	*Tootsie*	1987	Olympia Dukakis	*Moonstruck*
1983	Linda Hunt	*The Year of Living Dangerously*	1988	Geena Davis	*The Accidental Tourist*
1984	Peggy Ashcroft	*A Passage to India*	1989	Brenda Fricker	*My Left Foot*

Only one movie has received three nominations for "Best Supporting Actress" – Diane Cilento, Dame Edith Evans, and Joyce Redman for *Tom Jones*. The winners during the 1990s are: 1990 Whoopi Goldberg for *Ghost*; 1991 Mercedes Ruehl for *The Fisher King*; 1992 Marisa Tomei for *My Cousin Vinny*; 1993 Anna Paquin for *The Piano*; 1994 Dianne Wiest for *Bullets Over Broadway*; 1995 Mira Sorvino for the movie *Mighty Aphrodite*; and 1996 Juliette Binoche for *The English Patient*.

DENZEL WASHINGTON
Denzel Washington's Oscar-winning career spans movies from Glory, *to* Cry Freedom, *to* Much Ado About Nothing.

T O P 1 0

YOUNGEST OSCAR-WINNING ACTORS

	Actor/actress	Award/movie (where specified)	Year	Age
1	Shirley Temple	Special Award – outstanding contribution during 1934	1934	6
2	Margaret O'Brien	Special Award (*Meet Me in St. Louis*)	1944	8
3	Vincent Winter	Special Award (*The Little Kidnappers*)	1954	8
4	Jon Whitely	Special Award (*The Little Kidnappers*)	1954	9
5	Ivan Jandl	Special Award (*The Search*)	1948	9
6	Tatum O'Neal	Best Supporting Actress (*Paper Moon*)	1973	10
7	Anna Paquin	Best Supporting Actress (*The Piano*)	1993	11
8	Claude Jarman, Jr.	Special Award (*The Yearling*)	1946	12
9	Bobby Driscoll	Special Award (*The Window*)	1949	13
10	Hayley Mills	Special Award (*Pollyanna*)	1960	13

CHILD STAR
After winning an Oscar at the age of six, Shirley Temple's film career faded during the 1940s. In 1968 she found a new role as a diplomat, first with the UN and later as a US ambassador.

T H E 1 0

"BEST ACTOR" OSCAR WINNERS OF THE 1980s

Year	Actor	Movie
1980	Robert De Niro	*Raging Bull*
1981	Henry Fonda	*On Golden Pond* *
1982	Ben Kingsley	*Gandhi* #
1983	Robert Duvall	*Tender Mercies*
1984	F. Murray Abraham	*Amadeus* #
1985	William Hurt	*Kiss of the Spider Woman*
1986	Paul Newman	*The Color of Money*
1987	Michael Douglas	*Wall Street*
1988	Dustin Hoffman	*Rain Man* #
1989	Daniel Day-Lewis	*My Left Foot*

* Winner of "Best Actor" Oscar #Winner of "Best Picture" Oscar

"BEST ACTRESS" OSCAR WINNERS OF THE 1980s

Year	Actress	Movie
1980	Sissy Spacek	*Coal Miner's Daughter*
1981	Katharine Hepburn	*On Golden Pond* *
1982	Meryl Streep	*Sophie's Choice*
1983	Shirley MacLaine	*Terms of Endearment* #
1984	Sally Field	*Places in the Heart*
1985	Geraldine Page	*The Trip to Bountiful*
1986	Marlee Matlin	*Children of a Lesser God*
1987	Cher	*Moonstruck*
1988	Jodie Foster	*The Accused*
1989	Jessica Tandy	*Driving Miss Daisy* #

* Winner of "Best Actress" Oscar #Winner of "Best Picture" Oscar

The "Best Actor" Oscar-winners of the 1990s to date are: 1990 Jeremy Irons for *Reversal of Fortune*; 1991 Anthony Hopkins for *The Silence of the Lambs* (which also won "Best Picture" and "Best Actress"); 1992 Al Pacino for *Scent of a Woman*; 1993 Tom Hanks for *Philadelphia* – who also won the award in 1994 for *Forrest Gump* (also the winner of "Best Picture" Oscar); 1995 Nicolas Cage for *Leaving Las Vegas*; and 1996 Geoffrey Rush for *Shine*. Hanks's achievement in winning the award in two consecutive years is unique in Oscar history. Only four other actors have ever won twice: Marlon Brando (1954 and 1972), Gary Cooper (1941 and 1952), Dustin Hoffman (1977 and 1988), and Spencer Tracy (1937 and 1938).

As with the "Best Actor" award, only one actress has ever won in consecutive years – Katharine Hepburn in 1967 and 1968. Ten more have won twice: Ingrid Bergman, Bette Davis, Olivia De Havilland, Sally Field, Jane Fonda, Jodie Foster, Glenda Jackson, Vivien Leigh, Luise Rainer, and Elizabeth Taylor. The winners of "Best Actress" Oscars during the 1990s are as follows: 1990 Kathy Bates for *Misery*; 1991 Jodie Foster for *The Silence of the Lambs* (also the winner of "Best Picture" and "Best Actor" Oscars); 1992 Emma Thompson for *Howard's End*; 1993 Holly Hunter for *The Piano*; 1994 Jessica Lange for *Blue Sky*; 1995 Susan Sarandon for *Dead Man Walking*; and 1996 Frances McDormand for *Fargo*.

AND THE WINNER IS . . .

THE 10

FIRST RECIPIENTS OF THE AMERICAN FILM INSTITUTE LIFETIME ACHIEVEMENT AWARDS

1973	John Ford
1974	James Cagney
1975	Orson Welles
1976	William Wyler
1977	Henry Fonda
1978	Bette Davis
1979	Alfred Hitchcock
1980	James Stewart
1981	Fred Astaire
1982	Frank Capra

THE 10

LATEST RECIPIENTS OF THE AMERICAN FILM INSTITUTE LIFETIME ACHIEVEMENT AWARDS

1997	Martin Scorsese
1996	Clint Eastwood
1995	Steven Spielberg
1994	Jack Nicholson
1993	Elizabeth Taylor
1992	Sidney Poitier
1991	Kirk Douglas
1990	David Lean
1989	Gregory Peck
1988	Jack Lemmon

THE 10

FIRST GOLDEN GLOBE AWARDS FOR "BEST PICTURE"

1943	*The Song of Bernadette*
1944	*Going My Way**
1945	*The Lost Weekend**
1946	*The Best Years of Our Lives**
1947	*Gentleman's Agreement**
1948	*The Treasure of the Sierra Madre* and *Johnny Belinda*#
1949	*All the King's Men**
1950	*Sunset Boulevard*
1951	*A Place in the Sun*
1952	*The Greatest Show on Earth**

* *Also won "Best Picture" Academy Award*
\# *Joint winners*

The Golden Globe Awards are presented annually by the Hollywood Foreign Press Association, a group of US-based journalists who report on the entertainment industry for the world's press. Although the Golden Globe categories differ in some respects from those of the Academy Awards ("Oscars"), they are often seen as a prediction of Oscars to come: in the "Best Picture" category their awards were identical on six out of 10 occasions in the first 10 years, a coincidence rate that it has continued to maintain ever since.

THE 10

LATEST GOLDEN GLOBE AWARDS FOR "BEST MOTION PICTURE – DRAMA"

1996	*The English Patient*	1991	*Bugsy*
1995	*Sense and Sensibility*	1990	*Dances With Wolves*
1994	*Forrest Gump*	1989	*Born on the Fourth of July*
1993	*Schindler's List*	1988	*Rain Man*
1992	*Scent of a Woman*	1987	*The Last Emperor*

THE 10

FIRST CANNES FESTIVAL BEST FILM AWARDS

1949	Carol Reed, *The Third Man* (UK)
1951	Vittoria De Sica, *Miracle in Milan* (Italy), and Alf Sjöberg, *Miss Julie* (Sweden)*
1952	Orson Welles, *Othello* (Morocco), and Renato Castellani, *Two Cents Worth of Hope* (Italy)*
1953	Henri-Georges Clouzot, *Wages of Fear* (France)
1954	Teinosuke Kinugasa, *Gates of Hell* (Japan)
1955	Delbart Mann, *Marty* (US)
1956	Louis Malle and Jacques-Yves Cousteau, *World of Silence* (France)
1957	William Wyler, *Friendly Persuasion* (US)
1958	Mikhail Kalatozov, *The Cranes Are Flying* (USSR)

* *Prize shared*

THE 10

LATEST WINNERS OF THE CANNES *PALME D'OR* FOR BEST FILM

1997	Shohei Imamura, *The Eel* (Japan)/ Abbas Kiarostami, *The Taste of Cherries* (Iran)
1996	Mike Leigh, *Secrets and Lies* (UK)
1995	Emir Kusturica, *Underground* (Yugoslavia)
1994	Quentin Tarantino, *Pulp Fiction* (US)
1993	Chen Kaige, *Farewell My Concubine* (China)/ Jane Campion, *The Piano* (Australia)
1992	Bille August, *Best Intentions* (Sweden)
1991	Joel Coen, *Barton Fink* (US)
1990	David Lynch, *Wild at Heart* (US)
1989	Steven Soderbergh, *sex, lies, and videotape* (US)
1988	Bille August, *Pelle the Conqueror* (Denmark)

LATEST GOLDEN GLOBE AWARDS FOR "BEST PERFORMANCE BY AN ACTOR IN A MOTION PICTURE – DRAMA"

1996	Geoffrey Rush in *Shine*
1995	Nicolas Cage in *Leaving Las Vegas*
1994	Tom Hanks in *Forrest Gump*
1993	Tom Hanks in *Philadelphia*
1992	Al Pacino in *Scent of a Woman*
1991	Nick Nolte in *The Prince of Tides*
1990	Jeremy Irons in *Reversal of Fortune*
1989	Tom Cruise in *Born on the Fourth of July*
1988	Dustin Hoffman in *Rain Man*
1987	Michael Douglas in *Wall Street*

No fewer than eight of the 10 most recent Golden Globe Awards won by leading actors (those in 1987–88, 1990, and 1992–96) were subsequently mirrored by the same actors' Oscar wins.

LATEST GOLDEN GLOBE AWARDS FOR "BEST PERFORMANCE BY AN ACTRESS IN A MOTION PICTURE – DRAMA"

1996	Brenda Blethyn in *Secrets and Lies*
1995	Sharon Stone in *Casino*
1994	Jessica Lange in *Blue Sky*
1993	Holly Hunter in *The Piano*
1992	Emma Thompson in *Howard's End*
1991	Jodie Foster in *The Silence of the Lambs*
1990	Kathy Bates in *Misery*
1989	Michelle Pfeiffer in *The Fabulous Baker Boys*
1988	Jodie Foster in *The Accused* and Shirley MacLaine in *Madame Sousatzka**
1987	Shirley Kirkland in *Anna*

* *Prize shared*

LATEST GOLDEN GLOBE AWARDS FOR "BEST MOTION PICTURE – MUSICAL OR COMEDY"

1996	*Evita*
1995	*Babe*
1994	*The Lion King*
1993	*Mrs. Doubtfire*
1992	*The Player*
1991	*Beauty and the Beast*
1990	*Green Card*
1989	*Driving Miss Daisy*
1988	*Working Girl*
1987	*Hope and Glory*

LATEST GOLDEN GLOBE AWARDS FOR "BEST PERFORMANCE BY AN ACTOR IN A MOTION PICTURE – MUSICAL OR COMEDY"

1996	Tom Cruise in *Jerry Maguire*
1995	John Travolta in *Get Shorty*
1994	Hugh Grant in *Four Weddings and a Funeral*
1993	Robin Williams in *Mrs. Doubtfire*
1992	Tim Robbins in *The Player*
1991	Robin Williams in *The Fisher King*
1990	Gerard Depardieu in *Green Card*
1989	Morgan Freeman in *Driving Miss Daisy*
1988	Tom Hanks in *Big*
1987	Robin Williams in *Good Morning, Vietnam*

The Golden Globe "Musical or Comedy" awards tend to be presented to films that have received popular and commercial success. During the past 10 years, more than half the Golden Globe awards in this category went to the stars of movies that earned in excess of $100,000,000 apiece. *Mrs. Doubtfire* has made more than $400,000,000 globally, and *Four Weddings and a Funeral* is the highest-earning British film of all-time.

LATEST GOLDEN GLOBE AWARDS FOR "BEST PERFORMANCE BY AN ACTRESS IN A MOTION PICTURE – MUSICAL OR COMEDY"

1996	Madonna in *Evita*
1995	Nicole Kidman in *To Die For*
1994	Jamie Lee Curtis in *True Lies*
1993	Angela Bassett in *What's Love Got To Do With It*
1992	Miranda Richardson in *Enchanted April*
1991	Bette Midler in *For the Boys*
1990	Julia Roberts in *Pretty Woman*
1989	Jessica Tandy in *Driving Miss Daisy*
1988	Melanie Griffith in *Working Girl*
1987	Cher in *Moonstruck*

Although romantic comedies feature predominantly among the winners, a number of the successful actresses in this category received their awards for roles in movies that are either traditional musicals, or have a high musical content, including two musical biographies, *Evita*, and *What's Love Got To Do With It*. Among the most recent winners, Jessica Tandy also went on to win the "Best Actress" Academy Award for her starring role in *Driving Miss Daisy*.

MOVIE STARS – ACTORS

HARRISON FORD MOVIES

1	Star Wars	1977
2	Indiana Jones and the Last Crusade	1989
3	Return of the Jedi	1983
4	Raiders of the Lost Ark	1981
5	The Empire Strikes Back	1980
6	The Fugitive	1993
7	Presumed Innocent	1990
8	Clear and Present Danger	1994
9	Indiana Jones and the Temple of Doom	1984
10	Patriot Games	1992

Harrison Ford is in the fortunate position of having appeared in so many successful films that if any film were deleted from this Top 10, several similarly profitable films in which he starred could easily replace it, among them *Apocalypse Now* (1979) – although his role in it amounted to little more than a cameo, *Working Girl* (1988), *Witness* (1985), *Regarding Henry* (1991), and *Blade Runner* (1982). One film organization has recently voted Ford "Box Office Star of the Century".

SEAN CONNERY MOVIES

1	Indiana Jones and the Last Crusade	1989
2	The Rock	1996
3	The Hunt for Red October	1990
4	Thunderball	1965
5	Never Say Never Again	1983
6	Goldfinger	1964
7	First Knight	1995
8	Diamonds Are Forever	1971
9	You Only Live Twice	1967
10	From Russia with Love	1964

If Sean Connery's fleeting cameo entry in the final two minutes of *Robin Hood: Prince of Thieves* (1991) is taken into account, it would be placed 2nd in this list.

CLINT EASTWOOD MOVIES

1	In the Line of Fire	1993
2	Any Which Way You Can	1980
3	The Bridges of Madison County	1995
4	A Perfect World	1993
5	Every Which Way But Loose	1978
6	Unforgiven	1992
7	Sudden Impact	1983
8	Heartbreak Ridge	1986
9	Firefox	1982
10	The Enforcer	1976

MICHAEL DOUGLAS MOVIES

1	Basic Instinct	1992
2	Disclosure	1994
3	Fatal Attraction	1987
4	Romancing the Stone	1984
5	The War of the Roses	1989
6	The Jewel of the Nile	1985
7	The American President	1995
8	Black Rain	1989
9	Wall Street*	1987
10	Falling Down	1993

* Academy Award for "Best Actor"

ROBERT DE NIRO MOVIES

1	Heat	1995
2	Sleepers	1996
3	Mary Shelley's Frankenstein	1994
4	Cape Fear	1991
5	Backdraft	1991
6	The Untouchables	1987
7	The Godfather, Part II*	1974
8	Awakenings	1990
9	GoodFellas	1990
10	Casino	1995

* Academy Award for "Best Supporting Actor"

SYLVESTER STALLONE MOVIES

1	Rambo: First Blood Part Two	1985
2	Cliffhanger	1993
3	The Specialist	1994
4	Rocky IV	1985
5	Rocky III	1982
6	Rocky	1976
7	Judge Dredd	1995
8	Daylight	1996
9	Rocky II	1979
10	Assassins	1995

ARNOLD SCHWARZENEGGER MOVIES

1	Terminator 2: Judgment Day	1991
2	True Lies	1994
3	Total Recall	1990
4	Eraser	1996
5	The Last Action Hero	1993
6	Jingle All the Way	1996
7	Twins	1988
8	Kindergarten Cop	1990
9	Junior	1984
10	Predator	1987

SIR ANTHONY HOPKINS MOVIES

1	Bram Stoker's Dracula	1992
2	The Silence of the Lambs*	1991
3	Legends of the Fall	1995
4	A Bridge Too Far	1977
5	Magic	1978
6	Howards End	1992
7	The Elephant Man	1980
8	Shadowlands	1993
9	The Remains of the Day	1993
10	The Lion in Winter	1968

* Academy Award for "Best Actor"

TOP 10
JOHN TRAVOLTA MOVIES

1	Grease	1978
2	Saturday Night Fever	1977
3	Look Who's Talking	1989
4	Phenomenon	1996
5	Pulp Fiction	1994
6	Broken Arrow	1996
7	Staying Alive	1983
8	Get Shorty	1995
9	Michael	1996
10	Look Who's Talking Too	1990

TOP 10
TOM CRUISE MOVIES

1	Mission: Impossible	1996
2	Rain Man	1988
3	Top Gun	1986
4	The Firm	1993
5	A Few Good Men	1992
6	Interview with the Vampire	1994
7	Days of Thunder	1990
8	Jerry Maguire	1996
9	Cocktail	1988
10	Born on the Fourth of July	1989

TOP 10
JACK NICHOLSON MOVIES

1	Batman	1989
2	A Few Good Men	1992
3	One Flew Over the Cuckoo's Nest*	1975
4	Terms of Endearment#	1983
5	Wolf	1994
6	The Witches of Eastwick	1987
7	The Shining	1980
8	Broadcast News	1987
9	Reds	1981
10	Mars Attacks!	1996

* *Academy Award for "Best Actor"*
\# *Academy Award for "Best Supporting Actor"*

TOP 10
KEVIN COSTNER MOVIES

1	Dances with Wolves	1990
2	The Bodyguard	1992
3	Waterworld	1995
4	JFK	1991
5	Robin Hood: Prince of Thieves	1991
6	A Perfect World	1993
7	Tin Cup	1996
8	The Untouchables	1987
9	Field of Dreams	1989
10	The Big Chill	1983

TOP 10
MEL GIBSON MOVIES

1	Lethal Weapon 2	1989
2	Lethal Weapon 3	1992
3	Braveheart	1995
4	Ransom	1996
5	Forever Young	1992
6	Maverick	1994
7	Bird on a Wire	1990
8	Lethal Weapon	1987
9	Tequila Sunrise	1988
10	Mad Max Beyond Thunderdome	1985

TOP 10
TOM HANKS MOVIES

1	Forrest Gump*	1994
2	Apollo 13	1995
3	Sleepless in Seattle	1993
4	Philadelphia*	1993
5	Big	1988
6	A League of Their Own	1992
7	Turner & Hooch	1989
8	Splash!	1984
9	Dragnet	1987
10	Joe Versus the Volcano	1990

* *Academy Award for "Best Actor"*

T. HANKS SAYS "THANKS"
Tom Hanks won an Oscar for "Best Actor" in 1994 for his role in Philadelphia, *and the following year he was awarded an Oscar in the same category for his role in* Forrest Gump. *Hanks was the first actor to win an Oscar in two consecutive years since Spencer Tracy, who won "Best Actor" awards in 1937 and 1938.*

MOVIE STARS – ACTRESSES

T O P 1 0

SALLY FIELD MOVIES

1	Forrest Gump	1994
2	Mrs. Doubtfire	1993
3	Smokey and the Bandit	1977
4	Steel Magnolias	1989
5	Smokey and the Bandit II	1980
6	Hooper	1978
7	Eye for an Eye	1995
8	The End	1978
9	Absence of Malice	1981
10	Soapdish	1991

Sally Field provided the voice of Sassy in the animal adventure movies *Homeward Bound: The Incredible Journey* (1993) and its sequel *Homeward Bound II: Lost in San Francisco* (1996). If taken into account, they would appear in 10th and 8th places respectively, either side of *The End*, thereby evicting *Absence of Malice* and *Soapdish* from her Top 10.

SUPERSTAR SHARON STONE
Sharon Stone's movie career began in 1980 with her nonspeaking and brief appearance in Woody Allen's Stardust Memories *as "Pretty Girl on a Train."*

T O P 1 0

SIGOURNEY WEAVER MOVIES

1	Ghostbusters	1984
2	Ghostbusters II	1989
3	Aliens	1986
4	Alien	1979
5	Working Girl	1988

6	Dave	1993
7	Alien^3	1992
8	Copycat	1995
9	Gorillas in the Mist	1988
10	1492: Conquest of Paradise	1992

T O P 1 0

MICHELLE PFEIFFER MOVIES

1	Batman Returns	1992
2	Dangerous Minds	1995
3	Wolf	1994
4	The Witches of Eastwick	1987
5	Up Close and Personal	1996
6	Tequila Sunrise	1988
7	Scarface	1983
8	Dangerous Liaisons	1988
9	One Fine Day	1996
10	The Age of Innocence	1993

T O P 1 0

SHARON STONE MOVIES

1	Basic Instinct	1992
2	Total Recall	1990
3	The Specialist	1995
4	Last Action Hero	1993
5	Sliver	1993
6	Casino*	1995
7	Police Academy 4: Citizens on Patrol	1987
8	Intersection	1994
9	Action Jackson	1988
10	Above the Law	1988

T O P 1 0

MEG RYAN MOVIES

1	Top Gun	1986
2	Sleepless in Seattle	1993
3	French Kiss	1995
4	When Harry Met Sally	1989
5	Courage Under Fire	1996
6	When a Man Loves a Woman	1994
7	Joe Versus the Volcano	1990
8	The Doors	1991
9	I.Q.	1994
10	Innerspace	1987

T O P 1 0

SUSAN SARANDON MOVIES

1	The Rocky Horror Picture Show	1975
2	The Client	1994
3	The Witches of Eastwick	1987
4	Bull Durham	1988
5	Little Women	1994
6	Thelma & Louise	1991
7	Dead Man Walking*	1995
8	The Player	1992
9	White Palace	1991
10	The Great Waldo Pepper	1975

* *Academy Award for "Best Actress"*

Susan Sarandon also provided the voice of the spider in the animated movie of Roald Dahl's children's story *James and the Giant Peach* (1996). If included in the ranking, it would be in 8th place.

TOP 10

BARBRA STREISAND MOVIES

1	A Star is Born	1976
2	The Prince of Tides*	1991
3	What's Up, Doc?	1972
4	The Main Event	1979
5	Funny Girl	1968
6	The Mirror Has Two Faces*	1996
7	The Way We Were	1973
8	Yentl*	1983
9	Funny Lady	1975
10	Hello Dolly	1969

* Also directed

TOP 10

DEMI MOORE MOVIES

1	Ghost	1990
2	Indecent Proposal	1993
3	A Few Good Men	1992
4	Disclosure	1995
5	Striptease	1996
6	The Juror	1996
7	About Last Night	1986
8	St. Elmo's Fire	1985
9	Young Doctors in Love	1982
10	Now and Then	1995

Demi Moore provided the voice of Esmeralda in the animated movie The Hunchback of Notre Dame (1996). If included in her Top 10, it would be in 2nd place.

JULIA ROBERTS
Julia Roberts is best known for her role in Pretty Woman, *which made her one of the most highly paid actresses in Hollywood.*

TOP 10

JULIA ROBERTS MOVIES

1	Pretty Woman	1990
2	The Pelican Brief	1993
3	Sleeping with the Enemy	1991
4	Hook	1991
5	Steel Magnolias	1989
6	Flatliners	1990
7	Something to Talk About	1995
8	Dying Young	1991
9	I Love Trouble	1994
10	Michael Collins	1996

TOP 10

EMMA THOMPSON MOVIES

1	Junior	1994
2	Sense and Sensibility	1995
3	Dead Again	1991
4	Howard's End*	1992
5	In the Name of the Father	1993
6	The Remains of the Day	1993
7	Much Ado about Nothing	1993
8	Henry V	1989
9	Impromptu	1991
10	Carrington	1995

* Academy Award for "Best Actress"

TOP 10

MERYL STREEP MOVIES

1	The Bridges of Madison County	1995
2	Kramer vs. Kramer*	1979
3	Out of Africa	1985
4	Death Becomes Her	1992
5	The Deer Hunter	1978
6	Manhattan	1979
7	Postcards from the Edge	1990
8	Silkwood	1983
9	Sophie's Choice#	1982
10	Julia	1982

* Academy Award for "Best Supporting Actress"
# Academy Award for "Best Actress"

It is perhaps surprising that *Sophie's Choice*, the movie for which Meryl Streep won an Oscar, scores so far down this list, while one of her most celebrated movies, *The French Lieutenant's Woman* (1981), does not make her personal Top 10 at all.

TOP 10

NICOLE KIDMAN MOVIES

1	Batman Forever	1995	6	To Die For	1995
2	Days of Thunder	1990	7	Billy Bathgate	1991
3	Far and Away	1992	8	Dead Calm	1989
4	Malice	1993	9	Portrait of a Lady	1996
5	My Life	1993	10	Flirting	1991

COMEDY STARS

TOP 10

WHOOPI GOLDBERG MOVIES

1	Ghost	1990
2	Sister Act	1992
3	Made in America	1993
4	The Color Purple*	1985
5	Sister Act 2: Back in the Habit	1993
6	The Little Rascals	1994
7	Soapdish	1991
8	Star Trek: Generations	1994
9	Eddie	1996
10	National Lampoon's Loaded Weapon 1	1993

* Academy Award nomination for "Best Actress"

Whoopi Goldberg's appearance in *National Lampoon's Loaded Weapon 1* was an uncredited cameo; if excluded, her new No. 10 would be *Jumpin' Jack Flash* (1986). She provided the voice of Shenzi in *The Lion King* (1994). If that were taken into the reckoning, it would appear in No. 1 position in her Top 10.

TOP 10

EDDIE MURPHY MOVIES

1	Beverly Hills Cop	1984
2	Beverly Hills Cop II	1987
3	Coming to America	1988
4	Boomerang	1992
5	Harlem Nights*	1989
6	Trading Places	1983
7	Another 48 Hours	1990
8	The Golden Child	1986
9	48 Hours	1982
10	Eddie Murphy Raw	1987

* Also director

Eddie Murphy Raw is an unusual entrant in that it is not a feature film but a documentary featuring Murphy live on stage. It is one of an elite handful of "non-fiction" movies that rank alongside major feature films in terms of their earnings, from screenings, video sales, and rental.

TOP 10

GOLDIE HAWN MOVIES

1	The First Wives Club	1996
2	Bird on a Wire	1990
3	Private Benjamin	1980
4	Housesitter	1992
5	Death Becomes Her	1992
6	Foul Play	1978
7	Shampoo	1975
8	Seems Like Old Times	1980
9	Best Friends	1982
10	Deceived	1991

GOLDEN GIRL
Goldie Hawn (born Goldie Jean Studlendgehawn) made her first appearance in 1968 in the long-running TV series Rowan and Martin's Laugh-In. *She has effectively reprised her role as a zany, eternally youthful blonde in comedy films ever since, with* Private Benjamin *earning her a Best Actress Oscar nomination.*

TOP 10

WOODY ALLEN MOVIES

1	Manhattan*#✦	1979
2	Hannah and Her Sisters*#✦	1986
3	Annie Hall*#✦	1977
4	Casino Royale*	1967
5	Everything You Always Wanted to Know about Sex (But Were Afraid to Ask)*#✦	1972
6	What's New, Pussycat?*#	1965
7	Sleeper*#✦	1973
8	Crimes and Misdemeanors*#✦	1989
9	Radio Days*#✦	1987
10	Bullets over Broadway#✦	1994

* Appeared in
# Scriptwriter
✦ Directed

This list includes films that Woody Allen has either written, starred in, or directed. If it were restricted only to films he has directed, *Casino Royale* and *What's New, Pussycat?* would be dropped from the list, and the new 9th and 10th entries would be *Zelig* (1983) and *Love and Death* (1975), both of which he starred in, wrote, and directed. *Annie Hall* prompted the first occasion since 1941 on which one individual was nominated for "Best Picture," "Best Actor," "Best Director," and "Best Screenplay."

TOP 10

PETER SELLERS MOVIES

1	The Revenge of the Pink Panther	1978
2	The Return of the Pink Panther	1974
3	The Pink Panther Strikes Again	1976
4	Murder by Death	1976
5	Being There	1979
6	Casino Royale	1967
7	What's New, Pussycat?	1965
8	A Shot in the Dark	1964
9	The Pink Panther	1963
10=	Dr. Strangelove	1963
10=	The Fiendish Plot of Dr. Fu Manchu	1980

T O P 1 0

BETTE MIDLER MOVIES

1	*The First Wives Club*	1996
2	*Get Shorty*	1995
3	*Ruthless People*	1986
4	*Down and Out in Beverly Hills*	1986
5	*Beaches**	1988
6	*Outrageous Fortune*	1987
7	*The Rose*	1979
8	*Big Business*	1988
9	*Hocus Pocus*	1993
10	*Hawaii*	1966

* Also producer

Bette Midler's role in *Get Shorty* is no more than a cameo, and that in *Hawaii*, her first film part, is as an extra. If excluded, *Stella* (1990) and *For the Boys* (1991) would join the list. Her voice appears as that of the character Georgette in the animated film *Oliver and Company* (1988).

T O P 1 0

DANNY DEVITO MOVIES

1	*Batman Returns*	1992
2	*Romancing the Stone*	1984
3	*One Flew Over the Cuckoo's Nest*	1975
4	*Twins*	1988
5	*Terms of Endearment*	1983
6	*Junior*	1994
7	*The War of the Roses**	1989
8	*Get Shorty*	1995
9	*Ruthless People*	1986
10	*The Jewel of the Nile*	1985

* Also director

Danny DeVito had a relatively minor role in *One Flew Over the Cuckoo's Nest*. If this is discounted from the reckoning, his 10th most successful film is *Throw Momma from the Train* (1987). He directed, appeared in, and narrated *Matilda* (1996), which just fails to make his Top 10.

T O P 1 0

DAN AYKROYD MOVIES

1	*Ghostbusters*	1984
2	*Casper*	1995
3	*Indiana Jones and the Temple of Doom*	1984
4	*Ghostbusters II*	1989
5	*Driving Miss Daisy*	1989
6	*Trading Places*	1983
7	*Spies Like Us*	1985
8	*My Girl*	1991
9	*Dragnet*	1987
10	*The Blues Brothers*	1980

If his 20-second cameo appearance as Weber in *Indiana Jones and the Temple of Doom* is excluded, Aykroyd's next most successful film is *Sneakers* (1992). If his unbilled part (as Doctor Raymond Stantz) in *Casper* is eliminated, the Spielberg-directed *1941* joins the list – although it is technically regarded as a "flop" because it cost more to make than it earned at the box office. His directorial debut with *Nothing But Trouble* (1991), in which he also played the starring role, was his least commercially successful film.

T O P 1 0

BILL MURRAY MOVIES

1	*Ghostbusters*	1984	6	*What About Bob?*	1991
2	*Tootsie*	1982	7	*Scrooged*	1988
3	*Ghostbusters II*	1989	8	*Meatballs*	1979
4	*Stripes*	1981	9	*Caddyshack*	1980
5	*Groundhog Day*	1993	10	*Little Shop of Horrors*	1986

T O P 1 0

STEVE MARTIN MOVIES

1	*Parenthood*	1989
2	*The Jerk**	1979
3	*Father of the Bride*	1991
4	*Father of the Bride Part II*	1995
5	*Housesitter*	1992
6	*Planes, Trains, and Automobiles*	1987
7	*Dirty Rotten Scoundrels*	1988
8	*Roxanne*	1987
9	*Three Amigos!**	1986
10	*Little Shop of Horrors*	1986

* Also cowriter

Steve Martin was also one of the many "guest stars" in *The Muppet Movie* (1979). If included, it would appear in 4th place.

T O P 1 0

ROBIN WILLIAMS MOVIES

1	*Mrs. Doubtfire*	1993
2	*Jumanji*	1995
3	*Dead Poets Society*	1989
4	*The Birdcage*	1996
5	*Nine Months*	1995
6	*Good Morning, Vietnam*	1987
7	*Hook*	1991
8	*Jack*	1996
9	*Awakenings*	1990
10	*Popeye*	1980

T O P 1 0

JIM CARREY MOVIES

1	*Batman Forever*	1995
2	*The Mask*	1994
3	*Dumb & Dumber*	1994
4	*Ace Ventura: When Nature Calls*	1995
5	*Ace Ventura: Pet Detective*	1994
6	*Peggy Sue Got Married*	1986
7	*The Dead Pool*	1988
8	*Pink Cadillac*	1989
9	*Once Bitten*	1985
10	*Earth Girls Are Easy*	1989

DIRECTOR'S CUT

MASTER OF SUSPENSE
British-born Alfred Hitchcock directed almost 60 movies in his 50-year career, including some of the most popular thrillers of all time.

TOP 10

MOVIES DIRECTED BY ALFRED HITCHCOCK

1	*Psycho*	1960
2	*Rear Window*	1954
3	*North by Northwest*	1959
4	*Family Plot*	1976
5	*Torn Curtain*	1966
6	*Frenzy*	1972
7	*Vertigo*	1958
8	*The Man Who Knew Too Much*	1956
9	*The Birds*	1963
10	*Spellbound*	1945

TOP 10

MOVIES DIRECTED BY BLAKE EDWARDS

1	*10*	1979
2	*Revenge of the Pink Panther*	1978
3	*The Return of the Pink Panther*	1975
4	*The Pink Panther Strikes Again*	1976
5	*Blind Date*	1987
6	*Mickie & Maude*	1984
7	*The Great Race*	1965
8	*Victor/Victoria*	1982
9	*Operation Petticoat*	1959
10	*Skin Deep*	1989

TOP 10

MOST PROLIFIC DIRECTORS

	Director	Active period	No. films directed
1	D.W. Griffith	1908–36	545
2	Dave Fleischer	1918–48	392
3	Friz Freleng	1934–83	262
4	Chuck Jones	1938–	240
5	Theo Frenkel	1908–28	216
6	Allan Dwan	1911–61	189
7	Robert McKimson	1946–69	175
8	Sam Newfield	1933–58	165
9	William Beaudine	1917–66	156
10	Gilberto Martinez Solares	1936–94	150

TOP 10

MOVIES DIRECTED BY FRANCIS FORD COPPOLA

1	*Bram Stoker's Dracula*	1992
2	*The Godfather*	1972
3	*Jack*	1996
4	*The Godfather, Part III*	1990
5	*Apocalypse Now*	1979
6	*The Godfather, Part II*	1974
7	*Peggy Sue Got Married*	1986
8	*The Cotton Club*	1984
9	*The Outsiders*	1983
10	*Tucker: The Man and His Dream*	1988

TOP 10

MOVIES DIRECTED BY SIDNEY LUMET

1	*The Verdict*	1982
2	*Dog Day Afternoon*	1975
3	*Murder on the Orient Express*	1974
4	*Serpico*	1974
5	*Network*	1976
6	*The Wiz*	1978
7	*The Morning After*	1986
8	*Guilty As Sin*	1993
9	*Deathtrap*	1982
10	*A Stranger Among Us*	1992

Several of the most prolific directors, including D.W. Griffith, Theo Frenkel, Allan Dwan, and William Beaudine, spent at least the early years of their careers directing silent movies. In some instances, not all the films for which they were responsible have been identified, so the totals include certain "probable" but unconfirmed titles. Some directors worked in fairly narrowly defined genres, such as Sam Newfield, who was responsible for a large number of cowboy movies, while four included here were responsible chiefly for animated films: Dave Fleischer (*Popeye*), Friz Freleng (*Bugs Bunny*), Chuck Jones (*Tom & Jerry* and *Bugs Bunny*), and Robert McKimson (*Daffy Duck*, etc.).

THE GREAT DIRECTOR

David Lewelyn Wark (known as "D.W.") Griffith, who died 50 years ago, on July 23, 1948, was one of the most influential figures in the history of the cinema. Kentucky-born Griffith was an actor who turned to writing and directing in the early years of the cinema, pioneering such techniques as fades and flashbacks. The most prolific director of all time, he was making an average of 21 movies a week at one stage in his career. His movie *The Birth of a Nation* (1915) was the highest-earning movie made until 1937 (when Disney's *Snow White and the Seven Dwarfs* overtook it), while his controversial epic *Intolerance* (1916) was one of the first movies to have "a cast of thousands" – and the first major movie flop.

YEARS AGO • YEARS AGO • YEARS AGO
50

T O P 1 0

MOVIES DIRECTED BY JOHN HUSTON

1	*Annie*	1982
2	*The Bible*	1966
3	*Prizzi's Honor**	1985
4	*The Man Who Would Be King*#	1975
5	*Casino Royale*	1967
6	*The Life and Times of Judge Roy Bean*	1972
7	*Moby Dick*	1956
8	*Night of the Iguana*	1964
9	*Moulin Rouge**	1952
10=	*Heaven Knows, Mr. Allison*#	1957
10=	*Victory (or Escape to Victory)*	1981

* *Academy Award nomination for "Best Picture"*
\# *Academy Award nomination for "Best Screenplay"*

John Huston (1906–87) was a man of prodigious and diverse talents who wrote the scripts of some 30 movies, acted in 40, and directed more than 40. He is perhaps best remembered for films that were greater critical than commercial successes, among them *The Maltese Falcon*, *The Treasure of the Sierra Madre*, and *The African Queen*.

MOVIES DIRECTED BY HOWARD HAWKS

1	*Hatari*	1962
2	*Sergeant York*	1941
3	*El Dorado*	1967
4	*Rio Bravo*	1959
5	*Gentlemen Prefer Blondes*	1953
6	*The Outlaw**	1943
7	*Red River*	1948
8	*Rio Lobo*	1970
9	*I Was a Male War Bride*	1949
10	*To Have and Have Not*	1945

* *Codirected with Howard Hughes*

MOVIES DIRECTED OR PRODUCED BY GEORGE LUCAS

1	*Star Wars**	1977
2	*The Empire Strikes Back*#	1980
3	*Indiana Jones and the Last Crusade*#	1989
4	*Return of the Jedi*#	1983
5	*Raiders of the Lost Ark*#	1981
6	*Indiana Jones and the Temple of Doom*#	1984
7	*American Graffiti**	1973
8	*Willow*#	1988
9	*The Land Before Time*#	1988
10	*Tucker: The Man and His Dream*#	1988

* *Director*
\# *Producer*

George Lucas made the move from directing to producing after the phenomenal success of Star Wars, but he clearly has a Midas touch in both fields, the first five movies on this list ranking among the 25 highest-earning of all time, and his Top 10 earning more than $2.5 billion at the box office. Lucas was also responsible for writing the stories for the first 8 films in this catalogue of triumphs.

MOVIES DIRECTED BY MARTIN SCORSESE

1	*Cape Fear*	1991
2	*The Color of Money*	1986
3	*GoodFellas*	1990
4	*Casino*	1995
5	*The Age of Innocence*	1993
6	*Taxi Driver*	1976
7	*Raging Bull*	1980
8	*Alice Doesn't Live Here Anymore*	1975
9	*New York, New York*	1977
10	*New York Stories**	1989

* *Part only; other segments directed by Francis Ford Coppola and Woody Allen*

MOVIES DIRECTED BY STEVEN SPIELBERG

1	*Jurassic Park*	1993
2	*E.T.: The Extra-Terrestrial*	1982
3	*Indiana Jones and the Last Crusade*	1989
4	*Jaws*	1975
5	*Raiders of the Lost Ark*	1981
6	*Schindler's List*	1993
7	*Close Encounters of the Third Kind*	1977/80*
8	*Indiana Jones and the Temple of Doom*	1984
9	*The Lost World*	1997
10	*Hook*	1991

* *Reedited and rereleased as a "Special Edition"*

Steven Spielberg has directed some of the most successful movies of all time: the top four in this list appear among the top 13 films of all time. If his credits as producer are included, other blockbusters such as *The Flintstones*, *Casper*, *Twister*, *Gremlins*, and *Poltergeist* would also score highly.

OUT-TAKES

TOP 10

MOVIE-PRODUCING COUNTRIES

	Country	Movies produced p.a.
1	India	754
2	US	685
3	Japan	278
4	Hong Kong	154
5	France	134
6	UK	111
7	China	110
8	Italy	99
9	Spain	91
10	Pakistan	88

The list is of full-length (generally at least 5,250 ft/1,600 m) feature films, and for most countries is for numbers of movies produced in 1996. India has maintained its preeminence for several years, while the resurgence of the British film industry has elevated it from its former position at the bottom of the Top 10.

CINEMA GIANT
India's insatiable demand for movies has resulted in its film industry's outstripping even that of Hollywood.

TOP 10

MOVIE-GOING COUNTRIES

	Country	Annual theater visits per inhabitant
1	India	8.9
2	Singapore	6.4
3	US	4.8
4	Iceland	4.5
5=	Hong Kong	4.1
5=	New Zealand	4.1
7	Australia	3.9
8	Canada	3.0
9	Ireland	2.6
10	Norway	2.5

The popularity of movies on a country-by-country basis can be roughly measured by analyzing the average number of visits to the movies per head of the population. This analysis produces one of the very few world lists in which Iceland appears in close proximity to the United States.

TOP 10

MOVIES WITH THE MOST EXTRAS

	Movie/country/year	Extras
1	*Gandhi* (UK, 1982)	300,000
2	*Kolberg* (Germany, 1945)	187,000
3	*Monster Wang-magwi* (South Korea, 1967)	157,000
4	*War and Peace* (USSR, 1967)	120,000
5	*Ilya Muromets* (USSR, 1956)	106,000
6	*Tonko* (Japan, 1988)	100,000
7	*The War of Independence* (Rumania, 1912)	80,000
8	*Around the World in 80 Days* (US, 1956)	68,894
9=	*Intolerance* (US, 1916)	60,000
9=	*Dny Zrady* (Czechoslovakia, 1972)	60,000

TOP 10

COUNTRIES WITH MOST MOVIE THEATERS

	Country	Movie screens
1	China	100,000 *
2	US	27,805
3	India*	8,982
4	France	4,614
5	Germany	3,814
6	Italy	3,670
7	Spain	2,091
8	UK	2,052
9	Indonesia	1,800
10	Japan	1,776
	Canada#	*1,713*

* Estimated
\# 1990 figures; all others 1995

For many years UNESCO and other international agencies produced statistics for indoor theaters equipped to show 35 mm films and, in some instances, 16 mm films. The total for the former USSR, once said to be as high as 176,172, always seemed incredible, and was concluded to be a reflection of the value placed on film in the Soviet Union as a medium not only of entertainment but also political ideology. More believable figures are now emerging for the former Soviet republics.

TOP 10

COUNTRIES WITH THE MOST MOVIE SCREENS

	Country	Movie screens per million
1	Belarus	414.9
2	Sweden	137.8
3	US	105.9
4	Latvia	101.7
5	Norway	91.5
6	Iceland	86.3
7	France	80.0
8	Czech Republic	79.3
9	New Zealand	73.7
10	Switzerland	71.2

PRECIOUS RUBIES
The magical ruby slippers worn by Judy Garland in the 1939 film The Wizard of Oz were sold in 1988 for $165,000, making them the most expensive items of film costume ever sold at auction. As they were one of four pairs made for her role, history could yet repeat itself.

T O P 1 0

LONGEST MOVIES EVER SCREENED

	Title/country/year	Duration hr	min
1	*The Longest and Most Meaningless Movie in the World*, UK, 1970	48	0
2	*The Burning of the Red Lotus Temple*, China, 1928–31	27	0
3	****, US, 1967	25	0
4	*Heimat*, West Germany, 1984	15	40
5	*Berlin Alexanderplatz*, West Germany/Italy, 1980	15	21
6	*The Journey*, Sweden, 1987	14	33
7	*The Old Testament*, Italy, 1922	13	0
8	*Comment Yukong déplace les montagnes*, France, 1976	12	43
9	*Out 1: Noli me Tangere*, France, 1971	12	40
10	*Ningen No Joken (The Human Condition)*, Japan, 1958–60	9	29

The list includes commercially screened films, but not "stunt" films created solely to break endurance records (particularly those of their audiences), among which are the 85-hour *The Cure for Insomnia* and the 50-hour *Mondo Teeth*. Those in the list are no more watchable: *The Longest and Most Meaningless Movie in the World* was later cut to a more manageable 1 hr 30 min, and remained just as meaningless. Outside this Top 10, Abel Gance's *Napoleon* has not been shown at its full length of nine hours since it was first released, but as new segments of it have been discovered, it has been meticulously reassembled to a length approaching that of the original version. Among more conventional yet extremely long films of recent times are *Wagner* (UK/Hungary/Austria, 1983; 9 hr 0 min), *Little Dorrit* (UK, 1987; 5 hr 57 min), the colossally expensive and commercially disastrous *Cleopatra* (US, 1963; 4 hr 3 min) and the *Greatest Story Ever Told* (US, 1965), which was progressively cut from 4 hr 20 min to 2 hr 7 min, but in the end was no less tedious as a result.

T O P 1 0

MOST EXPENSIVE ITEMS OF FILM MEMORABILIA EVER SOLD AT AUCTION

	Item/sale	Price ($)
1	Vivien Leigh's Oscar for *Gone With the Wind*, Sotheby's, New York, December 15, 1993	562,500
2	Clark Gable's Oscar for *It Happened One Night*, Christie's, Los Angeles, December 15, 1996	607,500
3	Poster for *The Mummy*, 1932, Sotheby's, New York, March 1, 1997	453,500
4	James Bond's Aston Martin DB5 from *Goldfinger*, Sotheby's, New York, June 28, 1986	275,000
5	Clark Gable's personal script for *Gone With the Wind*, Christie's, Los Angeles, December 15, 1996	244,500
6	"Rosebud" sled from *Citizen Kane*, Christie's, Los Angeles, December 15, 1996	233,500
7	Herman J. Mankiewicz's scripts for *Citizen Kane* and *The American*, Christie's, New York, June 21, 1989	231,000
8	Judy Garland's ruby slippers from *The Wizard of Oz*, Christie's, New York, June 21, 1988	165,000
9	Piano from the Paris scene in *Casablanca*, Sotheby's, New York, December 16, 1988	154,000
10	Charlie Chaplin's hat and cane, Christie's, London, December 11, 1987, (resold at Christie's, London, December 17, 1993, for $86,900)	130,350

This list excludes animated film celluloids or "cels" – the individually painted scenes that are shot in sequence to make up cartoon films – which are now attaining colossal prices: just one of the 150,000 color cels from *Snow White* (1937) was sold in 1991 for $209,000 and in 1989 $286,000 was reached for a black-and-white cel depicting Donald Duck in *Orphan's Benefit* (1934). If memorabilia relating to film stars rather than films were to be included, Orson Welles' annotated script from the radio production of *The War of the Worlds* ($143,000 in 1988) would qualify for this Top 10. Among near-misses are posters for two 1933 films, *Flying Down to Rio* ($81,000) and *King Kong* ($79,500), both of which were sold in 1996, such costume items as the witch's hat from *The Wizard of Oz* ($33,000 in 1988) and Marilyn Monroe's "shimmy" dress from *Some Like It Hot* ($31,300 in 1988), and the stand-in model of Boris Karloff as Frankenstein's monster from the 1935 film *The Bride of Frankenstein* ($26,000 in 1988).

TV FIRSTS

T H E 1 0

FIRST GUESTS ON
THE TONIGHT SHOW –
STARRING JOHNNY CARSON

1	Groucho Marx	Comic actor
2	Joan Crawford	Actress
3	Rudy Vallee	Singer/actor
4	Tony Bennett	Singer
5	Mel Brooks	Comic
6	Tom Pedi	Actor
7	The Phoenix Singers	Vocal trio
8	Tallulah Bankhead	Actress
9	Shelley Berman	Comedian
10	Artie Shaw	Band leader

Source: Carson Productions

Originally a two-hour week-nightly show taped in New York, Carson took over *The Tonight Show* on October 1, 1962, with his final show airing on May 22, 1992.

T H E 1 0

FIRST MUSIC VIDEOS BROADCAST BY MTV EUROPE

	Video	Artist
1	*Money for Nothing*	Dire Straits
2	*Fake*	Alexander O'Neal
3	*You Got the Look*	Prince with Sheena Easton
4	*It's a Sin*	Pet Shop Boys
5	*I Wanna Dance with Somebody*	Whitney Houston
6	*I Want Your Sex*	George Michael
7	*Who's That Girl*	Madonna
8	*I Really Didn't Mean It*	Luther Vandross
9	*Misfit*	Curiosity Killed The Cat
10	*Higher and Higher*	Jackie Wilson

MTV Europe began its pan-European broadcasting on August 1, 1987.

T H E 1 0

FIRST MUSIC VIDEOS BROADCAST BY MTV

	Video	Artist		Video	Artist
1	*Video Killed the Radio Star*	Buggles	6	*We Don't Talk Anymore*	Cliff Richard
2	*You Better Run*	Pat Benatar	7	*Brass in Pocket*	Pretenders
3	*She Won't Dance with Me*	Rod Stewart	8	*Time Heals*	Todd Rundgren
4	*You Better You Bet*	Who	9	*Take It on the Run*	REO Speedwagon
5	*Little Susie's on the Up*	PhD	10	*Rockin' the Paradise*	Styx

50 YEARS OF TV

Television started on both sides of the Atlantic in the 1930s, but dates its inexorable rise as the world's foremost broadcast medium from the 1940s. The year 1948 was significant for a number of developments – not least the use of the abbreviation "TV," which first appeared in print in that year in the American magazines *Fortune* and *Time*. The first regular television news service broadcast in Britain was inaugurated on January 5, 1948 – although the first news casters were heard but not seen. In the US, *The Ed Sullivan Show* began its 23-year run on June 20, 1948. The first TV cartoon series, first animated TV commercial, and the first TV cowboy series (*Hopalong Cassidy*) shown in the US also all date from 1948.

10 US TV FIRSTS

1 The first President to appear on TV

Franklin D. Roosevelt was seen opening the World's Fair, New York, on April 30, 1939.

2 The first king and queen televised in the US

King George VI and Queen Elizabeth were shown visiting the World's Fair on June 10, 1939.

3 The first televised Major League baseball game

The game between the Cincinnati Reds and the Brooklyn Dodgers at Ebbets Field, Brooklyn, New York, was broadcast on August 26, 1939.

4 The first televised professional football game

The Brooklyn Dodgers vs. Philadelphia Eagles game at Ebbets Field was shown on October 22, 1939.

5 The first TV commercial

A 20-second commercial for a Bulova clock was broadcast by WNBT New York on July 1, 1941.

6 The first soap opera on TV

The first regular daytime serial, DuMont TV network's A Woman to Remember, began its run on February 21, 1947.

7 The first broadcast of a current TV show

NBC's Meet the Press was first broadcast on November 6, 1947.

8 The first televised atomic bomb explosion

An "Operation Ranger" detonation at Frenchman Flats, Nevada, on February 1, 1951, was televised by KTLA, Los Angeles.

9 The first networked coast-to-coast color TV show

The Tournament of Roses parade at Pasadena, California, hosted by Don Ameche, was seen in color in 21 cities nationwide on January 1, 1954.

10 The first presidential news conference televised live

President John F. Kennedy was shown in a live broadcast from the auditorium of the State Department Building, Washington, DC, on January 25, 1961. (A filmed conference with President Eisenhower had been shown in 1955.)

THE COMING OF TV

The arrival and spread of television is one of the most significant developments of the 20th century. Scottish electrical engineer John Logie Baird (1888–1946) is generally recognized as the pioneer of television. He first demonstrated low-definition broadcasts in 1926, and, although flawed, it was introduced in the UK by the BBC in 1929. Subsequent improvements led to the introduction of high-definition television in the UK on November 2, 1936, and in the US on April 30, 1939. World War II hampered developments until the 1940s, since when television has become established globally, to the extent that there are now scarcely any countries that do not have television.

PIONEER OF TELEVISION
Scottish inventor John Logie Baird seen demonstrating his original television system.

THE 10
FIRST COUNTRIES TO HAVE TELEVISION*

	Country	Year
1	UK	1936
2	US	1939
3	USSR	1939
4	France	1948
5	Brazil	1950
6	Cuba	1950
7	Mexico	1950
8	Argentina	1951
9	Denmark	1951
10	Netherlands	1951

* *High-definition regular public broadcasting service*

TV COMES OF AGE
By the 1950s, television was commonplace in many countries.

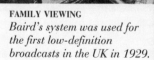

FAMILY VIEWING
Baird's system was used for the first low-definition broadcasts in the UK in 1929.

FIRST TVs
The earliest Baird television sets were cumbersome, unreliable, and expensive, but paved the way for all later developments.

TOP TELEVISION

WHO SHOT J.R.?
Viewers worldwide tuned in to the episode of
Dallas *that revealed it was Kristin Shepard –*
shown here – who shot J.R. Ewing.

CABLE TV COUNTRIES IN THE WORLD

	Country	Cable TV subscribers
1	US	60,495,090
2	Germany	14,600,000
3	Netherlands	5,700,000
4	Belgium	3,610,000
5	Switzerland	2,235,900
6	Sweden	1,850,000
7	France	1,620,000
8	Austria	1,000,000
9	UK	908,018
10	Finland	830,000

TV-OWNING COUNTRIES IN THE WORLD

	Country	Homes with TV		Country	Homes with TV
1	China	227,500,000	6	Germany	36,295,000
2	US	94,200,000	7	India	35,000,000
3	Russia	48,269,000	8	UK	22,446,000
4	Japan	41,328,000	9	France	21,667,000
5	Brazil	38,880,000	10	Italy	20,812,000

The estimated world total for TV households is 854,225,000, with the Top 10 countries accounting for almost 69 percent – a five-fold increase during the past 30 years and a rise of nearly 60 percent since 1984.

NIELSEN'S TV AUDIENCES OF ALL TIME IN THE US

	TV program	Date	Households viewing total	percent
1	*M*A*S*H* Special	Feb 28, 1983	50,150,000	60.2
2	*Dallas*	Nov 21, 1980	41,470,000	53.3
3	*Roots* Part 8	Jan 30, 1977	36,380,000	51.1
4	*Super Bowl XVI*	Jan 24, 1982	40,020,000	49.1
5	*Super Bowl XVII*	Jan 30, 1983	40,500,000	48.6
6	*XVII Winter Olympics*	Feb 23, 1994	45,690,000	48.5
7	*Super Bowl XX*	Jan 26, 1986	41,490,000	48.3
8	*Gone with the Wind* Part 1	Nov 7, 1976	33,960,000	47.7
9	*Gone with the Wind* Part 2	Nov 8, 1976	33,750,000	47.4
10	*Super Bowl XII*	Jan 15, 1978	34,410,000	47.2

© *Copyright 1997 Nielsen Media Research*

As more and more households acquire television sets (there are currently 94,000,000 "TV households" in the US), the most recently screened programs naturally tend to be watched by larger audiences, which distorts the historical picture. By listing the Top 10 according to percentage of households viewing, we get a clearer picture of who watches what.

PAY CABLE CHANNELS IN THE US

	Channel	Subscribers*		Channel	Subscribers*
1	Home Box Office	19,200,000	6	The Disney Channel	6,130,000
2	Encore Plex	8,969,000	7	Starz	3,279,000
3	Cinemax	8,900,000	8	The Movie Channel	3,100,000
4	Showtime	8,100,000	9	Encore/Westerns	1,517,000
5	Encore	6,868,000	10	Encore/Mystery	1,515,000

* *As of March 1997*

TOP 10
TV AUDIENCES OF ALL TIME IN THE UK

	TV program	Date	Audience
1	Royal Wedding of Prince Charles to Lady Diana Spencer	Jul 29, 1981	39,000,000
2	Brazil *vs.* England 1970 World Cup	Jun 10, 1970	32,500,000
3=	England *vs.* West Germany 1966 World Cup Final	Jul 30, 1966	32,000,000
3=	Chelsea *vs.* Leeds Cup Final Replay	Apr 28, 1970	32,000,000
5	*EastEnders* Christmas episode	Dec 26, 1987	30,000,000
6	*Morecambe and Wise Christmas Show*	Dec 25, 1977	28,000,000
7=	World Heavyweight Boxing Championship: Joe Frazier *vs.* Cassius Clay	Mar 8, 1971	27,000,000
7=	*Dallas* (episode revealing who shot J.R. Ewing)	Nov 22, 1980	27,000,000
9	*To the Manor Born* (last episode)	Nov 11, 1979	24,000,000
10	*Torvill and Dean Olympic Dance*	Feb 21, 1994	23,950,000

The November 22, 1980 screening of *Dallas* was the most-watched because it was the episode that revealed who shot J. R. Ewing. *To The Manor Born* gained its greatest-ever number of viewers for its last ever episode. The most-watched film of all time on British television is *Live And Let Die*. Although already seven years old when it was first broadcast on January 20, 1980, it attracted an audience of 23,500,000.

TOP 10
"BASIC" CABLE CHANNELS IN THE US

	Channel	Subscribers*
1	ESPN	71,100,000
2	CNN	71,000,000
3	TNT	70,549,000
4	TBS	69,920,000
5	C-SPAN	69,700,000
6	USA Network	69,677,000
7	The Discovery Channel	69,499,000
8	TNN	68,875,000
9	Lifetime	67,000,000
10	Family	66,900,000

* *Covering period January–February 1997*
Source: NCTA

Numbers 2, 3, and 4 are all owned by Turner Broadcasting System based in Atlanta, Georgia, where in 1993 he also successfully launched the Cartoon Network – which already has more than 11,000,000 subscribers.

TOP 10
BEST-SELLING BBC TV PROGRAMS*

	TV program	First UK transmission
1	*EastEnders*	1985
2	*The Living Planet*	1984
3	*The Trials of Life*	1990
4	*Miss Marple*	1984
5	*Police Rescue*	1991
6	*Tender Is the Night*	1985
7	*Elizabeth R*	1971
8	*Realms of the Russian Bear*	1992
9	*The Human Animal*	1994
10	*Pole to Pole*	1992

* *Ranked by total revenue earned*

BBC Worldwide Television is responsible for selling BBC TV programs to TV stations around the world. Drama, comedy, documentary and educational programs all feature strongly among their best-sellers – *Elizabeth R* (a documentary about Queen Elizabeth II) and *Miss Marple* have been sold in more than 50 countries.

TOP 10
FILMS OF ALL TIME ON PRIME-TIME NETWORK TV

	Film/year released	Broadcast
1	*Gone With the Wind Pt. 1 (1939)*	Nov 7, 1976
2	*Gone With the Wind Pt. 2 (1939)*	Nov 8, 1976
3	*The Day After**	Nov 20, 1983
4	*The Thorn Birds Pt. 3**	Mar 29, 1983
5	*The Thorn Birds Pt. 4**	Mar 30, 1983
6	*The Thorn Birds Pt. 2**	Mar 28, 1983
7=	*Love Story (1970)*	Oct 1, 1972
7=	*Airport (1970)*	Nov 11, 1973
9	*The Thorn Birds Pt. 1**	Mar 27, 1983
10	*The Godfather, Part II (1974)*	Nov 18, 1974

*Made-for-TV
Source: Nielsen Media Research

It is significant that all the most watched movies on TV were broadcast before the dawn of the video era, and attracted large audiences to whom this may have been the only opportunity to see a particular film that they might have missed.

TOP 10
TV SHOWS OF 1972–73 IN THE US

1	*All in the Family*
2	*Sanford and Son*
3	*Hawaii Five-O*
4	*Maude*
5=	*Bridget Loves Bernie*
5=	*The NBC Sunday Mystery Movie*
7=	*The Mary Tyler Moore Show*
7=	*Gunsmoke*
9	*The Wonderful World of Disney*
10	*Ironside*

The two most popular US TV shows of a quarter of a century ago were both adaptations of British series. *Gunsmoke*, for many years the top adult Western, began as a radio series starring William Conrad.

TOP VIDEO

COUNTRIES WITH MOST VCRs

	Country	Percentage of homes	No. video households
1	US	81.4	78,125,000
2	Japan	78.0	32,224,000
3	Germany	58.5	21,221,000
4	Brazil	42.8	20,458,000
5	UK	77.0	16,771,000
6	France	65.3	14,142,000
7	Italy	44.0	9,879,000
8	Canada	70.3	7,810,000
9	Spain	55.1	6,543,000
10	Russia	13.5	6,515,000

The 1980s have rightly been described as the "Video Decade." According to estimates published by *Screen Digest*, the period from 1980 to 1990 saw an increase in the number of video recorders in use worldwide of more than 27 times, from 7,687,000 to 210,159,000. The estimated 1994 total for the UK alone is more than double the entire world total for 1980. Since 1992 more than one-third of all homes throughout the world with TV have also had video.

VIDEO RENTAL CATEGORIES IN THE US, 1996

	Genre	Annual revenue ($)
1	Action	630,950,000
2	Comedy	611,450,000
3	Drama	219,830,000
4	Suspense	197,510,000
5	Family	194,270,000
6	Thriller	185,410,000
7	Romance	110,600,000
8	Science fiction	103,700,000
9	Humor	74,180,000
10	Animated	57,510,000

Source: Video Store Magazine

BEST-SELLING VIDEOS IN THE US*

	Title	Release	Label	Sales ($)
1	The Lion King	Mar 3, 1995	Buena Vista/Disney	27,500,000
2	Snow White	Oct 28, 1994	Buena Vista/Disney	27,500,000
3	Aladdin	Oct 1, 1993	Buena Vista/Disney	25,000,000
4	Independence Day	Nov 19, 1996	Fox Video	21,955,000
5	Jurassic Park	Oct 4, 1994	MCA/Universal	21,500,000
6	Toy Story	Oct 29, 1996	Buena Vista/Disney	21,000,000
7	Beauty And the Beast	Oct 30, 1992	Buena Vista/Disney	20,000,000
8	Pocahontas	Feb 26, 1996	Buena Vista/Disney	18,000,000
9	Star Wars Trilogy	Aug 29, 1995	Fox Video	15,300,000
10	Forrest Gump	Apr 27, 1995	Paramount	14,800,000

* Since 1992

Source: Video Store Magazine

MOVIE RENTALS ON VIDEO, 1996

	Film	Label	Release	Revenue ($)*
1	Twister	Warner	Oct 1	41,840,000
2	Independence Day	Fox Video	Nov 22	41,040,000
3	Broken Arrow	Fox Video	July 2	39,830,000
4	Ace Ventura: When Nature Calls	Warner	Mar 12	36,100,000
5	Toy Story	Buena Vista/Disney	Oct 29	34,480,000
6	Eraser	Warner	Oct 29	34,140,000
7	Babe	Universal	Mar 18	32,660,000
8	Braveheart	Paramount	Mar 12	32,640,000
9	Dangerous Minds	Buena Vista/Hollywood	Feb 12	31,970,000
10	A Time to Kill	Warner	Dec 31	30,390,000

* Spent by US consumers renting the title during its first four months of release

Source: Video Store Magazine

The success of movies on video closely mirrors the popularity of their theater release, the exception here being *Broken Arrow*, which would be in 9th place if ranked by US box-office income, but accelerates to 3rd place as a result of its popularity on video. Release date is also significant: *Independence Day* earned almost twice as much as *Twister* at the box office but was released after it on video, so was apparently less successful – a position that a longer-term analysis will almost certainly reverse.

TOP 10
MOST-RENTED HORROR VIDEOS IN THE US, 1996

	Title	Release	Label	Sales ($)
1	The Craft	Oct 8	Columbia TriStar	14,950,000
2	The Frighteners	Dec 17	Universal	14,500,000
3	Lord of Illusions	Jan 16	MGM/UA	12,410,000
4	Mary Reilly	Aug 27	Columbia TriStar	5,650,000
5	Tremors 2: Aftershocks	Apr 9	Universal	4,530,000
6	Sometimes They Come Back Again	Sep 3	Vidmark	3,220,000
7	Grim	Feb 26	A-Pix	2,890,000
8	Hellraiser : Bloodline	Nov 12	Buena Vista/ Dimension	2,770,000
9	Little Witches	Dec 24	A-Pix	2,540,000
10	Halloween 6: The Curse of Michael Myers	Sep 10	Buena Vista/ Dimension	2,340,000

Source: Video Store Magazine

TOP 10
MOST-RENTED SCIENCE FICTION VIDEOS IN THE US, 1996

	Title	Release	Label	Sales ($)
1	Independence Day	Nov 22	Fox Video	41,040,000
2	12 Monkeys	Jul 9	Universal	18,440,000
3	The Island of Dr. Moreau	Dec 24	New Line	17,630,000
4	Strange Days	Apr 2	Fox Video	9,670,000
5	The Arrival	Oct 22	LIVE	5,500,000
6	Lawnmower Man 2 : Jobe's War	Jun 11	New Line	3,900,000
7	Nemesis 3	Jun 18	WarnerVision	2,750,000
8	It Came From Outer Space 3	Oct 1	Universal	500,000
9	Forbidden Zone : Alien Abduction	Jun 25	Amazing Fantasy	470,000
10	The Silencers	Apr 23	PM	450,000

Source: Video Store Magazine

TOP 10
BEST-SELLING MUSIC VIDEOS OF ALL TIME IN THE US*

1 Hangin' Tough Live, New Kids on the Block
2 Hangin' Tough, New Kids on the Block
3 Step by Step, New Kids on the Block
4 Live Shit: Binge And Purge, Metallica
5 Moonwalker, Michael Jackson
6 In Concert, Jose Carreras, Placido Domingo, Luciano Pavarotti
7 Live At The Acropolis, Yanni
8 Garth Brooks, Garth Brooks
9 Justify My Love, Madonna
10 Video Anthology 1978–1988, Bruce Springsteen

* Excluding children's videos
Source: The Popular Music Database

In a diverse list ranging through opera, R&B, rock, and country, the three New Kids' titles are now joined by Metallica as the only music video releases to sell over 1,000,000 units each in the US.

TOP 10
BEST-SELLING CHILDREN'S VIDEOS OF 1995 IN THE US

1 Land Before Time II: The Great Valley Adventure
2 Land Before Time III: The Time of the Great Giving
3 Sing Along Disney: The Lion King
4 Dr. Seuss/ How the Grinch Stole Christmas
5 Rudolph the Red-Nosed Reindeer
6 Barney: Imagination Island
7 Winnie the Pooh: And Christmas Too
8 Barney's Alphabet Zoo
9 Barney Live! In New York City
10 Barney: Families Are Special

Dinosaurs not only once ruled the earth, but also dominate this Top 10: The Land Before Time, a successful animated film released in 1988, was followed by the two straight-to-video sequels that head this list. Videos featuring yet another popular dinosaur, Barney, occupy four slots.

TOP 10
BEST-SELLING EXERCISE VIDEOS OF 1995 IN THE US

1 Abs of Steel
2 Abs of Steel 2
3 Abs of Steel 3
4 Buns of Steel 3
5 Buns of Steel
6 Buns and Abs of Steel 2000
7 Susan Powter/Burn Fat & Get Fit
8 Kathie Lee
9 Denise Austin/Non Aerobic Work Out
10 Buns of Steel Step 20

The tapes featured in this Top 10 represent the best-sellers among a vast range of videos designed primarily to help the consumer reduce and tone his or her abdomen and other bodily parts. Although the vogue for aerobic exercise may have waned generally, the step-by-step programs and pacy workout routines presented by such keep-fit gurus as Tamilee Webb, have proved perennial bestsellers since their launch, some of them spawning as many as six sequels.

ON THE RADIO

GOING FOR A SPIN
The universal appeal of popular music of all types means that radio stations that play it dominate the world's airwaves.

TOP 10
RADIO FORMATS IN THE US

	Format	Share (percent)*
1	News/talk	16.8
2	Adult Contemporary	14.5
3	Country	10.5
4	Top 40	8.6
5=	Album Rock	7.2
5=	Urban	7.2
7	Spanish	6.2
8	Oldies	5.6
9	Modern Rock	4.1
10	Classic Rock	3.9

* *Of all radio listening during an average week, 6 am to midnight, fall 1995, for listeners aged 12+*

News/talk, only recently elevated to the top of this survey, has continued to maintain its premier position.

TOP 10
RADIO-OWNING COUNTRIES

	Country	Radio sets per 1,000 population
1	US	2,118
2	Guam	1,403
3	Australia	1,273
4	Bermuda	1,260
5	Gibraltar	1,173
6	Netherlands Antilles	1,165
7	UK	1,146
8	Monaco	1,126
9	Denmark	1,033
10	Canada	1,030

TOP 10
MOST LISTENED-TO RADIO STATIONS IN THE US

	Station	City	Format	AQH*
1	WKTU-FM	New York	Dance Contemporary Hit Radio	186,100
2	WQHT-FM	New York	Urban/Contemporary Hit Radio	160,400
3	KLVE-FM	Los Angeles	Hispanic Adult Contemporary	123,200
4	WLTW-FM	New York	Soft Adult Contemporary	136,200
5	WCBS-FM	New York	Oldies	135,500
6	WRKS	New York	Urban Adult Contemporary	126,300
7	WOR	New York	Talk	108,800
8	KFI	Los Angeles	Talk	107,300
9	KKBT-FM	Los Angeles	Urban Contemporary	105,700
10	KPWR-FM	Los Angeles	Urban/Contemporary Hit Radio	104,700

* *Average Quarter Hour statistic based on number of listeners aged 12+ listening between Monday and Sunday 6:00am to midnight*
Source: Duncan's American Radio from Spring 1996 Arbitron data

TOP 10
RADIO STATIONS IN THE US BY AUDIENCE SHARE

	Station	City	Format	Share (percent)
1	WTHI-FM	Terre Haute, IN	Country	32.5
2	WXBQ-FM	Bristol, TN	Country	29.0
3	WFGY-FM	Altoona, PA	Country	25.8
4	WDRM-FM	Huntsville, AL	Country	25.6
5	WQBE-FM	Charleston, WV	Country	24.9
6	WKSF-FM	Asheville, NC	Country	24.8
7	WIVK-FM	Knoxville, TN	Country	27.0
8	WOVK-FM	Wheeling, WV	Country	23.8
9	WIKY-FM	Evansville, IN	Adult Contemporary	22.0
10	WXHT-FM	Montgomery, AL	Urban Contemporary	20.8

Source: Duncan's American Radio from Spring 1996 Arbitron data

LATEST GEORGE FOSTER PEABODY AWARDS FOR BROADCASTING WON BY NATIONAL PUBLIC RADIO*

1996	*Remorse: The 14 Stories Of Eric Morse*
1995	*Wynton Marsalis: Making The Music/Marsalis On Music*
1994	*Tobacco Stories and Wade in the Water: African American Sacred Music Traditions (NPR/Smithsonian Institution)*
1993	*Health Reform Coverage 1993*
1992	*Prisoners in Bosnia*
1991	*The Coverage of the Judge Clarence Thomas Confirmation*
1990	*Manicu's Story: The War in Mozambique*
1989	*Scott Simon's Radio Essays on Weekend Edition Saturday*
1988	*Cowboys on Everest*
1983	*The Sunday Show and Taylor Made Piano: A Jazz History*

* *Includes only programs made or coproduced by NPR*

In 1938, the National Association of Broadcasters formed a committee to establish a "Pulitzer Prize" for radio. These were inaugurated the following year under the sponsorship of the Henry W. Grady School of Journalism at the University of Georgia, and named in honor of George Foster Peabody, a native Georgian and noted philanthropist. The first awards, for radio programs broadcast in 1940, were presented at a banquet at the Commodore Hotel in New York on March 31, 1941. The ceremony was broadcast live nationwide on CBS and included addresses by CBS founder and chairman William S. Paley and noted reporter Elmer David, the recipient of the first personal Peabody Award. The Awards are now regarded as the most prestigious in American broadcasting.

LONGEST-RUNNING PROGRAMS ON NATIONAL PUBLIC RADIO

1	*All Things Considered*
2	*National Press Club*
3	*Weekend All Things Considered*
4	*Marian McPartland's Piano Jazz*
5	*Morning Edition*
6	*NPR Playhouse*
7	*NPR World of Opera*
8	*St. Louis Symphony*
9	*Fresh Air*
10	*Weekend Edition Saturday*

Source: National Public Radio

All Things Considered, the longest-running NPR program, was first broadcast on May 3, 1971. Nos. 2 to 7 date from the 1970s, and Nos. 8 to 10 from the early 1980s.

STATES WITH MOST NATIONAL PUBLIC RADIO MEMBER STATIONS

	State	No. of stations
1	New York	33
2	California	23
3	Wisconsin	22
4=	Michigan	20
4=	Ohio	20
6	Minnesota	17
7=	Alaska	15
7=	Illinois	15
7=	Texas	15
10=	Colorado	14
10=	Florida	14
10=	Georgia	14
10=	Oregon	14

FIRST ARTISTS TO FEATURE IN A COCA-COLA RADIO COMMERCIAL

	Artist	Year
1	McGuire Sisters	1958
2	Limelighters	1963
3=	Four Seasons	1965
3=	Freddie & the Dreamers	1965
3=	Jan and Dean	1965
3=	Jay & The Americans	1965
3=	Tom Jones	1965
3=	Shirelles	1965
9=	Petula Clark	1966
9=	Lee Dorsey	1966
9=	Everly Brothers	1966
9=	Marvin Gaye	1966
9=	Gary Lewis & The Playboys	1966
9=	Little Milton	1966
9=	Roy Orbison	1966
9=	Supremes	1966

The list reads like a *Who's Who* of pop music in the 1960s. All the featured artists sang the jingle *Things Go Better With Coke*, with the exception of the McGuire Sisters who sang *Pause For A Coke*.

INDEX

ACKNOWLEDGMENTS

I would like to thank Caroline Ash for her unfailing assistance in compiling *The Top 10 of Everything*, along with Luke Crampton, Barry Lazell, Ian Morrison, Dafydd Rees, and the following individuals, organizations, and publications who kindly supplied the information to enable me to prepare many of the lists:

John Amos, Richard Braddish, Steve Butler, Shelly Cagner, Dr. Stephen Durham, Christopher Forbes, Darryl Francis, Max Hanna, Peter Harland, William Hartston, Duncan Hislop, Tony Hutson, Robert Lamb, Bernard Lavery, Allen Meredith, Giles Moon, Tim O'Brien, Adrian Room, Rocky Stockman MBE, James Taylor, Arthur H. Waltz

Academy of Motion Picture Arts and Sciences, AEA Technology, Airport Operators Council International, American Association of Botanical Gardens and Arboreta, American Automobile Manufacturers Association, American Forestry Association, American Kennel Club, American Library Association, American Society of Association Executives, *Amusement Business*, Angels & Bermans Fancy Dress Hire, *Animal World*, *Annual Abstract of Statistics*, Arbitron, Art Sales Index, Associated Press, Association of American Railroads, Association of British Investigators, Association of Comics Enthusiasts, Audit Bureau of Circulations, Automobile Association, BAFTA, Bank of England, BBC Publicity, BBC Radio, BBC Worldwide Television, BBC Written Archives, Ben & Jerry's, Beverage Marketing Corporation, *Billboard*, BMI, Bonhams, Bookwatch Ltd., *BP Statistical Review of World Energy*, British Astronomical Society, British Broadcasting Corporation, British Library, British Museum, British Rate & Data, British Video Association, Bureau of Engraving and Printing, Bureau of Federal Prisons, Bureau of Justice Statistics, Cablevision, Cadbury Schweppes Group, Cameron Mackintosh Ltd., Carbon Dioxide Information Analysis Center/Greg Marland/Tom Boden, Carson Productions, Cat Fanciers' Association of the USA, Central Intelligence Agency, Championship Auto Racing Teams (CART), Channel Four Television, Charities Aid Foundation, Chartwell Information, Christie's East, Christie's London, Christie's South Kensington, Civil Aviation Authority, *Classical Music*, Coca-Cola, Coca-Cola Great Britain and Ireland, Corporate Intelligence Ltd., Corporate Resources Group, Council for the Care of Churches, Countryside Commission, *Crime in the United States*, Criminal Justice Reference Service, *Criminal Statistics England & Wales*, Dateline, Death Penalty Information Center, Department of the Army, Corps of Engineers, Department of Health, Department of Trade and Industry, Department of Transport, Diamond Information Centre, Duncan's American Radio, Electoral Reform Society, Environmental Protection Agency, ESPNET Sports Zone, Euromonitor, Federal Bureau of Investigation, Feste Catalogue Index Database/Alan Somerset, Food and Agriculture Organization of the United Nations, Food Marketing Institute, *Forbes Magazine*, Ford Motor Company Ltd., Foundation Center, Generation AB, Geological Museum, London, George Foster Peabody Awards, Giga Information Group, Gideons International, Global Network Navigator, Inc., Gold Fields Mineral Services Ltd., Governing Council of the Cat Fancy, Hamleys of Regent Street Ltd., Harley Medical Group, Harrods Ltd., Health and Safety Executive, H.J. Heinz Co. Ltd., Higher Education Statistics Agency, Hollywood Foreign Press Association, Home Office, Indianapolis 500, Infoplan, Information Resources, Inc., Institute of Sports Medicine, International Civil Aviation Organization, International Cocoa Organization, International Coffee Organization, International Council of Shopping Centers, International Dairy Foods Association, International Ice Cream Association, International Monetary Fund, International Tea Committee, International Union for the Conservation of Nature, International Union of Geological Sciences Commission on Comparative Planetology, *International Water Power and Dam Construction Handbook*, ITV Network Centre, Kellogg Company of Great Britain, Kennel Club, John Lewis Partnership,

Library Association, Lloyds Register of Shipping, London Heathrow Airport, London Regional Transport, London Theatre Record, London Transport Lost Property, Magazine Publishers of America, Major League Baseball, Mansell Color Company, Inc., MARC Europe, *Market Focus*, Mars, Inc., Mars UK Ltd., Meteorological Office, Metropolitan Opera House, New York, *Modern Bride*, Modern Language Association of America, MORI, MRIB, MTV, NASA, National Association for Stock Car Auto Racing (NASCAR), National Basketball Association (NBA), National Canine Defence League, National Center for Education Statistics, National Center for Health Statistics, National Climatic Data Center, National Criminal Justice Reference Service, National Dairy Council, National Football League (NFL), National Gallery, London, National Gallery of Art, Washington, DC, National Grid Company plc, National Hockey League (NHL), National Oceanic and Atmospheric Association, National Piers Society, National Public Radio, National Railway Museum, National Retail Federation, National Safety Council, National Solid Waste Management Association, National Sporting Goods Association, NCAA, NCTA, Nestlé UK Ltd., New York Drama Desk, *New York Post*, New York Transit Authority, Niagara Falls Museum, A.C. Nielsen Co. Ltd., Nielsen Media Research, Nobel Foundation, *NonProfit Times*, Office of National Statistics, Ordnance Survey, Pasta Information Centre, PBS, *People*, Perrier UK Ltd., *Petfood Industry Magazine*, Pet Industry Joint Advisory Council, PGA Tour, Inc., Phillips West Two, Phobics Society, Popular Music Database, Produktschap voor Gedistilleerde Dranken, Professional Golf Association (PGA), Public Library Association, *Publishers Weekly*, *Railway Gazette International*, RAJAR, Really Useful Group, Recording Industry Association of America (RIAA), Registrar General, Relate National Marriage Guidance, Royal Aeronautical Society, Royal Mint, Royal Opera House, Royal Society for the Prevention of Cruelty to Animals, Royal Society for the Protection of Birds, RSA Examinations Board, Science Museum, London, Scotch Whisky Association, Scout Association, *Screen Digest*, Shakespeare Birthplace Trust, Siemens AG, Society of Actuaries, Sotheby's London, Sotheby's New York, *Spaceflight*, Spink & Son Ltd., Sports Council, *Statistical Abstract of the United States*, Sugar Bureau, Taylors of Loughborough, Telecom Security, Theatre Museum, Theatre Record, *Time*, *The Times*, Trebor Bassett Ltd., Tree Register of the British Isles, UNESCO, *Uniform Crime Statistics*, Union Bank of Switzerland, United Nations, Universal Postal Union, University of Westminster, University Statistical Record, US Board on Geographic Names, US Bureau of Labor Statistics, US Bureau of the Census, USCOLD, US Department of Agriculture, US Department of Agriculture Forest Service, US Department of Justice, US Department of Labor, US Department of the Interior, National Park Service/National Register of Historic Places, US Department of Transportation, Federal Aviation Administration, US Department of Transportation, Federal Highway Administration, US Department of Transportation, National Traffic Safety Administration, US Fish and Wildlife Service, US Geological Survey, US Immigration and Naturalization Service, US Mint, US Postal Services, US Social Security Administration, *USA Today*, *Variety*, *Video Store Magazine*, *Waste Age*, *Wines & Vines*, World Association of Girl Guides, World Bank, World Health Organization, World Tourism Organization, Zenith International,

PICTURE CREDITS

t=top left, c=center, a=above, b=below, l=left, r=right:
© Academy & Motion Picture Arts & Sciences ® 226 cla;
Allsport 118bc /Simon Bruty 129br /Dave Cannon 129crb, 137tr /J.D. Cuban 117ca;
BFI/United International Pictures 209bc;
Bridgeman Art Library/National Gallery, London 193br /Victoria & Albert 183tl;
British Museum front jacket cl;
Camera Press 1cr /Impress/N. Diaye 25crb;
Christie's Images 195br, 241tr;

Corbis/Bettmann 156tl /UPI 222tr, 243cla /Everett 223br, front jacket cra /Nasa, back jacket cra;
Ecoscene 1bc, 99br;
Mary Evans Picture Library 52bc, 157br, 190cb, 243clb;
FLPA 175tl;
Ford Motor Company 59br;
Getty Images 113cra, 129cra, 171br;
Glasgow Museum 209tr;
Robert Harding Picture Library /G & P Corrigan 96br, 160tl;
Image Bank 175br /Peter Hendrie 92bl /Bill Hickey 8cra /Laurence Hughes 153br /Bernard Roussel 191tr /Joe Szodzinski 21clb;
David King Collection 184tl;
London Transport Museum 60bl;
Los Angeles Police Department 144br;
Mary Evans 59acr;
Military Picture Library /Julie Collins 155tr /John Peart 154bl;
Nasa 70bl, 76bl /Finley-Holiday Films 71acr;
National Gallery, London 194tc;
National Maritime Museum 100tr;
National Motor Museum, Beaulieu 2clb, 59tr, 59 tr, 167cla, tr;
Peter Newark's Historical Pictures 108tl;
NHPA /Daryl Balfour 85bc;
Robert Opie 46tc;
Paramount /Courtesy of Kobal 209cra;
Range /Reuter /Bettmann 159tr;
Redferns /David Redfern 248tl;
© 1996 Les Editions Albert René Goscinny-Uderzo 185cra;
Rex Features 17bl, 55br, 111br, 187bc, 197tl, 202tr, 225br, 228bl, 229tr, 235tc, 236bl /Peter Brooker 1br, 233br /Frank Doran 209cla /Jim Graham 199tr /Charles Knight 132tc /Dave Lewis 234bl /Jim Selby 244cla /Sipa 102cra, 238tl, front jacket ca/ Peter Heimsath;
© Royal Geographical Society, London 113cr, 113br, 113bl;
Science Photo Library /J. Baum & N. Henbest 65crb /David A. Hardy 69tr /Nasa 2cra, 66tl, 67br;
Sotheby's 213tc;
South American Pictures /Tony Morrison 97cr;
Frank Spooner Pictures /Bassignac 2cl, 23tl /Alain Benainous 214tl /Clasos Press 173clb /Liaison 3bl, 68bc /Singh Spooner 240bl /Stills 219br;
Sporting Pictures (UK) Ltd 125tr, 129tr, 129bl, 136br;
Tony Stone Images /Doug Armand 21cl /Ben Edwards 9tr, 167clb /Tony Garcia 150cla /Bill Heinsohn 38–39tc /Arnulf Husmo 35tl /Chuck Keeler 167cra /Hideo Kurihara 18tr /Ben Osborne 169tl /Peter Pearson 3tc, 21bc /Jon Riley 31ca / Dave Saunders 37tl /Jack Vearey 37br /Terry Vine 179tr /Baron Wolman 29tr /Herbert Zetti 217br;
Syndication International 196br;
Text 100 /Microsoft 41br;
Topham Picturepoint 152ca, 164br, 165br, 201tr, 209br, 221cl;
Universal /Courtesy Kobal 209clb;
Zefa Pictures 1cl, 12bc, 21crb, 56tr, 57br, 73tr, 75tr, 80cb, 142cb, 143tr, 174bl, 177tc, 178cb.

Every effort has been made to trace the copyright holders, and we apologize for any unintentional omissions. We would be pleased to insert the appropriate acknowledgment in any subsequent edition of this publication.

ILLUSTRATIONS
Richard Bonson, Richard Ward, Mick Loates, Eric Thomas

PUBLISHER'S ACKNOWLEDGMENTS
Dorling Kindersley thanks the following people: Zirinnia Austin, Jason Little, Anna Youle. DK Publishing Inc. thanks Will Lach, Ray Rogers, Jill Hamilton, Nicole Zarick, Nicholas Sander, Phoebe Todd-Naylor.

INDEX
Susan Cawthorne